D0918262

Studies in Mother–Infant Interaction

Studies in Mother–Infant Interaction

PROCEEDINGS OF THE LOCH LOMOND SYMPOSIUM
ROSS PRIORY, UNIVERSITY OF STRATHCLYDE,
SEPTEMBER, 1975

Edited by

H. R. SCHAFFER
University of Strathclyde
Glasgow, Scotland

1977

ACADEMIC PRESS
London New York San Francisco
A Subsidiary of Harcourt Brace Jovanovich, Publishers

ACADEMIC PRESS INC. (LONDON) LTD.
24/28 Oval Road,
London NW1

United States Edition published by
ACADEMIC PRESS INC.
111 Fifth Avenue
New York, New York 10003

Second Printing 1978

Library of Congress Catalog Card Number: 77-71649
ISBN: 0-12-622560-5

Printed in Great Britain by
Whitstable Litho Ltd.,
Whitstable,
Kent.

Contributors

B. BEEBE, *College of Physicians and Surgeons, Columbia University, New York, U.S.A.*

S. L. BENNETT, *College of Physicians and Surgeons, Columbia University, New York, U.S.A.*

J. S. BRUNER, *University of Oxford, Oxford, England.*

G. M. COLLIS, *University of Strathclyde, Glasgow, Scotland.*

W. S. CONDON, *University of Boston, Boston, Mass., U.S.A.*

J. B. DUNN, *University of Cambridge, Cambridge, England.*

A. FOGEL, *University of Chicago, Chicago, Illinois, U.S.A.*

J. HERRMANN, *University of Cambridge, Cambridge, England.*

R. A. HINDE, *University of Cambridge, Cambridge, England.*

J. JAFFE, *College of Physicians and Surgeons, Columbia University, New York, U.S.A.*

O. H. M. JONES, *University of Nottingham, Nottingham, England.*

K. KAYE, *University of Chicago, Chicago, Illinois, U.S.A.*

D. J. MESSER, *University of Strathclyde, Glasgow, Scotland.*

C. M. MURPHY, *University of Strathclyde, Glasgow, Scotland.*

J. L. NEWSON, *University of Nottingham, Nottingham, England.*

H. PAPOUŠEK, *Max-Planck Institut für Psychiatrie, Munich, Germany.*

M. PAPOUŠEK, *Max-Planck Institut für Psychiatrie, Munich, Germany.*

G. PARSONS, *University of Strathclyde, Glasgow, Scotland.*

S. J. PAWLBY, *University of Nottingham, Nottingham, England.*

M. P. M. RICHARDS, *University of Cambridge, Cambridge, England.*

H. R. SCHAFFER, *University of Strathclyde, Glasgow, Scotland.*

D. N. STERN, *New York Hospital, Cornell Medical Center, New York, U.S.A.*

C. TREVARTHEN, *University of Edinburgh, Edinburgh, Scotland.*

A. WHITEN, *University of St. Andrews, St. Andrews, Scotland.*

Preface

The contributions to this volume are based on papers presented at a conference, financed by the Social Science Research Council, on Mother–Infant Interaction. Referred to as the Loch Lomond Conference (after its venue at Ross Priory, a country house owned by the University of Strathclyde on the shores of Loch Lomond), it provided its participants with the opportunity, over a number of days, to exchange ideas and findings, to show films and video-tapes, and to learn from each other about new methods and techniques as well as to hear substantive research reports. The aim of this book is to share this experience with a wider audience, and the papers originally presented have therefore been revised with this aim in mind.

The infant's interaction with his mother (and let us say straight away that that term is used in its widest sense, referring to the child's principal caretaker rather than implying any biological constraints) has been a topic of great fascination—to theoreticians, to research workers, and, of course, to practitioners. It is certainly one of the liveliest of present-day research topics to be found in the developmental sciences, but recently the approach to it has undergone some fairly drastic changes in both the questions being asked and the methods used to answer them. The nature of these changes is outlined in the Introduction; here let us merely register the belief that it is timely to draw attention to these changes by means of this publication, and express the hope that thereby others will be inspired to further this exciting and socially important topic.

I warmly acknowledge the invaluable help with the conference arrangements that my colleagues Glyn Collis, David Messer, Stuart Millar, Catherine Murphy, and Norman Sharp provided. I am also grateful to Brian Foss for helping to chair the meeting, and finally I wish to express my gratitude to Margaret Hunter and Elizabeth Reid for taking so much care in preparing the final manuscript.

University of Strathclyde,
Glasgow, Scotland.
November 1976.

H. R. SCHAFFER

Contents

I | Introduction

1 | Early Interactive Development

H. R. Schaffer

What are the characteristics of social behaviour in infancy? In the past the motivation for enquiry has come mostly from the intrinsic interest of the problem itself, in that evidence was looked for regarding the capabilities at the beginning of life for what is surely one of the most complex of skills, namely that of forming interpersonal relationships. It is true that some had hoped to find in the first bond formed by the infant with another person the prototype of all subsequent relations: as yet, however, there is no substantiating evidence whatever for such an association. Rather, the primary relationship is an intriguing event in its own right, forming but the first though crucial step in the socialization process.

Increasingly, however, an additional reason for interest in this area has appeared in recent years. It stems from the realization that many functions traditionally treated in psychology as though they "belonged" to individuals and could thus be studied purely as intrapersonal events generally occur within an *inter*personal context and that it is from this context that they derive their functional meaning. Abstraction is, of course, not only permissible but necessary in scientific enquiry; however, the study of early development in particular has furnished us recently with a number of examples showing how vital it is to extend the traditional focus and take note of the *social* dimension of behaviour patterns.

Of these examples that of language is no doubt the best known.

Conceived initially as a beneath-the-skin system, as a set of behavioural patterns explicable purely in terms of the psychological organization of the individual, it has increasingly been recognized as in fact deriving its significance primarily from its communicative function and as in need consequently of study in dyadic settings. The change of emphasis from syntactic to semantic features no doubt made this inevitable, but its implications have been explored in particular amongst those attempting to comprehend the very first stages of language acquisition. Instead of seeing language arising *de novo* at the beginning of the second year, it is now being related to the pre-verbal communication patterns that are already established between mother and infant in the early months of life (see Bruner, Chapter 11). Language acquisition, in other words, has been firmly placed within a social setting.

Amongst other functions in the study of which we see a similar change are concept formation, which Katherine Nelson (1974) in particular has treated in terms of the child's encounters with the people and things that constitute his social environment; the acquisition of skills and of problem solving ability that Kaye (1976) and Wood and Middleton (1975) have described as occurring within a dyadic context; and even attention—surely, according to its traditional treatment, one of the most private of an individual's functions, but now given an interpersonal slant by describing the role of mutuality of attentive focus that develops among mothers and infants (see Collis, Chapter 14). And as a final example let us note that in the considerable body of literature on the sucking response there has until recently been virtually no acknowledgement of the fact that sucking generally implies the presence of another person actively involved in the feeding process—an omission only now beginning to be rectified by work such as that of Kaye (Chapter 5).

Changes in Approach

As a result of this trend, an increasing number of investigators are turning to an examination of the earliest social relationship in their search for the developmental antecedents of particular functions. And with this new impetus the study of early social behaviour has begun to take a new direction in terms of both the questions being asked and the techniques being used. A considerable body of data is, of course, already in existence on social development (see the reviews by Maccoby and Masters, 1970, and Ainsworth, 1973)—much of it based on the concept of attachment, to which ethological (Bowlby, 1969), cognitive-developmental (Schaffer, 1971) and social learning (Gewirtz, 1972) interpretations have variously been given. More recent studies, however, are distinguished by the following features:

(1) *Treatment of social behaviour in dyadic terms.* That infants are capable of organized, spontaneous behaviour from the very beginning of life is now richly documented; the implications for the study of early social behaviour are that a dyadic orientation is essential. Thus the mother's task in interacting with her baby is seen to be not one of creating order out of chaos; it is rather a matter of fitting her behaviour in with an already existing organization. Interactions, even the earliest, are thus two-way affairs in which mutual interchange takes place (Bell, 1968).
(2) *The need to postulate some degree of social pre-adaptation.* A neonate may be an essentially a-social creature, in the sense of not being capable as yet of truly reciprocal social relationships and of not yet having the concept of a person. However, the nature of his early interactive behaviour is such that it is increasingly difficult to avoid the conclusion that in some sense the infant is already prepared for social intercourse (see Chapters 3 and 10). Not that this should surprise us: if an infant arrives in the world with a digestive system to cope with food and a breathing apparatus attuned to the air around him, why should he not also be prepared to deal with that other essential attribute of his environment, people?
(3) *Emphasis on temporal relationships in interactive situations.* As we shall see below, the nature of the infant's pre-adapted organization can, in part, be described in terms of temporal parameters. Behaviour is chunked in time, and dyadic interactions are thus based on an elaborate interweaving of the participants' behavioural flow. Techniques of sequential analysis rather than indices based on total amounts of behaviour collated over time accordingly become the principal means of data reduction.
(4) *The use of microanalytic techniques.* Experience has shown that the temporal relationships just referred to become most evident at micro-levels of analysis. This applies, of course, to adult communicative behaviour too (see Chapter 7), but, as many of the following contributions indicate, this level of analysis has been found to be a particularly

fruitful one for exploring the manner in which the infant's behaviour meshes with that of his caretakers.

(5) *An interest in processes rather than products.* Whereas the focus of previous work tended to be on the nature of attachment behaviour in its developed form, recent work has concerned itself more with the processes underlying the formation of social relationships, and accordingly questions have been asked as to how these come about rather than when they appear, towards whom they are manifested, or in what way they change across time and situation.

Methodological Issues

New questions often necessitate the use of new methods and techniques. However, in one respect at least the microanalytic examination of mother–infant interaction has been fortunate, namely in the availability of a wide range of technological aids for recording and analysing in great detail behavioural sequences. Papoušek in particular, in Chapter 4, shows well what ingenious use can be made of film and television equipment in order to deal with new problems.

One of the disadvantages of microanalytic investigations lies in their labour-intensive nature, for a session lasting just a few minutes can generate a considerable amount of data when analysed in units of a fraction of a second. Under these circumstances it is not surprising to find samples generally to be small (sometimes involving only single cases) and observation sessions to be limited. This makes the problem of generalizing findings thus obtained an acute one—particularly so when the observations are carried out in the laboratory or, for that matter, in a home converted into a laboratory by the presence of obtrusive equipment and even more obtrusive personnel to operate the equipment. The need for replication becomes accordingly an even more urgent one than it normally is.

The problem of replication also looms large with regard to the choice of the units into which behaviour may be analysed. Going to more microscopic levels of analysis inevitably means that conventional response indices and categories are no longer applicable—or at least need to be supplemented by units of a more appropriate scale. But what are these to be? In their respective contributions here Condon, Fogel, and Stern all make interesting suggestions as to ways found helpful by them in ordering their data. But clearly some agreement has to be reached among investigators for units to assume scientific reality and to be more than something in the beholder's eye.

Interactive studies are, however, throwing up a further class of new variables, namely those that transcend the behaviour of individuals and instead are defined by the responses of both participants in a dyadic situation. Stern (1974), for example, has shown the usefulness of such dyadic states in the study of mutual gazing among mother–infant pairs, employing the four-fold classification given by *both* partners looking at the other, neither looking, or only one or the other doing so. Similarly Duncan (1973) has used the four possible combinations of speaker–auditor behaviour to yield dyadic states, and yet another example is provided by Collis in this volume with the concept of visual co-orientation. Such variables have heuristic value; their particular importance lies, however, in their demonstration that interactive situations need not be reduced to variables pertaining only to individuals but may be treated in terms peculiar to themselves. Not that interactive situations have not given rise to their own sets of terms and concepts: it is indeed difficult to discuss interactions without resorting to words like smooth, synchronized, or successful. Such notions tend to be both complex and value-laden, making agreement as to their usage difficult. Yet, as Hinde (1976) has shown, there is no reason why a relationship cannot be analysed into its constituents and be provided with meaningful indices (see Hinde and Herrmann, this volume), and though some of the more global concepts like communication or reciprocity are still used in an intuitive and sometimes all-embracing fashion, the advent of dyadic state variables points at least to one way of describing interactions in more acceptable objective fashion.

The use of dyadic states does not, however, solve a further problem raised by the study of interactions, namely that of describing and analysing the sequential flow of interactive behaviour. It is only comparatively recently that the nature of this flow has become of interest, particularly in ethological studies (Slater, 1973), and the statistical methods available for sequential analysis are still at a very early stage of development. On the whole these have concerned themselves with intra-individual sequences in order to establish whether an animal's successive responses are independent or whether each is influenced by one or more preceding responses. While in theory the same principles could hold for inter-individual data (Altmann, 1965), in practice such data raise certain extra problems. One of these is that the behaviour of an individual in an interaction sequence is generally dependent not only on the immediately preceding response of his partner but also on his own previous behaviour. Indeed it seems likely that a *cumulative* effect of previous events in a far from simple additive manner ought ideally to be taken into account, thus making simple Markov chain models even less applicable. Taken in conjunction with the likelihood that social behaviour (just like linguistic behaviour) is arranged in complex hierarchical structures about which we know little as yet, it is apparent that there is a considerable need for purely descriptive accounts of interactive structures quite apart from the provision of the necessary statistical tools for their analysis. That this task has already begun can be seen in some of the contributions to this volume: see, for example, Fogel's account of "framing" structures to describe the way in which maternal behaviour may provide a context for infant behaviour, or Stern's hierarchically arranged three levels of maternal behaviour. Nevertheless, a great deal more remains to be established about the various sequential arrangements that can be found among the constituents of social behaviour, at both intra- and interpersonal levels.

Themes in the Study of Early Interactive Development

Some general trends are already beginning to emerge from studies that have undertaken the detailed examination of early interactive behaviour. What follows is an attempt to sketch an outline provided by this work and draw attention to some of the themes highlighted so far.

SOCIAL PRE-ADAPTATION

Given the need for some degree of preparedness for social interaction, how does it manifest itself?

There are two aspects that may be usefully distinguished, namely *structural* and *functional* pre-adaptation. The former refers to the availability of certain structural mechanisms of endogenous origin that serve to bind the young to its caretaker. Thus, just as the infant rhesus monkey is provided with a strong grasping reflex that ensures its hold on the mother's fur, so the human baby comes into the world with an oral apparatus precisely adapted to cope with the nipple and food that the mother will provide, a set of visual structures highly sensitive to those aspects of stimulation that emanate from other people's faces, and auditory equipment selectively attuned to the human voice. A basic compatibility of inherent origins thus exists between the baby and his caretakers that is shown from the first day of life.

Interactions are, however, never static: the baby's mouth is used for sucking, its sensory apparatus for processing information. Functional compatibility is shown in the way these structures are used, and seen in particular in the temporal relationships between the infant's and the adult's responses. There is now an impressive body of evidence to show that from the beginning an infant's behaviour is organized in time and that the periodicity thus found is mostly dependent on centrally regulated microrhythms (as seen in scanning and in sucking) or macrorhythms (as seen, for example, in state changes). These are at first internally regulated but very soon after birth become linked to external events, particularly to caretaker activities (Schaffer, 1977). How this process of entrainment occurs remains one of the main outstanding questions in this field; that it does occur is shown in the finely synchronized interpersonal exchanges described for sucking (Kaye, Chapter 5), vocal behaviour (Schaffer *et al.*, Chapter 12), and visual interaction (Stern, 1974). To some extent, as we shall see below, the resulting "smoothness" of the relationship is a function of the adult's sensitivity to the on–off flow of the baby's behaviour; to some extent also, however, the entrainment may be based on inherently determined interpersonal synchronies of movement patterns (as suggested by Condon, Chapter 7). The complex rules which are subsequently found to regulate the temporal use of communication channels can thus be said to arise from such inherent compatabilities.

THE INFANT'S INTERACTIVE ACHIEVEMENTS

The realization in the last decade or so that the young infant, far from being a *tabula rasa*, is even at birth already endowed with an impressive set of competencies, should not, of course, blind one to the considerable task ahead of him in reaching full social status. As Ashley Montagu (1950) has put it, "The wonderful thing about a baby is its promise, not its performance—its promise to perform under certain auspices." What then does it still have to achieve in the course of the first year or two to fulfil that promise?

The child's major achievement lies in attaining what we may call the *concept of the dialogue*. There are two aspects to this development, expressed respectively by the notions of *reciprocity* and of *intentionality*.

Reciprocity refers to the role which the infant plays in an interaction sequence. There are numerous indications (provided here in particular in the contributions by Newson, Trevarthen, Kaye and Whiten) that early dialogues are at first one-sided affairs (*pseudo-dialogues*), that they are sustained only through the mother's initiative in replying to the infant's responses *as if* they had communicative significance. It is not till the end of the first year that the infant will learn that dialogues are two-sided, that they are based on roles which are both reciprocal and interchangeable (actor–spectator, giver–taker, speaker–auditor), and that the playing of these roles and their periodic exchange are managed according to certain rules to which both partners must adhere. Bruner's description (Chapter 11) of give-and-take games shows this development clearly: action patterns of a *joint* nature cannot appear until the infant has mastered the idea of reciprocity.

The related notion of intentionality develops once the infant realizes that his behaviour has communicative value and can be used purposively to affect the behaviour of others and to bring about desired results. Intentionality (as Trevarthen and Collis here show) is a slippery concept that cannot easily be defined in operational terms, yet it is useful in expressing the strong impression one gains when observing older infants that they act in full awareness of anticipated goals. The contrast is between the baby who cries because he has a pain and the baby who cries in order to summons his mother to deal with the pain: the one responding reactively, the other with an eye to the future. Through having been involved in dialogues all along and through the consistent responses of others contingent on his behaviour the infant learns that his smiles, vocalizations, gestures and movements are attended to by others and produce particular effects. In time they will therefore be used purposively with the anticipation that others will respond in certain specific ways. Just when the infant becomes capable of such an achievement is still far from certain. However, the argument advanced by Bates *et al.* (1975) is convincing, namely that intentionality does not become evident till the end of the first year, when on attaining sensori-motor stage V the infant becomes capable of differentiating ends from means and thenceforth is able to use objects to interact with adults and adults as a means of obtaining objects. From that stage on he can point for things out of reach, cry for attention, raise his arms to be lifted, repeatedly drop toys out of his pram for the sheer sadistic pleasure of seeing his mother pick them up again, and eventually use words capable of producing a great range of diverse effects.

It becomes apparent that two further developments are closely related to attaining the concept of the dialogue. In the first place, it is necessary for certain *cognitive mechanisms* to develop so that dialogic ability can appear at all. The differentiation of ends from means is only one such mechanism; a more basic one is the differentiation of self from other (without which a dialogue would obviously be an absurdity) and the related growth of object permanence and of representational skills generally. If, moreover, the child is to deal with social events in terms of a remembered past and an anticipated future and not relate them merely to the here-and-now, an expansion in memory capabilities is clearly required. And yet another example is the growth of attention span which will enable the infant to relate to two objects simultaneously and thus, for example, play ball with the mother rather than, as earlier, play with *either* the mother *or* a ball.

The other development refers to the expansion that takes place in the number of *communication channels* available to the child. Some, such as smiling and crying, are present from the early weeks on, but throughout the first year or two an increasing number make their appearance. Gestures such as pointing (see Murphy and Messer, Chapter 13) and demand movements, the ability to follow the other person's gaze, vocalizations of one kind or another and finally the appearance of words all combine to increase vastly the range of subtle meanings which the child can eventually both convey and comprehend.

THE MOTHER'S DYADIC BEHAVIOUR

What is it that enables an infant eventually to become an accomplished participant in dialogues? Given an inherent basis of pre-adaptation and the necessary cognitive means, the additional factor required seems to be just the sheer opportunity, repeated day after day for month after month, of taking part in dialogue-like exchanges. And it is here that the mother's ability to set up and sustain such exchanges becomes so important.

Mothers need to call upon a variety of dyadic techniques in relating to their infants. For convenience sake these have been classified as phasing, adaptive, facilitative, elaborative, initiating and control techniques and are discussed in these terms in greater detail elsewhere (Schaffer, 1977). For our present purposes it is the first of these, the mother's phasing techniques, that are of relevance. A repeated theme that emerges from the observations reported in the following pages is that early interaction sequences generally begin with the infant's own spontaneous behaviour, that the mother then chimes in to support, repeat, comment upon and elaborate his response, that she holds herself ready to let the infant resume as soon as he wishes, and that in this way she makes it possible for a dialogue-like interaction to be set in motion. Newson (Chapter 3) in particular stresses how mothers tend to act as though the infant were already an active communicative partner, endowing his responses with a signal value which, seen from his point of view, they do not in fact possess. The mother thus allows herself to be paced by the infant. She fills in the pauses between his response bursts, and to do so successfully she needs, of course, sensitivity and an exquisite sense of timing.

It is here that we see the importance of the turn-taking pattern found by a number of the contributors in various early interactive situations, for such a pattern is particularly suited to let the infant find out that his behaviour can be used as a means of interacting with another person. It maximizes the opportunity for him to learn that his behaviour is of interest to the mother, that it will be attended to and elicit a response from her, and that it is worth his while to attend to her response in turn. Routine sequences of a predictable nature thus become built up. And it is here that a further phenomenon becomes important, namely that of imitation: as Pawlby (Chapter 9) shows, whatever the facts of infants' imitation, imitation *by mothers* is a very common occurrence and accounts for a relatively high proportion of interaction sequences. By repeating the infant's response the mother not only reflects back to him his own behaviour but also produces a stereotyped and therefore predictable form of interaction. And let us also note the extent to which the mother ensures that the infant gets maximum benefit of the information content of her behaviour by exaggerating, repeating, and slowing down her actions and using all the other techniques to which Stern (Chapter 8) draws attention.

No wonder that mothers (as pointed out by several of the contributors) spend so much of any interactive situation in visually attending to the infant, for the appropriateness of their timing and of the nature of their contribution is essential to the continuation of the dialogue. Looking patterns are thus very different from those found in adult dyads, for the mother is holding herself in almost constant readiness to intervene at appropriate moments, without the benefit of the much more varied cues that an adult partner would provide. Far from arbitrarily imposing her behaviour upon the child, she is engaged in continuously monitoring his activities so that she can then time her own interventions in precise synchrony with his. The *when* of her behaviour is thus every bit as important as the *how* if she is to achieve a predictable outcome to the encounter.

Conclusions

How do patterns of communication manifest themselves in the pre-linguistic stage? What compatibility is there between the infant and the adult with respect to the mode of communication and its topics? What is the compatibility based on and how is it fostered? These are questions to be answered if we are to explain how the infant becomes capable of participating in interactive situations and growing increasingly skilled at manipulating and recombining social sequences.

In this book a variety of attempts are made to deal with such questions. The answers they produce are by no means unanimous; furthermore it is apparent that the methodological problems to be overcome are still considerable. Nevertheless, it is significant that the findings obtained are already being applied to two further issues that are also discussed in this volume.

The first refers to the application of knowledge about normal interactive processes to the course of development in atypical children. The contributions of both Jones and Whiten illustrate this—one by a comparison of Down's Syndrome infants with a normal group, the other by examining infants who had experienced separation in early post-natal life.

The second issue refers to the implications of early interactive events for later behaviour. There are few who would now subscribe to a critical period model of human development according to which early experiences have some decisive long-term effect just because they are early; there are also few, however, who would not agree that in some sense such early patterns do not set the scene for what follows by guiding (though by no means irreversibly) the infant in one direction rather than another. The contributions by Dunn and by Dunn and Richards examine this very difficult theme in their follow-up study, searching for the consistencies that would enable one to predict across time on the basis of either individual or dyadic measures.

More recently, however, the continuities issue has taken on a new significance with the debate about the precursors of language acquisition. As Bruner (Chapter 11) argues, there are strong indications that language skills, far from arising *de novo*, have their roots in earlier interactive events and that the development of verbal communication in the second year must thus be related to the infant's ability to participate in sequences of interpersonal behaviour already evident in the course of the first year. If, as Rommetveit (1968) has put it, one's real concern in learning a language is to communicate messages, and if we follow Halliday (1975) in believing that messages can be meaningfully conveyed long before the child speaks his first word, then the basic problem becomes one of understanding the development of the communicative process in general, with language acquisition being seen as but one offshoot (albeit the most vital one) of this development.

Yet how we can convincingly show that there is indeed a continuity between the pre-verbal and the verbal communicative level, in the sense that the former constitutes a necessary precondition to the latter, remains a problem. One of the customary methods of demonstrating a connection between two developmental events A and B, namely experimentally to deprive the organism of A and see if B still occurs, is obviously not feasible in this instance. The deprivation technique in any case does not provide a pure test, in that it introduces various confounding influences. Similarly another approach, the correlational technique, is not wholly convincing, in that it consists in examining the relationship between parameters of the two functions involved (their age at onset, their amount, and so on) in order to detect similarities, but is then unable to proceed to making statements about the aetiological factors at work.

Under the circumstances it is not surprising to find a tendency to resort to arguments based on the similarity in topography of the functions under discussion, and this may well be as far as we can take it at present. But however persuasive the similarity, one should bear in mind that it provides an argument based on analogy—no more. Developmental continuity therefore remains an assumption. At any rate let us be clear that there are at least three senses in which one may talk of continuity: first with regard to the *functions* of communication (the wish to obtain certain objects, to affect the other person's behaviour, and so on); second with regard to the *constituent skills* required for communication (such as intentionality, role alternation, etc.); and third, with regard to the *situation* in which communication occurs. The last can be particularly misleading: vocal turn-taking, for instance (see Schaffer *et al.*, Chapter 12), may be found in quite early interactions, providing them with the "mature" appearance of later verbal exchanges, and yet this may be brought about entirely by the mother's skill at inserting her vocalizations at appropriate moments into the child's sequence of vocal activity. The continuity, that is, is in this instance inherent in the dyadic situation and does not refer to a constituent skill of the child's.

Any attempt to "explain" the onset of language in terms of its developmental precursors is thus still fraught with difficulties. But what cannot be doubted is that mother and infant come to share a code of conduct long before they share a linguistic code, that this code has its rules—some universal, some idiosyncratic—which the child acquires in a way that is still far from clear, and that the characteristics of this rule-governed behaviour are now clarifying the processes that underlie the formation of the child's primary social bond.

References

Ainsworth, M. D. S. (1973). The development of infant-mother attachment. In B. M. Caldwell and H. N. Ricciuti (Eds), *Review of Child Development Research Vol.* **3**. University of Chicago, Chicago.

Altmann, S. A. (1965). Sociobiology of rhesus monkeys, II. Stochastics of social communication. *J. theor. Biol.* **8**, 490–522.

Bates, E., Camaioni, L. and Volterra, V. (1975). The acquisition of performatives prior to speech. *Merrill-Palmer Q.* **21**, 205–226.

Bell, R. Q. (1968). A reinterpretation of the direction of effects in studies of socialization. *Psychol. Rev.* **75**, 81–95.

Bowlby, J. (1972). *Attachment and Loss, Vol. I. Attachment.* Hogarth, London.

Duncan, S. (1973). Toward a grammar for dyadic conversation. *Semiotica* **9**, 29–46.

Gewirtz, J. L. (1972). Attachment, dependence, and a distinction in terms of stimulus control. In J. L. Gewirtz (Ed.), *Attachment and Dependency*. Wiley, New York.

Halliday, M. A. K. (1975). *Learning How to Mean*. Arnold, London.

Hinde, R. A. (1976). On describing relationships. *J. Child Psychol. Psychiat.* **17**, 1–19.

Kaye, K. (1976). Infants' effects upon their mothers' teaching strategies. In J. C. Glidewell (Ed.), *The Social Context of Learning and Development*. Gardner, New York.

Maccoby, E. and Masters, J. C. (1970). Attachment and dependency. In P. H. Mussen (Ed.), *Carmichael's Manual of Child Psychology*, 3rd edition. Wiley, New York and London.

Montagu, A. (1950). *On Being Human*. Abelard-Schuman, New York.

Nelson, K. (1974). Concept, word, and sentence: interrelations in acquisition and development. *Psychol. Rev.* **81**, 267–285.

Rommetveit, R. (1968). *Words, Meanings, and Messages*. Academic Press, New York and London.

Schaffer, H. R. (1971). *The Growth of Sociability*. Penguin, Harmondsworth, Middlesex.

Schaffer, H. R. (1977). *Mothering*. Open Books, London; Harvard University Press, New York.

Slater, P. J. B. (1973). Describing sequences of behavior. In P. P. G. Bateson and P. H. Klopfer (Eds), *Perspectives in Ethology*. Plenum, New York.

Stern, D. N. (1974). Mother and infant at play: the dyadic interaction involving facial, vocal, and gaze behaviors. In M. Lewis and L. A. Rosenblum (Eds), *The Effect of the Infant on its Caregiver*. Wiley, New York and London.

Wood, D. and Middleton, D. (1975). A study of assisted problem-solving. *Br. J. Psychol.* **66**, 181–192.

II | Describing the Relationship

2 Frequencies, Durations, Derived Measures and their Correlations in Studying Dyadic and Triadic Relationships

R. A. Hinde and Joan Herrmann

Introduction

A recurring problem is how to select items for recording or measurement from the continuous stream of behaviour which passes before our eyes. One set of criteria is based on the reliability with which they can be recorded. Another, clearly of primary importance but often conflicting with the first, concerns their relevance to the problem in hand. In studies of the development of social behaviour a variety of issues may be important here—for instance the predictive value of the measures, or the extent to which they represent enduring characteristics of a relationship or contribute towards an understanding of its dynamics.

In attempting to answer such questions, it is common practice to rely primarily on measures of the frequency and/or duration of the various activities. However, it is not necessarily the case that such measures are the most pertinent. It could well be that, for instance, the *absolute number* of ventro-ventral contacts that a mother monkey initiates with her infant has less predictive value for the future course of the relationship than the proportion of all the contacts that occur for which she is responsible. Intuitively one might expect such a "Derived Measure" to be at least as valuable as measures of absolute frequency or duration.

This issue is discussed in the first part of this paper with reference to the measures used in some recent studies of the development of mother–infant relationships in rhesus monkeys. It reviews (with hindsight) how these measures were chosen, their limitations, and the ways in which they have been used to tackle a number of problems for which they were not originally intended. Its aim is not to provide examples to be followed, but rather to make explicit some of the difficulties and basic assumptions in this type of research, and perhaps to indicate some principles that may be useful for choosing and using other measures in comparable contexts.

In one respect, perhaps best made explicit from the start, these studies have differed from many other studies of the development of social behaviour (though see Dunn, 1975). It has not been assumed that any of the measures assesses individual characteristics of the behaviour of *either* the mother *or* the infant: rather we have presumed that each measure assesses an aspect of *the relationship*, influenced by the behaviour of both partners. The latter sections of the paper therefore involve consideration of how such measures can contribute towards understanding of the roles of the two partners in the relationship.

Although the paper is based on data on rhesus monkeys, we believe that the principles involved have much wider applicability: we hope that those who read it will think in terms of the dependent variables in which they are interested, substituting, for instance, for "mother initiates ventro-ventral contact", "mother initiates mutual gaze" or whatever seems appropriate.

Some Background Issues

Since the work was concerned with a problem in social development, the monkeys were kept in small social groups each consisting of a male, a few females and their offspring. The situation was intended as a compromise, permitting moderate experimental control and moderately precise recording of behaviour in a moderately complex social group.

During the period under review budgetary considerations limited us to check-sheet recording techniques (Hinde, 1973). More recently we have substituted a keyboard technique which produces a record on magnetic tape susceptible to direct computer analysis (White, 1971). Whilst this refinement permits us to record finer details than was possible previously, and to analyse data more rapidly, it does not necessarily out-date discussion of measures obtainable with cruder techniques. For one thing, the efficiency or inefficiency of detailed methods in different situations is an empirical matter and must await further data: for some problems a gross measure may take one more quickly to the nub of the issue than very detailed material. For another, keyboard techniques are not suitable for all situations—for instance keyboards may be difficult to use for human mother–infant interaction in the home.

The Measures

The measures to be discussed here, which are selected from those used in the original studies, fall into three categories.

(i) *Duration measures*
The two principle ones discussed here are (a) Total Time Off Mother (or T.T. off) and (b) Time At A Distance (i.e. out of arm's reach of the mother, or more than 60 cm from her, abbreviated to > 60 cm). In practice the data were recorded on check-sheets with half-minute time intervals, and the measures actually used were "Number of half-minutes in which the infant was off its mother, expressed as a percentage of the number observed", and "Number of half-minutes in which the infant was more than 60 cm from its mother, expressed as a percentage of the number in which it was off her at all". (It will be noted that the two measures are independent of each other: we are asking what proportion of the time observed the infant was off its mother, and what proportion of *that* time off it was at a distance from her.) The method, involving the recording of whether or not a particular condition (e.g. infant off mother) occurs in successive time intervals, leads to an overestimation of durations, since a bout of, for example, time off which lasts for less than or extends into a half-minute unit is recorded as involving that unit (Altmann, 1974; Hinde, 1974; Simpson and

Simpson, in press). However, in the present case the slight errors thus introduced do not affect the conclusions drawn.

In addition to the two duration measures described above, the number of half-minutes in which the mother groomed the baby, as a percentage of those observed (M.G.B.) is mentioned briefly.

(ii) *Occurrence measures*

These include (a) *Rejections:* the number of occasions on which an infant attempted to make ventro-ventral contact with its mother and was rejected by her (R);

(b) *Maternal contacts:* the number of occasions on which contact was made on the mother's initiative (Mk_M);

(c) *Infant contacts:* the number of occasions on which contact was made on the infant's initiative (Mk_I);

(d) and (e) *Approaches:* the number of times the distance between mother and infant decreased from more than 60 cm to less because of movement by the mother (Ap_M) or infant (Ap_I);

(f) and (g) *Leavings:* the number of times that the distance between mother and infant increased from less than 60 cm to more because of movement by the mother (L_M) or infant (L_I).

In all these cases the measure used was the absolute number of occurrences per standard period of observation.

(iii) *Derived measures*

It is often presumed that the closer a measure is to what the subjects actually did, the more useful is that measure likely to be. Although this is an important basic principle, from an early stage in our work we felt some departures from it were justified, for two reasons. First, there is no way to predict which measures will have a high consistency or a high predictive value. It thus seemed important to explore the usefulness not only of direct assessments of duration or frequency, but also of measures derived from them. Thus we felt intuitively that for some problems, rather than asking only how often an infant's attempts to gain ventro-ventral contact were rejected, it might be profitable also to assess what proportion of the contacts he made or attempted were rejected. The mother–infant relationship of an infant which tries to make contact with its mother ten times and is rejected ten times must surely be different from that of an infant which tried to make contact 100 times and was rejected ten times. Either we must assess this difference by keeping both measures in mind simultaneously, or we must attempt to combine them. The following ratios are discussed in the present paper:

(a) The proportion of ventro-ventral contact makes due to the mother ($Mk_M/(Mk_I + Mk_M)$).

(b) The ratio of unsuccessful to successful infant attempts to make ventro-ventral contact (R/Mk_I).

(c) The ratio of the number of rejected attempts to make contact by the infant to the total number of contacts or attempted contacts ($R/(Mk_I + Mk_M + R)$).

(d) The proportion of approaches due to the infant ($Ap_I/(Ap_I + Ap_M)$).

(e) The proportion of leavings due to the infant ($L_I/(L_I + L_M)$).

The second reason for using derived measures is one of convenience. It is useful to be able to summarize, for instance, the relative contribution of the infant to the maintenance of proximity with the mother in one index. In this context we have used the difference between the percentage of approaches due to the infant and the percentage of leavings due to the infant:

$$\{100Ap_I/(Ap_I + Ap_M)\} - \{100L_I/(L_I + L_M)\}, \text{ abbreviated to } \%Ap_I - \%L_I.$$

This index is negative if the mother is primarily responsible for the maintenance of proximity (i.e. infant responsible for a higher proportion of leavings than of approaches), and positive if the infant is. The properties and limitations of the index have been discussed elsewhere (Hinde and Atkinson, 1970; Hinde, 1975; see also discussion of a similar index for assessing the infant's role in ventro-ventral contact in Hinde and White, 1974).

Many workers do not use ratio or derived measures either because they feel that they are too remote from the actual behaviour, or because of the misleading properties that ratios can have. However, as already mentioned, we have taken it as axiomatic that no measure is a direct measure of the behavioural propensities of either mother or infant. Thus how long the infant spends off the mother depends on the behaviour of both, and how often the mother rejects the infant depends on how often the infant attempts to make contact. Indeed we find it difficult to envisage a behavioural measure that is relevant to the relationship that may not depend on the behaviour of both participants. In our view the same applies to many measures that are treated as "baby" or "mother" measures in studies of human mother–infant relationships. For instance the latency with which a mother goes to her baby when it cries (Bell and Ainsworth, 1972) must depend on how often the baby has cried recently. And if one accepts that such measures are measures of the relationship rather than of the behavioural propensities of either individual, ratio measures are intuitively at least as likely to be relevant as absolute frequencies.

To some extent the effects of the scaling distortions inherent in the use of ratio measures are minimized if results are assessed with non-parametric statistics. The consistency of direct (duration and occurrence) and derived measures are assessed in the next section.

The age changes in some of these measures are shown in Figs 1 and 2.

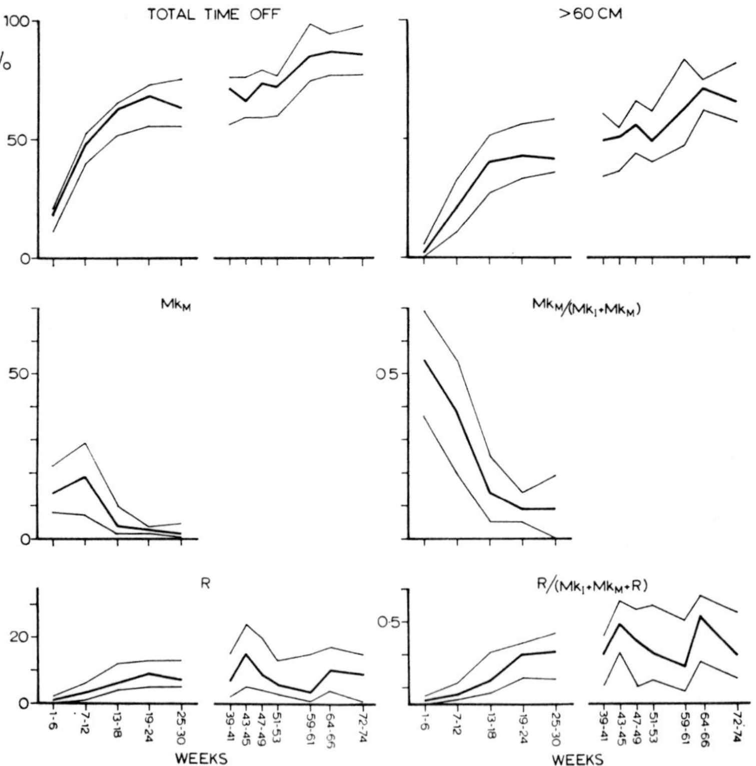

Fig. 1. Medians and interquartile ranges of some measures of the mother–infant relationship. Data are grouped over 6 or 3-week intervals. Abscissae indicate percentage, value of ratio or index, or total occurrences in 6 hours.

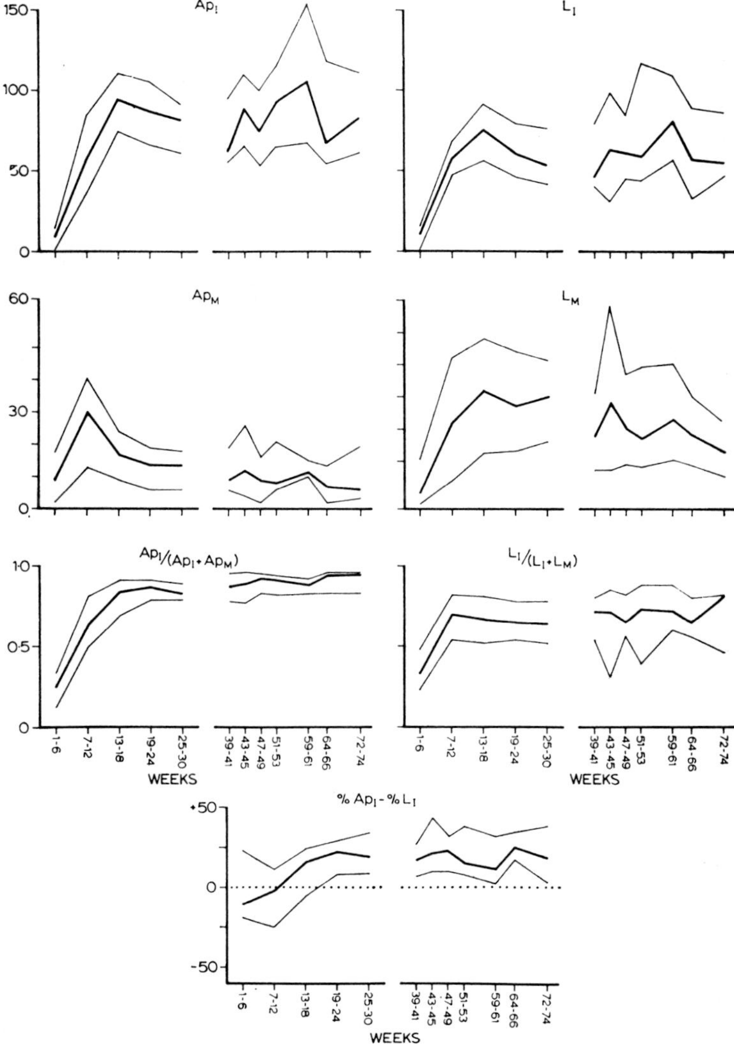

Fig. 2. Medians and interquartile ranges of some measures of the mother–infant relationship. Data are grouped over 6 or 3-week intervals. Abscissae indicate percentage, value of ratio or index, or total occurrences in 6 hours.

Comparison of Direct and Derived Measures

RANK ORDER CONSISTENCY OVER SUCCESSIVE AGE PERIODS

We shall here consider the extent to which the various measures are consistent over successive age periods. For this we have used the following data:

(a) Data from 26 mother/infant dyads observed over the first 24 weeks of life. Each dyad was watched for six morning hours per week, weekly or fortnightly. Data have been grouped into six-week age periods.

(b) Similar data from 16 of these dyads for weeks 25–28.

(c) Data on a smaller number of measures for 9–22 animals observed during weeks 39–41, 43–45, 47–49, 51–53, 59–61, 64–66 and 72–74. Some of these animals had been separated for 6–13 days from their mothers between weeks 24 and 31 (Hinde and Spencer-Booth, 1971a).

In addition certain other data, to be specified later, are used to make specific points.

Rank order correlation coefficients between individual values of the same measure in successive time periods are shown for the younger animals in Table I and for the older ones in Table II. The following points emerge:

(i) In general, consistency between each six-week period and the next was high. Thus, considering all measures, 82 of the 104 correlation coefficients between the values of a measure in one six-week period and the next (excluding those based on samples of less than 14) were significantly positive. Not surprisingly, consistency becomes lower over longer time intervals.

(ii) Maternal initiative in ventro-ventral contact becomes rare after the first 20 weeks (Fig. 1), and so data are available only in Table I. The ratio measure showed at least as much individual consistency as the absolute measure (correlation coefficients for $Mk_M/(Mk_I + Mk_M)$ higher or less negative than those for Mk_M in six out of ten comparisons).

(iii) With maternal rejections, the ratio measures again showed as much individual consistency as the absolute measures (correlation

Table I

Rank order correlations (Spearman) over successive age periods, weeks 1–30

Correlation of rank in:	Weeks 1–6				Weeks 7–12			Weeks 13–18		Weeks 19–24
With weeks:	7–12	13–18	19–24	25–30	13–18	19–24	25–30	19–24	25–30	25–30
T.T. off	0·52[b]	0·35[a]	0·35[a]	−0·04	0·40[a]	0·29	−0·11	0·45[a]	0·36	0·47[a]
> 60 cm	0·59[b]	0·21	0·27	−0·10	0·65[b]	0·32[a]	−0·06	0·36[a]	0·30	0·40
M gms B	0·65[b]	0·33[a]	−0·02	−0·04	0·64[b]	0·52[b]	0·52[a]	0·68[b]	0·62[b]	0·73[b]
Mk_M	0·32	0·27	0·30	−0·31	0·64[b]	0·63[b]	0·37	0·71[b]	0·24	0·46[a]
$Mk_M/(Mk_I + Mk_M)$	0·15	0·21	0·54[b]	−0·20	0·78[b]	0·62[b]	0·38	0·69[b]	0·33	0·74[b]
R	0·52[b]	0·50[b]	0·30	0·27	0·77[b]	0·47[b]	−0·20	0·36[a]	0·18	0·33
R/Mk_I	0·48[b]	0·40[a]	0·22	0·35	0·79[b]	0·57[b]	−0·18	0·76[b]	0·27	0·41
$R/(Mk_I + Mk_M + R)$	0·51[b]	0·44[a]	0·20	0·32	0·79[b]	0·64[b]	−0·13	0·80[b]	0·36	0·38
Ap_I	0·63[b]	0·19	0·01	0·13	0·31	0·09	0·13	0·41[a]	0·25	0·29
Ap_M	0·31	0·27	0·26	0·14	0·77[b]	0·60[b]	0·69[b]	0·72[b]	0·31	0·40
$Ap_i/(Ap_I + Ap_M)$	0·50[b]	0·23	0·27	0·45[b]	0·69[b]	0·63[b]	0·64[b]	0·73[b]	0·75[b]	0·72[b]
L_I	0·53[b]	0·14	0·07	0·03	0·12	0·21	−0·02	0·38[a]	0·28	0·36
L_M	0·59[b]	0·32	0·27	0·71[b]	0·75[b]	0·63[b]	0·34	0·95[b]	0·68[b]	0·65[b]
$L_I/(L_I + L_M)$	0·48[b]	0·37[a]	0·42[a]	0·44[a]	0·62[b]	0·77[b]	0·43[a]	0·74[b]	0·77[b]	0·74[b]
$\%Ap_I - \%L_I$	0·48[b]	0·53[b]	0·44[a]	0·36	0·61[b]	0·63[b]	0·27	0·79[b]	0·65[b]	0·70[b]
N =	26	26	26	16	26	26	16	26	16	16

[a] $p < 0·05$.
[b] $p < 0·01$.

Table II

Rank order correlations (Spearman) over successive age periods, weeks 39–74

Correlation of rank in:	Weeks 39–41						Weeks 43–45				
With weeks:	43–45	47–49	51–53	59–61	64–66	72–74	47–49	51–53	59–61	64–66	72–74
Total Time off	0·21	0·45[a]	0·53[a]	0·62[a]	−0·12	−0·04	0·38[a]	0·28	−0·04	−0·45	−0·44
> 60 cm	0·38[a]	0·69[b]	0·62[b]	0·69[b]	0·10	−0·15	0·71[b]	0·62[b]	0·68[b]	−0·36	−0·27
R	0·47[a]	0·14	0·46[a]	0·22	0·33	0·53	0·30	0·58[b]	0·44	0·07	0·11
$R/(Mk_I + Mk_M + R)$	0·57[b]	0·22	0·32	0·22	0·26	0·38	0·47[a]	0·59[b]	0·42	0·10	0·43
Ap_I	0·19	0·19	0·10	0·01	−0·57	−0·18	0·33	0·45[a]	−0·37	−0·01	−0·40
Ap_M	0·65[b]	0·68[b]	0·73[b]	−0·04	0·74[a]	0·53	0·64[b]	0·77[b]	−0·11	0·73[a]	0·55
$Ap_I/(Ap_I + Ap_M)$	0·84[b]	0·80[b]	0·78[b]	−0·15	0·55	0·14	0·71[b]	0·76[b]	−0·12	0·58	0·24
L_I	0·48[a]	0·41[a]	0·39[a]	0·03	−0·67[a]	0·12	0·59[b]	0·61[b]	−0·25	−0·26	−0·10
L_M	0·71[b]	0·69[b]	0·74[b]	0·65[b]	0·73[a]	0·64[a]	0·66[b]	0·81[b]	0·77[b]	0·85[b]	0·89[b]
$L_I/(L_I + L_M)$	0·83[b]	0·66[b]	0·79[b]	0·65[b]	0·95[b]	0·90[b]	0·75[b]	0·85[b]	0·70[b]	0·82[a]	0·90[b]
$\%Ap_I - \%L_I$	0·60[b]	0·43[a]	0·39[a]	0·50[a]	0·83[b]	0·87[b]	0·66[b]	0·75[b]	0·74[b]	0·76[a]	0·69[a]
N =	22	19	19	14	8	9	19	19	14	8	9

[a] $p < 0{\cdot}05$.
[b] $p < 0{\cdot}01$.

Table II (continued)

Correlation of rank in:	Weeks 47–49				Weeks 51–53			Weeks 59–61		Weeks 64–66
With weeks:	51–53	59–61	64–66	72–74	59–61	64–66	72–74	64–66	72–74	72–74
Total Time off	0·45[a]	0·33	0·31	0·08	0·38	0·50	−0·18	0·90[a]	1·0[b]	0·47
> 60 cm	0·62[b]	0·56[a]	0·33	0	0·64[b]	0·31	−0·03	−0·30	−0·40	0·50
R	0·45[a]	0·53[a]	0·69[a]	0·45	0·69[b]	0·60	0·23	0·62	0·60	0·59
$R/(Mk_I + Mk_M + R)$	0·39[a]	0·58[a]	0·71[a]	0·44	0·12	0·50	0·31	0·60	0·30	0·76[a]
Ap_I	0·39	−0·10	−0·17	−0·23	0·18	0·21	−0·18	0·50	0·60	0·57
Ap_M	0·75[b]	0·16	0·54	0·24	0·04	0·55	0·48	−0·36	−0·21	0·16
$Ap_I/(Ap_I + Ap_M)$	0·68[b]	−0·36	0·43	0·44	0·12	0·56	0·59	−0·21	−0·30	−0·02
L_I	0·60[b]	0·03	−0·26	−0·08	0·52[a]	0·05	−0·50	0·10	−0·41	0·19
L_M	0·70[b]	0·67[a]	0·78[a]	0·74[a]	0·57[a]	0·74[a]	0·85[b]	0·80	0·60	0·69[a]
$L_I/(L_I + L_M)$	0·71[b]	0·52[a]	0·95[b]	0·79[b]	0·55[a]	0·86[b]	0·85[b]	0·80	0·90[a]	0·91[b]
$\%Ap_I - \%L_I$	0·57[b]	0·41	0·76[a]	0·66[a]	0·49[a]	0·86[b]	0·75[a]	1·0[b]	0·90[a]	0·81[a]
N =	18	13	8	9	14	8	9	5	5	8

[a] $p < 0{\cdot}05$.
[b] $p < 0{\cdot}01$.

coefficients for R/Mk_I and $R/(Mk_I + Mk_M + R)$ higher or less negative than that for R in seven out of ten comparisons in Table I; coefficients for $R/(Mk_I + Mk_M + R)$ higher or equal to that for R in 11 out of 21 comparisons in Table II).

(iv) Comparing maternal and infant approaches and leavings, the (absolute) maternal measures were more consistent than the infant's in 24 out of 31 comparisons for approaches and in every case for leavings. This is of course a reflection of the fact that the frequency of the infant's approaches and leavings were affected by its tendencies to explore its environment and play with social companions as well as its relationship with its mother.

(v) Comparing absolute and ratio measures of the infant's approaches and leavings, the ratio measures gave higher coefficients in 24 out of 31 comparisons for approaches and 30 out of 31 for leavings. Thus here the ratio measures clearly showed greater consistency than the absolute ones.

(vi) The difference between the proportion of approaches and leavings due to the infant tended to be about as consistent as the two ratios from which it was derived (correlation coefficients for $Ap_I/(Ap_I + Ap_M)$ and $L_I/(L_I + L_M)$ higher than those for $\%Ap_I - \%L_I$ in 12 out of 31 cases and 23 out of 31 cases respectively).

These results indicate that the ratio measures in general show at least as much rank order consistency as the absolute measures from which they are derived. To that extent, and in that sense, they effectively represent durable properties of the relationship. What precisely does this mean? We may consider two alternatives.

First, greater consistency of the ratio measures could have been a mathematical consequence of the nature of the measures on which the ratios were based. Thus if Mk_I were much greater and more consistent than Mk_M, individual differences in Mk_I could swamp those in Mk_M. In practice, although Mk_I was greater than Mk_M over most of the period covered here (Fig. 1), the correlation coefficients between successive age periods were similar for the two measures (r_s for $Mk_M >$ r_s for Mk_I in five out of ten comparisons). Again, $Ap_I/(Ap_I + Ap_M)$ could show greater consistency than Ap_I because Ap_M was much greater than and more consistent than Ap_I. In fact Ap_M was only about one-sixth of Ap_I (Fig. 2): so that, although it showed greater consistency (Table I), this would be swamped by the difference in absolute values. In any case, the ratio measure tends to show rather more consistency than either Ap_I or Ap_M. Similar considerations apply to the measures of leavings.

Since the rank order consistency of the derived measures is not to be explained away in such terms, it can be concluded that the differences to which they are addressed (see above) show at least as much consistency over age as do the absolute measures on which they are based.

CORRELATIONS BETWEEN DIRECT AND DERIVED MEASURES

Correlations between different measures of a relationship are often used to assess the extent to which the several measures are redundant and reflect a common underlying property. For instance, in so far as maternal initiative in ventro-ventral contact is positively correlated with the time the mother spends grooming the baby (Table V), the two can be regarded as manifestations of "maternal warmth" (see Hinde and Simpson, 1975). Here we are concerned with a comparable issue—namely the extent to which the derived measures assess characteristics that are in fact different from the absolute measures on which they are based. For this we consider first whether the median values of absolute and derived measures show similar age changes (Figs 1 and 2); and second whether, at any one age, individuals who score high on the absolute measures also score high on the derived measures, or whether there is no correlation between them (Table III). In some instances we shall also look at the effects of experimental treatments on the relations between them. In the interests of brevity, only some of the pairs of measures given in Table I and II are discussed here.

Mk_M and $Mk_M/(Mk_I + Mk_M)$. The age changes in the absolute and derived measures were closely similar, except that the absolute measure showed an initial rise rather than a continuous fall. This initial rise in the absolute measure was merely a consequence of the increase in the number of bouts that the infants spent off their mothers. Within each of the six-week periods between weeks 1 and 30 the rank order correlations between individuals were high (Table III). Both measures were near zero in older age groups. Thus in this case the ratio measure is largely redundant, though the age changes in the mother's role in ventro-ventral contact are perhaps more accurately portrayed by the continuous fall of the ratio measure than by the initial rise of the absolute one.

R and $R/(Mk_I + Mk_M + R)$. Figure 1 shows that the age changes in

Table III

Rank order correlations (Spearman) between absolute measures and ratio measures derived from them

Correlations between:	Weeks 1–6	7–12	13–18	19–24	25–28	39–41	43–45	47–49	51–53	59–61	64–66	72–74
Mk_M and $Mk_M/(Mk_I + Mk_M)$	0·52[b]	0·86[b]	0·89[b]	0·87[b]	0·92[b]							
R and R/Mk_I	0·95[b]	0·96[b]	0·91[b]	0·78[b]	0·81[b]	0·83[b]	0·78[b]	0·86[b]	0·87[b]	0·96[b]	0·76[b]	0·75[b]
R and $R/(Mk_I + Mk_M + R)$	0·94[b]	0·98[b]	0·91[b]	0·79[b]	0·82[b]	0·81[b]	0·79[b]	0·86[b]	0·85[b]	0·96[b]	0·77[b]	0·73[b]
Ap_I and $Ap_I/(Ap_I + Ap_M)$	0·73[b]	0·60[b]	0·08	0·07	0·55[a]	0·47[a]	0·11	0·04	0·32	0·64[a]	−0·48	−0·37
Ap_I and $\%Ap_I - \%L_I$	0·10	0·77[b]	0·36[a]	0·11	0·01	−0·47[a]	−0·21	−0·21	−0·35	0·10	0·36	0·63[a]
L_I and $L_I/(L_I + L_M)$	0·59[b]	0·07	0·42[a]	0·31	0·67[b]	0·76[b]	0·72[b]	0·46[a]	0·75[b]	0·36	−0·64	0·27
L_I and $\%Ap - \%L_I$	0·21	0·09	−0·01	−0·30	−0·38	−0·79[b]	−0·74[b]	−0·52[a]	−0·74[b]	−0·23	0·19	−0·10
N =	26	26	26	26	16	22	22	19	19	14	8	9

[a] $p < 0{\cdot}05$.
[b] $p < 0{\cdot}01$.

these two measures were closely similar, and Table III that the rank order correlations within each age range were high. Thus here again the ratio measure appears to be largely redundant. However, in an earlier sample of data extending to week 100 the relative frequency of rejections remained high though the absolute frequency fell to near zero (Hinde, 1969). A reasonable interpretation is that the older infants maintained their demands at such a level that a more or less constant proportion were rejected; in the face of more rejecting mothers they could do this only by reducing the absolute number of attempts, and thus of rejections. That the rank order correlations within each age range remained high is in harmony with this interpretation. If further data should confirm this dissociation between the two measures in older age groups, the use of both might thus provide useful insights into the dynamics of the relationships.

Ap_I and $Ap_I/(Ap_I + Ap_M)$. After the first few weeks, the medians of both measures fluctuated about a steady level, but the ratio measure fluctuated less violently (Fig. 2). The latter, however, was in part a consequence of the difference in absolute values of the number of approaches by mother and infant, the ratio approaching its ceiling. Within each age period the correlations were erratic: up to week 12 the infants that made the most approaches also made the highest proportion of approaches, but thereafter only three of the ten correlations were significantly positive. This is presumably a reflection of the fact that the absolute number of approaches may be profoundly influenced by the frequency with which the infant leaves its mother to play or explore: unless the mother is very restrictive, such sallies usually require a subsequent approach. The relative measure is affected more directly by the behaviour of the mother.

L_I and $L_I/(L_I + L_M)$. The relations between these measures are essentially the same as those between the absolute and ratio approach measures, though strong positive correlations appeared in weeks 39–53.

Absolute measures of Approaches and Leavings, and $\%Ap_I - \%L_I$. It is not meaningful to compare the age changes in these measures, since the scales are not comparable. It will be seen, however, that the correlation coefficients within age periods were very variable. Although there were clear tendencies for those infants who approached their mothers most often in weeks 7–18 to rank highly on $\%\mathrm{Ap_I} - \%\mathrm{L_I}$, and for those who left often in weeks 39–53 to rank lowly, the correlations were otherwise erratic. This again is a reflection of the fact that the frequency of approaches and leaves depended on the tendencies of the infant to play with other animals and to explore its environment as well as on its relationship with its mother.

That absolute or ratio measures of approaches or leaves could not by themselves provide evidence on the role of the infant in maintaining proximity is evident from the correlations between them. If they did, we should expect those infants who approached often to leave seldom, and vice versa. In fact the correlations between them are negative only in the early weeks, and then not significantly: later they are strongly positively correlated (Hinde and White, 1974). This is of course a reflection of the fact that both are influenced by how much the infant plays away from its mother.

The same point was demonstrated clearly in experiments involving removal of the mother for six or 13 days whilst the infant stayed behind in the social group. When the mother was returned the infants both approached and left their mothers less than before separation—an aspect of their "depression". However, their role in proximity, as assessed by $\%Ap_I - \%AL_I$, almost invariably increased (Hinde and Spencer-Booth, 1971a).

In summary, this analysis suggests that we have so far not lost greatly, and may have profited slightly, by using the ratio measures of maternal initiations of ventro-ventral contact and maternal rejections. With the measures of approaching and leaving, however, the ratio measures showed greater individual reliability. Furthermore the ratio measures of the infant's approaches and leavings bear more directly on the nature of the mother–infant relationship than the absolute measures, which are affected by other aspects of the infant's social behaviour. Finally, the derived measure $\%Ap_I - \%L_I$ provides a useful measure of the infant's role in proximity which has considerable independence from the absolute level of activity.

Correlations between Measures and the Dynamics of the Relationship

If the measures we use refer to properties of the relationship, and not specifically to the behavioural propensities of either participant, how can we assess the contributions of those participants to the relationship?

Since we are dealing with continuing interactions within a relationship, problems in this area are unlikely to have easy answers: the infant may show behaviour that affects the mother's behaviour, but only because the mother had previously done something else. A productive approach is to ask questions about *differences* in mother–infant relationships between dyads, or about *changes* in a relationship with age or treatment. The method has been described in a number of other contexts (Hinde, 1969, 1974, in press), so discussion here is brief. It depends on the

Table IV

Model for predicting the effects of four simple types of change in mother or infant (left-hand column) on four measures of the mother–infant relationship

		T.T.off	R	>60cm	$\%Ap_I - \%L_I$
$\underset{\rightarrow}{M}$	I	−	−	−	−
$\underset{\leftarrow}{M}$	I	+	+	+	+
M	$\underset{\leftarrow}{I}$	−	+	−	+
M	$\underset{\rightarrow}{I}$	+	−	+	−

simple model in Table IV. The left-hand column indicates four types of change in mother or infant—namely an increase or decrease in the tendency of mother or infant to respond positively to the other. The hypothesis that changes in the relationship depend on only four types of basic change is of course too simple but provides a convenient starting point. The body of the table shows the predicted directions of change in four measures of the mother–infant relationship consequent upon each of these changes in the participants. It will be seen that where the change is due to the infant, time off the mother changes in the opposite direction to the frequency of rejections, and time at a distance from the mother in the opposite direction to the infant's role in proximity. Where the change is in the mother, changes within each pair of measures occur in the same direction. Thus by examining the relation between changes in or differences between pairs of measures, it is possible to make some progress in analysing the dynamics of the relationship.

Some examples of the application of this model are summarized below.

(i) *Age changes in the mother–infant relationship*
As the infant develops, it spends less time on its mother. The changes seem to be related to the growth and development of the infant, but is their rate controlled primarily by changes in the mother or by changes in the infant? The data (Fig. 1) show that, up to the age of one year, increase in median time off is associated with an increase in both the absolute and the ratio measures of rejections. Thus, from Table IV, the rate of change in the time the infant spends off its mother is determined primarily by changes in the mother. Of course the changes in the mother may in their turn be determined by changes in the infant's behaviour: we are concerned here with only the first stage in teazing apart the contributions of changes in the two participants to the changes in the relationship (see discussions in Hinde, 1969, 1974). With infants over one year-and-a-half the time off increases only slowly, the absolute measure of rejections may fall and the ratio measure stay fairly constant. Here, then, the model breaks down, for the simple hypothesis of changes in mother *or* infant could not predict a dissociation of the direction of changes in the absolute and relative frequency of rejections. The extent to which this dissociation between absolute and relative measures may provide insight into the dynamics of the relationship has already been mentioned.

(ii) *Inter-dyad differences at one age*
Are differences in the mother–infant relationship at any one age due more to differences between mothers or to differences between infants? The model predicts that if those mother–infant dyads in which the infants spend most time off the mother are also those in which the mothers reject the infants most, the inter-dyad differences are primarily due to differences between the mothers, and vice versa. The correlations are in fact low (Table V), indicating that inter-mother and inter-infant differences are both important. But they do show interesting and consistent age changes. Whereas the coefficients are initially positive, around week 30 they become negative and remain so throughout the period for which data are available. Thus while inter-mother differences are more important than inter-infant differences with young infants, later the reverse is the case. Similar trends are evident for the control

Table V

Rank order correlation coefficients between duration and occurrence measures

	Weeks											
	1–6	7–12	13–18	19–24	25–30	39–41	43–45	47–49	51–53	59–61	64–66	72–74
$Mk_M/(Mk_I + Mk_M)$ with MGB	0·50[b]	0·32[a]	0·36[a]	−0·08	−0·21	—	—	—	—	—	—	—
T.T. off with R	0·30	0·24	0·20	0·45[a]	−0·30	−0·30	−0·14	−0·43[a]	−0·38[a]	−0·53[a]	−0·29	−0·70[a]
T.T. off with R/ $(Mk_I + Mk_M + R)$	0·19	0·24	0·31	0·24	−0·04	−0·19	−0·03	−0·28	−0·14	−0·48[a]	−0·05	−0·21
T.T. off with $Mk_M/(Mk_I + Mk_M)$	0·21	−0·07	−0·29	−0·42[a]	−0·54[a]	—	—	—	—	—	—	—
> 60 cm with $\%Ap_I - \%L_I$	0·07	0·64[b]	0·19	−0·14	−0·39	−0·26	−0·24	−0·39[a]	−0·50[a]	0·14	−0·26	0

[a] $p < 0{\cdot}05$.
[b] $p < 0{\cdot}01$.
MGB = Mother Grooms Baby.

of the time the infant spends at a distance from its mother (Hinde and Spencer-Booth, 1971b; Hinde, 1969).

One further point here perhaps deserves comment. After weeks 25–30 the correlations between time off and the absolute frequency of rejections are consistently more negative than those with the ratio measure. In the first place, this means that those infants which were off their mothers least (i.e. on most), were on in spite of the fact that they tended to be rejected most often. But it was slightly less the case that they were on in spite of the fact that they tended to have a greater proportion of their attempts rejected. Thus those who ranked high on rejections ranked slightly less high on the relative frequency of rejections. In so far as those who were on their mothers most wanted to be on most, they were apparently able to be so in spite of a higher ranking on absolute rejections than on the relative measure. Does this mean that a high rank on relative frequency of rejections is a more potent deterrent than a high rank on absolute frequency?

We could of course go on to ask whether inter-dyad differences in a particular measure at one age are related to inter-dyad differences in *another* measure at a later age. Use of the cross-lagged correlational technique to this end is exemplified in the monograph by Clarke-Stewart (1973). We would, however, reiterate the need for caution in regarding measures as referring to either mother or infant, rather than to their relationship.

(iii) *Inter-group differences related to treatment differences*

Rhesus infants living alone with their mothers were off their mothers in more half-minutes than infants living with their mothers in groups in similar cages. Was this due primarily to a difference between the mothers in the two situations, or to a difference between the infants? Since the frequency of rejections was higher in the dyads living alone, Table IV indicates that the differences were primarily due to differences between mothers (Hinde and Spencer-Booth, 1967).

That this approach permits only the first step towards understanding the relevant dynamics of the relationship has already been emphasized (see also the other papers cited). However, one further example will show how the analysis can be pursued. If the mothers of group-living rhesus infants are removed for six days and then returned, the mother–infant relationship in the immediately post-separation period differs from the pre-separation relationship in the following ways (Spencer-Booth and Hinde, 1971):

(a) The infants spend less time off their mothers.

(b) They tend to be rejected less by their mothers.

(c) They spend a smaller proportion of their time off their mothers more than 60 cm from her.

(d) They play a greater relative role in staying near her.

From the model in Table IV, (a) and (b) suggest that the decrease in time off is due primarily to a change in the mother. However, consideration of other measures, such as the rate of distress calling and the frequency of tantrums shown by the infant, indicate that the infant changes dramatically in demanding more ventro-ventral contact with its mother. Thus the decrease in time off is initiated at least in part by greater demands for contact from the infant, and it is likely that signals from the infant affect the mother's tolerance of his demands. However, the mother could respond to the increased demands by either increasing or decreasing the proportion of attempted contacts rejected. If the ratio measure of rejections had increased, we could have argued unequivocally that the reduction in time off was due primarily to a change in the infant's demands, and occurred despite the increase in rejections. In the present case, where rejections decrease, we should argue that the decrease in time off, although perhaps initiated by the infant's demands, is permitted by, and thus controlled by, the mother through a reduction in the proportion of attempted contacts rejected. Here we have used at least three measures (Tantrums, Time off and Rejections), and the argument exemplifies the manner in which, as more measures are added, we can get farther in teazing apart the dynamics of the relationship.

We can go one stage further by considering points (c) and (d) above. That the infant's role in maintaining proximity should increase when rejections decrease is apparently incompatible with any of the simple changes shown in Table I. However, the two halves of the diagram must be considered independently. Whilst (a) and (b) together indicate the importance of maternal changes in control of time off, (c) and (d) indicate the importance of changes in infant behaviour in controlling time at a distance. Further discussion involving yet further measures is given in Hinde and Spencer-Booth (1970, 1971a) and Hinde and White (1974).

Triadic Relationships

Another context in which relationships between measures can be useful is in the understanding of triadic relationships. If X associates more with A than with B, what is the basis for the difference? To be more specific, is it due to differences between X's responses to A and to B, or to differences between the ways in which A and B respond to X, or both? And if the difference lies primarily between X's responses to A and B (or vice versa), do they involve more positive responses to A, more negative responses to B, or etc.?

Let us consider only the case where strength of association is assessed in terms of the number of bouts spent in proximity. The various possibilities summarized above could be teazed apart by examination of the number of approaches and leavings made by each member of each dyad. However, this presents some difficulties, especially when the activity levels of the members of dyads are markedly different. Considerable progress can be made by using the proximity index already discussed.

Assume (i) that X, A and B are all moderately active, for the index is misleading at low levels of Ap and L (Hinde and Atkinson, 1970); and (ii) that the time spent together by the members of one dyad does not materially affect that spent by the other. Suppose that X initially associates equally with A and with B, and that changes then occur as indicated in column 1 of Table VI. The successive rows in this column indicate that X approaches A more, avoids B more, approaches B more, and so on. We can then predict the consequences of these changes on the association of X with A and B, and on X's roles in proximity with A and B, as shown in columns 2 and 3. Thus if X approaches A more, X will spend more bouts with A than with B, and play a greater role in the maintenance of proximity with A than with B. It will be apparent that, if the change in the relationship is due to a change in X, the difference in the number of bouts in proximity and that in X's role in proximity with A and with B lie in the same direction (i.e. A $>$ B for both or B $>$ A for both, top four rows). But if the change is due to a change in A or B, the differences lie in opposite directions (bottom four rows) (column 4).

So far we have predicted from hypothesized changes (column 1) the

Table VI

Some possible changes in preferences and aversions between X, A and B, their consequences on measures of the relationship, and the interpretation of such measures

Changes in responsiveness (1)	Difference between number of bouts with A and B (2)	Difference in %Ap–%L of X to A and to B (3)	Difference in number of bouts primarily due to (4)	Absolute values of (5) %Ap–%L to A	%Ap–%L to B	Primary responsibility for proximity (6)	Difference in number of bouts due to (7)
X → A; B	A > B	A > B	X	++	+	X with A and B	X seeks A more than X seeks B (1)
				+	–	X with A, B with X	X seeks A and avoids B (2)
← X; A; B	A > B	A > B	X	–	––	A and B with X	X avoids A less than X avoids B (3)
X → B; A	B > A	B > A	X	+	++	X with A and B	X seeks A less than X seeks B (4)
				–	+	A with X, X with B	X avoids A and seeks B (5)
← X; A; B	B > A	B > A	X	––	–	A and B with X	X avoids A more than X avoids B (6)
X ← A; B	A > B	B > A	A/B	––	–	A and B with X	A seeks X more than B seeks X (7)
				–	+	A with X, X with B	A seeks X and B avoids X (8)
X; A; B →	A > B	B > A	A/B	+	++	X with A and B	A avoids X less than B avoids X (9)
X ← B; A	B > A	A > B	A/B	–	––	A and B with X	A seeks X less than B seeks X (10)
				+	–	X with A, B with X	A avoids X and B seeks X (11)
X; A →; B	B > A	A > B	A/B	++	+	X with A and B	A avoids X more than B avoids X (12)

consequent changes in our measures of the relationship (columns 2 and 3). In practice we want to proceed from the measures to an understanding of whether the difference in proximity is due primarily to differences between X's responses to A and to B, or theirs to him. Consider for example the hypothetical data in Table VII, where X represents a mother and A and B her twins. X is near A more than B, but her role in proximity is greater with B than with A. Thus the difference in proximity is due primarily to a difference in the twins' behaviour to the mother. (It must be emphasized that this argument applies only to the particular measure of association used. In such a case data on the amount of ventro-ventral contact showed that one twin spent more time in ventro-ventral contact with the mother primarily because of a difference in the way the mother behaved to the twins, but less of its time off near the mother primarily because of a difference in the twins' behaviour to the mother (see Spencer-Booth, 1968). A similar issue was discussed in the preceding section with reference to the effects of separation.)

This argument can be extended to assess not only whether changes in X or changes in A or B are responsible for the observed changes in the relationship, but also the nature of those changes in the participants. Here we must consider the absolute values of the proximity indices (i.e. of the measures of X's role in maintaining proximity to A and to B). For each two rows in column 1 of Table VI, column 5 shows three possibilities for the absolute values of X's role in proximity (cases in which %Ap − %L are 0 are omitted for brevity). The last column shows how data of the type shown in each row would be interpreted. In the case shown in Table VII, we have already seen that we must refer to the lower half of the table. Since A and B are primarily responsible for proximity with X (i.e. X's role is negative), with A

Table VII

Hypothetical data on proximity relations between a mother (X) and her twins (A and B)

X with	Measure of proximity	Measure of X's role in proximity
A	43	−12
B	28	− 4

playing a greater role than B, the difference is primarily due to A seeking X's proximity more than B sought it.

It is of course possible that a difference in association is due to more than one of the factors indicated in column 1 of Table VI. It is possible to proceed some way towards unravelling such cases by examining the relative magnitude of the differences in proximity and role in proximity measures. Furthermore, the method can be used to help understanding of changes in a relationship with time, A and B being successive states of one individual. This and other related issues are discussed in more detail elsewhere (Hinde, in press).

Discussion

The course of any interaction may affect the course of subsequent ones within the same relationship (see discussion in Hinde and Stevenson-Hinde, 1976). That being so, measures of the behaviour of either participant may be affected by influences from the other. Such measures will thus have reference to the *relationship* but not to behavioural characteristics of either *individual* uncontaminated by the other.

Starting from this point of view, we have tried to make two main points in this paper. First, measures of the absolute duration or frequency of particular types of behaviour are not necessarily more "absolute", more reliable or more illuminating than ratios or indices derived from them. Indeed, such ratios or indices can sometimes provide information which either is simply not available in the so-called "absolute" measures, or can only be obtained from them by simultaneous assessment of two or more measures—which means in effect holding them in one's head and doing the mental equivalent of computing the derived measure.

Of course, given that the number of things one could measure or count in a series of behavioural interactions is large, the number of derived measures one could compute from them is many times larger still. Inevitably, and properly, intuition plays a not inconsiderable part in the initial selection of derived measures, just as it does in the selection of absolute ones. However, that intuition may suggest that some derived measures are more pertinent to some questions than some absolute measures is not the point: the ultimate test must lie with the data—

which measures are the most reliable, most predictive, or most revealing.

The ratios used in this paper have been relatively simple in that they have involved comparable events—for instance, the number of contacts made on the mother's initiative and the number made on the infant's initiative. It would, however, be possible to go further than that. For example, the supposition that two infants which score similarly on rejections (in absolute or relative terms) are equally "frustrated" (speaking loosely for the moment) depends on the presumption that they have equal "needs" for ventro-ventral contact. But it is reasonable to assume that, all else being equal, infants would differ in the time they spent off their mothers. Perhaps, therefore, a measure of frequency of rejections *in relation* to Time off would provide a measure more closely related to fundamental aspects of the infant's experience. Two procedures spring to mind. One could assess, for each infant, the number of rejections experienced per unit time of ventro-ventral contact gained. Alternatively, one could argue as follows. If differences in the (absolute or relative) frequencies of maternal rejections were solely responsible for differences in Time off the mother, there would be an absolute rank order correlation between the two measures. In practice the correlations, though positive, are not high (Table V). An infant ranking lower on Rejections than on Time off is achieving its ventro-ventral contacts with fewer rejections than would be expected on this hypothesis, and vice versa. Then (Rank on the Rejection measure) minus (Rank on Time off) would give an index which would be positive if the infant were rejected frequently relative to the time off the mother, and vice versa. In practice we found the consistency of such a "Rejection Index" from one age period to the next to be lower, though only slightly so, than those of the ratios shown in Tables I and II. The same was true for indices derived from differences between ranks on Maternal initiations of contact and Time off, and Infants role in proximity and Time at a distance. For that reason these indices have not been discussed here, but comparable indices could prove to be useful in other contexts.

We may mention one further issue here. Some of the judgements we make about relationships depend on more than one type of interaction. For instance, we might say that a mother–infant relationship involved a possessive mother if the mother initiated contact often (though of course without the necessary implication that this individual mother would be possessive in another mother–infant relationship), or a rejecting mother if she often rejected the infant's approaches. But if she did both, or neither, we might label her behaviour in this relationship respectively as "controlling" or "permissive". These latter properties emerge from comparing data on two types of interaction. This could be done by, for instance, comparing ranks on a rejection measure and a maternal initiation measure. It is at least possible that such qualities of relationships, which we have names for in everyday life, are important for the behavioural development of the participants. They could not be assessed simply by examining individual measures (Hinde, in 1976).

The second point we have tried to make concerns the dynamics of the relationship. Even though our measures refer to the relationship as a whole rather than to the behavioural propensities of the individuals, it is possible to use them to gain some insight into their respective roles. While correlations between two measures can help us with only the first stage in teazing apart the roles of differences or changes in the participants, use of relationships between more than two measures can give deeper understanding. We believe that this method is not limited to the mother–infant relationship, but could be applied in any context in which measures comparable to those in Table IV are available. Furthermore, as we have indicated, correlations between measures can also bring us some understanding of the nature of triadic relationships.

References

Altmann, J. (1974). Observational study of behaviour: sampling methods. *Behaviour* **49**, 227–267.

Bell, S. M. and Ainsworth, M. D. S. (1972). Infant crying and maternal responsiveness. *Child Dev.* **43**, 1171–1190.

Clarke-Stewart, K. Allison (1973). Interactions between mothers and their young children: characteristics and consequences. *Mong. Soc. Res. Child Devel.* 38 Serial No. 153, Nos 6–7.

Dunn, J. (1975). Consistency and change in styles of mothering. *Ciba Foundation Symposium—Parent-Infant Interaction*, ASP, Amsterdam. pp 155–176.

Hinde, R. A. (1969). Analysing the roles of the partners in a behavioural interaction —mother-infant relations in rhesus macaques. *Ann. N. Y. Acad. Sci.* **159**, 651–667.

Hinde, R. A. (1973). On the design of check-sheets. *Primates* **14** (4), 393–406.

Hinde, R. A. (1974). *Biological Bases of Human Social Behaviour*. McGraw-Hill, New York.

Hinde, R. A. (1975). Mothers' and infants' roles: distinguishing the questions to be asked. In M. O'Connor (Ed.), *Parent-Infant Interaction*. Elsevier, Amsterdam.

Hinde, R. A. (1976). On describing relationships. *J. Child Psychol. Psychiat. 17*, 1–19.

Hinde, R. A. (In press). Assessing the bases of partner preferences. *Behaviour*.

Hinde, R. A. and Atkinson, S. (1970). Assessing the role of social partners in maintaining mutual proximity, as exemplified by mother-infant relations in rhesus monkeys. *Anim. Behav.* **18**, 169–176.

Hinde, R. A. and Simpson, M. J. A. (1975). Qualities of Mother-Infant Relationships in Monkeys. In M. O'Connor (Ed.), *Parent-Infant Interaction*. Elsevier, Amsterdam.

Hinde, R. A. and Spencer-Booth, Y. (1967). The effect of social companions on mother-infant relations in rhesus monkeys. In D. Morris (Ed.), *Primate Ethology*. Weidenfeld and Nicolson, London.

Hinde, R. A. and Spencer-Booth, Y. (1970). Individual differences in the responses of rhesus monkeys to a period of separation from their mother. *J. Child Psychol. Psychiat.* **11**, 159–176.

Hinde, R. A. and Spencer-Booth, Y. (1971a). Effects of brief separation from mothers on rhesus monkeys. *Science* **173**, 111–118.

Hinde, R. A. and Spencer-Booth, Y. (1971b). Towards understanding individual differences in rhesus mother-infant interaction. *Anim. Behav.* **19**, 165–173.

Hinde, R. A. and Stevenson-Hinde, J. (In press). Towards understanding relationships: Dynamic stability. In P. P. G. Bateson and R. A. Hinde (Eds), *Growing Points in Ethology* pp. 451–479. Cambridge University Press, Cambridge.

Hinde, R. A. and White, L. E. (1974). Dynamics of a relationship: rhesus mother-infant ventro-ventral contact. *J. comp. physiol. Psychol.* **86**, 8–23.

Simpson, M. J. A. and Simpson, A. E. (In press). The use of scan and one-zero sampling. *Anim. Behav.*

Spencer-Booth, Y. (1968). The behaviour of twin rhesus monkeys and comparisons with the behaviour of single infants. *Primates* **9**, 75–84.

Spencer-Booth, Y. and Hinde, R. A. (1971). Effects of 6 days separation from mother on 18 and 32 week old rhesus monkeys. *Anim. Behav.* **19**, 174–191.

White, R. E. C. (1971). WRATS: A computer compatible system for automatically recording and transcribing behavioural data. *Behaviour* **40**, 135–161.

3 An Intersubjective Approach to the Systematic Description of Mother–Infant Interaction

John Newson

Orientation

In all empirical scientific work the strategies of recording and the methods adopted for analysing observations are bound to reflect certain underlying theoretical preconceptions of the investigators. One aim of this paper is therefore to make explicit certain common features of the approach which underpins the other two contributions from members of the Child Development Research Unit at Nottingham to this volume. In particular, it needs to be emphasized that we view mother–baby interaction as an attempt by the mother to enter into a *meaningful* set of exchanges with her infant, despite the fact that she herself will often be aware that the semantic element in any resulting communication lies more in her own imagination than in the mental experience of her baby. That our primary concern is with the semantic aspects of the communication taking place between mother and infant, even during the pre-verbal stage of development, needs to be fully understood and appreciated because, in our opinion, there is a fundamental distinction which needs to be made between the techniques which one employs in studying infant "behaviour" and those which are appropriate in attempting to investigate the emergence of cognitive and linguistic understanding in infants (Piaget, 1970).

The broader theoretical stance from which our research efforts derive have now been outlined in a number of different papers (Newson, 1974; Newson and Shotter, 1974; Newson and Pawlby, 1975; Newson and Newson, 1976). One basic assumption is that communication necessarily implies both a *process* and a *content*; and that the infant begins by becoming actively involved in the "process" of communicative interaction as a step towards acquiring "content" in the form of mental constructs or understandings, which he begins to share with persons only as he regularly engages in communication. From this point of view the mother's task is seen to be one of organizing her own activity in synchronous alternation with certain discrete actions produced by her baby, so as to establish temporally linked patterns of reciprocation which continually recur in the baby's experience in the course of ordinary human caretaking. It is in this organization, in the temporal domain, of the infant's otherwise unrelated action patterns that we think we have the key to understanding that mysterious process whereby shared mental constructs begin to emerge in human development.

A second assumption is that even newborn babies share with their mothers an ability to generate activity of a distinctly non-random kind, which takes the form of discrete actions interspersed with natural breaks. Thus when we observe infants we notice a sequence of separate and clearly distinguishable actions, e.g. yawns, gurgles, hand swipes, grimaces, sucking bouts, startle reactions, etc., and these actions make up a finite set (or vocabulary) of distinct elements which can easily be noted as they continually recur within the ongoing stream of infant activity (Trevarthen, 1974; Trevarthen *et al.*, 1975). That human beings so readily recognize and respond to such actions as discrete implies in turn that our human attentional capacities are similarly organized into acts of looking, listening etc., which resonate in harmony with the actions of other members of our own species. The present approach takes it for granted that newborn babies share with their mothers a capacity to produce strings of discrete actions. Moreover, some of these actions denote attentional states. It is only, however, when the discrete actions of two separate individuals become interlinked and interdependent, as a result of repeated temporal entraining, that communication as such can begin to take place.

The Social Precocity of Human Infants

That babies can be objects of compelling social interest to their doting parents, and to friends and relations, has up to now been regarded by serious students of early human development as a kind of whimsical aberration on the part of the adults themselves. This, however, may be a serious mistake.

One important outcome of the current upsurge of interest in the systematic study of infants in the presence of their mothers has been the realization that they are, in a sense, hugely precocious socially. This is obvious in the selective attention they pay to *people* (as opposed to inanimate objects), and in the way they are able to combine appropriate looking behaviour with an elaborate repertoire of gesture-like bodily and facial activity. In fact it is remarkable that babies are somehow intrinsically capable of emitting, and responding to, very complex signals which are precisely mimetic of a range of human feeling states from boredom through to interest and from anxiety to blissful content-ment. All this "protosocial" activity contrasts sharply with a baby's physical immaturity as revealed in such simple matters as holding up his head, sitting without support or manipulating inanimate objects. A possible reason for the previous neglect of this disparity may be the surprisingly recent recognition of the fact that it is only when the young baby is being physically supported in an upright posture by a socially responsive caretaker, who can maintain him in a state of contented alertness, that he is able to demonstrate his most sophisticated behaviour.

Our own attempts to look at mother–child interaction and to describe it carefully and systematically has led towards a broad agreement with the standpoint of Trevarthen *et al.* (1975). Their evidence suggests that the human infant is biologically primed, or pre-tuned, to enable him to communicate with other human beings. He has all the basic equipment he requires to begin to engage in face-to-face interpersonal communication—initially of a non-verbal kind—right from birth. This perspective is one which emphasizes the temporal and dynamic aspects of those forms of stimulation which so obviously and automatically engage the attention of all normal babies whenever they are fully awake and held comfortably upright. It is also clear that, right from birth, they can participate in two-person exchange rituals which, because they include turn-taking, have a distinctly conversational quality. It is in practice almost impossible (or one might say pathological) for a mother to react to her baby as if it were merely an inanimate "thing". The moment he opens his eyes and looks at her, she will almost inevitably begin to engage in ritual social exchanges with him; and when these are examined in detail it immediately becomes clear that the baby himself is by no means a passive or non-participant partner.

Some observers, faced with the social complexity of the exchanges which ordinarily occur all the while between mothers and babies, are inclined to say that what takes place can be accounted for as a reflection of ordinary maternal skill in maintaining the *appearance* of a conversational exchange when no real communication is actually taking place (Schaffer, 1974). Certainly to begin with it is possible to argue that many ordinary mothers incline towards flagrant over-interpretation of any gestures which their babies may spontaneously emit. Two points need to be emphasized however: one is that the exchanges clearly do become meaningful to the child, as well as to the mother, well before verbal language can be considered to be the operative factor; the second is that the exchanges themselves are typically highly repetitive. Thus a baby learns to play an active role in an oft-repeated exchange by virtue of the fact that he is caught up in the same ritual sequence, with the same person, over and over again. This makes it less surprising that he begins to offer with some certainty the appropriate actions which are required of him to sustain the chain of reciprocal activity. It must be conceded, however, that this transition between mutual involvement and mutual understanding remains a highly mysterious process.

Our approach began with an attempt to describe these recurrent interaction sequences in minute detail. To do this the observer needs to be able to switch his attention rapidly between the individual roles being played by each partner in turn, and this requires a certain amount of self-discipline to avoid falling into the trap of merely describing the general drift of the joint production to which one is ordinarily inclined to attend as an interloper on a private conversation between two other people. This total drift is, of course, one level at which the interaction certainly needs to be described, but there is another at which we can attempt to identify and describe the precise signals which are being offered by each partner moment by moment, and to which the alternate partner is in fact paying attention turn by turn. Here the problem for the observer is the extraordinary speed with which signals are typically exchanged, so that even with very young infants it seems to be essential to capture the communication sequences on film or video, allowing the observer to review them repeatedly in context and from the standpoint of each of the participants independently. For this form of micro-analysis it is sometimes necessary to have slow motion replay facilities, and it is generally desirable to incorporate a digital time display accurate to the nearest tenth of a second.

Given that it is possible to engage infants in social interchanges with adults which develop progressively greater communicative significance throughout the whole of the first year of life, the implications are profound. Infants are repeatedly and massively involved in structured forms of interaction. Such "forms" reflect—and are in part governed by—the intentions, expectancies and understanding (both rational and intuitive) of the more sophisticated partner who is interacting with the baby; and it seems likely, by analogy with what we now know about the transmission of rules of syntax in linguistic interchanges later on in development, that such dialogues promote shared understandings of what are eventually understood as significant events, happenings and expected outcomes in the combined experience of both partners, though to begin with they may only be significant in the mind of the adult partner. Undoubtedly it is true that during the second six months of life many babies have developed levels of mutual understanding which enable them not only to respond to shared conceptions of reference, but also to share jokes and teasing interludes about the behaviour of objects or the meanings of actions in a way which implies a very high degree of communicative competence on the part of the baby, though he may not yet have uttered even his first most primitive "word".

The exciting prospect is, then, that we are now "eavesdropping" on a fundamental process of human acculturation or "socialization-through-interaction", of whose very existence developmental psychologists have previously been unaware. We feel confident, moreover, that in opening up this area for systematic investigation we are likely to throw a great deal of light upon the establishment in infants of those mental processes which must precede and prepare the way for language development proper.

The Structure of Communication Sequences

To elaborate our approach in more practical terms, it is convenient to spell out in a somewhat didactic fashion a number of the assumptions which have already been referred to. We are, however, conscious of the need at this stage to keep theoretical speculation down to a bare minimum, in order to allow the further development of our thinking to be as responsive as possible to what can be observed in practice.

A communication sequence between two partners can be described as an alternating chain of communication gestures. It may be convenient to illustrate this chain diagrammatically, using single letters to refer to the person who is emitting a communication gesture at any point within a sequence which can be read from left to right across the page. Thus if the partners are "m" (mother) and "c" (child) the alternation of communication gestures between the two can be symbolized as follows:

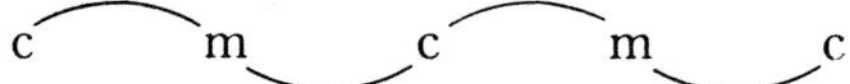

Communication gestures between mothers and babies are many and various. They may, for instance, be vocal utterances (not necessarily words) or they may be gestural signals comprising hand movements, changes in facial expression or merely adjustments of bodily posture. Many gestures in fact consist of simultaneous co-ordinations of several such actions. However, it is not in our view possible to compile an exhaustive list or dictionary of communication gestures having universal meanings; and we would take issue with those who are attempting to apply an ethological approach to young children with this aim in view. Our reasons are firstly that, in practice, almost any action on the part of one partner can be put to use by being assigned a new meaning for the purposes of communication; and secondly, that many of the gestures used in practice only have specific object reference in the particular context of the moment. All that is required for meaning to be transmitted is that the partners are both prepared to accept the action in question as some kind of a signal in relation to the ongoing pattern of communication in which they are both involved. From this standpoint, the *timing* of the gesture and its contextual significance will often be much more important than the precise movements of which it is made up.

With acknowledgement gestures, for instance, a nod may indeed be as good as a wink. Also, when two persons become sophisticated in the art of close interpersonal communication, they may begin to use gestures which are deliberately opaque to social view—like kicking someone under the dinner table to mark a social gaffe. And there is nothing to prevent the use of private pre-arranged signals which can *only* be understood by those who originally negotiated their meaning: as when the chairman blows his nose to indicate to other members of an interviewing panel that further questioning must close.

Such examples from adult communication should alert us to the fact that the meaning of signals can never be assumed from their physical form alone. They can often only be understood by the partners themselves by virtue of sharing a particular history of previous communication with one another. In attempting to describe mother–baby communication, we may thus expect to find that at least some of the gestures which are used will only be understandable to the participants. Babies and their regular caretakers do normally share a massive and continuous history of previous attempts at communication, in the course of which they have negotiated a flexible repertoire of specific gesture signals. As observers, we often have to concede the status of a gesture simply because it appears to have functional significance within the chain of communicative acts which we are attempting to describe.

This is not to say, of course, that all movements which mothers and babies make are equally probable, nor does it discount the notion that many human gesture signals seem to operate across cultures. There is bound to be some basic lexicon of likely gestures which mothers and babies traditionally employ, and it is a matter for empirical research to determine the relative probability of the various commonplace communication gestures which mothers and babies use during the preverbal stage of infant development, and how far these are idiosyncratic to a specific partnership. To the extent that it is possible to identify and clarify signals, the types of gestures used by each partner can be given coding symbols and displayed as subscripts or superscripts to the letters shown in the chain, but this is merely a shorthand alternative to providing a full running descriptive account; and for some purposes a fuller protocol will need to be given below the letters which form the chain.

Most communication gestures within any chain serve a dual function. They operate as answering signals to the preceding gesture and also as eliciting signals inviting some further communication gesture from the other partner. Logically, the exceptions must be the initiating signals for any new communication sequence which do not serve to answer any preceding communication gesture, and terminating signals which do not invite any further communication gesture from the other partner and which therefore may be indicated by placing a full stop after a letter. There are, however, special problems in assigning responsibility for the initiation and continuation of communication sequences and these are discussed below.

The simplest communication sequence is one in which one partner emits a communication gesture which merely receives some acknowledgement from the other partner.

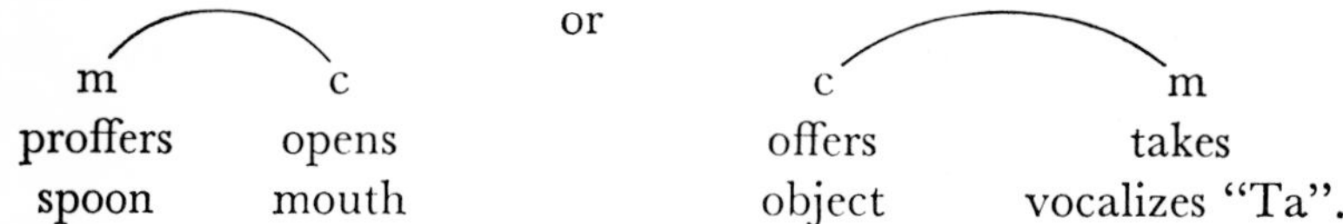

Using this system it is also possible to distinguish between two superficially similar sequences which ought not to be confused, e.g.:

In the first example the mother's initial gesture only required a simple acknowledgement from the child, after which both partners turned their attention elsewhere. In the second case, the mother signals, the child replies with a further signal to which the mother might have been expected to reply in her turn, but her reply was not in fact forthcoming and the child was left in the air. A further possibility arises when one partner emits a gesture which is in effect ambiguous in relation to termination. It can either be replied to or not as the partner chooses.

That we can distinguish these various instances depends upon our ability, as observers, to note not only the communication gestures made by each partner, but also at least some of the reciprocal attention-paying activity of the other partner which is obviously equally important if the dialogue is to be sustained. A more comprehensive model to describe communication sequences must therefore involve the simultaneous recording of these attention-paying gestures. The difficulty is, however, that mothers and babies do not necessarily signal to us that they have heard or seen certain cues, even though these cues may be vital in sustaining the sequence. For instance, we may have no immediate indication that a child has in fact heard some vocalization made by his mother, or that he has seen in peripheral vision some significant movement such as her bending towards him expectantly. In practice this may even mean that as observers we can sometimes only reconstruct dialogues-of-action in retrospect, as it were, by noting the continuity of succeeding events which make up the overall pattern of communication gestures supported by such accompanying attention-paying gestures as can be observed.

In the case of mothers and babies, the two communicating partners are operating at very different levels of competence and this has both advantages and disadvantages for the reconstruction of the dialogue sequence. On the one hand, it is difficult to know how far the baby understands the significance either of his own actions or of the signals with which his mother responds. Fortunately, however, the actions of the mother are often deliberately dramatized and exaggerated, as part of her strategy for maintaining the attention of the baby, and this makes the task of observation and analysis simpler than it might otherwise be.

The observer will also tend to rely heavily on any verbal commentary which the mother makes. And it is fortunate that, in practice, this too is often extensive and very explicit. This may be partly because the mother knows she is being observed and is trying to justify her behaviour to a third party; but it is also not uncharacteristic for mothers to talk a lot to their babies even when they are not in a formal observation situation and it may well be that they need to comment out loud simply to reassure themselves about the meaning content of the dialogue which they are trying to sustain. In this sense it is the mother herself who provides us with the most secure evidence about the content of communication; the job of the observer becomes considerably more complicated when the mother is speaking in a foreign language. The procedure we are describing thus relies quite heavily on our ability to exploit the mother's natural tendency to offer indirectly her own spontaneous comments, and indeed for certain purposes we may even find it useful to re-play the video-recording to her and ask her to explain exactly what her intentions were at certain points of the dialogue.

These practical strategies capitalize upon the fact that the observer is a member of the same linguistic community as the mother. Our primary concern, as I have said, is with the semantic aspect of whatever communication is taking place, even though its semantic potential is, to begin with, only fully understandable to one of the two participants, namely the mother. How, then, can we introduce an element of scientific empiricism which will allow us to test the validity of any description we give? Here we rely upon the experience that certain signals do frequently recur and are objectively verifiable by an external observer.

A rather dramatic example is the use which babies make of referential glances. As Schaffer *et al.* have noted (Chapter 12), mothers continually monitor the activity of their infants; and this means that when the baby looks towards them it is highly probable that eye-to-eye contact will take place. One of Olwen Jones' concerns (see Chapter 15) is to understand the when and how of referential eye-contact, and the assumption is that its occurrence can only be understood if it is related in a precise temporal sense to its semantic context (i.e. the meaningful exchange which is taking place between the partners around that point in time).

If a specific gesture (such as the referential glance) occurs repeatedly, and can be objectively defined, this immediately allows us the strategy of collecting a large sample of such signals and of analysing the sample in relation to the contexts in which each signal was emitted. We can then begin to make statements about the nature of the contexts within which they typically occur. It may also be possible to link the use of one signal with the simultaneous occurrence of other gesture signals (for instance a referential glance with an offering gesture), and it may be possible to evaluate the likelihood of such contingencies against the null hypothesis of a non-contingent joint occurrence. Here we would follow Wright (1960) in stressing that, whereas the "stream of behaviour" can only be understood in intersubjective terms, this need not preclude our using any of the conventional statistical techniques in order to document the occurrence of different types of events or their association with other meaningful events within some representative sample of records of ongoing activity.

Broadly, we may adopt one of two empirical approaches. The first is to sample reasonably sized "chunks" of dialogue from a representative sample of mother–infant pairs and then to identify and count the frequency of different types of signals. This would lead us to generalization about the extent to which infants make use of different gesture-signals at different age stages, for instance. The second is to examine a much larger sample of all instances which conform to a given definition —e.g. Susan Pawlby's work (Chapter 9) which focuses upon instances of "imitation" in mother–infant free-play sessions. These instances can then be divided into sub-types and further analysed into categories according to who initiated them.

Some Complicating Factors

Because our focus is upon mothers and infants—and because mothers are more sophisticated in the art of communication than their infants—special problems inevitably arise concerning the initiation of communication sequences. Among the many communication gestures which are used by babies, some are not deliberately aimed at communication from the infant's point of view. For example, he may simply switch his attention to some new object and his mother, noticing this, may decide to use his attentional shift in the interests of sustaining communication with her baby. An example of such a sequence can be described symbolically as follows:

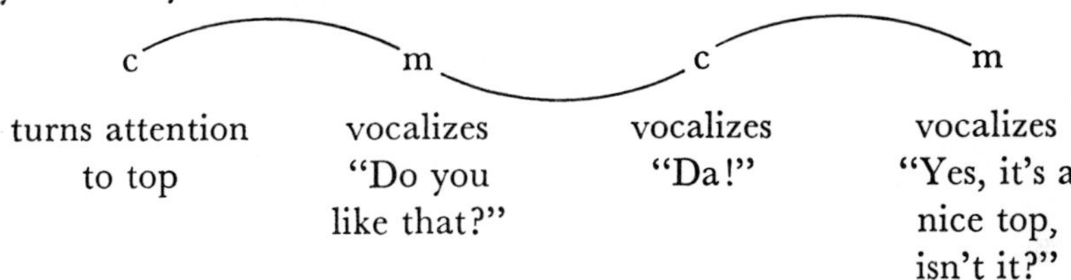
c
m
c
m
turns attention to top
vocalizes "Do you like that?"
vocalizes "Da!"
vocalizes "Yes, it's a nice top, isn't it?"

In this instance the mother has capitalized upon a non-initiatory, and perhaps quite unpremeditated, action of the child, but she responds to it as if it were a deliberate comment by the child. It is she, however, who must be credited with having built upon the action to initiate communication. This example also brings out two further points: firstly, that the child's early communications are often situation-dependent, in the sense that the same action in a different situation might mean something different; and secondly that, to begin with, many of the gestures which young infants emit only have the status of communication gestures to the extent that the mother imputes that status to them.

One point deserving emphasis is that the regular spacing of the symbols along the line need not correspond in any very accurate way with the passage of equal amounts of real time. The reason for this is that the communication gestures which the partners use take varying times to complete. Furthermore, they are sometimes responded to even before they have formally ceased or, alternatively, a brief action may be followed by a "pregnant pause", inviting a reply from the other partner. In the latter case it is the combined act + pause which seems to function as the communication gesture. If this method of tapping-in to the intersubjective process lacks the semblance of "objectivity" of the kind traditionally demanded by behavioural scientists, this is probably a price that has to be paid for the sake of understanding the signal-mediated transactions or negotiations in which the participants themselves are clearly involved.

Again, it is important to point out that there is no one-to-one correspondence between simple behavioural acts and communication gestures. Thus a smile once initiated may be sustained for varying lengths of time by a continuing adjustment of head and eye directional movements; and a single imitative gesture of rhythmic tapping may require a whole chain of discrete hand-and-finger movements. In fact, what we call communication gestures are nearly always based upon patterns of movement through time, such that the rhythm of the complete gesture is often one of its most identifiable parameters.

For the non-participating observer, then, it may be true that certain communication gestures can only be understood by virtue of the fact that such an observer has himself had much previous experience as a participant communicator in similar situations. And in some cases the adequate identification of particular communication gestures may have to rest upon confirmation in terms of succeeding gestures given by the other partner before the whole sequence can be recorded with reasonable confidence.

Finally, it should be noted that this particular system for recording a dialogue was specifically devised for observing mothers and babies at an age where the baby is assumed to be operating at a pre-verbal level. Between adults, an analysis of communication sequences based on such conceptions would be manifestly inadequate. For one thing, adults habitually resort to words in addition to gesture language; words free the partners from the need to rely on these non-verbal signals. This "freedom" is in fact imposed when conversations take place by telephone; and still more so when correspondence is conducted by an exchange of written messages which largely eliminate signals that depend upon intonation and changes in pace. Yet in both cases adequate communication can be sustained. In mother–baby communication, by contrast, gestural, facial and non-linguistic vocal cues provide the only means by which communicative contact can be established or maintained.

Conclusion

What has been presented in this paper is merely the skeleton of *one* system which we have used in describing mother–child interaction so as to preserve those properties which characterize it as a form of intersubjective communication. It at least makes it possible for us to code and classify episodes according to the types of gesture signals which mothers and babies employ and according to the number of alternations through which they were sustained, paying due regard to the real-life complexities which occur when, as is often the case, it is difficult to attribute responsibility for initiation and termination. It is already clear to us that early on in development there are a very large number of instances of attempted exchanges where communication is only transitory. This shows up in analysis as a large number of simple two-or-three-turn alternations which fail because the expected response, particularly from the child, is not forthcoming, or because attention has arbitrarily shifted to some new focus of joint reference. Mothers are not, however, discouraged by this relative lack of success in babies under four months. They are strongly motivated to persevere, and they eagerly look for signs of increasing communication competence as an indication that their babies are developing normally by progressively becoming more like human beings with whom at least some primitive shared understandings are possible.

At the early levels it is also clear that success and failure in keeping communication going is not to be judged in all-or-nothing terms. Mothers are continually learning how to structure the communication situation more effectively so as to capitalize on whatever the infant himself spontaneously brings to it. Being able to "read" the infant so as to anticipate from past experience what he is likely to do in certain situations, and knowing what gestures will engage the immediate attention of this particular child at this particular stage of development, may be more important than having a knowledge of babies in general.

To begin with, in fact, mothers seem to provide an elaborate framework or "scaffolding" for keeping the dialogue going. Within this, almost any gesture which the baby might emit can be given a role, so as to make the alternating role sequence first possible and then familiar. Later, as the child becomes more adept and secure in playing his part, the props may be gradually removed. Always, however, the goal is communication so that still more communication becomes possible. Once begun the process is not only continuous but cumulative. Thus, by the time the normal child has been the subject of ordinary family caretaking for, say, nine months, he will almost inevitably have a considerable history of involvement in two-way communication episodes simply as an indirect consequence of being given the minimal care and protection necessary to keep him alive and well. In making such assertions, however, we are probably pushing theoretical speculation rather too far in the light of existing knowledge about how ordinary babies are treated in everyday circumstances. All we can say is that a theoretical standpoint of the kind outlined opens up all sorts of new questions about the nature of the relationship between social deprivation and subsequent cognitive deficiency. A theory of this kind also touches upon other questions in the applied field: how deafness or blindness may affect later linguistic performance, for example, and what remedial strategies may be most appropriate. At this stage of the game we would merely like to suggest that we are taking seismic soundings of what appears to be an extraordinarily rich seam of empirical investigation.

References

Newson, J. (1974). Towards a Theory of Infant Understanding. *Bull. Br. Psychol. Soc.* **27**, 251–257.

Newson, J. and Newson, E. (1976). On the social origins of symbolic functioning. In V. P. Varma and P. Williams (Eds), *Piaget, Psychology and Education.* Hodder and Stoughton, London.

Newson, J. and Pawlby, S. (1975). On imitation. (Paper presented to an inter-university colloquium at Nottingham University.)

Newson, J. and Shotter, J. (1974). How babies communicate. *New Society* **29**, 345–347.

Piaget, J. (1970). Piaget's theory. In P. H. Mussen (Ed.), *Manual of Child Psychology,* 3rd edition. Wiley, New York and London.

Schaffer, H. R. (1974). Behavioural synchrony in infancy. *New Scientist* **62**, 16–18.

Trevarthen, C. (1974). Conversations with a one-month-old. *New Scientist* **62**, 230–235.

Trevarthen, C., Hubley, P., and Sheeran, L. (1975). Les activités innées du nourrisson. *La Recherche* **6**, 447–458.

Wright, H. F. (1960). Observational Child Study. In P. H. Mussen (Ed.), *Handbook of Research Methods in Child Development*. Wiley, New York and London.

4 | Mothering and the Cognitive Head-start: Psychobiological Considerations

Hanuš Papoušek and Mechthild Papoušek

Introduction

The central aim of our research has been to study how mothering may influence the infant's cognitive development. The effects of maternal deprivation on cognitive development are well known, although the mechanisms of these effects still lack a satisfactory explanation.

As learning and cognition develop rapidly in the first six months of life, we have concentrated our attention particularly on this age, in the hope that more can be learned about the role of mothering if we analyse it at its very beginning.

Here we will refer to two kinds of observations that have contributed to the conceptual framework for our programme of work: (1) studies of pre-verbal learning and cognitive capacities in human infants, and (2) studies of mother–infant interaction. We have seen certain important connections between these two areas. For instance, the behavioural states of the infant that clearly influence the course of mother–infant interaction can be analysed more easily with the tools of learning experiments. Similarly, it is easier to understand the development of vocalization and facial expressions, both relevant components of social communication, if we know the predictability with which they accompany certain phases of learning or problem solving in the absence of a social partner.

Parallel studies of both cognitive development and social interactions in the same subjects gave our findings a broader validity and pointed to new ways of interpreting the general regulation of the infant's behaviour (for more details see Papoušek and Papoušek, 1975). Here we will briefly comment on those aspects which concern our view of the structure of pre-verbal social interaction, its relation to intrinsic motivation, the roles of visual and vocal communication, and imitation.

Subjects and Methods: General Remarks

Our interest in the detection and analysis of adaptive processes rather than in normative descriptions of certain populations called for access to healthy infants whom we could observe repeatedly and thus become familiar with their individualities.

For the earlier studies we used infants whom we could accept from birth with their mothers at a special lying-in research unit for up to six months. Reliable information on the duration and course of both prenatal and post-natal periods of development and daily control of the infant's state and of many environmental factors was available, as well as the possibility of carrying out parallel observations five times a week for several months (Papoušek, 1967a). In the later studies, healthy mature infants were either observed in their homes or repeatedly invited to our laboratories.

In learning experiments, head-turning conditioned to acoustic signals and reinforced with a contingent delivery of milk was used for analyses of the course of and inter-individual variability in different conditioning procedures (Papoušek, 1967b).

Shaping of the head-turns into movements switching on a rewarding visual display served as a basic response in problem solving studies in which the infant had to adjust his responses to different rules in order to achieve a reinforcement (Papoušek and Bernstein, 1969).

In the analysis of social interactions between infants and adults we used both filming and video-taping of behaviour. Both methods were modified in ways that deserve a few comments.

Since the majority of responses involved in infant–adult interaction lasted more than 0·5 second, we could save a lot of film material by using time-lapse filming at a speed of 100 frames per minute. This also allowed us to use up to four cameras simultaneously.

For the purpose of multiple synchronization we constructed a synchronizer triggering up to four cameras (Nizo-Braun S-800) at speeds of 1, 2, 5, 10, 20, 50, and 100 frames per minute. Simultaneous with every signal, numbers from 00 to 99 were displayed by a noiseless light-counter which could be filmed together with the subjects to label each frame. Simultaneous with every tenth signal, an on-line signal was sent into a three-track tape-recorder to enable matching of the film analysis with the analysis of vocalization and with the comments of a hidden observer. Two additional spotlight signals on the counter could serve as event-markers photographed on each frame (Fig. 1).

Another specialized device (designed for us by Schmidt Co., Straubing, F.R. Germany) allows easy analysis of up to four synchronized films at once. It consists of four professional Super-8 projectors housed in pairs in two twin cases. Each projector can be used separately or any combination of them can be synchronized and operated with a single button. Both single-frame steps and continuous projection in either direction at different speeds are possible. Each projector has its own counter.

Time-lapse filming makes movements discontinuous, thus facilitating their detection and evaluation in frame-by-frame analysis even when the observed movements are slow. In each individual frame we tried to analyse behaviour into basic motor components, using descriptive rather than interpretative categories. To facilitate a structural analysis of social interactions we evaluated the basic motor components using a strictly binary description.

Modern video-recorders allow the use of time-lapse recording, thus reducing the high expense of video-tapes. Both video-recording and filming have advantages and disadvantages which we have discussed elsewhere (Papoušek and Papoušek, 1974a). Built-in date generators allowing time measurement in hundredths of a second, and mixers combining pictures obtained by two cameras on one monitor certainly open new technical possibilities in video-recording. Television also enabled us to produce social stimulation mediated by live or playback display on a T.V. monitor. We found, for example, that four-month-old infants responded to such stimuli with vivid interest, and discriminated

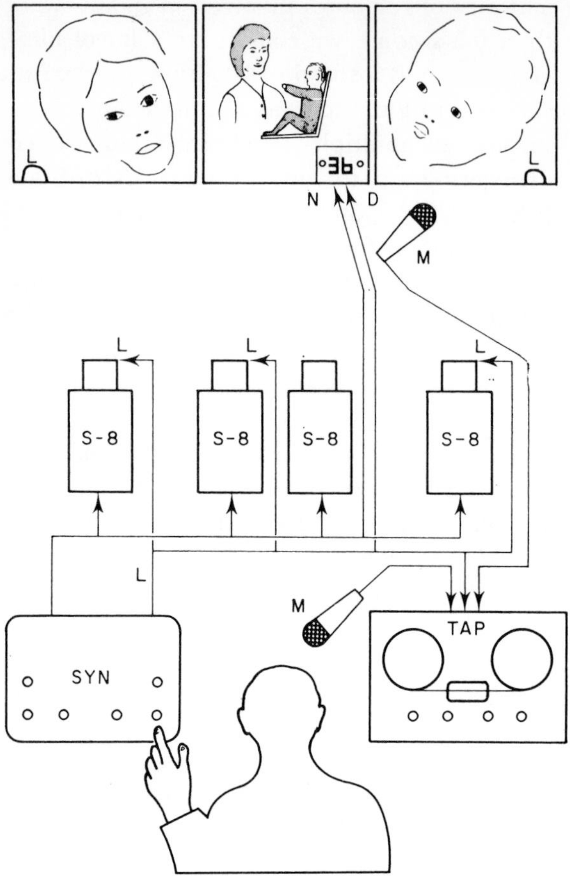

Fig. 1. Experimental set-up using multiple synchronization of cameras and tape-recorder. SYN = synchronizer for speeds of 1, 2, 5, 10, 20, 50, and 100 frames/min; S-8 = super-8 cine cameras; L = light signals coming with every 10th triggering signal; ND = numbering device displaying numbers from 00 to 99 for individual frames on film; M = microphones; TAP = tape-recorder (3 tracks).

meaningful differences in the displayed stimulation (Papoušek and Papoušek, 1974a).

Figure 2 demonstrates a combination of video-recorders and film cameras which allowed us to show the infant two matching images in a typical two-choice preference design where the critical variable between the two images consisted only of the difference in a cue-component of behaviour. Thus differences between the infant's responses to the two images, such as differences in visual attention,

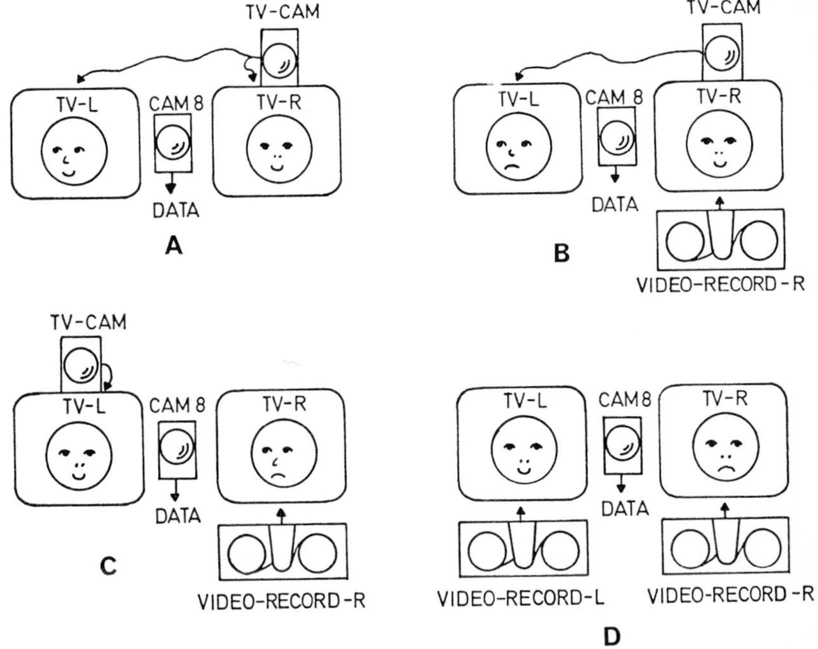

Fig. 2. Variations in the combination of video-recorders in a two-choice analysis of preferences. A: for the evaluation of eye-to-eye contact; B or C: for the evaluation of contingency; D: for the evaluation of discriminants between two T.V. movies.

vocalization, smiling or motor activities, may indicate whether the infant is capable of responding to the critical variable and in what modality he responds to it.

We used such an arrangement to study the development of self-recognition in infants in a mirror situation (Papoušek and Papoušek, 1974a), which at the same time allowed us to study the role of visual contact.

The first variation schematically presented in Fig. 2A enables the infant to observe televised images of himself on both monitors, the distinguishing variable being eye-to-eye contact which is possible on the right monitor only.

In the second variation (Fig. 2B, C) we can match the live image of self with a playback of self video-taped prior to experimental stimulation. In this way, the contingency of the televised mirror image on the subject's behaviour becomes the critical variable.

In the third variation (Fig. 2D) two different playbacks can be matched so as to make various other behavioural components the important variables, e.g. the image of self versus that of a strange baby, babyishness versus adultness, etc.

Analysing the infant's behaviour along these lines, we used the following list of behavioural patterns for a binary evaluation:

(1) looking in the direction of the central camera;
(2) looking in the direction of the left T.V. monitor;
(3) looking in the direction of the right T.V. monitor;
(4) looking at what the infant was touching;
(5) sucking the fingers;
(6) both fists firmly closed;
(7) motor activity very intense;
(8) motor activity reduced to a minimum;
(9) smiling;
(10) fussing or crying;
(11) frame not analysable according to preceding patterns.

Combinations of individual patterns yielded new, more complex categories of behaviour or differences in gradation. For instance, item 8 indicated increased attention to the T.V. image if combined with item 2 or 3, whereas alone it would indicate a decreased alertness and looking away (see the section on the fundamental regulation of behaviour).

Psychobiological Processes Underlying Pre-verbal Social Interaction

THE ROLE OF BEHAVIOURAL STATES

As part of his natural environment, the infant is exposed to different factors causing seasonal periodicities, circadian or ultradian biorhythms. As a result of his adaptation to them, his behavioural states show periodical fluctuations as well. For example, at certain intervals the infant must be fed and then left in peace for a nap several times a day during the first months of life.

In our previous studies, we analysed the level of learning in relation to changes of behavioural state in infants, using the percentage of correct responses and the latencies of responses as the critical parameters

(Papoušek, 1969). As shown in Fig. 3, the degree of wakefulness prior to the conditioning stimulus significantly influenced the responses.

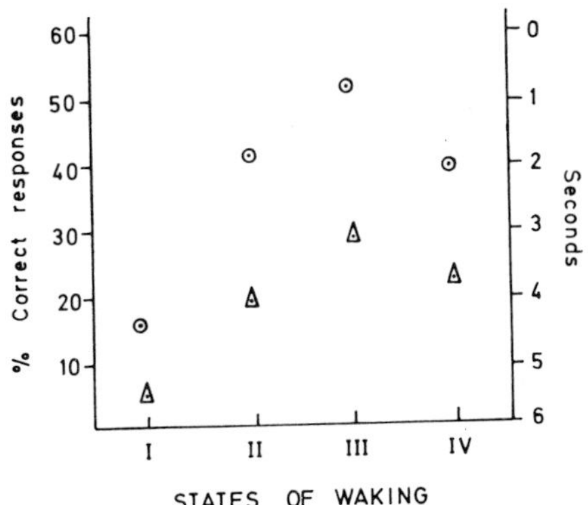

Fig. 3. Conditioning in different states of waking. ○ = percentage of correct CRs; △ = latency of CRs.

Another member of our team, Koch (1968), analysed changes in the level of learning in a similar way during the interval of time between two feedings and between two day-naps. In a bifactorial design, he showed that a relatively low level of conditioning after feeding improved significantly, reaching a maximum at approximately 40 minutes after feeding and then decreasing again with the increasing hunger of the infant. An analogous correlation was demonstrated by Koch in relation to sleep. Thus, the capacity of individual infants to perform conditioned responses can be shown to vary according to the sequence and temporal relation of their sleep and feeding patterns (Fig. 4).

We may assume that the course of social interactions may also be influenced by these two factors. Actually, in our films we found evidence

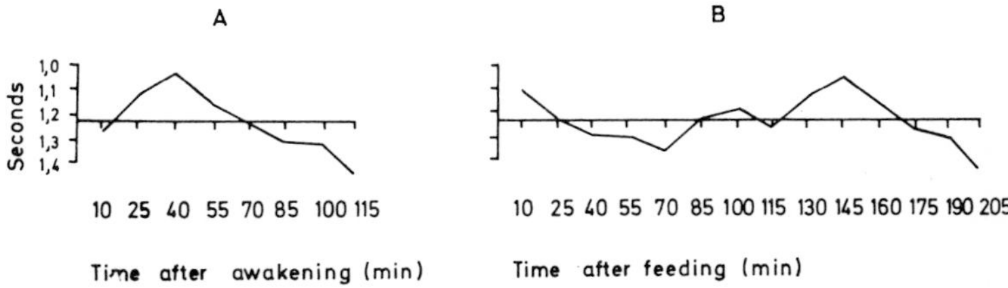

Fig. 4. The change of latency in conditioned responses affected by the state of wakefulness (A) and by the state of hunger (B) according to Koch (1968).

that during mother–infant interactions mothers respond to changes in the infant's behavioural state. This is apparent even during the first post-natal weeks where these changes are more frequent, less obvious, and less predictable.

This raises a question of what cues the mother may use. There are obvious cues signalling sleep, e.g. closed eyes, absence of movements and vocalization, and regular breathing. It is more difficult to find out what cues prompt the mother to increase or modify her stimulation of the infant in order to regain his attention, and why she stops playing and prepares her infant for sleep at other times. She is in fact seldom aware of her reasons for doing so, as we learned in subsequent interviews.

The mother may actually be using criteria similar to those we used in previous learning experiments (Papoušek, 1969); i.e. observational parameters of motor behaviour. The position and activity of the infant's hands alone would give her sufficient information, as indicated in Fig. 5.

During the infant's transition from lively waking activities to sleep we may see the hands first raised and partly stretched towards the mother, the fingers moving, and the palms open. Then the finger movements decrease, the hands are held stationary for increasing periods of time until they start dropping lower and finally rest motionless at the sides of the infant. Fists closed for more than several seconds indicate increasing fatigue or distress caused by unusual or discomforting circumstances. When interviewed, mothers typically claim to be unaware of this cue, although in film records they may be seen touching the closed fists, trying to open them slightly and to find out reasons for the infant's discomfort.

Probably the most sensitive parameters indicating to the mother even slight changes in the behavioural states are changes in the infant's facial expressions, type of vocalization, and interruption of visual attention. The mother's words and modifications in her stimulation behaviour indicate that she interprets such changes as changes of interest on the part of the infant. She responds to them very regularly.

THE FUNDAMENTAL REGULATION OF BEHAVIOUR

Paying attention to the relations between the course of learning and the level of alertness, we found that they can affect each other in both directions, i.e. that the course of learning may also influence the subsequent behavioural states in a predictable way (Papoušek, 1969).

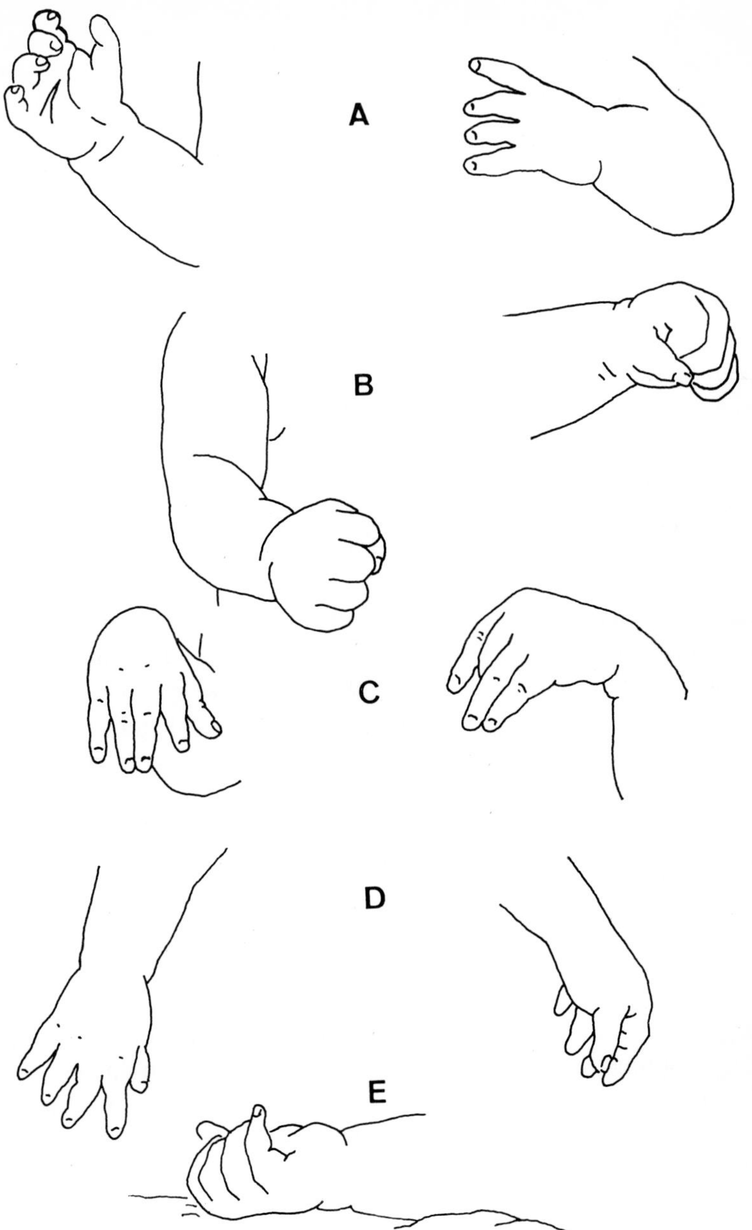

Fig. 5. The position of hands in different behavioural states of infants. A = alert waking state; B = closed fists in uncomfortable or distressing situations; C = passive waking state; D = transitional states to sleep; E = sleep.

Further evidence led us to the following assumptions regarding the regulation of behaviour in infants (Papoušek and Papoušek, 1975):

(1) Differences in waking behavioural states actually reflect different degrees of activation of behavioural mechanisms and strategies controlling the input and processing of information on the one hand, and the organization of adaptive responses on the other.

(2) There is a fluent transition evident between the activation of such behavioural mechanisms leading to increasing attention, orientation, approach, exploration, and experimenting in one direction and the inhibition of these mechanisms leading to decreasing attention, to habituation, avoidance and complete inner detachment in the other direction.

(3) Parallel to the mechanisms named above, corresponding changes may be seen in the autonomic system and in the behavioural responses interpretable as signals emitted for the social environment. Autonomic activation or inactivation controls the readiness for gross physical activity, among other things. Vocal signals and facial expressions may be differentiated only in rough categories in the first months of life, e.g. as signs of beneficial experience or pleasure, or as signs of displeasure, rejection or distress. Nevertheless, in a predictable way, they are also related to the discovery of a novel stimulus, an unexpected outcome of the infant's behaviour, the inability to find a solution in a problem situation as well as the achievement of such a solution (i.e. to the phenomena marking the course of the mechanisms named above).

Thus, behaviour consists not only of specific patterns such as appetitional, avoiding or communicative patterns, but also includes non-specific patterns common to all life situations, which control the input and processing of information and thus represent important fundamental mechanisms of cognitive processes. These non-specific mechanisms can be observed distinctly in infancy because infants do not inhibit or disguise them for social reasons, as adults commonly do. In their basic modes they may be found in the infant at the beginning of post-natal life.

According to actual needs, the non-specific fundamental cognitive mechanisms may be activated in order to facilitate optimal adaptation.

Or they may be moderated in order to protect the inexperienced infant against a flood of information or against stresses resulting from his inability to cope with too difficult situations.

In our studies of learning in infants we often saw that the activating or inactivating effects of stimuli were also determined by circumstances such as the infant's preceding experience with them, their contingency upon the infant's behaviour, or by the infant's behavioural state. These arguments resulted from experiments that represented non-social situations. Let us, therefore, consider the applicability of our model to social interactions.

Cognitive Aspects of the Structure of Pre-verbal Social Interaction

Social interactions are now commonly viewed as a chain of interlocking behavioural patterns representing responses and, at the same time, acting as stimuli initiating the next step in the interaction. Each behavioural pattern gains new dimensions which result from its position in such a chain and from its preceding history as well.

Two dimensions require particular attention: the degree of the infant's familiarity with a given behavioural pattern on the part of his social partner, and the contingency of that pattern on the infant's own activity.

At the very beginning of a mother–neonate relationship both partners are unknown to each other and have, therefore, good reasons for observing each other as much as possible in order to become familiar with the other's behaviour and to find out how his or her behaviour can be manipulated.

This process of familiarization is obviously relatively slow in the infant and requires many repetitions of the stimulation, according to all that we know about neonatal learning. It is interesting to observe that mothers tend to modify their behaviour into repeated simple patterns while mothering. However, the further development of the interaction may give those repeated patterns very different meanings. They may become merely repetitious and the response to them may decrease, they may become signals of other rewarding events through associative conditioning, or they may in some way depend on the infant's activity, so that he learns to elicit them himself in the sense of operant conditioning.

Needless to say, from this point of view, social interaction represents innumerable learning situations requiring different levels of cognitive processes. The infant's ability to determine whether or not an environmental change depends on his own activity has been demonstrated even in neonates (Papoušek, 1961; Siqueland and Lipsitt, 1966; Sameroff, 1968). However, his adaptation develops in several phases in such a case, and may thus be accompanied first by signs of distress, then later by signs of pleasure.

In order to facilitate such adaptive processes in her infant, the mother seems to be capable of very sensitive evaluation of all significant cues, and to reward richly any sign of the observed adaptation. The facial and vocal expressions of pleasure or distress and visual contact obviously play particularly important roles. We therefore want to discuss them in more detail.

SOME REMARKS ON INTRINSIC MOTIVATION IN RELATION TO SOCIAL INTERACTION

In mother–infant interaction we saw many examples where some new type of stimulation, repeatedly offered by the mother, first elicited orienting responses and then, after several repetitions, facial or vocal signs of pleasure in her infant. Such an emotional response may be even more striking if the mother repeatedly responds in some particular way to the infant's movements or vocal sounds, i.e. when her repetitive stimulation is contingent on the infant's own behaviour.

In such cases we may ask what aspect of the mother's stimulation is responsible for triggering signs of pleasure in her infant. It is not necessarily the fact that such stimulation has been produced by his mother. Toys or other non-social types of novel stimulation may elicit similar effects, although habituation soon leads to a decrement in emotional responses. The mother, however, stops repeating her stimulation if the infant's pleasure in it decreases, and starts using another kind of repetitive stimulation.

Two circumstances appeared to be particularly capable of eliciting the infant's signs of pleasure: familiarization with the repeated stimulation, and the contingency of the stimulation on the infant's own activity. The first has been analysed by McCall and Kagan (1967) and by Lewis and Goldberg (1969). The second one became apparent in our experiments during the final phases of learning or problem solving, where infants showed facial and vocal signs of pleasure in the absence of social partners when carrying out correct responses (Papoušek, 1967b; Papoušek and Bernstein, 1969).

The predictability of this observation led us to the hypothesis that, in accordance with Bernstein's model (Bernstein, 1967) of the regulation of movements, the congruence between the intended outcome (Soll-Wert) and the real outcome (Ist-Wert) of a movement alone elicits rewarding pleasant feeling, which plays an important role in intrinsic motivation (Papoušek and Papoušek, 1974b, 1975). Such an assumption has also been formulated in the theories of cognitive development of Piaget (Piaget, 1952; Piaget and Inhelder, 1969) and Bruner (1966).

In general we might say that the effective circumstance eliciting the infant's pleasure during a social interaction is related to the fulfilment of the infant's prediction that an event is going to be repeated or, in other cases, that his own activity will elicit a relevant event. Thus smiles or other signs of pleasure in the infant may first appear as responses caused by confirmation of predictions, fulfilment of expectations or correct outcome of movements. From the very beginning, however, they also act as stimuli eliciting changes in the mother's behaviour, and the infant may soon discover that through this kind of activity he can manipulate behaviour in his mother. The role of emotional signs may thus soon become very complex and can hardly be understood if we do not have sufficient insight into their earliest post-natal development.

VISUAL COMMUNICATION

Unlike other mammals, including the non-human primates, direct eye-to-eye contact in man represents a frequent and meaningful means of inter-individual communication. With reference to the regulation of behaviour in infants we mentioned visual contact as a basic mechanism of orientation, indicating what the infant pays attention to or what he wants to avoid. Eye movements preceding conditioned movements of the head can be seen even in neonates (Papoušek, 1967b). Rheingold (1961) and Robson (1967) consider visual contact one of the most important components of social behaviour in infants.

Using the design described schematically in Fig. 2 we found that of two matching movies of himself (variation B), the infant preferred the movie allowing eye-to-eye contact to an identical movie in which eye-to-eye contact was excluded (Papoušek and Papoušek, 1974a).

In this study, 11 infants at five months of age were observed during three 2-minute periods:

(1) pre-experimental behaviour (recorded with the central camera);
(2) first experimental stimulation: the televised mirror image of self without eye-to-eye contact was matched with a movie of self (i.e. the playback of the pre-experimental record) where eye-to-eye contact was possible;
(3) second experimental stimulation: with the same but laterally reversed images as in (2) above.

The results are shown in Table I.

Table I

Infant's visual attention to televised movies in a two-choice study of preference at 5 months (percentage of time)

Behavioural patterns	Pre-experimental	During experimental stimulation I	II
Looking at central camera	14·18	4·45	5·86
Looking at left monitor	19·14		
Looking at right monitor	14·18		
Looking at mirror image		27·59	17·19
Looking at movie of self		54·18	50·14
Looking at object of touch	8·77	3·87	7·63
Looking at other things	43·73	9·91	19·18
Intensive motor activity	24·73	14·00	24·46
Smiling	0·27	1·68	3·51

Both types of experimental stimulation attracted so much attention that infants looked most of the time at the T.V. monitors. However, the movie of self allowing eye-to-eye contact attracted significantly more attention ($p < 0{\cdot}01$) than the televised mirror image of self without eye-to-eye contact (though contingent on the infant's own activity).

The significance of contingency appeared only when we divided the 2-minute samples into four 1/2 minute blocks and found the following trends: visual attention to the movie of self decreased from 68·36% to 39·64% (Friedman analysis of variance: $X_r{}^2 = 15{\cdot}8$, df=3, $p < 0{\cdot}01$), whereas visual attention to the mirror image increased from 14·54% to 26·73% ($X_r^2 = 9{\cdot}46$, df $= 3$, $p < 0{\cdot}05$). These trends support the assumption that the infant can detect the contingency of the mirror image on his own activity only after a certain amount of experience.

The role of visual communication between the infant and his mother in natural interactions appeared in our film records to be complex. However, it is difficult to quantify it without gross intervention or to apply statistics rather than individual analyses of simple cases.

The experience accumulated until now has led us to the following conclusions:

(1) The mother regularly carries out many movements of which she may be largely unaware, which are interpretable as attempts to achieve mutual visual contact with her infant, particularly in the first months of his life. She keeps moving her head to stay centred in the infant's visual field, with her eyes in the same plane as his eyes. She also tries to maintain the optimal distance (20–25 cm in the first two or three weeks) as if respecting the infant's limited capacities for focusing and convergence. This may be observed even in mothers who do not expect their infants to be capable of seeing, according to their statements in interviews following our observations.

(2) Having achieved eye-to-eye contact with her infant, the mother often responds with what we call "greeting behaviour". She lifts her head slightly for a fraction of a second, raises her eyebrows or opens her mouth, perhaps calling the infant by his name. The change in facial expression or vocalization may be individually very different, of course, from minute to quite dramatic responses. Gentle smiles usually follow such a "greeting". If the infant is awake and starts responding to the mother's behaviour, she seldom interrupts her looking at him.

(3) At the beginning of his life the infant is obviously less able to maintain prolonged visual contact. His behavioural state fluctuates more frequently and with larger amplitudes so that the periods of optimal waking are very short. In addition, he may easily lose visual contact with his mother if the distance between them changes. In any case he starts scanning and often turns his head aside in such a situation. The length of the infant's periods of observing his mother increases, though, in a few weeks, as does his capacity to observe the mother under less favourable circumstances, e.g. while she moves about or changes the infant's position during different activities.

(4) The mother's proximity plays a special role here. Measuring the length of time during which the infant observes his mother we found

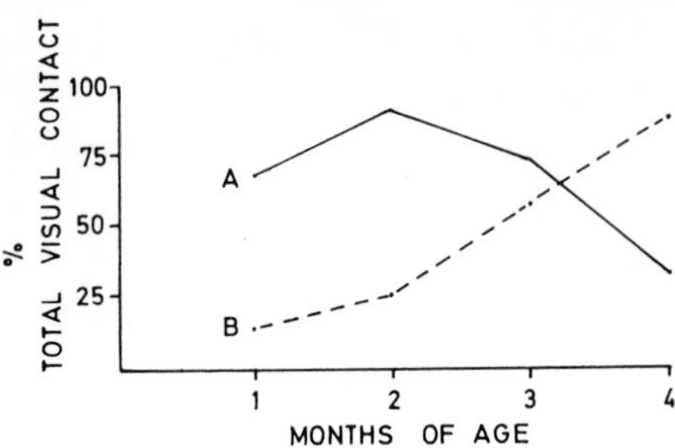

Fig. 6. Visual contact with mothers in infants one to four months of age being held by mothers (A) or 1·5m distant from mothers (B).

two different curves of development (Fig. 6) corresponding to two different situations:

(a) when the infant was held by his mother in a position optimal for visual contact;

(b) when the mother stayed 1·5 m away from the infant, however under circumstances favourable for visual contact.

Obviously, some kind of contact with the mother is so important for the infant that, in the latter situation (b), the infant needs to observe her. It seems that he is free enough to observe other things only when other means of contact, such as tactile, are available.

In infants above six months of age this situation looks quite different. The infant can concentrate his attention on other objects of interest in the presence of his mother, independent of her distance from him. The length of his visual attention seems to be determined by novelty or by certain needs of the infant. He may observe his mother longer if he is hungry or distressed, as well as in situations where his mother is involved in unusual activities.

(5) All our experience indicates that the infant's visual contact plays an important role as feedback information for the mother, telling her whether her mothering is being performed in the right way and at the right time. We will recall here what we said about visual attention in relation to the fundamental mechanisms of cognition. Visual orientation seems to be a very sensitive indicator not only of what the infant is interested in, but also of what he wants to avoid. He tries to turn away

from objects he cannot reach after repeated efforts, from persons behaving in a strange way, or from situations which are different from his expectations or beyond his capabilities.

In any case, such an interpretation best explains the different situations observed in our studies of pre-verbal social interaction. Thus we saw mothers changing their repetitive behavioural patterns as soon as the infant had stopped looking at them. We also saw infants four months of age turning away from their mothers and resisting their attempts to re-establish contact in experiments where mothers repeatedly left infants for a short time in three-second periods of darkness, i.e. in a fashion unknown to the infants (Papoušek and Papoušek, 1974b, 1975).

VOCAL COMMUNICATION

The first half of the first year of life may seem to deserve little attention from the point of view of vocal communication, since only in the fifth or sixth month do the first more or less distinct syllables appear, obviously as incidental products of the speech organs, associated with no particular objects or situations.

Yet a closer look at the earliest vocalization soon reveals three pathways of development playing different roles in social interactions:

(1) Crying, thereby alarming the social environment in all situations in which the further existence or integrity of the infant might be threatened. Crying is present at birth and temporarily prevails as the only form of vocal communication.

(2) Fundamental vowel-like sound produced with only minimal contribution of the relaxed speech organs during quiet waking states of the infant, with his mouth either closed or slightly open.

(3) Syllabic sounds consisting of consonants followed by increasingly differentiated vowels which are often repeated in bursts, e.g. "gah-gah-gah-gah" or "duh-duh-duh".

The latter two categories gradually emerge in a similar fashion to the newly learned responses in conditioning studies described in preceding sections: as single responses at first, and only after a certain interval (lasting sometimes just a few days) with increasing frequency. However, there are substantial differences between these two categories in several respects.

The fundamental pre-verbal vocalization appears earlier, i.e. between the second and fifth week of life, and changes only little during the pre-verbal period. It may have an iterative character as well; however, the rhythm then is slower, remaining usually within the limits of 40 to 60 utterances per minute.

The syllabic sounds, on the contrary, typically appear in the fifth or sixth month of life, are frequently combined into bursts of several repetitions of the same pattern at a rhythm twice as fast as the fundamental vowel-like sounds. Also, after a week or two, they are usually replaced by groups of other syllables and may disappear for weeks. Parents often imitate such a syllabical vocalization, using the pauses between individual bursts and thus giving the interaction the semblance of a dialogue, pleasing to both partners. However, below seven to nine months the syllabic sounds bear the character of incidental and passing products of the developing speech organs and do not represent any objects or situation.

The fundamental pre-verbal sounds attracted our attention for two reasons in particular: their relative stability, and the predictability with which their main variations accompany certain characteristic situations. They vary more significantly in length and intonation than in other phonological qualities. These variations appear to be very relevant for social communication.

The mother interprets the individual variations of the fundamental pre-verbal sounds as signals related to different everyday life situations, e.g. in the following terms: the infant likes his meal, his play or the mother's stimulation, he enjoys the expected outcome of his play with a favourite object, he is taken by surprise at an unexpected outcome of his activity, he feels relief at having overcome some difficulty, he tries to draw attention to himself, he asks for help, he provokes another repetition of a pleasant stimulation, he calls the absent caretaker, he is becoming tired, upset or sleepy, etc.

In our learning experiments we had a convenient chance to analyse the relationship between such fundamental vocal sounds and the individual phases of learning processes. In their simplest forms such sounds appeared in the second or third week of life. At this age, their relation to learning can be detected only in such experiments. Actually, at such an early age it is in fact easier to detect due to the slower course of learning.

The occurrence and differentiation of such fundamental vocalization was typically related to the following experimental situations: the initial unsuccessful attempts to carry out the adequate response, the final phases of successful acquisition of correct responses, the first omissions of reinforcement during extinction procedures, changes of the principles of reinforcement during reversals of conditioned discriminations. The individual variations of vocalization resembling signs of discomfort, distress, pleasure, surprise, or disappointment were appropriate to the experimental situations named above.

Thus, before the infant has learnt the first meaningful words, this fundamental vocalization seems to be the relevant means of pre-verbal communication informing the infant's social environment on the course of his adaptive behaviour. The more differentiated syllabic sounds cannot replace the fundamental vocalization, although they may please the adults as signs of the prospective higher level of communication.

IMITATION

The infant's ability to imitate his caretaker represents an important point in the relationship between mothering and cognitive development. In Chapter 9 Pawlby analyses its communicative aspects in infants of 17 to 43 weeks of age. We can therefore limit our comments to the earliest period of the development of social interaction and to the question of the first evidence of imitation. Our experience may contribute to the clarification of this problem for two reasons: first, because of our extensive opportunity to observe infants and their mothers daily from birth to six months, and secondly, because of the applicability of our concept concerning the structure of social interaction to the problem of imitation.

In the literature the earliest manifestations of imitation, its reflexive character and motivational structure and its relation to observational learning remain unclear. We were surprised to find that in previous studies on early imitation in infants only the infant has been expected to learn, to imitate, and to adapt his behaviour. He is capable of learning in the first days of life, that is true, although his adaptive capacities are still very poor. But it is his caretaker who must adapt his behaviour first to facilitate the infant's cognitive start and to arrange for him the first optimal learning situations. There is no doubt that the mother is best prepared for this role through both the biological processes of pregnancy and her social and cultural motivation.

In the repertoire of maternal behaviour two components deserve special attention from the point of view of imitation: *her* increased readiness to imitate her infant's facial expressions, vocal sounds, and movements, and her tendency to demonstrate to him the desired outcomes of his behaviour. Both components are present during the first days after delivery.

According to our observations the mother more often imitates the activity occurring in the area of mouth, nose, and eyes as well as whatever new behavioural patterns develop in her neonate. Here the mother's "instructions", i.e. models demonstrating the desired outcome of the infant's behaviour, also first appear. Opening her eyes before her infant can fully open his eyes after a nap or opening her mouth when bringing a spoon to her infant's mouth can be given as examples of such early instructions. A similar readiness can be observed in fathers and strangers, but is weaker there.

Thus the first step in the development of early imitation is actually made by the mother. From the first days she offers her infant what we call "a biological mirror". By imitating him she gives him a chance to associate his interoceptive information about his own movements with their visual external representation. In facial expressions or mouthing he cannot yet find the evidence of similarity between his and the mother's behaviour. The first chance comes when he produces sounds which his mother imitates or later when he can observe the similarity of hand movements. However, these first steps may soon lead to the next important point.

Recalling what we said about the structure of social interaction, we would like to point out another aspect of the mother's imitative behaviour. When imitating her infant the mother often joins his ongoing activity and initiates a sequence of interlocking mutual acts in which, for example, they both alternatively protrude tongues. The similarity of their acts may be insignificant for the infant, but he may detect that his act elicits a response in his mother with a certain regularity, and the contingency of this response alone may be enough first to initiate operant learning in him, and second to elicit a smile from him when the congruency between "Soll-Wert" and "Ist-Wert" of his movement has been confirmed.

It is interesting to note that the infant does not smile when the mother gives him "instructions" on opening the mouth or other oral activities which are not contingent of the infant's own behaviour, but that he often smiles when the mother imitates his oral activities so that her actions become contingent on his behaviour.

Thus Piaget (1951) may well be right when he labels as "pseudo-imitation" what is otherwise interpreted as genuine imitation of the protrusion of the tongue at the age of two to four months (Piaget's second stage of imitation), in spite of evidence on the earliest imitative behaviour in infants that was accumulated by his student Maratos (1973).

Concluding Remarks

Social interaction often represents complex situations where sets of events are chained without any easily detectable rules and where most relations among these events have only a probabilistic character. Moreover, they depend on individual peculiarities of both partners and change with their accumulating experience, so that the actual meaning of social interaction can hardly be interpreted without a good knowledge of the whole course of such interaction.

It is no wonder, then, that the role of mothering has been so difficult to interpret. Even the mere description of human maternal behaviour is still far from satisfactory. Yet, with all due respect to the unique position of the biological parents in the social world of a child, we do not believe in anything mystical that escapes scientific analysis and makes it impossible to prevent the syndrome of deprivation in the absence of the biological parents.

However, we still have much to learn in order to understand fully the significance of a good parent or a good caretaker. Very likely we will have to continue to combine experimental analysis with good naturalistic observation where experiments are hardly possible, be it for technical or ethical reasons. At the same time, though, we certainly need new methods for a rational utilization of naturalistic observations.

During our presentation at the Loch Lomond Symposium we were able to offer a film illustrating some of the arguments set out in individual sections of this chapter. We showed one infant—Tanya—in different behavioural states with different levels of readiness to respond. We also demonstrated the difference with which a stimulus changed the behavioural state in relation to its contingence on Tanya's behaviour.

One part of the film showed an uninterrupted double sequence of repeated protrusions of tongue in Tanya and her mother, the first sequence initiated by the mother, the second one by Tanya. It was clearly evident how much Tanya enjoyed the mother's responses to her in contrast to feeding situation where the mother's oral activities, in the form of "instructions", were non-contingent.

This one case study is typical of many of our other observations and allows one to show easily what might otherwise be difficult to demonstrate in written form. Unfortunately there is no substitute for a film that is acceptable to publishers.

Acknowledgements

The individual studies discussed in this paper were partly supported by grants from the General Research Support (Gov. No. 5 SO 1 RP-05482) to the Children's Hospital Medical Centre, from the National Institute of Mental Health (12623) and the Carnegie Foundation (B 3233) to the Center for Cognitive Studies, both at the Harvard University in Cambridge, Mass., and from the Deutsche Forschungsgemeinschaft (Pa 208/1) to the Max-Planck-Institute for Psychiatry in Munich, F.R. Germany. The generosity of Professor Peter H. Wolff, Professor Jerome S. Bruner, and Professor Detlev Ploog is very much appreciated. We also owe special thanks to Dr Hana Krulišová and Jarmila Melicharová, the former collaborators of the first author at the Research Institute for the Care of Mother and Child in Prague, Czechoslovakia, to Dr Marc H. Bornstein and his wife Helen, and to Anne Fernald for their devoted help.

References

Bernstein, N. (1967). *The Coordination and Regulation of Movement.* Pergamon Press, New York.

Bruner, J. S. (1966). On cognitive growth I and II. In J. S. Bruner, R. R. Olver, and P. M. Greenfield (Eds), *Studies in Cognitive Growth.* Wiley, New York.

Koch, J. (1968). The change of conditioned orienting reaction in 5-month-old infants through phase shift of partial biorhythms. *Human Devel.* **11**, 124–137.

Lewis, M. and Goldberg, S. (1969). Perceptual-cognitive development in infancy: A generalized expectancy model as a function of mother-infant interaction. *Merill-Palmer Q.* **15**, 81–100.

Maratos, O. (1973). The origin and development of imitation in the first six months of life. Ph. D. Thesis, University of Geneva.

McCall, R. B. and Kagan, J. (1967). Attention in the infant: effects of complexity, contour, perimeter, and familiarity. *Child Dev.* **38**, 939–952.

Papoušek, H. (1961). A physiological view of early ontogenesis of so-called voluntary movements. *Plzeň. Lék. Sb. Suppl.* **3**, 195–198.

Papoušek, H. (1967a). Conditioning during postnatal development. In Y. Brackbill and G. G. Thompson (Eds), *Behavior in Infancy and Early Childhood.* The Free Press, New York.

Papoušek, H. (1967b). Experimental studies of appetitional behavior in human newborns and infants. In H. W. Stevenson, E. H. Hess, and H. L. Rheingold (Eds), *Early Behavior: Comparative and Developmental Approaches.* Wiley, New York.

Papoušek, H. (1969). Individual variability in learned responses in human infants. In R. J. Robinson (Ed.), *Brain and Early Behaviour.* Academic Press, London and New York.

Papoušek, H. and Bernstein, P. (1969). The function of conditioning stimulation in human neonates and infants. In A. Ambrose (Ed.), *Stimulation in Early Infancy.* Academic Press, London and New York.

Papoušek, H. and Papoušek, M. (1974a). Mirror image and self-recognition in young human infants: I. A new method of experimental analysis. *Dev. Psychobiol.* **7**, 149–157.

Papoušek, H. and Papoušek, M. (1974b). Die Mutter-Kind-Beziehung und die kognitive Entwicklung des Kindes. In R. Nissen and P. Strunk (Eds), *Seelische Fehlentwicklung im Kindesalter und Gesellschaftsstruktur.* Luchterhand, Neuwied.

Papoušek, H. and Papoušek, M. (1975). Cognitive aspects of preverbal social interaction between human infants and adults. In M. O'Connor (Ed.), *Parent-Infant Interaction.* Elsevier, Amsterdam.

Piaget, J. (1951). *Play, Dreams and Imitation in Childhood.* Heinemann, London.

Piaget, J. (1952). *The Origins of Intelligence in Children.* International Universities Press, New York.

Piaget, J. and Inhelder, B. (1969). *The Psychology of the Child.* Basic Books, New York.

Rheingold, H. L. (1961). The effect of environmental stimulation upon social and exploratory behavior in the human infant. In B. M. Foss (Ed.), *Determinants of Infant Behavior,* Vol. I. Wiley, New York.

Robson, K. S. (1967). The role of eye-to-eye contact in maternal-infant attachment. *J. Child Psychol. Psychiat.* **8**, 13–25.

Sameroff, A. J. (1968). The components of sucking in the human newborn. *J. exp. Child Psychol.* **6**, 607–623.

Siqueland, E. R. and Lipsitt, L. P. (1966). Conditioned headturning behavior in newborns. *J. exp. Child Psychol.* **3**, 356–376.

III | The Organization of Dyadic Behaviour

5 | Toward the Origin of Dialogue

Kenneth Kaye

Clov: What is there to keep me here?
Hamm: The dialogue.
Samuel Beckett, *Endgame*

Introduction

There is an obvious similarity between the burst-pause pattern in sucking during the first month of human life and later burst-pause cycles of activity. These are found in visual attention to objects (alternating with gaze aversion), face-to-face interaction (cycles of arousal and passivity), trials in skill acquisition, turns in instructional interaction, and language. Is there a developmental course, from burst-pause or on-off cycles in the individual to turn-taking and dialogue in social systems?

Orienting to the breast, sucking and swallowing are precocious in comparison with other skills—developing from reflexes to organized intentional schemata in a matter of days rather than months after birth. This precocity explains the long history (e.g. Marquis, 1931) and recent proliferation of experimental studies of classical conditioning and reinforcement in the newborn, using sucking as the critical response (cf. Kaye, 1967; Kessen *et al.*, 1970; Millar, 1974).

Investigators differ from one another in the size of the lenses through which (literally or figuratively) they view the phenomena of sucking. Experimental studies invariably focus upon the infant alone, usually his mouth alone; while students of socialization and attachment regard the mother–infant dyad as their subject, and anthropologists may concern themselves with the nuclear or even the extended family as it involves itself in the care and feeding of new members. Clearly there is an inverse relation between the width of one's view and the sharpness of focus as well as the experimental control one can manage. Nonetheless, the different types of investigation have much to offer one another in the way of cross-validating theoretical interpretations and refining hypotheses. Microanalysis is to no avail without the accompaniment of macroanalysis.

I presume that the mechanisms of early learning which evolved for our species and which are available to the newborn infant are just those which serve the needs of early development and survival in the social systems into which human infants are born. A good example is the infant's pre-adapted capacity to learn phonemic discriminations and to segment perceptual continua categorically (e.g. Eimas *et al.*, 1971). We may also presume that some social systems evolved as a consequence of the human infant. And in the case of an individual family, the systems which develop partly for the goal of producing a child now develop further as a consequence of the infant's birth. Patterns of child-rearing, cultural expectations for newborn infants, and differentiated child-care roles which human societies have created—diverse as they may appear to be—could only survive if they allowed infants' innate programmes to interact with the environment so as to acquire conceptual, social, and linguistic skills in an orderly and productive way. Thus the "environment" of the infant is more than just a given reality with which he has to deal; and his innate equipment is more than just a given reality to which his parents have to accommodate themselves. The environment and the newborn infant are in a sense made for each other, and our job is to understand the whole system as a set of mutual causes and consequences.

Our own work falls in the category of naturalistic observations of the dyad or "nursing couple" (Middlemore, 1941), with an emphasis upon what we believe to be species-universal patterns of behaviour and development. We are using a zoom lens, narrowing in for the details while trying to retain an awareness of the wide-angle picture.

BURST-PAUSE PATTERNS

Virtually the entire literature on burst-pause patterns is based upon artificial feeding or non-nutritive sucking under laboratory conditions. When the infant* sucks on a pacifier or blind nipple, his pauses in sucking tend to be at least as long, or longer than, his bursts of sucks. The bursts consist of four to ten sucks at a rate usually somewhat less than one per second, never faster than two per second. Thus the bursts may last between three and about 15 seconds, with the pauses in pacifier sucking having about the same range. The pattern is least variable over time if the infant is asleep. There are obvious differences in the parameters (both central tendency and variability) of the burst-pause pattern between one session and another, but whether there are stable individual differences in infants across sessions is still problematic. Kron *et al.* (1968) reported individual consistencies in sucking rate and pressure, but not in bursts or pauses. Studies of individual differences in sucking rate (e.g. Balint, 1948) are unhelpful because the rate is typically averaged over a session without regard to the bursts (Kaye, 1967).

When the nipple delivers milk or water at a normal level of flow, the burst:pause ratio increases. There are fewer bursts of only three to five sucks, but the upper limit remains (typically) about nine or ten sucks. The pauses are almost all shorter (in seconds) than the bursts. When the flow is very rapid, as with a full breast or a nipple whose hole is too large, the pauses may disappear entirely and one sees bursts as long as one or two minutes. This fact, and the difference between nutrient delivery systems in one laboratory and the next, apparently led to the erroneous equation of the burst-pause pattern with "non-nutritive" sucking. Actually, the infant always sucks in bursts and pauses; rapid milk flow may tend to prolong the bursts and shorten or eliminate some pauses; while, on the other hand, very short bursts can be and are used by mothers as a clue that something is occluding the nipple. (Kaye, 1972; and additional subsequent observations.)

When milk delivery is made contingent upon some component of the infant's sucking, he appropriately modifies the length of his bursts (Bosack, 1967; Hillman and Bruner, 1972). When some external reinforcer (other than delivered fluid) has been made contingent upon

* This paper deals exclusively with the first few weeks of life; unless specified otherwise, by "infant" we mean "newborn infant".

his sucking, the pause durations have been modified (Brassell, 1971). Speaking very generally we might infer that the bursts are modified by nutrient delivery (Kaye, 1972) while the pauses depend upon other factors. Unfortunately, bursts cannot so easily be separated from pauses since the onset of one is the point of termination of the other. Is it correct to say, for example, that the infant shortens his bursts when there is no milk? Or should we say that he pauses more often? One is really dealing with the organization of events in time, in this case sucks, and when we treat the pause or even the somewhat arbitrarily defined burst as an event in itself we are doing so only as a matter of convenience.

Yet bursts and pauses *seem* like events to an observer. Although the suck is obviously the appropriate unit of behaviour for recording, the fact remains that the designations "he is sucking" (burst) and "he is waiting" (pause) feel right subjectively. Thus the question arises, does the infant's mother perceive his sucking as being organized in this way? Does she behave any differently during bursts vs. pauses? If so, does this possibly have any consequences for their later interaction?

Several years ago we reported data from ten infants in Cambridge, Mass. and Cambridge, England, observed three to five times during the first month of life (Kaye and Brazelton, 1971). The fact that their mothers tended to jiggle them (or their bottles) during pauses in sucking, and expressed a belief that this "wakes them up" or elicits a resumption of sucking, led us to test whether jiggling indeed had such an effect. Contrary to the mothers' belief, the midwives' and nursery nurses' advice, and the bulk of the literature (e.g. Middlemore, 1941), we found that the pauses were longer if mothers jiggled than if they did nothing. Furthermore, it was not a matter of their having jiggled in the especially long pauses; the mean latency from onset of pause to jiggle was nearly always less than the mean duration of pauses without jiggles. Our principal hypothesis in the present study was that we would replicate the Kaye and Brazelton findings: that jiggling would increase rather than decrease the pause, postpone rather than hasten the next burst.

No physiological function suggests itself for the pauses in sucking, at least from the baby's point of view. He swallows and breathes concurrently with his sucking. He pauses no longer on the second breast than on the first, nor do we typically see any increase in the pause durations over the course of a session; thus fatigue seems to be ruled out. It is possible that the pauses evolved to allow the flow of more milk, but their temporal parameters are longer than would be suggested by the physiology of the mother's breast (Ardran *et al.*, 1958). Accordingly, we speculated that a possible adaptive function of pauses might be their one most striking effect: to elicit a response from the mother. This hypothesis demanded that we study neonatal feeding from the point of view of interactive behaviour and learning in a natural social context.

TURN-TAKING

Two distinct themes in recent research gave further impetus to our analysis of early feeding. One was the interest in exchange of speaking turns, signalled by an orderly set of partly conventionalized, partly universal rules among adult speakers (Duncan, 1972). Certain specific types of signal, notably eye-contact, are shown to be important in the studies of adults by Duncan, by Kendon (1967) and Argyle (1972), and in studies of mother–infant dyads (Jaffe *et al.*, 1973; Robson, 1967; Schaffer *et al.*, this volume). This naturally leads us to ask whether the rules for exchange of turns may be learned in early infancy, and if so how; or whether on the contrary they may characterize communication in the human species at any age, irrespective of learning.

A second theme has to do with the development of language acquisition proper. A large number of investigators have begun to focus upon the interactive contexts in which linguistic relations are presumably learned. One (and only one) of the necessary precursors of language development is the alternation-of-comments-upon-a-common-topic discussed by Bruner (1975), deLaguna (1927), and Macnamara (1972) among others. The crucial proviso is that a learner of a language must be able to alternate his own attempts at expressing propositions, semantic relations, etc., with the attempts of a model. Such alternation may serve a number of functions, including some which provide information to the child and some which provide information to his mother. For the sake of this paper, it will be sufficient to point out that turn-taking is more than just a characteristic of language, whether learned or unlearned; it is a necessity for the *acquisition* of language. A child will be able to extract little information from adult utterances, or from the mismatch between his own utterances and those of adults, unless there is some high probability he and they are talking about the same thing. This is where gaze direction becomes especially important.

The evidence that mothers tend to look where their infants are looking (Collis and Schaffer, 1975) suggests that the infant may have at least one means of eliciting utterances about an object in which he is interested, long before he can produce even a poor verbal reference to that object.

Similar arguments can be made about the acquisition of skills such as reaching for a toy behind a detour (Kaye, 1976). The infant's gaze movements elicit appropriate object-directed interventions by adults. In all such tasks, there needs to be temporal proximity between the trials of the learner and the model. Timing is crucial in the effect of any feedback—reinforcing, comparative or corrective—upon learning. Thus dialogue ought to be acquired or built into the system first, so that the specifics of language, object manipulation, social ritual, or whatever can then be learned efficiently. Put this way, we can think of dialogue as a necessary context for language acquisition as well as other kinds of learning, and we would be inclined to pursue any phenomenon in early infancy which bears a resemblance to dialogue.

Method

The subjects for this study were 30 healthy full-term infants delivered by vaginal route in Columbus Hospital, Chicago, and their mothers. The mothers included 15 primiparae and 15 multiparae, 12 breast- and 18 bottle-feeders; all were Caucasian, English-speaking, U.S.-born women. There were 18 boys and 12 girls. The feeding sessions for this analysis were the first 40 sessions which we happened to have coded, cleaned up, and stored in a computer disk, out of an eventual 100 sessions with 50 subjects in a longitudinal study.

Half the sessions took place on the second full day of the infants' lives, between 36 and 60 hours after delivery. All of these sessions were in the mothers' rooms in the hospital, sitting up in bed, between 5.00 and 5.30 p.m. The mothers had just eaten dinner; the infants had been examined, at about 4.30, using the Brazelton Neonatal Assessment procedure (Brazelton, 1973). None of the male infants had yet been circumcised. All were discharged from the hospital within two days after this session.

The other 20 sessions took place at age 12–18 days, in the subjects' homes. There were some morning, some afternoon, and a few evening feedings at this age. Some fathers, siblings, and an occasional neighbour were present. The Brazelton examination was usually administered before, but in some cases not until after the feeding. However, all observations took place at a time and place in which the mother said she would have been feeding her infant, even if the observers had not been present. (Some mothers know when this time will be, several days in advance; others do not know even when the next feeding will be. This is true of both breast- and bottle-feeders, and does not correspond very well to mothers' claims as to whether they feed by "schedule" or "demand". Both the mother who can and the one who cannot accurately tell us in advance what time the baby will be fed on a subsequent day, appear to regard this as a matter of course.)

For the present preliminary analysis of our data, we have a cross-sectional and a longitudinal sample. Only 10 of our subjects are represented in the two-day as well as the two-week sessions. (This explains how the 40 sessions happen to come from 30 subjects.) The other subjects, on whom we cannot do a longitudinal analysis here, are mainly cases in which the computer-readable transcripts for the other session were not yet ready. When we refer to the "longitudinal sample" in this paper, we shall mean the 10 subjects observed twice. When we refer to the "cross-sectional sample" we shall mean the other 20 subjects, plus half the longitudinals randomly assigned to the two-day group (their two-week sessions being ignored) and the other half assigned to the two-week group (their two-day sessions being ignored). This gives us a total of 30 independent sessions for cross-sectional analysis, 15 at each age.

There were two observers at each feeding, one looking at the mother and one at the infant. Each observer held a digital keyboard attached to a portable cassette recorder (Datamyte, Electro General Corp., Hopkins, Minnesota). Depressing any combination of the numerical keys caused those digits to be recorded, and depression of the "Time" key caused the elapsed time to be recorded, to a precision of 0·2 seconds. Since their two clocks were synchronized (by simultaneously coding the beginning and end of each session), the coders were able to make independent observations of mother and infant, preserving the sequence of events in the dyad.

Observer 1 coded (1) the mother's placement of the nipple in her infant's mouth (ONBT), and its removal (OFBT); (2) her direction of gaze, at (LOOK) or away from (AWAY) the baby's head; (3) the beginning (JIGG) and end (STOP) of bouts of jiggling, defined as any displacements of the baby's body or cheek, the breast, or the bottle which would have the effect of moving the nipple with respect to his mouth; and (4) the beginning (STRK) and end (STOP) of bouts of stroking, defined as all forms of touching which could be sensible to the infant yet not affect the relative positions of mouth and nipple. Among the events which we ignored, the most salient ones were (1) the mother's vocalizations to the baby, observers, and other people; (2) the type of jiggling, whether moving the bottle in and out or from side to side, pressing on part of the breast, tickling the baby's cheek, or jiggling his body; and (3) rocking her own body together with the baby's, normally in a rocking chair.

Observer 2 coded the baby's taking of the nipple (ONBT), and any rejection of it (OFBT); and each individual suck (SUCK). The sucks were coded at the point of maximum closure (expression), with no regard for swallowing and no information, obviously, about suction. Of behaviour which the observer unfortunately had to ignore, the most promising would have been whether the infant's eyes were open or closed. (It was not possible to crowd the room with a third observer.)

To avoid having to depress two keys for every suck, we used the "Time" key alone. This difference between the tasks of the two observers had the effect of giving Observer 2 a shorter response time. Furthermore, the regularity of the sucking rate within bursts—along with the fact that she was coding the downward, or last visible phase of the suck—enabled her to code each suck just about simultaneously with its occurrence. In fact, a 16mm, 24 frames/s film of one of our sessions indicated that her finger depressed the key only 5 ± 1 frames after the event. Observer 1, however, was 35 ± 10 frames late—due to the fact that he was coding less predictable events. We therefore subtracted 1·2 seconds from all of the coded events for each mother, before mixing the two codings into a single transcript. This gives us our "best estimate" of the actual time of occurrence of events; however, the variability in response times when one is coding live sessions makes it imperative to remember that any inter-event latency A–B of less than about one second could easily have been a sequence B–A, or a simultaneous occurrence of B and A. (Reliability tests on video-tapes of newborn feedings indicate a "confidence interval" or mean deviation of 1·4 seconds for recordings of maternal categories and 0·9 seconds for onset of bursts and pauses in sucking.)

As for the simple reliability of coding vs. failing to code an event, our comparison of the coding of the filmed mother with the live coding made while we were filming was only 0·85. However, this does not reflect the true reliability of coding. Comparison of *two* codings made from the film or video-tapes yields reliability coefficients greater than 0·90, and we believe this would also be true of two live coders who were somehow made deaf and blind to one another's presence. (The Datamyte makes a slight click, apparently ignored by our subjects but sufficiently audible to us (along with the information from peripheral vision) so that we never regard codings of the same events at the same time as being independent; therefore at the moment we do not have data on the reliability of live codings.) One can see better live, of course, than from a film—but it is possible that ambiguous events are lost or disambiguated by the camera angle. This would have the effect of giving codings from a film a higher reliability coefficient. Yet the live coder, who can change his position and use extra cues outside the camera's vision, is surely the more valid one so long as events are not happening too rapidly to be coded live.

A third type of reliability which concerned us was of the specific measures to be derived. Between two codings of the same video-tape by different observers, for example, the duration of jiggling (JIGG-to-STOP) correlated 0·92. Correlation of individual observations between observers *within* a session does not give a good estimate of the reliability of derived measures (such as the median jiggle durations analysed later in this paper) *across* subjects. However, the latter can be assumed to be at least as high or higher than the former, if between-subject variability in the durations themselves is at least as great as within-subject variability. Thus a reliability test of this type, the only practical one under the circumstances, is fairly conservative.

Table I shows a sample computer transcript of one of our sessions. To save paper we do not print these transcripts with constant time scale. Instead we print a line every time a new event is coded. As a visual aid we print AWAY continually until it is ended by LOOK; JIGG or STRK (stroking) continually until ended by STOP. The events labelled SUCK, however, are discrete events. BRST and PAUS will be explained in the following section.

Our preferred method of analysis is to eschew time-sampling. When possible we live with the complexity of real time, segmenting our sessions into units which are behaviourally defined (such as JIGG-to-STOP

Table I

Two-minute excerpt from a transcript

Time (sec)	MOBT	MOJG	MOLK	BABY	BTPS
274·6	ONBT			SUCK	BRST
275·6				SUCK	
276·6				SUCK	
278·6					PAUS
286·8				SUCK	
287·6				SUCK	
293·8				SUCK	
294·4				SUCK	
298·9		JIGG			
301·0		JIGG		SUCK	BRST
301·6		JIGG		SUCK	
302·6		JIGG		SUCK	
302·8		STOP			
304·6					PAUS
307·8		JIGG			
308·2		JIGG		SUCK	BRST
308·4		JIGG		SUCK	
309·2		STOP			
309·4				SUCK	
311·4					PAUS
313·6		JIGG			
314·0		JIGG		SUCK	
314·6		JIGG		SUCK	
314·8		STOP			
320·2		JIGG			
320·4		JIGG		SUCK	BRST
321·0		STOP			
321·2				SUCK	
322·2				SUCK	
323·4				SUCK	
325·4					PAUS
326·8			AWAY		
328·7			LOOK		
329·2				SUCK	HFBS
329·8				SUCK	
331·2				SUCK	
331·4	OFBT				
339·0	ONBT				
340·8				SUCK	
344·8				SUCK	
348·8				SUCK	BRST
349·6				SUCK	
350·4				SUCK	
351·4				SUCK	
352·6				SUCK	
353·4				SUCK	
354·2				SUCK	
356·2					PAUS
357·8				SUCK	BRST
358·8				SUCK	
359·4				SUCK	
361·0				SUCK	
363·0					PAUS
365·4				SUCK	
366·0				SUCK	
374·8		JIGG			
375·3		STOP			
380·6				SUCK	
381·6				SUCK	
383·5		JIGG			
385·2		JIGG		SUCK	BRST
385·8		STOP			
386·0				SUCK	
386·8				SUCK	
388·8					LAST
389·0		JIGG			
390·4		JIGG		SUCK	
391·2		JIGG		SUCK	
396·0		STOP			
397·4				SUCK	
398·0				SUCK	
402·2	OFBT				

and PAUS-to-BRST) and asking questions about their temporal organization.

Results

A monograph in preparation will take the High Road to understanding our full corpus of data: analysing first the organization of sucking at each age; then the intrinsic organization of the mothers' jiggling at each age; then the relation between jiggling and sucking and its possible development over the first two weeks; then (by comparison) the relation between stroking, jiggling, and sucking; and finally the possible role of the mother's gaze direction in affecting her interaction with the infant. Fortunately for the reader of this paper, economy of time and space demand that we take the Low Road. Thus in addition to limiting ourselves to the 40 sessions explained above, we shall also ignore the mothers' stroking and looking behaviour. Since these subjects were involved in an intensive longitudinal study including neonatal assessment and video-tapes of interaction at home through the first six months of life, a large number of additional variables have yet to be studied. We found no differences by sex or by feeding method in any of the measures to be discussed here.

THE BURST-PAUSE PATTERN

The precise number and durations of the bursts and pauses in any sucking session depends upon the criterion one uses. Figure 1 shows the distribution of all SUCK-to-SUCK intervals in the first 400 seconds of a single session. This bottle-feeding at two weeks was chosen because it happens to be both our longest session and the one with the least amount of maternal activity. The pattern, however, is the same in all our sessions. One sees a bimodal distribution with most intervals less than 2·0 seconds, and substantial variance among the intervals longer than 2·0. As is the case in this session, we almost never see an interval of exactly 2·0 seconds between sucks, and therefore this was our criterion value; intervals greater than 2·0 were regarded as pauses. Furthermore, we required at least three sucks, or two consecutive intervals of 2·0

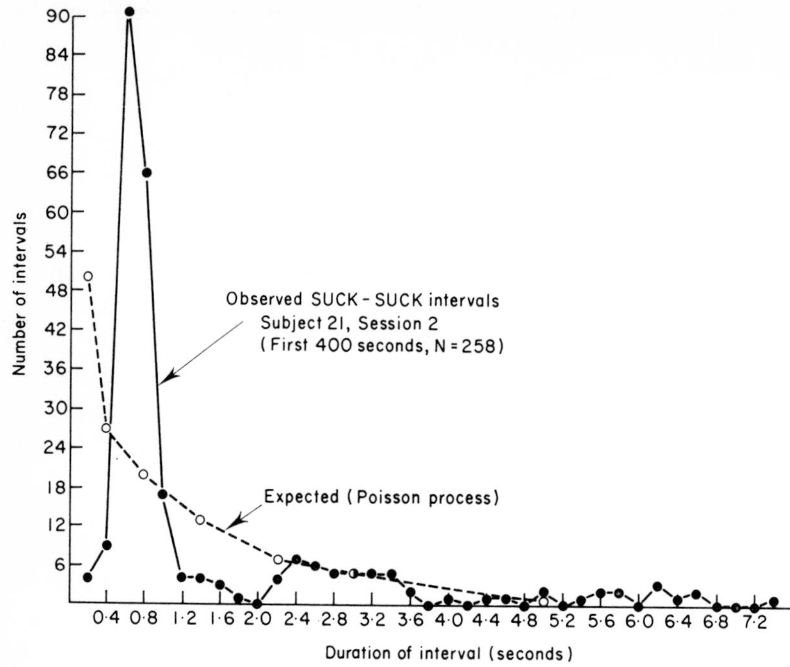

Fig. 1. SUCK-to-SUCK intervals found in the first half of a long bottle-feeding session, at two weeks. Expected values are based on an exponential distribution where N = 258 and $\lambda = 0{\cdot}70$.

seconds or less, as criterion for a burst. Others have arrived at these same criteria (Sameroff, 1967; Kaye, 1967).

Thus the event BRST was written at the first SUCK of each burst, and PAUS 2·0 seconds after the last SUCK of each burst as shown in Table I. A SUCK-to-SUCK interval of 3·6 seconds would become a PAUS-to-BRST of 1·6 seconds, and so on. If OFBT (off-breast or off-bottle) came after a PAUS, we changed that PAUS to LAST. If OFBT came after a BRST and before the PAUS, we changed the BRST to HFBS (half-burst) and deleted the PAUS. For analysis we exclude the time after LAST or HFBS (i.e. while the nipple was being withdrawn), and also exclude the time between ONBT and the first BRST.

Pauses, the PAUS-to-BRST intervals, may contain one or more isolated sucks. However, in the full 15-minute session of Fig. 1, only 11 of the 82 pauses contained isolated sucks. This is representative of the typical pattern. More troublesome is the fact that a rigid criterion such as 2·0 seconds inevitably omits some very short pauses, and introduces some which are not "really" pauses or which would not be perceived by the mother as pauses. What we defined as (for example) bursts of 6·0 and 5·0 seconds, separated by a 1·0-second pause, might "really" have been a 12-second burst. However, these errors, like the variability in observer response time, will work against any significant findings. The only systematic distortion to be kept in mind is that the shorter the criterion interval for pauses, the shorter both the median bursts and the median pauses will appear to be.

Figure 1 shows the deviation of SUCK-to-SUCK intervals from an exponential distribution. Many intervals cluster around 0·8 seconds, the median for this session; the intervals greater than 2·0 seconds are essentially a random distribution except that there are more very long ones, which of course are pauses.

Figure 2 is a plot of the BRST-to-BRST and PAUS-to-PAUS intervals from the same session as Fig. 1. These events also deviate from the exponential distribution; the onset of a burst or pause is obviously not a Poisson process. However, these intervals are not distributed bimodally like the SUCK-to-SUCK intervals in Fig. 1. There is periodicity, or uniformity in the intervals.

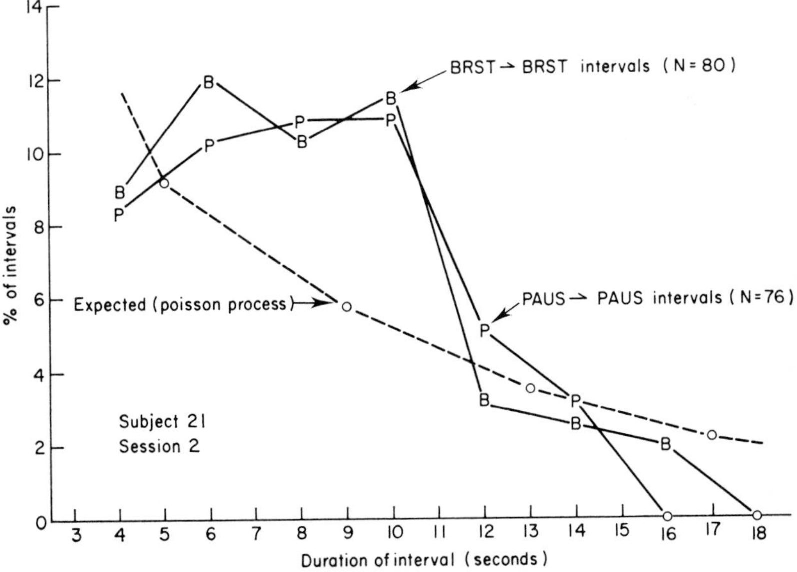

Fig. 2. BRST-to-BRST and PAUS-to-PAUS intervals. N = 82, $\lambda = 0{\cdot}012$ for both curves.

There is no reason *a priori* for the BRST-to-BRST curve in Fig. 2 to fit so closely the PAUS-to-PAUS curve. If the pauses were rests we might expect them to be correlated positively with the lengths of the preceding bursts, making the BRST-to-BRST intervals less uniform than the PAUS-to-PAUS. If on the other hand the natural function of the pauses were to let milk collect in the nipple, then at least in breast-feeding we might expect the pauses to be positively correlated with the following bursts. This would make the PAUS-to-PAUS intervals less uniform. Alternatively, the bursts and pauses might be hypothesized to have an inverse relation: if the pause somehow compensated for the duration of the preceding burst, then BRST-to-BRST would be much more uniform than PAUS-to-PAUS. Such hypotheses, however, find no support in our data. The correlation is zero between pauses and their preceding bursts (N = 1147, across all sessions) and zero between pauses and their following bursts.

Is there any stability in the individual infant's burst-pause pattern? Certain parameters of sucking, such as pressure and per minute efficiency, have been shown to distinguish individual infants over several feedings through laboratory apparatus (designed to monitor pressure, rate, etc.) (Balint, 1948; Kron *et al.*, 1968). But these investigators have failed to show any stability in the burst-pause pattern. Nor is there evidence that the individual consistency in the infant's response to such apparatus is matched by a corresponding consistency in his feeding under normal (interaction) conditions. We as yet have no substantial evidence supporting individual consistency in our dyads. There was a reduction in pause length by the time our longitudinal infants were two weeks old, as shown in Table II. Despite this general reduction there seems to be some significant correlation in individual dyads' median pause lengths. If supported by our data yet to be analysed, this would be consistent with a view of pauses as relating to the mother–infant interaction rather than the flow of milk (which differs greatly between hospital at two days and home at two weeks).

JIGGLING

Sixty-two per cent of the jiggles in all of our sessions came during pauses, despite the fact that just under 45% of the elapsed time was pause time. Figure 3 compares the probability of one or more jiggles

Table II

Comparison of two-day and two-week sessions

	Median burst length (N)		Median pause length		Proportion of session, jiggling		Median JIGG-STOP duration	
	Two-day	Two-week	Two-day	Two-week	Two-day	Two-week	Two-day	Two-week
Cross-sectional (Mean of 15 Ss at each age)	8·2 (26)	7·1 (27)	4·7	5·7	0·150	0·123	2·25	1·69
t-test	N.S.		N.S.		N.S.		N.S.	
Longitudinal Ss:	Two-day	Two-week	Two-day	Two-week	Two-day	Two-week	Two-day	Two-week
03	7·6 (34)	4·3 (9)	13·5	17·0	0·278	0·072	3·50	0·75
04	3·9 (26)	6·4 (31)	8·5	3·7	0·411	0·056	3·50	1·00
09	8·8 (7)	7·5 (34)	6·0	2·3	0·112	0·025	3·00	0·50
16	5·9 (10)	18·8 (12)	18·3	2·3	0·213	0·175	4·25	1·50
21	7·8 (9)	5·1 (82)	2·6	2·5	0·106	0·038	1·00	1·50
25	5·6 (13)	4·7 (26)	6·6	4·5	0·142	0·097	1·88	1·00
28	5·7 (13)	[a](0)	11·3	[a]	0·136	0·199[b]	(1·23)	[a]
31	5·4 (56)	6·2 (47)	1·7	1·6	0·194	0·114	4·50	0·75
32	5·4 (11)	7·2 (11)	6·8	4·4	0·162	0·060	2·25	0·75
36	5·7 (11)	6·9 (40)	2·3	2·0	0·228	0·128	3·13	2·00
(mean)	6·18	7·46	7·76	4·48	0·198	0·096	3·00	1·08
Rank order correlation	$r_s = 0{\cdot}04$		$r_s = 0{\cdot}53$, p = 0·05		$r_s = 0{\cdot}24$		$r_s = -0{\cdot}21$	
Binomial sign test	2-tailed N.S.		2-tailed $p = 0{\cdot}039$		1-tailed $p = 0{\cdot}010$		1-tailed $p = 0{\cdot}019$	
t-test (Wilcoxon):	N.S.		N.S.		$t = 2{\cdot}75$, $p < 0{\cdot}05$		$t = 4{\cdot}23$, $p < 0{\cdot}001$	

[a] One subject is omitted because his session at two weeks contained never more than one burst per ONBT-to-OFBT period, thus no official pauses (the bottle was removed during each of four pauses).
[b] Jiggling occurred only during excluded parts of the session (see text).

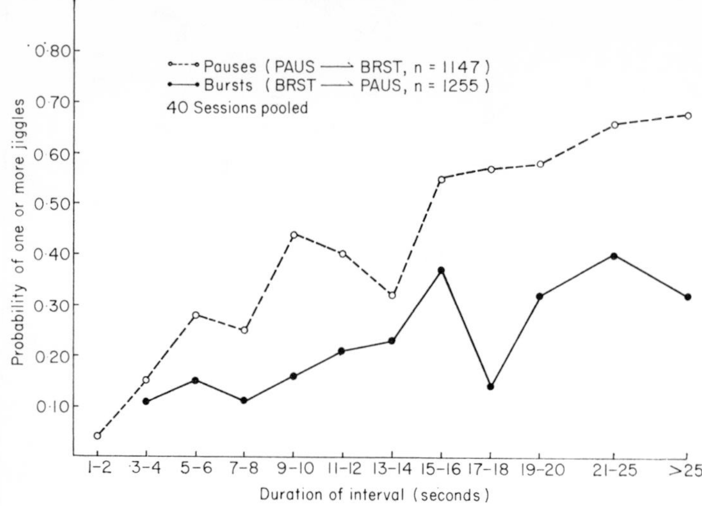

Fig. 3. Probability that at least one jiggle will fall into an interval, depending upon the length of the interval; bursts compared with pauses.

falling into a pause of any length, with their probability of falling into a burst of the same length.

As reported by Kaye and Brazelton (1971), the pauses containing jiggles were significantly longer than those without. In the earlier study, we compared the *logs* of pause durations (raw durations do not meet the assumption of homogeneous variance) by a t-test for each subject at each session, finding a preponderance of significant differences all in the same direction. With much more data now we are dissatisfied with central tendencies like the mean of logs or the median, preferring instead to look at the whole distribution. Figure 4 compares pauses with one or more jiggles, and pauses with none, over all sessions. The data on each group—two-day breast, two-day bottle, etc.—look the same.

One might expect pauses with jiggles to be longer just because there is a greater chance of any random event falling into an interval, the longer the interval. But we can show in a simple way that this is not the explanation. The median duration of the 896 pauses without jiggles was 2·5 seconds (mean = 4·4). The median duration of pauses with jiggling was 10·2 seconds (mean = 15·0). Even the portion of these pauses that *followed* the first JIGG had a median of 5·5 seconds (mean = 9·7), significantly longer than the pauses without jiggles ($t = 6{\cdot}1$,

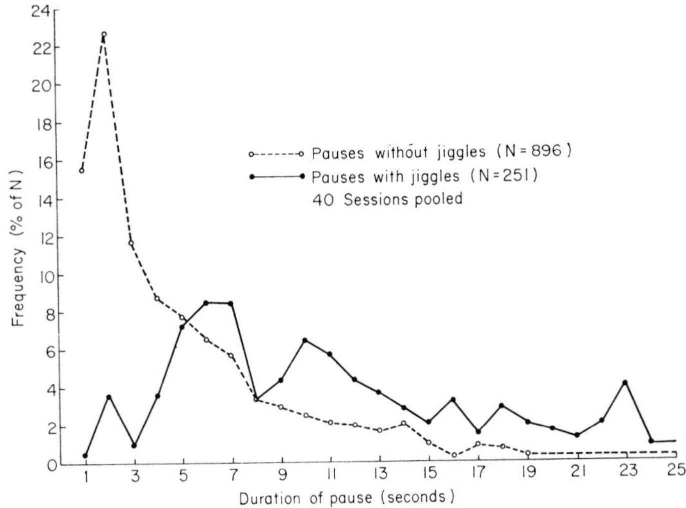

Fig. 4. Duration of pauses with and without jiggling.

$p < 0{\cdot}001$). I interpret this as sufficient evidence that jiggling *lengthens* the pause.

STOPPING

It is mildly interesting that mothers' jiggling is contingent upon the pauses in their infants' sucking, and that they are wrong in believing the infants' BRST to be contingent on the jiggling. However, in the data presented so far we do not have an interaction. We have simply the behaviour of one person organized biologically, and the behaviour of another person fitting into the organization somewhat. It is a one-way direction of effect, and furthermore it is simply a response—nothing we would call learning.

If, however, the behaviour of mother and infant were to be thought of as turn-taking, then we should not consider JIGG as the mother's turn. JIGG, the onset of jiggling, is only the beginning of her turn which has a duration JIGG-to-STOP just like BRST-to-PAUS. The event STOP can be thought of as comparable to a speaker's yielding the floor. Is a BRST any more likely to occur immediately after a STOP than at other times? The answer is yes.

If an event such as BRST is *not* contingent in any way upon another event such as JIGG, then the latencies JIGG-to-BRST should be distributed as a Poisson process, fitting the exponential distribution as they do in fact in Fig. 5. These latencies are from the last JIGG in a pause to the

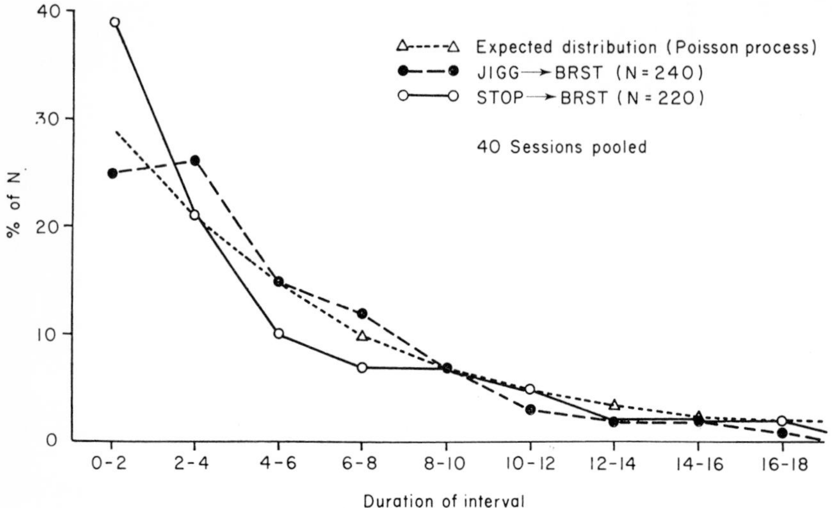

Fig. 5. Latencies to BRST from last JIGG in a pause, and from last STOP.

next BRST, regardless of what intervenes. The sequence may be JIGG-STOP-BRST, or it may be JIGG-BRST, followed only later by a STOP. Similarly, the last STOP in a pause can precede the last JIGG: the sequence can be JIGG-STOP-JIGG-BRST. *A priori*, the STOP-to-BRST times could be longer or shorter than the JIGG-to-BRST times. However, the issue is not which is longer or shorter on the average, but how each of them compares with a random or Poisson process. The STOP-to-BRST latencies in Fig. 5 do not coincide with the expected values. There are many more short ones than expected, and many more than there are of the short JIGG-to-BRST latencies.

The statistical significance of the STOP-to-BRST curve's deviation from an exponential distribution can be tested by a statistic $\Sigma|x-\bar{x}|/2\Sigma x$ whose expected value is equal to $1/e$ and which is normally distributed with calculable variance (Cox and Lewis, 1966). For four sub-samples of our data—the longitudinal and cross-sectional groups at each of two ages—this statistic is always between $1z$ and $3z$ above the expected value. The graphs all have the form of Fig. 5, with visibly more of the very short waiting times (0–2·0 seconds) between STOP and BRST than we could expect by chance. Thus we can conclude that a mother is more likely to elicit a BRST within two or three seconds when she stops jiggling than when she starts jiggling.

THE MOTHER'S TURN

The preceding sentence expresses a conclusion from our data in terms that cannot help but raise the further question of reinforcement. If indeed mothers begin by thinking of (or unconsciously relying upon) the jiggle as an elicitor of sucking bursts, and if indeed the burst is more often contingent, especially in the critical range of 1–2 seconds, upon the STOP than upon the JIGG, should we not predict a change in the duration of jiggling? Instead of jiggling and watching for the next burst, mothers might learn to jiggle and stop. This would be reflected in a number of changes in the many types of sequence found in our data. But if it were a fundamental and robust phenomenon, it ought to be reflected in the simple durations of jiggling, throughout the session. We can hypothesize that jiggling in general becomes shorter in duration over the first two weeks. Table II presents the data. These values are not to be regarded as precise. In fact, there were many latencies recorded as 0·0, when the observer saw that the jiggling had ended by the time he had entered JIGG. The data reflect more of these at two weeks. For the cross-sectional sample a t-test comparing median JIGG-to-STOP durations fell short of significance at 1·28 ($p = 0{\cdot}213$). For the longitudinal sample a matched t-test showed a highly significant change ($t = 4{\cdot}23$, $p < 0{\cdot}001$). The two-day latencies of 2·25 or 3·0 seconds may seem quite short, but the medians themselves range from 1·0 to 4·5; at two weeks the range is 0·5 to 2·0.

The difference was evident in the cross-sectional comparison, but individual variation prevented its reaching significance. This fact itself is interesting, suggesting the possibility of stable individual differences in jiggling duration which we were able to test in our longitudinal sample. Using the median JIGG-to-STOP duration we found a correlation of only −0·35 between two days and two weeks. But the STOP-to-BRST latencies at two days predicted the JIGG-to-STOP latencies at two weeks. The correlation of 0·53 (N.S.) is merely suggestive, since it is based on a small N. But the amount of variance accounted for is surprising, and we look forward most of all to replicating this particular finding with our larger corpus of data. It would suggest not just that mothers learn shorter bursts of jiggling, but that those mothers change the most whose infants reinforced them the most.

Lest we seem to suggest that all of the effects in early feedings are those of the infant upon his mother, attention should be directed back to the other side of the story. Pauses were shorter at two weeks than they had been at two days. And there were more of the short STOP-to-BRST latencies at two weeks. These exceeded the frequency of short JIGG-to-BRST latencies by 25% at two days and by 50% at two weeks. The rule "you end your turn and I'll start mine" was being learned by the infants as well as by the mothers. It is not a matter of a new rule suddenly emerging. The learning in this case seems to consist in heightening the frequency of certain interactive sequences which occur naturally with some probability and then are selected by the dyad-system.

Discussion

MICROANALYSIS

In contrast to the complexity of our analysis (much of which still remains to be done) the results appear to be rather straightforward. Mothers begin by interpreting their infants' pauses as signs of flagging and as occasions for stimulation. Gradually, apparently under the influence of a tendency on the infant's part to respond to the *end* of jiggling by a resumption of sucking, the mothers change their response during pauses from "jiggle" to "jiggle-stop". By two weeks both the duration of jiggling and the duration of pauses are shorter.

This suggests a degree of symmetry between the behaviour of both partners. When her baby pauses the mother might jiggle, or she might not. When his mother stops jiggling the infant might suck, or he might not. While he is in the midst of a burst she is unlikely to jiggle—though the likelihood increases as the bursts get very long. While she is in the midst of jiggling he is less likely to resume sucking—though the likelihood goes up if she continues too long.

There is also, however, some important asymmetry. The smooth alternation of turns comes about, when it does come about, by the mother's accommodating her turns to the temporal organization imposed by the infant. Her turns get shorter and so (therefore) do his pauses. His bursts do not depend upon her intervention at all. If she does nothing, he will organize his sucking in essentially the same manner. There is merely a slight tendency to delay the onset of a burst, all other things being equal, until after her jiggling stops; or to hasten the onset of some of the bursts so that they come right after she stops.

We do not suggest that the infant is in any way conscious of the effect his behaviour may have, or that he intends to reinforce his mother. Nonetheless, because jiggling tends to prolong the pauses, and jiggle-stop tends to elicit a resumption of sucking, the potential reinforcement is there. "Tends to elicit" does not mean every time, of course; but partial reinforcement is the best kind. It seems to be only a matter of the number of very short-latency "responses" of BRST following a STOP. One way of reading Fig. 5 is that there are about one-third more STOP-to-BRST latencies under two seconds than we should expect by chance. This may well be sufficient to shape a tendency on the mother's part to STOP jiggling, and thus to reduce the duration of JIGG-to-STOP over the course of many feeding sessions.

Two sessions, approximately the seventh and the seventieth times the mother feeds her infant, certainly do not make a learning curve. We are currently making video-tapes of a few mothers, every other day during this period, to see if we can see the changes in jiggling and in the burst-pause pattern over a gradual period and despite each day's new disruptions. (One of the striking things about the first two weeks is that, on balance, there is very little "routine". The homes of our subjects are certainly very different from a well-controlled animal laboratory, and if consistent trends survive the exigencies of each new day and the various sources of unsystematic error, they must be robust trends indeed.)

The fact that STOP does increase the probability of BRST—or, put another way, that it sometimes has no effect and sometimes is followed by an immediate BRST, is not difficult to understand when we consider the nature of neonatal reflexes. This response seems to lie somewhere between a reflex like the Moro which is externally-stimulated but still depends upon the infant's state and activity, and a primary circular reaction like vocalization. By the second month an adult can substitute his own "ahhh" for the infant's, filling the pause, and elicit a repetition of the sound from the infant. This is reminiscent of the burst-jiggle-burst sequence. Since sucking is different in form from jiggling, neither we nor the mother perceive her infant's behaviour as imitation. Yet her belief that the bursts are contingent upon jiggling is about as well founded as her later belief that his "ahhh" is an imitation.

MACROANALYSIS

It is necessary now to present a view of the broader context in which our observations have been made. My interpretation draws upon some additional observations in the course of this study as well as the theoretical issues and biases my students and I have been developing.

The newborn infant and his mother have very different agendas. The infant responds to hunger as to pain, cold, or distention of his bowel: he is equipped with certain reflexes, and he gradually becomes able to anticipate what the sequence of events will be as those reflexes occur. His time-frame expands slowly from seconds to fractions of a minute. Even as we see intentional breast-seeking replace rooting, anticipatory tonguing replace crying, we still see an organism which is concerned only with getting control over whatever is immediately necessary to obtain the goal when the time comes. He is learning, but it is a matter of being conditioned by very immediate results in his environment. The infant is responsive to, and affected by his experience of, the transition points from hunger to feeding, from cold to warm, etc.

With the mother the situation is very different. While we may casually use the term reinforcement, the fact remains that we can point to no intrinsic reward for her in the infant's bursts. If this event has meaning for her it is only because she is concerned with a larger picture. More than any other topic in these early weeks of her baby's life, the mother talks about his cycles (Sander, 1962). "When will he sleep?; how long will he sleep?; when will he be hungry again?; what is it that probably explains his crying at this time of day?; how much milk will he take at this feeding?; what does his behaviour now tell about what he is going to do or want next?" She needs to see regularity in his behaviour if for no other reason than to feel she understands him. His way of controlling the uncertainty in the world is to develop appropriate techniques for responding to whatever unpleasantness may arise. Her way is to develop a theory of the infant, and one (we believe) which is really a theory of the infant-in-time or time-in-the infant.

Yet it is not enough for her to be able to anticipate the infant's cycles. The mother (if you will permit some speculation) wants to see herself as a *participant* in the organization of his day. Without disrupting his cycles she wants to make them contingent upon her own schedule, or at least to see herself as having made him accommodate himself to her. Some of our mothers fantasize accommodations by their infants: reporting strict schedules when they are clearly on demand, claiming credit for altering the infant's sleeping or attentional behaviour when they have actually accommodated their own techniques by trial and error. Other mothers express frustration at not yet regaining any sense of control over their lives.

I think a similar process is occurring within the narrower time-frame of the feeding session. The mother is not satisfied with perceiving a burst-pause pattern innately wired into her infant. In fact, it is surprising how few mothers express any awareness of this regular cycle. Their awareness is largely subconscious, and it takes the form of seeing regularity in the interaction rather than in the infant. "Don't go to sleep, now" (jiggle, jiggle). The jiggling behaviour itself is less important than the function it serves, which sometimes takes other forms such as calling the infant's name, clicking the tongue, or perhaps stroking. It is a strange sort of researcher who tries to report what he thinks his subjects are trying to say in their behaviour. But as Emerson said, "Words are also actions and actions are a kind of words." During early feedings, in the first month before mutual smiling and other games begin, the mothers' actions express to me: "I'm not just sitting here holding this bottle. I'm *feeding* my baby."

The infant, let me reassure you, does not inspire me to paraphrase. Yet he is the one with the remarkably organized behaviour. We must assume that a variety of adaptive functions affected the evolution of his behaviour. One set of functions have to do with obtaining food. But his behaviour affects his social environment as well, and these effects have in turn had evolutionary consequences. When we think of the infant's differentiation of reflexes into skills, etc., as accommodation to an environment, we need also to be aware of how the environment is differentiating itself, at least partly as an accommodation to the infant. The reflexes with which he is born are appropriate ones given the nutritive social environment into which he is born, which may include sets of "reflexive" built-in responses of its own. However, the organization of the infant's behaviour will itself impose and elicit an organization in the environment.

It is true that the human newborn is "autistic" (Mahler *et al.*, 1975) and "subcortical" but it is a mistake to regard that fact strictly as a matter of "helplessness". Surely the immaturity in which our species delivers its young is no mere accident of premature parturition. The newborn's immaturity at birth may be his most important asset—for it guarantees a degree of salient regularity, rhythmicity, and predictability to his behaviour which will not again be possible once higher cortical processes take over. The human mother apparently makes use of the fact that she can predict the temporal structure of her infant's behaviour. She uses it to build, through mutual differentiation of responses, a basic pattern of interaction which will *not* depend upon biological clocks but upon mutual monitoring and feedback.

It may be that a species which is going to rely so heavily upon communication and co-operation, and in which such a vast amount of knowledge and basic skill is going to be passed on through interaction and discourse, needs to deliver its young while they still have the capacity to teach their parents how to interact with them. The biological clocks of the newborn are indeed remarkable as is the co-ordination of sucking at birth; but they are not a matter of precocity. Whatever their mechanisms, these clocks are characteristic of things that have been going on in the fetus's nervous system during most of his gestation. They represent the very opposite of precocity. The fact that the most neurologically advanced organism is born in a neurologically primitive state needs explaining. Only by looking at the psychological development of the dyad can we begin to explain it.

I should not like to limit the relevance of our findings to turn-taking alone. Although it has intrinsic importance for linguistic dialogue and for instruction, turn-taking is only one aspect of the enormously rich exchange that goes on between infants and other people. True, the infant and his mother learn to take turns and to read one another's signals about the beginnings and ends of turns. But at a more general level they are learning how to anticipate one another's behaviour, which is just as important in simultaneous activities, such as smiling, as it is in the alternation of turns. Similarly, as their interaction continues in subsequent feedings and other situations, they learn to read intentions; to interpret affect; and perhaps most important to read the signs of how the other partner is interpreting their own behaviour (Winnicott, 1967).

Previous authors have used the word "dialogue" to describe early mother–infant interaction, often with respect to breast-feeding (e.g. Resta, 1955). The literature is old and diverse, and I cannot do justice to it here. However, the notion has been much more general than simply "turn-taking". For Spitz (1963a, b, 1964) the exchanges between mother and infant gave the infant a sense of being responded to, of having his action completed in a context, and thus were seen as crucial in establishing his well-being and sense of identity:

> ". . . my proposition is that the mutual exchanges between mother and baby consist in a give and take of action and reaction between the two partners, which requires from each of them both active and passive responses. These responses form series and chains, the single links of which consist in what I call 'action cycles', each completed in itself and at the same time anticipating the next link. I designated these seriated response exchanges as the 'precursor of dialogue', as a primal dialogue."
>
> Spitz, 1964, p. 774

Both kinds of dialogue (simultaneous and alternating) provide for joint engagement in a task and the opportunity for mutual imitation—which are necessary if language and conceptual development are to proceed. In addition, the various forms of dialogue share two other important features. These features tie together the several tasks—feeding, face-to-face play, stranger-interaction, bathing, and teaching—in the longitudinal project from which the present data are drawn. One feature is the strengthening of a cathexis between the two partners. It is a bond consisting of affect plus rules, and we consider its main significance to lie in its transfer outside the mother–child dyad. Each partner develops skills and expectations which he will at least try to apply with this same partner in other situations, and also with other partners. Thus we conceive of the child's development of a *self*, as well as the mother's continued development of her own self-concepts, as a matter of transfer of learning from the dyad-role to other roles in which each of them will become engaged. For the infant these will include interaction with other adults, peer play, and eventually schooling. For the mother they include experience with her subsequent infants, but also nurturant, tutorial, and accommodative roles with her husband, her parents, etc.

A second feature of both simultaneous and alternating dialogue is the provision of a stable context within which one partner or the other can introduce variation (Stern, Fogel, this volume).

Within the interactive situations we are studying microanalytically I expect to find recurrence of the general phenomenon discovered in early feeding: first a phase in which the mother tries to fit in to her infant's more or less autonomous patterns of behaviour, then a phase in which they achieve a mutual contingency or "game". What happens subsequently is well-known, at least for later face-to-face interaction and peekaboo-type games. The contingent sequence becomes a goal in itself for both partners, and they attempt to initiate it and prolong it (Brazelton *et al.*, 1974; Bruner and Sherwood, 1974). Finally, there is the phase in which one or the other partner violates the rule (Stern, 1975). Probably a major function of this violation (and part of its intrinsic humour) is the verification and mutual confirmation of the fact that the rule really was what he or she thought it was. But an effect of violation is to disrupt the ongoing sequence, and sometimes to *disconfirm* the other partner's expectancies. So the stage is set again for phase one, finding regularity, and phase two, establishing mutual contingencies, each time at a slightly more sophisticated level. If this theory is valid, then with each elevation of the dialogue there is acquisition of skills which are potentially transferable beyond the dyad.

Are phases three and four found in sucking as well, or do they depend upon more cognitive apparatus and a higher level of communication than the infant has attained in the first month? We do not yet know. Our notion is that the advanced phase of interaction with respect to sucking serves as a very primitive phase with respect to mutual smiling and other facial communication. Much the same processes are recapitulated in the development of one domain of interaction after another. Thus the communicative successes or failures of a dyad multiply as time passes.

Conclusions

1. When feeding under natural conditions in the first few weeks of life, infants suck in bursts of fairly regular duration separated by pauses of fairly regular duration. There is no correlation between the duration of a pause and that of the burst immediately preceding or immediately following it.

2. Findings in this and other studies are consistent with—but do not firmly establish—the idea that duration of bursts depends more upon milk flow while duration of pauses depends upon other factors including interaction with the mother.

3. Mothers tend to jiggle their infants, stroke the mouth area, retract

the nipple, or jiggle the bottle more during pauses than during bursts of sucking.

4. Contrary to the mothers' (and nurses') beliefs jiggling reduces the probability of an immediate burst of sucking.

5. The cessation of jiggling slightly increases the probability of an immediate burst of sucking.

6. Between two days and two weeks post partum, mothers reduce their duration of jiggling so that there are far more short jiggles, and the behaviour basically becomes "jiggle and stop" rather than "jiggle until he starts sucking again".

7. This phenomenon is the earliest example of infants and mothers learning to take and give turns.

Acknowledgements

This study, supported by a grant from the Spencer Foundation, is the work of many people. I am grateful to Marsha Brumfield, project secretary; to Mary Wanserski who recruited the subjects; to Marilyn DeBoer and Alan Fogel for serving as observers and kibbitzers; to Ralph Baskett and Stephen Muka for programming; to Cheryl Fish, David Schwartz, and especially Anne Wells for collaboration in the analysis. Richard Nachman, M.D., Nancy Barabesi, R.N., and the staff of Columbus Hospital's nursery and obstetric ward were extraordinarily co-operative.

References

Ardran, G. M., Kemp, F. H. and Lind, J. (1958). A cineradiographic study of bottle feeding. *Br. J. Radiol.* **31**, 11–12, 156–162.

Argyle, M. (1972). Non-verbal communication in human social interaction. In R. A. Hinde (Ed.), *Non-verbal Communication.* University of Cambridge Press, London.

Balint, M. (1948). Individual differences of behavior in early infancy, and an objective method for recording them: II. Results and conclusions. *J. Genet. Psychol.* **73**, 81–117.

Bosack, T. N. (1967). The effects of fluid delivery on the sucking response of the human newborn. Unpublished Ph.D. dissertation, Brown University.

Brassell, W. R. (1971). The relationship between feedback from the sucking environment and subsequent modification of sucking behavior in the human neonate. Unpublished Ph.D. dissertation, Emory University.

Brazelton, T. B. (1973). *Neonatal Behavior Assessment Scale.* Lippincott, Philadelphia.

Brazelton, T. G., Koslowski, B. and Main, M. (1974). The origins of reciprocity. In M. Lewis and L. A. Rosenblum (Eds), *The Effect of the Infant on Its Caregiver,* pp. 49–76. Wiley, New York.

Bruner, J. S. (1975). The ontogenesis of speech acts. *J. Child Lang.* **2**, 1–19.

Bruner, J. S. and Sherwood, V. (1974). The game of Peekaboo. (mimeo, Oxford University).

Collis, G. and Schaffer, H. R. (1975). Synchronization of visual attention in mother-infant pairs. *J. Child Psychol. Psychiat.* **16**, 315–320.

Cox, D. R. and Lewis, P. A. (1966). *Statistical Analysis of Series of Events.* Halsted Press, New York.

Duncan, S. (1972). Some signals and rules for taking speaking turns in conversation. *J. Pers. soc. Psychol.* **23**, 283–292.

Eimas, P. D., Siqueland, E. R., Jusczyk, P. and Vigorito, J. (1971). Speech perception in infants. *Science* **171**, 303–306.

Hillman, D. and Bruner, J. S. (1972). Infant sucking in response to variations in schedules of feeding reinforcement. *J. exp. Child Psych.* **13**, 240–247.

Jaffe, J., Stern, D. N. and Peery, J. C. (1973). "Conversational" coupling of gaze behavior in prelinguistic human development. *J. Psycho-linguistic Res.* **2**, 321–330.

Kaye, K. (1967). Infant sucking behavior and its modification. In L. P. Lipsitt and C. Spiker (Eds), *Advances in Child Development and Behavior,* Vol. 3, pp. 1–52. Academic Press, New York and London.

Kaye, K. (1972). Milk pressure as a determinant of the burst-pause pattern in neonatal sucking. *Proceedings,* 80th Annual Convention, APA, 83–84.

Kaye, K. (1976). Infants' effects upon their mothers' teaching strategies. In J. C. Glidewell (Ed.), *The Social Context of Learning and Development.* Gardner Press, New York.

Kaye, K. and Brazelton, T. B. (1971). Mother-infant interaction in the organization of sucking. Paper delivered to the Soc. Res. Child Dev., Minneapolis.

Kendon, A. (1967). Some functions of gaze-direction in social interaction. *Acta Psychologica* **26**, 22–63.

Kessen, W., Haith, M. M. and Salapatek, P. H. (1970). Human infancy. In P. H. Mussen (Ed.), *Carmichael's Handbook of Child Psychology,* Vol. I, pp. 329–339. Wiley, New York.

Kron, R. E., Ipsen, J. and Goddard, K. E. (1968). Consistent individual differences in the nutritive sucking behavior of the human newborn. *Psychosom. Med.* **30**, 151–161.

deLaguna, G. (1927). *Speech: Its Function and Development.* Indiana University Press, Bloomington.

Macnamara, J. (1972). Cognitive basis of language learning in infants. *Psychol. Rev.* **79**, 1–13.

Mahler, M. S., Pine, F. and Bergman, A. (1975). *The Psychological Birth of the Human Infant.* Basic Books, New York.

Marquis, D. P. (1931). Can conditioned responses be established in the newborn infant? *J. Genet. Psychol.* **4**, 163–168.

Middlemore, M. P. (1941). *The Nursing Couple.* Hamish Hamilton, London.

Millar, W. S. (1974). Conditioning and learning in early infancy. In B. Foss (Ed.), *New Perspectives in Child Development*, pp. 53–84. Penguin, Baltimore and London.

Resta, G. (1955). L'allattamento come dialogo mimico nutricelattante. *Infanz. Anorm.* **11**, 107–16.

Robson, K. (1967). The role of eye-to-eye contact in maternal-infant attachment. *J. Child Psychol. Psychiat.* **8**, 13–25.

Sameroff, A. J. (1967). Non-nutritive sucking in newborns under visual and auditory stimulation. *Child Dev.* **38**, 443–452.

Sander, L. W. (1962). Issues in early mother-child interaction. *J. Am. Acad. Child Psychiatry* **1**, 141–166.

Spitz, R. (1963a). Life and the dialogue. In H. Gaskill (Ed.), *Counterpoint*. International University Press, New York.

Spitz, R. (1963b). The evolution of the dialogue. In M. Schur (Ed.), *Drives, Affects, Behavior*, Vol. 2. International University Press, New York.

Spitz, R. (1964). The derailment of dialogue: stimulus overload, action cycles, and the completion gradient. *J. Am. Psychoanal. Assn.* **12**, 752–775.

Stern, D. (1975). Infant regulation of maternal play behavior and/or maternal regulation of infant play behavior. Paper delivered to the Soc. Res. Child Dev., Denver.

Winnicott, D. W. (1967). Mirror-role of mother and family in child development. In P. Lomas (Ed.), *The Predicament of the Family*, pp. 26–33. International University Press, New York.

6 | Temporal Organization in Mother–Infant Face-to-Face Interaction

Alan Fogel

Introduction

Past work on mothers' and infants' attention to each other's faces in the early months has suggested that there is an asymmetry of timing and duration between the partners' periods of gazing—either at or away from the other—and that this asymmetry serves an important functioı in the development of the infant's control over what he looks at, when, and for how long. Studies of early face-to-face interaction by Brazelton *et al.* (1974) done in a laboratory setting, and by Stern (1974) done in the home, show that periods of mother and infant gazing have the relationship shown in Fig. 1.

The baby's mother is almost always looking at him, whether he is looking at her or not. In other words, the baby may look away at any time, but as long as he continues to look at his mother she will remain

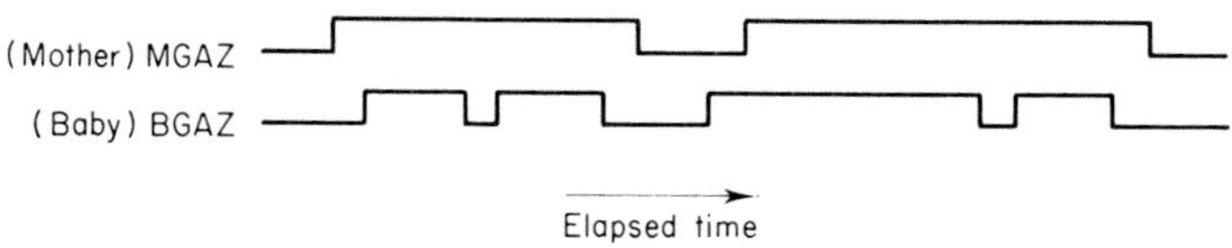

Fig. 1. "Framing" relationship between mother gaze (MGAZ) and infant gaze (BGAZ). Raised segments represent gazing "AT" the other, lowered segments gazing "AWAY".

looking at him. When she does look away it is almost always while her baby is looking away, and she tends to look back relatively soon ("gazing away" intervals are much shorter than "gazing at" intervals). If the baby should look back at her first, she will quickly return to "gazing at".

This type of asymmetrical relationship between two individuals is a part of many caretaker–child activities: the mother creates a "frame" for the up and down fluctuations which are common to the activity of infants and children. "Framing" can occur in a variety of behavioural forms. An example is the conceptualization by Ainsworth *et al.* (1971) of the mother as secure basis for exploration. She found that a toddler's excursions into the environment have a "toward or away" relationship with a more or less stationary mother. An obvious example from early infancy is the mother's physical holding and cradling of her baby during feeding. In this case maternal physical holding provides a stable context within which the infant can indulge in various cycles: go off and on the nipple, start and stop sucking, doze and awaken.

The term "framing" can also be applied to the early mother–child relationship as a whole. Spitz (1965) speaks of the mother as the child's "external ego"; the buffer which shields and provides structure for the child's emergent psyche. In the first months a "symbiotic unity" (Mahler, 1968) is established between mother and child, a unity in which many aspects of a mother's behaviour—her voice, her physical presence, her eyes, her smile—are available to the infant.

Out of this "framing" relationship the infant emerges with his own controls over what previously were inexorable cycles. Hunger and sleep cycles are familiar examples. Attention is another such periodic process, with much shorter limits on the infant's span. The attention–withdrawal cycle is seen in its natural context most clearly in face-to-face interaction.

This paper reports some of the results of a study designed to investigate the relationship between various mother and infant behavioural modalities during face-to-face interaction—in particular gazing, facial expressions, vocalizations and head movements. It grew out of some casual observations of the relationship between mothers and infants during episodes of mutual visual attention. Activities during this period, like smiling and cooing, seemed to bear a somewhat more symmetrical relationship to each other than the one already described between mother and infant gazing.

Furthermore, a study by Kaye (Chapter 5) suggested that even during the feeding interaction in the first few weeks mother and infant appear to be engaged in something like a dialogue between baby's sucking and mother's jiggling. Turn-taking in the oral-vestibular modalities and "framing" in the postural modalities formed two inseparable aspects of the same total mother–infant feeding interaction; the "framing" providing a context to facilitate turn-taking which then provided the source of enjoyment necessary to sustain further "framing" for the same interaction, and possibly for other interactions as well.

A single mother–infant pair was video-taped in our laboratory ten times over a seven-week period starting when the infant was six weeks old, the purpose being to replicate the findings of Brazelton *et al.* (1974) and Stern (1974) on gazing, and to study the relationship between faces and voices within the "framing" relationship of mutual gazing. A further purpose of the present case study was to obtain an in-depth sense of the *process*, rather than simply the *progress*, of development in face-to-face interaction. Our investigation of intra-individual and intra-dyad relationships asks the following questions. Do mother and infant behave differently when they are gazing at each other than when they are not? Does a mother's facial expression bear the same relationship to her infant's as her gaze does to his gaze? Does the "framing" relationship change over time and if so, how?

Method

TRANSCRIPTION

Details of the method—taping, coding and reliability—are presented more extensively elsewhere (Fogel, 1976). A brief summary follows here. The infant, Quinn, was already seated in an infant seat when he was approached by his mother who interacted continuously with him for about ten minutes. Two video-tapes recorded (a) a close-up of the faces using a split-screen technique and (b) a full view of the infant with the upper half of the mother.

These tapes were coded using a magnetic-tape event recorder (Datamyte, Electro General Corp.) which recorded the category plus time of entry. Behaviour was divided into modalities such as mouth, gaze, head movement, and vocalization. Each of these was categorized in such a way that no categories within a modality—such as "gazing at" and "gazing away"—could ever occur simultaneously. Each modality was then coded independently in a separate run through the video-tape. When coding mother's face we obscured the baby and vice versa. We coded sound with the picture off and the picture always without sound. We can thus state with some confidence that relationships found between modalities, whether within one individual or between mother's and baby's behaviour, were valid for this dyad rather than being dependencies built into our coders.

Table I

Modalities and categories used in the analysis. "Type" refers to the method of coding: continual (C) records onset and offset; instantaneous (I) records onset only

Modality	Category	Type	Description
MOTHER GAZE	"AT"	C	Mother looks at infant's face or body
	"AWAY"	C	Mother looks away from infant
MOTHER MOUTH	"EXAGGERATED"	C	Smile, "oooo", surprise
	"REST"	C	Rest-mouth, normal speech
MOTHER VOCAL	"MOTHER VOCALIZE"	I	Onset of individual vocalizations
MOTHER HEAD	"NOD"	I	Onset of individual head nod
	"SHAKE"	I	Onset of individual head shake
MOTHER DISTANCE	"NEAR"	C	Mother's face less than 20 cm from baby
	"NORMAL"	C	Mother's face greater than 20 cm from baby
INFANT GAZE	"ATTENTIVE"	C	Infant looking at mother
	"WITHDRAWN"	C	Infant looking away or eyes closed
INFANT MOUTH	"OPEN"	I	Onset of wide, sustained (for more than 2 seconds) mouth opening
INFANT VOCAL	"INFANT VOCALIZE"	I	Onset of positive vocalizations

Out of the original set of modalities coded, a smaller sub-set was chosen for the purposes of the present analysis. As listed in Table I, they are the modalities involving gaze, facial expression and voice. This leaves out all modalities involving body and limb activity. Within this smaller set of modalities, further simplifications were made by combining the originally coded categories.

Some of this recoding was due to unreliable discriminations. An originally coded distinction between mother's "broad smile" and "narrow smile" proved to be such a case. These two categories were collapsed into "smile". Another reason for recoding was to concatenate several reliably coded categories into a larger unit in order to simplify analysis. This was the case for categories like MOTHER MOUTH "EXAGGERATE" and INFANT GAZE "ATTENTIVE".

Table I shows only those categories used in the present analysis. For the purposes of clarity, modalities will be written with small capital letters. Categories within modalities will be written with small capital letters and enclosed in quotes. The modalities discussed in this report are labelled: MOTHER GAZE, INFANT GAZE, MOTHER MOUTH, INFANT MOUTH, MOTHER VOCAL, INFANT VOCAL, MOTHER HEAD, MOTHER DISTANCE. For MOTHER GAZE the categories are "AT" and "AWAY". "AWAY" is counted only if the mother turns her head and eyes fully away from the baby. Brief glances down at his body, which are infrequent, are ignored. Since INFANT GAZE combines head direction with eye openness, the two categories were called "ATTENTIVE" and "WITHDRAWN".

MOTHER MOUTH has been recoded as either "EXAGGERATED" or "REST". "EXAGGERATED" includes smiling, mouth rounding, as in "oooo", and wide mouth opening as in mock surprise. "REST" includes true rest-mouth as well as normal mouth movements during speech. "REST" also includes a lips-compressed expression signifying mild frustration and a mock pout. These are included in "REST" because they did not normally occur in the "high" periods of the interaction—places in which this mother typically exaggerated her face (cf. Stern, 1974 and Chapter 8). INFANT MOUTH is limited (in the present analysis) to a single type of infant behaviour: a wide, mouth open expression which was sustained for two to four seconds ("OPEN"). We were unable to get high reliability for any other infant mouth movement, including smiling.

Both INFANT VOCAL and MOTHER VOCAL were coded for only the onset of individual vocalizations, thus treating them as instantaneous rather than continual categories. This turned out to be a better approximation for Quinn than for his mother. Although she often emitted runs of brief vocalizations such as "Hi!", "Yes", "oh, yes" or "oh, that's great" (each segment within quotes, in our method, would have been coded as a single vocalization), she sometimes uttered rather long unbroken strings in an adult-like fashion, or else chorused the baby's short coo's with one long "OOooOOooOO".

The MOTHER HEAD categories of "NOD" and "SHAKE"—both instantaneous—were included because they were part of the total configuration of the mother's facial movement presented to the infant. For the same reason MOTHER DISTANCE is included in the present analysis: the subjectively judged distance between mother's and infant's faces. The category of particular interest is "NEAR" during which the mother remained in close proximity (less than about 20 cm) to the baby's face—sometimes stationary, sometimes touching his face with her nose or lips, and sometimes bobbing in and out. This bobbing is different from "NOD" in the MOTHER HEAD mode, which could occur at any distance. In bobbing the head remains stationary with respect to the body.

Inter-coder category agreement reliability (proportion of agreements) was better than 0·85 for all the modalities and categories discussed here. Furthermore, for those cases in which the coders agreed on a category, the mean discrepancy of the times of entry of that category between the two codings of the same video-tape ranged from 0·5 to 2·0 seconds, depending on the particular category. This means that we should not make any statements about relationships between coded events if the time interval between them is less than two seconds.

Ten sessions were coded in this manner for the first eight minutes, or less if the session terminated sooner. The age of the infant at each session was: 6·5, 7·0, 8·0, 8·5, 9·5, 10·5, 11·0, 11·5, 12·0, and 13·0 weeks.

MEASURES

The measures derived from the transcription fall into three classes: proportions of time based on continual categories, frequency proportions based on instantaneous categories, and mean durations of event-to-event intervals.

T (Time Taken Up by a Particular Category). The total time a category is "ON" during a session, expressed as a proportion of the total. This is always measured with respect to a single category.

M.D. (Mean Duration). This is given in seconds and computed for all onset-to-offset or onset-to-onset intervals of a particular category observed during a session.

CO_o *(Observed Co-occurrence)*. The total time during which two continual categories are simultaneously "ON", expressed as a proportion of the session.

ON_0 *(Observed Co-onset).* The number of onsets of one category (continual or instantaneous) which occur during the "ON" phase of a different, continual category, expressed as a proportion of the total number of such onsets.

OFF_0 *(Observed Co-offset).* The number of offsets of one category which occur during the "ON" phase of a different, continual category, expressed as a proportion of the total number of such offsets.

The Organization of Behaviour in Time

When the baby is looking at his mother, does he behave differently than when he looks away? How do the various modalities of the mother's expression relate to each other? To answer these questions it is necessary to examine how the behaviour of each individual is distributed in time.

RUNS AND TIME-OUTS

All of the various forms of activity of either individual can be described as either "ON" or "OFF" at any given moment. This is obvious for continual categories like gazing, for each individual vocalization or for each "OPEN". Observations of the video-tapes revealed that "MOTHER VOCALIZE", "INFANT VOCALIZE", "OPEN" and "NOD" sometimes cycle "ON" and "OFF" in rapid succession. This creates the impression of a *run*; a whole, higher order unit which is "ON" as long as the repetition of the same activity continues at the same high rate, and "OFF" when it falls markedly below that rate.

Kaye's work cited earlier, showing that bursts and pauses in sucking are not strictly characteristics of the infant, but affect and are affected by the behaviour of the mother, led to an investigation of the possible dyadic significance of the runs in face-to-face interaction.

As an example of a category which was observed to occur at relatively high rates of repetition, consider "INFANT VOCALIZE". In Fig. 2 the solid line is the distribution of all onset-to-onset intervals for the 136 infant vocalizations found in the transcripts. Similar distributions were also produced (but not shown here) for "MOTHER VOCALIZE", "NOD" and "OPEN". They all share the same characteristic: a relatively high,

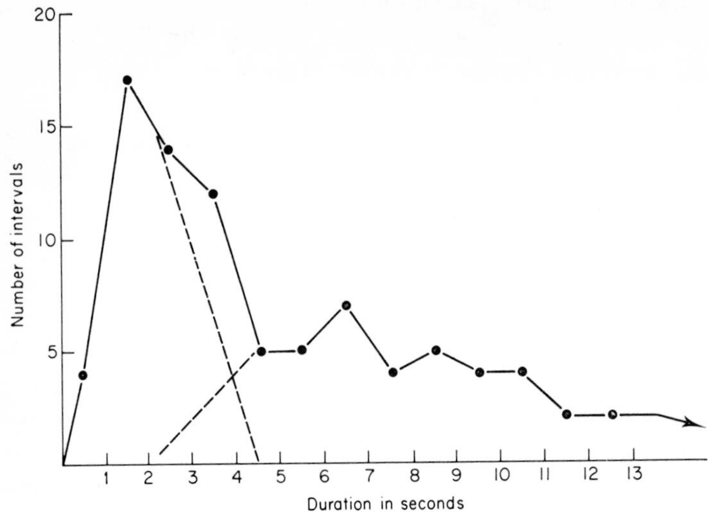

Fig. 2. Distribution of onset-to-onset intervals for "INFANT VOCALIZE" (solid line). Broken lines represent two hypothetical components of the original distribution.

narrow peak for smaller intervals, and a relatively long, flat tail for the longer intervals.

A random (Poisson) set of intervals, ordered from smallest to largest, is distributed as an exponential distribution, skewed to the left. The peak-tail shape of Fig. 2 suggests a non-random deviation from the Poisson process: one population of "long" intervals, and another of "short" intervals. We can assume that there are two component distributions representing these two populations, the tails of which overlap somewhat as indicated by the dashed line in Fig. 2.

A run is essentially a sequence of events from the same category separated by "short" intervals. The point where the peak joins the tail was used as the criterion interval for inclusion in a run. If a vocalization began within four seconds of the previous one, this was considered to be a run of two vocalizations. As long as successive vocalizations came within four seconds of their immediate predecessors the run was considered to be continually "ON". Vocalization runs began at the onset of the first event in the series and ended four seconds after the onset of the last event in the series.

A *time-out* was defined as the interval between the offset of a run and the next onset. Time-out intervals may contain one or more isolated events of the same class as the runs. For "INFANT VOCALIZE", using a four-second criterion, 53% of Quinn's vocalizations occurred in runs. The average run duration was 10·4 seconds, or about three or four vocalizations per run. The remaining 47% of vocalizations were isolated from each other by more than four seconds. The mean duration of these runs did not systematically change over the sessions, although there were three sessions in which none of Quinn's vocalizations met the criterion for runs.

The eight-second criterion interval chosen for "OPEN" yielded a mean run duration of 16·7 seconds, with 68% of the "OPENS" occurring in runs. For "MOTHER VOCALIZE", using a four-second criterion and "NOD" using a five-second one, the mean durations were 13·6 seconds and 13·9 seconds respectively. "NOD" runs included both "NOD" and "SHAKE" events. The proportions occurring in runs using these criteria were 84% for "MOTHER VOCALIZE" and 83% for "NOD". There were no systematic changes over the sessions in any of these means or proportions.

TEMPORAL LEVELS

Inspection of the distributions of onset-to-offset intervals for the categories listed in Table I, and for the runs of "OPEN", "INFANT VOCALIZE", "MOTHER VOCALIZE" and "NOD", leads us to consider these categories as falling into four distinct temporal levels, the lowest containing intervals of several seconds, the highest composed of intervals lasting several minutes. At the briefest level (level 1) were individual acts of "MOTHER VOCALIZE", "INFANT VOCALIZE", "OPEN" and "NOD". These acts typically had "ON" times of about two seconds. In rare cases a single "MOTHER VOCALIZE" or "INFANT VOCALIZE" may have lasted as long as 10 seconds.

Table II presents the mean duration (*M.D.*), standard deviation and range of the onset-to-offset intervals for those categories that fell into the middle and highest levels. At the middle level (level 2) were runs of "OPEN", runs of "INFANT VOCALIZE", runs of "MOTHER VOCALIZE", runs of "NOD", "EXAGGERATE" and "NEAR". Their mean durations ranged from five to 16 seconds with a range from one to 77 seconds.

At the highest levels were MOTHER GAZE "AT" and INFANT GAZE "ATTENTIVE". "ATTENTIVE" intervals were typically 45 seconds in duration and ranged from two seconds to five minutes. In spite of some overlap with level 2 intervals, "ATTENTIVE" intervals (level 3) form a

Table II

Mean duration (*M.D.*), standard deviation and range of onset-to-offset intervals for selected categories in seconds. Intervals are pooled from all ten sessions.

	MOTHER GAZE "AT"	INFANT GAZE "ATTENTIVE"	MOTHER HEAD "NOD" RUNS	MOTHER MOUTH "EXAGGERATE"	MOTHER VOCAL "VOCALIZE" RUNS	MOTHER DISTANCE "NEAR"	INFANT MOUTH "OPEN" RUNS	INFANT VOCAL "VOCALIZE" RUNS
M.D.	207·3	45·8	13·9	7·3	13·6	5·7	16·7	10·4
Standard deviation	168·2	58·1	10·3	6·8	8·3	6·0	8·1	5·1
Smallest interval	3	2	7	1	5	2	10	5
Largest interval	480	305	70	77	67	34	48	28
Number of intervals	20	69	107	269	221	34	35	39

separate population. A comparison between *M.D.* for "ATTENTIVE" and the pooled *M.D.* for level 2 intervals yields $t = 4{\cdot}93$, significant at the 0·001 level. MOTHER GAZE "AT" intervals (level 4) were significantly greater than "ATTENTIVE" intervals ($t = 4{\cdot}22$, $p < 0{\cdot}001$), placing the former at a higher level. "AT" had a *M.D.* of 207 seconds, compared to the "ATTENTIVE" *M.D.* of 45 seconds.

If we make the assumption that these levels are important for the organization of the interaction, it follows that temporal level and behavioural modality are two somewhat independent dimensions of that organization. The same modality may be distributed into different temporal levels. This is the case for individual vocalizations, and for runs of vocalizations. On the other hand, mother and infant gazing appear to be confined to one level each. In general the possibility exists for intervals between events at a given level to be distributed in a non-random way, thus forming new units at higher levels.

It then becomes possible to conceptualize interaction in terms of both behavioural modality and temporal level. Furthermore, several measures can be derived for each modality-level within the individual. The individual (as opposed to dyadic) measures used here are the time taken up by a particular continual category (T) and the mean duration (*M.D.*) of the onset-to-offset intervals of that category.

This suggests a model by which modality, level and individual measure can be varied with respect to dyadic measures of the mother–infant interaction. Two dyadic measures are used in this report: (1) the proportion of a session during which one continual category of the mother co-occurs with one of the infant's continual categories (CO_o) and (2) the frequency of onset (ON_o) or offset (OFF_o) of a mother category during the "ON" phase of a baby category and vice-versa. By using a longitudinal case-study design we hope to discover how behaviour is organized within and between the individuals.

WITHIN-INDIVIDUAL ORGANIZATION OF THE MOTHER'S BEHAVIOUR

Whereas the distribution of onset-to-onset intervals of the acts within a run always showed a "peak-tail" form like that of Fig. 2, the distributions of this mother's run durations were more or less smoothly skewed to the left, typical of durational data. The durations of the time-outs between the mother's runs were also distributed in this fashion. Thus there was no systematic organization at a higher temporal level of the mother's run or time-out intervals.

Since each modality within the individual was coded independently of the others, we can derive measures of the temporal relationship between any two within-individual modalities which are the same measures that will be used for the dyadic relationships (CO_o, ON_o and OFF_o). We can then apply the model discussed in the previous section to "NOD" runs, "MOTHER VOCALIZE" runs and "EXAGGERATE".

Table III shows the co-occurrence, co-onset and co-offset relationships for these three categories. For the purposes of this analysis the function $(CO_o–CO_e)/CO_e$ is a measure of the proportion by which the

Table III

The proportions by which observed measures (o) exceed expected values (e). CO_o = proportion of co-occurrence by session, ON_o = proportion of onsets of category "1" which occur during the "ON" phase of category "2"; OFF_o = proportion of offsets of category "1" which occur during the "ON" phase of category "2"; $CO_e = T_1 \times T_2$; $ON_e = T_2$; $OFF_e = T_2$. Abbreviations used are "EXAG" = "EXAGGERATE", "MVOC" = "MOTHER VOCALIZE".

	$(CO_o–CO_e)/CO_e$ for:			$(ON_o–ON_e)/ON_e$ for:		$(OFF_o–OFF_e)/OFF_e$ for:	
Category "1"	"EXAG"	"EXAG"	"MVOC" RUNS	"NOD" RUNS	"EXAG"	"NOD" RUNS	"EXAG"
	with	with	with	during	during	during	during
Category "2"	"MVOC" RUNS	"NOD" RUNS	"NOD" RUNS	"EXAG"	"NOD" RUNS	"EXAG"	"NOD" RUNS
Session 1	+0·05	−0·10	−0·07	+0·15	+0·10	−0·10	+0·38
2	+0·17	+0·08	+0·13	+0·87	+0·12	−0·08	+0·52
3	+0·01	+0·22	+0·04	+0·04	−0·15	−0·15	−0·03
4	+0·02	+0·33	+0·33	+0·73	−0·25	+0·10	+0·04
5	+0·03	+0·07	−0·03	+0·36	−0·12	−0·20	+0·08
6	−0·09	+0·06	−0·04	−0·58	+0·11	−0·17	−0·19
7	+0·02	+0·47	+0·14	+0·52	−0·17	−0·09	+0·19
8	+0·02	+0·13	−0·02	+0·16	−0·17	−0·26	−0·04
9	+0·07	+0·14	−0·18	+0·11	+0·09	−0·06	+0·09
10	+0·03	+0·43	+0·25	+0·04	+0·46	−0·27	+0·62
Binomial sign test (two-tailed) p =	0·021	0·021	N.S.	0·021	N.S.	0·021	N.S.

observed co-occurrence exceeds or falls below what could be expected due to chance alone. The functions $(ON_o–ON_e)/ON_e$ and $(OFF_o–OFF_e)/OFF_e$ are similarly defined. This number has the property of preserving the sign of the difference between observed and expected, as well as making all the cells comparable in terms of strength of association.

In the case of co-occurrence, the expected values are the conditional probabilities obtained by a pair-wise multiplication of the proportions of each session taken up by the two categories in question (the T values for each category). The proportion of a session taken up by a particular category (T) is itself the expected value for the co-onsets and co-offsets with that category.

A binomial sign test (two-tailed) was used to calculate the probability that the number of (+) signs (the observed proportion exceeded the expected) for all sessions could have occurred by chance. A statistical test across sessions, rather than one applied within each session, was used to get a level of statistical significance for the CO_o, ON_o, and OFF_o measures. This is because these measures were derived from continual categories. Therefore whole blocks of time, limited by the total time of the session, were the subjects of analysis. The amount of time taken up by one individual block of time is not independent of the time taken up by another block in the session. To the extent that each session as a whole can be considered independent from all the others, the sign test across sessions is applicable. Our population, therefore, consists of Quinn and his mother.

Since all the modalities used in this analysis were categorized dichotomously, only the "ON" phases are given in the tables. A column which as a significant sign test probability for negative signs implies a positive relationship with the "OFF" phase.

The results of Table III can be summarized as follows:

(1) There was a greater than chance co-occurrence of "EXAGGERATE" with "MOTHER VOCALIZE" runs and with "NOD" runs. The two latter categories, however, did not necessarily co-occur.

(2) "NOD" runs tended to begin and end during "EXAGGERATE", but not necessarily during the same "EXAGGERATE" unit. "NOD" may have started in one "EXAGGERATE", remained "ON" during the subsequent "REST", and ended regularly during "NOD" time-outs. Nodding tended to be something this mother did only after she had already started to "EXAGGERATE".

Quinn's mother used her face, voice and head movement in varying combinations while maintaining an almost unbroken gaze contact with Quinn. All combinations were theoretically possible, but certain ones predominated: she tended to nod and vocalize in runs when her face was exaggerated, usually beginning "NOD" runs only during "EXAGGERATE", rather than during the previous "REST".

WITHIN-INDIVIDUAL ORGANIZATION OF THE INFANT'S BEHAVIOUR

The infant categories of "OPEN" and "INFANT VOCALIZE" were defined as mutually exclusive, since "OPEN" included only movements wider than those of vocalization. However, there was no logical reason that runs of "OPEN" and "INFANT VOCALIZE" could not overlap; yet they never did. In all ten sessions there was not a single case of a run of "INFANT VOCALIZE" co-occurring with a run of "OPEN". However, there were cases where a run of one type was immediately followed by the other. This contrasts with the results obtained for the mother. In her case there was a great deal of co-occurrence between categories. The result for the infant may be an artifact of the kind of INFANT MOUTH category that was coded. For example infant smiling, although unreliable and therefore not included, was observed sometimes to co-occur with "INFANT VOCALIZE" runs.

The durations of Quinn's runs were distributed exponentially, as were his mother's. However, the time-outs between the infant's runs, ignoring whether they were runs of "OPEN" or "INFANT VOCALIZE", were distributed more like a peak-tail (Fig. 3). Some of these time-outs were as long as three minutes. Figure 3 shows that there were more infant runs of any kind in the later than in the earlier sessions, and that especially in the later sessions most runs began within 30 or 40 seconds after the end of the previous run.

Did the "shorter time-outs" (defined as being less than 35 seconds) serve a different function for the infant than the "longer time-outs"? For this particular infant, during a total of 526 seconds of "shorter time-outs", there were only 24 seconds of co-occurrence with "WITHDRAWN". This is much less than the 117 second co-occurrence which might have occurred by chance.

Since "WITHDRAWN" occurs typically during "longer time-outs" (968 seconds of observed overlap compared to 614 seconds of expected) it means that the latter are closely related to the function of the former;

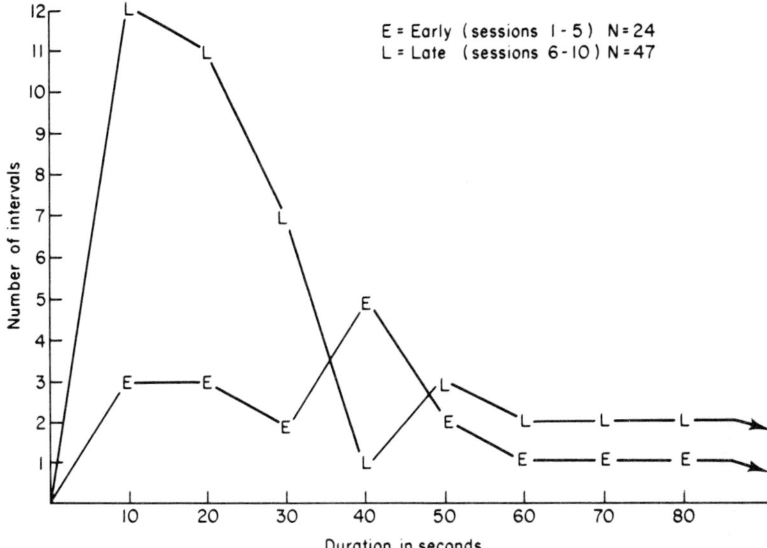

Fig. 3. Distribution of time-out intervals between any two infant runs of either "OPEN" or "INFANT VOCALIZE".

some kind of "break" from the interaction. During the "shorter time-outs" Quinn remained attentive to his mother, thus suggesting that he used them to take in information about her, or perhaps in order to wait until she had completed a segment of behaviour. This relationship is shown in Fig. 4.

Quinn's "shorter time-out" intervals had the same distribution as his "OPEN" and "INFANT VOCALIZE" run intervals. This means that infant runs and "shorter time-outs" had roughly the same duration providing

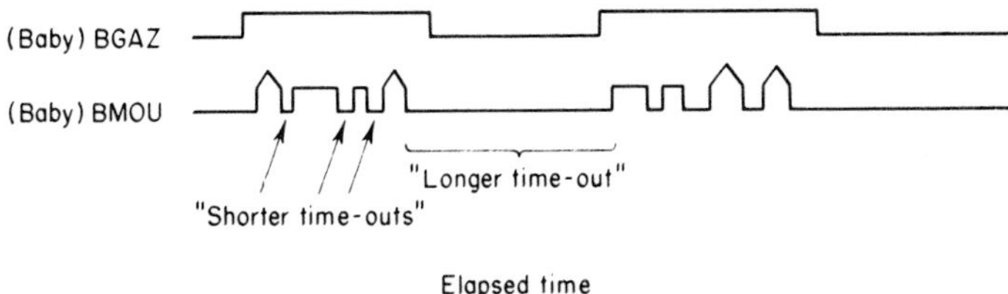

Fig. 4. Within-infant relationship between INFANT GAZE (BGAZ) and INFANT MOUTH (BMOU). Raised portions of INFANT GAZE represent "ATTENTIVE" periods, lowered portions "WITHDRAWN" periods. Raised portions of INFANT MOUTH represent "OPEN" runs (with caps) and "INFANT VOCALIZE" runs (flat).

for a somewhat regular "ON"–"OFF" cycling of runs with "shorter time-outs". The "ON"–"OFF" cycling of Quinn's face and voice is then embedded into the "ON" phase of the "ON"–"OFF" cycle of Quinn's attention to his mother.

Dyadic Relationships

Having examined the within-individual organization of behaviour, we now turn to look at co-occurrence, co-onset and co-offset relationships between modalities taken from both individuals. We are confining our analysis to the relationships between the three highest temporal levels: between mother gaze (level 4) and infant gaze (level 3), between the level of infant gaze and that of runs, "EXAGGERATE" and "NEAR" (level 2), and between modalities within level two.

A glance back at Table II will remind the reader that MOTHER GAZE "AT" had a mean duration of about three minutes, INFANT GAZE "ATTENTIVE" a mean duration of about one minute, the mean durations of runs, "NEAR" and "EXAGGERATE" being of the order of 10 seconds.

Table IV presents summary information on the session proportions

Table IV

Mean, standard deviation and range of T, pooled from all sessions, for each category used in the analysis. Values expressed as a proportion of the session. Abbreviations used are "ATTN" = "ATTENTIVE", "EXAG" = "EXAGGERATE", "BVOC" = "INFANT VOCALIZE", "MVOC" = "MOTHER VOCALIZE".

	Infant			Mother			
	"ATTN"	"OPEN" RUNS	"BVOC" RUNS	"EXAG"	"MVOC" RUNS	"NEAR"	"NOD" RUNS
Mean	0·76	0·14	0·10	0·55	0·71	0·05	0·37
Standard deviation	0·10	0·09	0·10	0·03	0·07	0·05	0·13
Smallest proportion	0·60	0·03	0·00	0·39	0·61	0·00	0·13
Largest proportion	0·89	0·28	0·30	0·66	0·83	0·14	0·54

(T) of the categories used in this analysis, pooled for all sessions. Expected values in subsequent tables were calculated on the basis of the value of T for each session. However, since there were no systematic trends over sessions in T for any category, only the pooled data are provided.

MOTHER AND INFANT GAZE

The total duration of the transcriptions is 4250 seconds, summed for all ten sessions. In that period this mother was judged as "AWAY" for a total of 13 seconds. This was composed of several glances away, lasting no more than a second or two. INFANT GAZE changed from "ATTENTIVE" to "WITHDRAWN" more frequently, with total "WITHDRAWN" time taking up as much as 40% of some sessions (see Table IV). The mean MOTHER GAZE "AT" duration was 207 seconds compared to a mean of 45 seconds for INFANT GAZE "ATTN".

This implies that the relationship between their gazes was as depicted in Fig. 1. Although the proportion of "ATTENTION" was different for each session, the relationship between "ATTENTION" and "AT" did not change.

Our observations of naturally occurring face-to-face interaction in the home suggest that such long infant-directed gazes are not uncommon. The best predictor of when a mother looks away seems to be the activity of another person in the same room, especially the entrance of a sibling. In the laboratory situation as we constrained it there were virtually no distractions.

This finding for the gazing relationship of Quinn and his mother replicates the results of Stern (1974) and Brazelton *et al.* (1974), cited earlier. Quinn's gaze cycled on and off while his mother maintained virtually continual gaze contact, so we can say that mother gaze "frames" infant gaze. The constancy of the mother's gaze—and consequently of the mutual gazing relationship—suggests that gaze "framing" was a stable characteristic of their interaction during the entire seven-week period of observation.

By virtue of this result it is important while reading subsequent sections to keep in mind that the relations between mother's activity and infant "ATTENTIVE" are not isolated phenomena. More appropriately we should refer to "infant 'ATTENTIVE'-as-'framed'-by-mother 'AT' " as the category under analysis.

THE RELATIONSHIP BETWEEN INFANT "ATTENTIVE" AND MATERNAL ACTIVITY AT THE LEVEL OF RUNS

We now consider INFANT GAZE in its temporal relationship to the mother modalities of VOCAL, HEAD, MOUTH, and DISTANCE. Table V presents data on the extent to which infant "ATTENTIVE" co-occurred with

Table V

Proportion by which observed exceeds expected co-occurrence. CO_o = proportion of actual co-occurrence in session; $CO_e = T_1 \times T_2$. Abbreviations used are "ATTN" = "ATTENTIVE", "EXAG" = "EXAGGERATE", "BVOC" = "INFANT VOCALIZE", "MVOC" = "MOTHER VOCALIZE".

		$(CO_o - CO_e)/CO_e$ for:				
Category 1			"ATTN" with:			
Category 2	"EXAG"	"OPEN" RUNS	"BVOC" RUNS	"MVOC" RUNS	"NEAR"	"NOD" RUNS
Session 1	−0·02	+0·12		−0·16	−0·36	−0·14
2	+0·13	+0·70		+0·18	−1·00	+0·40
3	+0·06	+0·14	+0·14	+0·14	−0·25	+0·10
4	+0·32	+0·63	+0·80	+0·03	−1·00	+0·64
5	+0·14	+0·18	+0·17	+0·07		+0·07
6	+0·11	+0·31		+0·06	+0·30	−0·02
7	+0·20	+0·32	+0·31	+0·08		+0·07
8	+0·15	+0·28	+0·40	+0·03	+0·11	+0·18
9	+0·17	+0·39	+0·42	+0·04	+0·22	+0·17
10	+0·04	+0·23	+0·22	+0·08	−0·10	+0·09
Binomial sign test (two-tailed) p =	0·021	0·002	0·02	0·021	N.S.	N.S.

mother "EXAGGERATE", "NEAR", "MOTHER VOCALIZE" runs and "NOD" runs. Table VI shows the co-onset and co-offset relationships for the same categories. "NEAR" is excluded because it occurred too infrequently for this sort of analysis. These two tables can be interpreted in the same way as Table III. The same kinds of comparisons of observed to expected proportions found in Table III for within-mother

Table VI

Proportion by which observed exceeds expected. ON_o = proportion of onsets of category "1" during category "2"; OFF_o = proportion of offsets of category "1" during category "2"; $ON_e = T_2$; $OFF_e = T_2$.

		$(ON_o–ON_e)/ON_e$ for:				$(OFF_o–OFF_e)/OFF_e$ for:			
Category	"1" / "2"	"EXAG" during "ATTN"	"NOD" RUNS during "ATTN"	"ATTN" during "EXAG"	"ATTN" during "NOD" RUNS	"EXAG" during "ATTN"	"NOD" RUNS during "ATTN"	"ATTN" during "EXAG"	"ATTN" during "NOD" RUNS
Session	1	+0·01	−0·03	+0·15	+0·79	+0·03	−0·03	−0·04	+0·28
	2	+0·17	+0·22	+0·28	−0·61	+0·17	+0·22	−0·05	−0·24
	3	+0·09	+0·14	−0·72	−0·76	−0·05	+0·05	−0·54	−0·48
	4	−0·05	+0·48			+0·02	+0·67		
	5	−0·06	+0·09	−0·18[a]	−0·29[a]	−0·02	+0·09	−0·68[a]	−0·54[a]
	6	+0·13	−0·21			+0·13	+0·05		
	7	−0·04	+0·05			−0·04	+0·05		
	8	+0·01	−0·18	−0·12	−0·44	+0·06	−0·18	−0·12	−0·44
	9	−0·14	+0·14	−0·05	−0·59	−0·10	+0·26	−0·33	−0·66
	10	−0·20	+0·23	−0·11	+0·31	−0·02	+0·02	−0·23	+1·23
Binomial sign test (two-tailed) $p =$		N.S.	N.S.	N.S.	N.S.	N.S.	N.S.	0·02	N.S.

[a] Sessions 4, 5, 6 and 7 lumped due to small number of observations of "ATTN" onsets and offsets in each session.

modality relationships are applied in Tables V and VI to between-individual relationships. Again, a binomial sign test across sessions was used to determine the level of significance of the findings.

Summarizing these two tables, the following major points can be made.

(1) There was a high degree of co-occurrence of "ATTENTIVE" with the maternal modalities of "EXAGGERATE" and "MOTHER VOCALIZE" runs, but not with "NOD" runs or "NEAR"—higher, that is, than would be predicted by chance. This means that Quinn's mother invested more time in "MOTHER VOCALIZE" runs and in "EXAGGERATE" when Quinn was looking at her and, conversely, Quinn tended to look at her when her face and voice were particularly active.

(2) The presence of infant "ATTENTIVE" had no effect on when the mother began and ended her "EXAGGERATE" or her "NOD" runs. She was just as likely to begin and to end these activities in "WITHDRAWAL" as in "ATTENTIVE".

(3) Quinn had a tendency to end "ATTENTIVE" units during MOTHER MOUTH "REST". This means that "EXAGGERATE" could sustain, but not initiate, "ATTENTIVE". Although there were no other significant results for co-onsets and co-offsets of "ATTENTIVE" over sessions, there was a consistency across the two co-onset measures (during "EXAGGERATE" and "NOD") and the two co-offset measures (during "EXAGGERATE" and "NOD") within sessions 3 to 9. In those sessions Quinn was more likely to begin and end "ATTENTIVE" during a "REST" or during a time-out. In other words, Quinn's mother was more likely to attract his gaze if she was quiet and attentive, but she had to become facially active to sustain that gaze.

Even though the co-occurrence of "ATTENTIVE" and "EXAGGERATE" was high, it is notable that this mother began and ended "EXAGGERATE" just as often during "ATTENTIVE" as during "WITHDRAWN". A comparison between the mean durations of "EXAGGERATE" and "REST" under each of these infant conditions is enlightening. The mean duration of all the "EXAGGERATE" units taken together was 7·3 seconds. However, the mean duration of those "EXAGGERATE" units which occurred during infant "ATTENTIVE" was 9·6 seconds while the mean duration of "EXAGGERATE" during infant "WITHDRAWN" was 3·9 seconds ($t = 4{\cdot}71$, $p < 0{\cdot}001$). For "REST" the mean durations were 5·7 seconds during "ATTENTIVE" and 7·5 seconds during "WITHDRAWN"

($t = 1{\cdot}73$, $p > 0{\cdot}10$). For "NOD" runs, a similar pattern held: mean duration during "ATTENTIVE" was 13·5 seconds, during "WITHDRAWN" was 6·7 seconds ($t = 2{\cdot}68$, $p < 0{\cdot}02$). The mean duration of "NOD" time-outs during "ATTENTIVE" vs. "WITHDRAWN" was not significant.

Thus if Quinn was withdrawn, the mother seemed to make attempts to engage him using facial activity. Since these attempts were typically unsuccessful (the baby did not usually look back unless she was behaviourally quiet), they ended on the average after 4 seconds. On the other hand, Quinn's mother would prolong her "EXAGGERATE" episodes and "NOD" runs during "ATTENTIVE" periods. This is shown in Fig. 5.

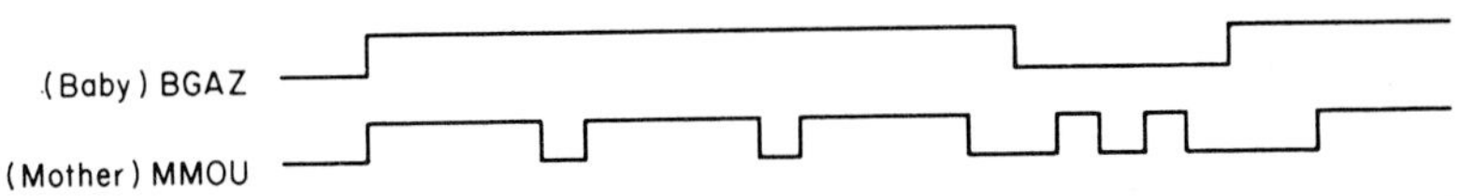

Fig. 5. Relationship between INFANT GAZE (BGAZ) and MOTHER MOUTH (MMOU). INFANT GAZE is either "ATTENTIVE" (raised) or "WITHDRAWN" (lowered); MOTHER MOUTH is either "EXAGGERATE" or "REST".

"Framing", defined in terms of co-occurrence, co-onset and co-offset, may not be the most appropriate way to describe the relationship between infant "ATTENTIVE" and the maternal categories examined in this section. There was a greater than chance co-occurrence as in a "framing" relationship. Also, as in "framing", there was a temporal level difference which provided for the "ON"–"OFF" cycling of "EXAGGERATE" and "NOD" runs during a continual period of infant "ATTENTIVE". But unlike cycles which are completely "framed" by the "ON" phase of another, these maternal activities continued to cycle during periods of infant "WITHDRAWAL".

We cannot say that INFANT GAZE "framed" maternal activity, but INFANT GAZE regulated that activity in an important way. Specifically, the "ON" phase of the mother's cycles was systematically expanded during "ATTENTIVE" while being contracted during "WITHDRAWAL". Conversely, the extension of the mother's "ON" phases may have functioned to prolong infant "ATTENTIVE" periods while the contraction of the "ON" phases during "WITHDRAWN" may have kept the "WITHDRAWN" periods shorter.

DYADIC RUNS: THE RELATIONSHIP BETWEEN MOTHER AND INFANT FACIAL ACTIVITY DURING MUTUAL GAZING

In this section we will focus on the infant's facial activity during "ATTENTIVE" periods. We ask whether those portions of the "ATTENTIVE" period in which the infant is facially active accounted for a significantly greater share of the co-occurrence with maternal facial activity than the quiet "ATTENTIVE" periods.

Measures for co-occurrence, co-onset and co-offset were computed for the period during which the infant was "ATTENTIVE". Since "ATTENTIVE" always took up less than 100% of the sessions and since the mother's and infant's activity at the level of runs tended to co-occur with "ATTENTIVE", the values of *T* based on "ATTENTIVE" were all somewhat greater than those given in Table IV.

Tables VII and VIII present the results. Blanks indicate that, for those sessions, *T* was zero for either one of the categories specified in the second row. In Table VIII, "OPEN" and "INFANT VOCALIZE" were lumped because there were so few onsets and offsets per session of either category taken individually. Tables VII and VIII were derived in the same manner as Tables V and VI, the difference being that the proportions in Tables V and VI were based on the duration of the entire session, whereas the proportions in Tables VII and VIII were based only on the total duration of infant "ATTENTIVE".

The results from these two tables are as follows:

(1) A different set of maternal categories was associated with infant "OPEN" runs than with "INFANT VOCALIZE" runs. In particular, "EXAGGERATE" co-occurred often with "OPEN" runs, yet it did not co-occur at more than a chance level with "INFANT VOCALIZE" runs. On the other hand, "NEAR" co-occurred with "INFANT VOCALIZE" time-outs slightly more often than expected (not significant), but "NEAR" bore no significant relationship to "OPEN" runs or time-outs. There were no other consistent relationships between infant runs and "MOTHER VOCALIZE" runs or "NOD" runs.

Since "INFANT VOCALIZE" runs and "OPEN" runs did not have the same relationship to the mother's behaviour, it means that both mother and infant were responding selectively to each other's behaviour. Of course that is what we mean when any observed measure exceeds its expected value. We could say that the mother selectively exaggerated

Table VII

Proportion by which observed exceeds expected co-occurrence. CO_o = proportion of actual co-occurrence; $CO_e = T_1 \times T_2$.

	$(CO_o - CO_e)/CO_e$ for:							
Category "1"	"OPEN" with:				"BVOC" with:			
Category "2"	"EXAG"	"MVOC" RUNS	"NEAR"	"NOD" RUNS	"EXAG"	"MVOC" RUNS	"NEAR"	"NOD" RUNS
Session 1	+0·35	+0·14	−0·19	+0·44				
2	+0·57	+0·05		+0·94				
3	+0·37	+0·04	−1·00	+0·89	+0·38	−0·41	−1·00	+0·19
4	+0·15	+0·25		+0·45	+0·06	+0·59		+1·70
5	+0·13	+0·48		+0·10	−0·21	−0·73		−0·74
6	+0·12	−0·03	+1·23	+0·59				
7	+0·11	+0·12		+0·64	+0·16	−0·14		+0·10
8	+0·12	+0·01	−1·00	−0·11	−0·13	−0·34	−0·80	+0·27
9	+0·02	−0·04	+1·86	−0·36	−0·28	−0·27	−1·00	+0·15
10	+0·36	+0·36	+3·48	+1·79	+0·08	+0·12	−1·00	+2·80
Binomial sign test (two-tailed) $p =$	0·002	N.S.	N.S.	N.S.	N.S.	N.S.	0·084	N.S.

Table VIII

Proportion by which observed exceeds expected. ON_o = proportion of onsets of category "1" during category "2"; OFF_o = proportion of offsets of category "1" during category "2"; $ON_e = T_2$; $OFF_e = T_2$.

		$(ON_o–ON_e)/ON_e$ for:				$(OFF_o–OFF_e)/OFF_e$ for:			
Category	"1"	"EXAG"	"NOD"	"OPEN" or "BVOC"	"OPEN" or "BVOC"	"EXAG"	"NOD"	"OPEN" or "BVOC"	"OPEN" or "BVOC"
		during	during	during	during	during	during	during	during
	"2"	"OPEN" or "BVOC"	"OPEN" or "BVOC"	"EXAG"	"NOD"	"OPEN" or "BVOC"	"OPEN" or "BVOC"	"EXAG"	"NOD"
Session	1	−0·05	+0·41	+0·20	+0·18	+0·18	+0·41	−0·20	+0·18
	2,3,4[a]	−0·31	+0·47	+0·41	+0·15	+0·11	−0·11	+0·05	−0·03
	5	−0·10	+0·43	+0·18	−0·46	+0·08	+0·45	−0·41	−0·46
	6	−0·17	−0·06	+0·06	+0·19	−0·17	+0·06	+0·06	−0·19
	7	−0·33	+1·04	+0·05	−0·43	−0·33	+0·03	+0·05	+0·16
	8	−0·20	+0·35	+0·38	−0·02	−0·03	−0·50	+0·11	+0·26
	9	−0·07	+0·16	+0·13	−0·03	−0·35	+0·05	−0·08	+0·21
	10	+0·17	+1·17	−0·34	+0·78	−0·43	+2·48	+0·29	−0·07
Binomial sign test (two-tailed) $p =$		0·07	0·07	0·07	N.S.	N.S.	N.S.	N.S.	N.S.

[a] These sessions lumped due to small number of observations of "BVOC" and "OPEN" runs in each session.

her face when the baby looked at her, or that Quinn only performed "OPEN" runs when his mother was "EXAGGERATED".

Selection implies a process of narrowing down a large set of response alternatives. A good deal of the selection process between the temporal level of infant "ATTENTIVE" and the level of mother runs "EXAGGERATE" and "NEAR" has been pre-adapted or culturally determined. Facial exaggeration, head movement, and increased vocal activity are fairly standard adult responses to infant looking in middle-class, white, English-speaking communities (Stern, 1974).

Within the level of runs, however, one gets the impression that each mother and baby pair develop their own distinctive routines or games. Informally, we have observed the use of highly idiosyncratic rituals in other mother–infant pairs. In the vocalization modality alone the variety of individual difference abounds: coos, clicks, hums, whistles, excerpts from songs, stories and verse.

We were fortunate to capture on video-tape a segment in which Quinn and his mother seem to have been engaged in a process of selection at the level of runs. This occurred in session 9 (at age 12 weeks) between the categories of "OPEN" and "NEAR". Early in that session the mother bobbed in and out briefly with no apparent relation to Quinn's behaviour. At one point she suddenly moved in and touched her nose to his lips. As she moved back he closed his mouth and then quickly opened it again. She repeated the nose-to-mouth movement and then a rather long "nose-in-mouth" game ensued.

To the eye of the observer, the "nose-in-mouth" game was a non-overlapped exchange of turns: "OPEN"-touch mouth-"OPEN"-touch mouth. Unfortunately, the transcripts are not precise enough to determine the actual extent of overlap vs. alternation (Duncan, 1974; Schaffer *et al.*, Chapter 12). What has been called a co-occurrence at the level of runs may be a non-overlapped exchange at the level of individual acts.

(2) Did infant runs account for a significantly greater share of the co-occurrence with maternal activity than infant time-outs? On the whole, the answer is no. Maternal activity tended to co-occur at a chance level with runs and with time-outs. The mother's activity at the level of runs appeared to be distributed in a fairly unsystematic manner across the infant "ATTENTIVE" periods, and conversely the infant tended to engage in run behaviour whether his mother's face and voice were active or not.

The notable exception was the co-occurrence of "EXAGGERATE" with "OPEN". In comparison to "INFANT VOCALIZE" runs, where the infant would vocalize at any time, he tended to "OPEN" in the presence of a comparable mouth exaggeration on the mother's part.

(3) Table VIII is notable for its lack of significant results. The first three columns of the co-onset relationships just fall short of a 0·05 level of significance, the other columns are clearly not significant. There were no systematic co-onset and co-offset relationships at the level of runs.

Did MOTHER MOUTH and MOTHER HEAD "frame" INFANT MOUTH? Since the mean durations of the categories representing these modalities were roughly equal, we do not get the sense that INFANT MOUTH runs were free to cycle on and off during a continual period of maternal facial activity. There were only some relationships in which co-occurrence and co-onset measures were greater than expected, reminiscent of "framing". A further difference between this and "framing" is the co-offset results. Quinn's mother did not consistently end her activity with respect to Quinn's, nor did he with respect to hers.

This may be due to the fact that it is more difficult, and perhaps less desirable, for the mother to maintain indefinitely long episodes of smiling, cooing, nodding and bobbing as she did for gazing. Many factors may be at work here: fatigue, boredom, uncertainty about her effect on the infant. There is also the possibility that Quinn's mother was attempting to regulate his level of excitement by slowing down (ending a run) or stopping her activity at appropriate times.

Our interpretation of Quinn's co-offset behaviour is again different from the interpretation of the mother's co-offsets. We know that the "ON"–"OFF" cycling of infant facial activity was not independent of his attention cycles. Since these latter cycles are limited in span by neurological immaturity it is not unlikely that the facial activity cycle has a limited, though briefer, span. These cycles, like bursts and pauses in sucking simply have to go "OFF" after a determined interval (Wolff, 1967), without regard to the mother's behaviour. Another way of saying this is that the mother is capable of a greater range of expansion and contraction of her intervals than is the infant.

In general, the categories examined at the level of runs had few consistent relationships with each other. There was no "framing" and little co-occurrence, but on the other hand, no alternation either. This may reflect the highly tentative nature of the games that Quinn and his mother played during this period. The gaze "frame" served to define a realm of "playing around" in which both partners offered and responded. Usually this give and take was random. But at times they did have moments of a mutually satisfying mesh between their actions (cf. the nose-in-mouth game). Fully developed games like "peek-a-boo" or "give and take" as described by Bruner (Chapter 11) for older infants were extremely rare.

Discussion

In this section three points will be made with respect to the data: (1) mother and infant accommodate each other, but in very different ways; (2) the consideration of various levels and modalities within the same subject pair may lead to a better understanding of the relationship between the mother–infant interaction and cognitive–social development; (3) maternal repetition can sustain an infant's attention and elicit his facial activity, increase redundancy for the sake of his immature information processing capacities, and create a more predictable environment for the infant. Infant repetition can provide a mother with a confirmation of the effects of her interventions, and with the ability to anticipate what the infant might do.

MUTUAL ACCOMMODATION: SYMMETRY AND ASYMMETRY

We now have some data to show that there is more symmetry in this mother–infant interaction than would have been expected if the "framing" relationship were the main form of dyadic integration. MOTHER GAZE "framed" INFANT GAZE, but MOTHER MOUTH and HEAD in relation to INFANT MOUTH, and INFANT GAZE in relation to MOTHER MOUTH were more complex relationships.

Both mother's and infant's individual facial and vocal acts tended to be organized into runs, showing the same non-random onset-to-onset interval distribution. Furthermore, both mother and infant activity cycled "ON" and "OFF" at all temporal levels. The high incidence of co-occurrence between mother and infant continual categories indicated a mutual, symmetrical contribution to the sustenance of the interaction. For those categories coded as runs, it was suggested (based on informal observations of the video-tapes) that co-occurrence of runs may consist of an alternating exchange of turns at the level of individual acts.

Nevertheless, there is an important sense in which mother and infant have asymmetrical roles. By looking at the distribution of behaviour in time as it differs from a random process, we have refined our view of this asymmetry.

At the level of runs, this mother's runs and time-outs had random interval distributions. Quinn's run durations were randomly distributed but his time-out intervals were non-randomly distributed (Fig. 3). The time-outs between face and voice runs were linked to changes in infant gaze (see Fig. 4).

Stern (1974) found that even though infant "gazing at" time increased with age, the increase was always relative to a decrease in time "gazing away". This suggests that the whole cycle, from the onset of one "ATTENTIVE" period to the onset of the next, is subject to internal limitations. The infant has the capacity to delay or to hasten looking away within these limits, but he could not maintain either for an indefinite period.

The burst-pause phenomenon in sucking is another example of a cycle which is constrained to operate within narrowly defined internal limitations. The infant will suck in bursts and pauses whether the mother intervenes or not. If she does intervene, the baby may have a tendency to inhibit the onset of the next burst for a short time (see Kaye, Chapter 5).

Compared to these probably neurological limits on the range of accommodation of infant attention and oral activity, the mother is much more flexible. It therefore does not seem unlikely that the mother has a greater share in the mutual accommodation than has the infant.

The mother is more free to place various modalities of her behaviour in various relationships with the baby's and she does so simultaneously across levels. She is more free to expand and contract the on and off phases of her cycles as the need arises. She is still subject to internal constraints, but they are less narrow than those of her infant.

That the infant is more regular and predictable, the mother more flexible, leads us to consider another important maternal function reflected in these data: that of selection. The infant's cycles are not independent across all of his modalities. Rather, cycles of attention, face, voice, arms, legs and posture are all behavioural manifestations of underlying cycles of arousal or need.

We assume that the mother's and the infant's main goal is not to respond to or to elicit particular behavioural forms, but rather to maintain some optimal level of excitement or arousal, or to satisfy some other important need. In order to accomplish this goal the mother is forced to select from that array of stimuli a small sub-set. Or she may choose to respond to the most salient aspect of behaviour at a given point in time.

There are segments of the video-tapes during which Quinn was facially quiet and attentive. In some of those segments we have seen his mother respond to a run of arm movements as though it were a run of vocalizations. And Quinn in turn built up a characteristic level of excitement in response to her. The cooing game and the "nose-in-mouth" game which they played were no doubt results of a selection process, but we know little about the mechanisms of such selection and elaboration.

INDIVIDUAL DEVELOPMENT IN THE SOCIAL CONTEXT

The studies by Brazelton *et al.* (1974) and by Stern (1974) suggest a relationship between infant attentiveness and the mother–infant interaction. Infants whose mothers did not allow them to cycle their gaze at and away, as in the "framing" relationship, tended to spend less time looking at their mothers than infants who were allowed free access to the mother's face. The studies cited lead us to ask how infant attention is prolonged.

First, there is the "frame". A "frame" can be social, as in the "framing" of infant gaze by mother gaze. "Frames" can also exist within the individual. We gave the example of infant gaze as a "frame" for infant facial and vocal activity. The function of the "frame" is to contain or indulge cycles of activity. "Frames" serve to define the situation as a whole. A maternal gaze "frame" reminds the infant: "now we are engaged in joint visual activity". Schaffer *et al.* (Chapter 12) find that mothers of older infants—infants who rarely look at their mothers and who spend most of their time playing with objects—continue to provide gaze "frames" that contain vocal interchanges about the infant's activity.

Once a social "frame" is provided, all other "individual" activity within that "frame" can take on possible social significance. Quinn's mother's gaze "frame" served the particularly valuable function of allowing mother and infant some room to "play around" or to experiment with novel combinations of the mutual contributions at the level of runs (see Tables VII and VIII). Bruner (Chapter 11) refers to the mother as the "buffer" who sets the stage for social play. In that play the variables are the rules of interaction. It is out of social play that new rules or games are developed. And as games develop, so do the players.

How does an infant's attention become prolonged? We cannot conclusively answer this question with the results presented here. But this study does suggest that more modalities than simply gazing may be involved. A "frame" which permits the offering, modification and substitution of shared activity may be an essential factor in psychological development.

THE ROLE OF REPETITION

These results suggest some possible functions of repetition in the mother–infant interaction. Although the discussion here is focused on the repetition of acts taken from the same category within a run (level 1), it would also apply to "ON"–"OFF" cycling at any temporal level.

Stern (Chapter 8) shows how maternal repetition in naturally occurring interactions can sustain infant gaze, provide a basis for a theme-and-variation format, and present information in small doses with high redundancy for the benefit of an immature infant's cognitive apparatus. This explains why it might be adaptive for a mother to organize her activity into runs while in the presence of an infant. With each new presentation of the same stimulus, or with each new variation, the adult increases the probability of getting an infant's response.

Schleidt (1973) presents evidence that an immediate repetition of the same act will enhance the probability of response in a receiving communicant. For example, a receiving rooster usually will not respond until he hears at least two or three crows of a conspecific male.

The same limitations of information processing apply to the mother as well. The human infant is remarkable in the extent to which repetition is used for communication. An isolated cry would not get a mother's attention in the same manner as an insistent series of cries. But this example only speaks to the function of repetition as a *beacon* or signal.

There are two other possible functions of infant repetition for the mother which can be discussed without assuming any conscious intent on the part of the infant. These are *confirmation* and *anticipation*. Due to the asymmetries already discussed, Quinn's mother behaved "as if" he had certain capacities, such as, for example, the ability to make his runs simultaneous with hers. In the course of creating this "as if" co-occurrence it became necessary to confirm her effect on maintaining infant arousal. She did this by making inferences from repetition—the infant's use of the same act in the same way as before.

The infant's repetition then became an incentive to the mother to maintain her own repetitive series of acts. The example of the "nose-in-mouth" game shows that the repeated maternal bobbing and touching of her nose to the infant's mouth (coded as "NEAR") was a result of the infant's "asking for more" simply by repeating his mouth opening.

On the other hand, during infant "ATTENTIVE" periods the individual acts within a run were occurring at a rather high rate of repetition, so it is unlikely that even an adult would have time to react to each infant act as a separate stimulus. The more likely explanation is that the repetition allowed the mother to plan her next "response" even before the baby had emitted the "stimulus". Response and stimulus are used metaphorically; the real point is that something much more complex than a simple signal–response chain must be at work in order to sustain dyadic runs of any duration.

Studies of the relation between reaction time and prior anticipation of a stimulus (Poulton, 1950) have been interpreted similarly. That is, the ability to anticipate a sequence of acts is what unites them into a whole, integrated skilled performance. Once this is accomplished the subject can then divide his attention in order to accommodate to slight variations of the individual events in the series with little or no reaction time lag.

There is also something to be said about the pleasure which derives from doing the same thing over and over again, so long as it keeps working. Most parents and children repeat the same game as many times as it continues to be fun for them both. It may even be the case that the mother's repetitions allow the infant to confirm his own hypotheses about the interactions. And the mother's repetitions provide anticipation for the infant in the form of a somewhat stable, predictable pattern amidst a great deal of change.

Conclusions

This study suggests that it may be fruitful to view mother–infant (indeed any) interaction as a complex unfolding of events in time. The basic tool for this approach is the temporal interval distribution. Used in combination with the atemporal frequency distribution it may give us a means of sorting out cause and effect in naturally observed sequences of behaviour.

Further, our understanding of intra-subject and intra-dyadic organization may be improved by the use of analytic models which address the complexity of the naturally occurring process. This should be seen as a needed accompaniment to, rather than a substitute for, experimental manipulation of that process. By examining relationships between temporal levels, behavioural modalities and derived measures we have reduced the field of variation to three dimensions without sacrificing the complexity of the phenomenon.

With a single case no claims can be made for the universality of the particular findings. However, the demonstration of a complex interdependence of behaviour in a single case does suggest new approaches in future work. The use of dyadic concepts like symmetry and asymmetry, co-occurrence and co-onset, "framing" and turn-taking may lead us from a "direction of effects" approach to a more holistic view of human development in its social context.

Acknowledgements

This study was funded by a grant to Kenneth Kaye from the Spencer Foundation. I wish to thank Kenneth Kaye for his support and for his astute contributions to all phases of this work. I am also grateful to Starkey Duncan and Susan Stodolsky. They have served as encouraging and conscientious critics. I am indebted to Lynn Barker, Marilyn DeBoer, David Schwartz and Anne Wells for their assistance in making and coding the video-tapes, and of course, to Quinn and his mother.

References

Ainsworth, M. D. S., Bell, S. V. and Stayton, D. J. (1971). Individual differences in strange-situation behavior of one-year-olds. In H. R. Schaffer (Ed.), *The Origins of Human Social Relation.* Academic Press, London and New York.

Brazelton, T. B., Koslowski, B. and Main, M. (1974). The origins of reciprocity: the early mother-infant interaction. In M. Lewis and L. Rosenblum (Eds), *The Effect of the Infant on its Caregiver.* Wiley, New York.

Duncan, S. (1974). On the structure of speaker-auditor interaction during speaking turns. *Language in Society* **2**, 161–180.

Fogel, A. (1976). Gaze, face and voice in the development of the mother-infant face-to-face interaction. Unpublished Doctoral Dissertation, University of Chicago.

Mahler, M. (1968). *On Human Symbiosis and the Vicissitudes of Individuation.* International Universities Press, New York.

Poulton, E. (1950). Perceptual anticipation and reaction time. *Q. Jl exp. Psychol.* **2**, 99–112.

Schleidt, W. (1973). Tonic communication: continual effects of discrete signs in animal communication systems. *J. theor. Biol.* **42**, 359–386.

Stern, D. (1974). Mother and infant at play: the dyadic interaction involving facial, vocal and gaze behaviors. In M. Lewis and L. Rosenblum (Eds), *The Effect of the Infant on its Caregiver.* Wiley, New York.

Spitz, R. (1965). *The First Year of Life.* International Universities Press, New York.

Wolff, P. (1967). The role of biological rhythms in early psychological development. *Bull. Menninger Clin.* **31**, 197–218.

7 A Primary Phase in the Organization of Infant Responding Behaviour

William S. Condon

Introduction

Many years have been spent studying the micro-organization of human behaviour and interaction utilizing a frame-by-frame analysis of sound film, and this work is now presented to form a contribution to the study of the earliest period of interaction: that of the infant and its caretakers. The following discussion will seek to achieve a relatively integrated perspective or overview of the results of that inquiry, including several observations and tentative theoretical formulations which might prove useful to students of infant–caretaker interaction. Retrospectively, the microanalysis appears to have been an incipient ethology of "information processing" as this could be detected from the analysis of human behaviour in natural "response" to the surroundings, especially during communicational interaction. The fundamental impression to emerge from the microanalysis of human behaviour was one of the organized continuity of human beings with Nature and with each other. Man's ability to know and Nature's ability to be known seem to involve a mutual and reciprocal integrity.

The process of being born and growing up is natural. It is being accomplished daily and has been accomplished for thousands of years. There is a suspicion, however, that man sometimes tends to view this process as something which *he* accomplishes, as something beyond Nature's ability. The process of knowing is felt to be his possession and not a natural process linked with other natural processes. There has been a long epistemological tradition of isolating man and his abilities from Nature. Yet if we seek to study Nature as if she were separate from us, how can we then make contact with her—and with each other? When one considers what is required for a creature to have perceptions and knowledge, then one is struck by the profound continuity of man with Nature and with other human beings. The emphasis here will be on that *continuity*, particularly as illustrated by observations from the microanalysis of both normal and pathological behaviour and interaction. The thesis will be presented that the ethological microanalysis of human interaction may have unwittingly revealed a primary phase in the adult response process. This thesis emerges from the hypothesis of *interactional synchrony* between interactants. This hypothesis will be discussed below. The postulation of such a primary phase also implies that there may be other phases, suggesting that response is more an ongoing process than an event. Some tentative statements will be made about the nature of this postulated primary phase. The central thesis, however, is that the infant, as early as the day of birth, exhibits this early response phase at a high level of ability. Responding, particularly as it occurs during interaction when adults speak to the infant, can be studied in a relatively natural, non-laboratory style. An important question for students of infant behaviour is how much information processing ability the infant has, the nature of that ability, and how it functions in subsequent development.

PERSPECTIVE AND METHOD

A study of people in their natural state, as they talk and move together, shows that many aspects of their behaviour overlap. One of them may be speaking, accompanying his speech with various gestures. At the same time there are also varied movements on the part of the listeners and all of them will be sustaining certain postures in relation to each other. They will be in a certain situation, wearing certain styles of clothing, and relate to each other differently, yet within a framework of predictable behaviours, depending on sex and status. Each has a psychological make-up with its own complex history which will also influence the nature of their participation in the interaction. The following is a paraphrase of the work of philosopher F. J. E. Woodbridge which is relevant to the study of such complexity (Woodbridge, 1940). Any analysis of behavioural interaction is complicated by the fact that it is all intertwined. Nature does not put the events together as if they were originally separate. We discriminate between them and attend now to one and now to another, so that each of them is analysed, not by itself, but in the context of the others. In Nature there are no events so isolated that we could study them as if there were nothing else, although analysis proceeds as if this were possible. We analyse Nature into bits and pieces and then believe that we have discovered original elements which were somehow combined to become what Nature *is* in her encompassing unity. There is a paradox about inquiry. Analysis begins naturally with an inquirer who is part of and sustained within a vast universe of complex, vital connections. He grew up, went to school and studied various subjects and became an investigator rather than a poet. His analysis leads him to discriminate between aspects of his universe and these now isolated features are then assumed to be the pieces which were originally combined to make up the vital interconnections all around him by which he is being sustained as he conducts his very analysis for pieces.

Things are said to be composed of, to be elements of, to be parts of, other things. Much of our way of talking about things suggests a profoundly disjointed view of Nature's structure. It is difficult, for example, to conceptualize a person's behaviour as being an integrated and wholistic unity and at the same time to conceptualize that behaviour as having discrete sub-forms. The unity of the totality is often forgotten in an emphasis on the sub-forms. But there is no privileged position when describing the nature of the organization of behaviour. The total behaviour is there just as much as the sub-forms. We discriminate the sub-forms, to repeat, by attending now to one and now to another, so that they are analysed, not by themselves in isolation, but in relation to each other within the ongoing unity of the total behaviour. The analysis of human communication begins with people interacting with each other. Succeeding analyses do not arrive at pieces of people or of interaction which were somehow combined to be communication. The people are wholly there during the interaction and an aspect of behaviour isolated for study does not thereby become separate or cease its participation in the complex organization of that totality (Husserl, 1913).

The above perspective and method used by the author are outgrowths of each other. The method has primarily been that of viewing sound films of human behaviour and interaction again and again until a variety of forms of order begin to emerge. The "units" or "categories" in terms of which the analysis is to proceed are themselves the result of intensive analysis and are not postulated arbitrarily in advance. To a certain extent the most arduous and time-consuming task is the discovery of what might constitute the natural "units" or "sub-forms" within the process being investigated. This continues to remain the primary method. In this approach the investigator is required to continually question and often change his views about the structure of the process. In essence, the "units" are discovered and modified during the inquiry as a function of the inquiry itself. Even the notational categories, in terms of which the data are described, emerge during this inquiry process.

"Units as Forms of Organization"

The actual units of behaviour are usually not examined critically. They are often assumed *a priori* (or only after a cursory analysis) in advance of inquiry as the basis on which any discovered, correlated relationships can then be considered to define the nature of the total process. What is at issue is the method by which such units are determined to be units in the first place. Very often the uncritical acceptance of prevailing views about the nature of things can be misleading. This is particularly true when dealing with complex behavioural and interactional processes.

SPEAKING BEHAVIOUR

As indicated, a speaker while talking often moves several parts of his body at the same time. He may gesticulate this way and that, shift in his chair, cross and uncross his legs, reach for a pipe, etc. Thus several body parts are usually moving together at the same time and this is occurring at the same time that the speaker is articulating his syllables, words, and phrases. It is this temporal quality of behaviour which cannot be reduced to discrete segments of which it can then be said to be composed. If varying body parts are varying movement together over time, which one of them can be said to deserve unit status in preference to the rest? Many years of frame-by-frame analysis of sound films of human behaviour and interaction finally led to the observation of "forms-of-order" or patterns in the way these simultaneously moving body parts of the speaker changed in relation to each other and to speech. In brief, the "units" of behavioural organization are postulated to be "forms-of-order" or sub-organizations. At the micro-level, then, the investigator seems constrained to analyse organized behaviour as forms of organization.

Self Synchrony. Figure 1 is from a film of two male adults discussing their work. The speaker says, "I was going to ask you why do you . . . um . . . have difficulty with your late appointments?" The word "ask" and the co-occurring speaker's body motion illustrate the characteristic

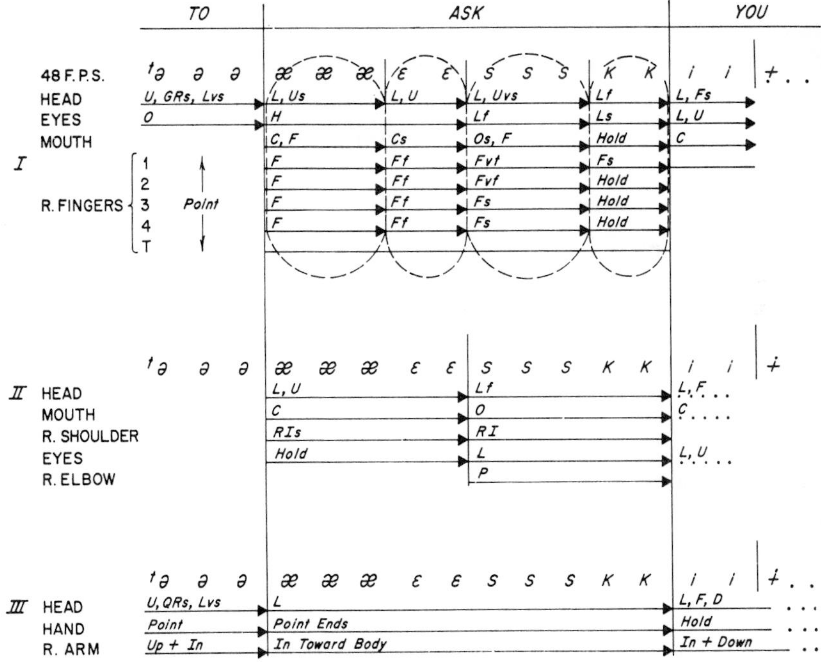

Fig. 1. The sustained relationship of change between different moving body parts and speech, forming a micro-behavioural unity in speaker behaviour. The following transcription notation symbols apply to all figures: U = up; D = down; L = left; R = right; AD = adduct; AB = abduct; S = supinate; P = pronate; RI = rotate in; RO = rotate out; F = flex; E = extend; C = close (mouth); O = open (mouth); Q = incline (head); H = hold, or still; B = back. The subscripts describe the relative velocity, from very slow to very fast—vs, s, f, vf.

self synchrony that has been observed in normal speaker behaviour. This has been consistently observed in the over 200 films studied so far, including speakers from a variety of other cultures. The word "ask" exhibits four speech features with four isomorphically co-occurring body motion configurations. The /s/ sound from part I at the top which lasts 3 frames will be used for illustration. During the emission of /s/ the head moves left and up very slightly, while the eyes move left rapidly, while the mouth opens slightly and comes forward, while fingers one and two flex very fast, while fingers three and four flex slightly. These are the most minimally detectable changes in the body at that time. A relationship is being sustained between these moving body parts during the three frames of the emission of /s/. This gives rise to a "relational configuration" or sustained unitary form defined by their durating together. The relation or order between the different directions and speeds of movement of different body parts is being sustained together and is doing so isomorphically with the duration of the /s/. There are four such configurations co-occurring with the four speech features of "ask". Such shared orderedness would apparently represent an *organized* process of the CNS (Central Nervous System). The head moving left does not cause the eyes to move left or the fingers of only the right hand to flex or conversely. Their doing this together synchronously comes from a central organizing process.

This characteristic and precise isomorphism of body motion configurations with the articulatory features of speech further supports the hypothesis of micro-behaviour as quantal forms of organization. The content forming the relationship sustaining across /s/ differs from that sustaining across /k/. A unifying recurrence in behaviour, which is always there as a basis for unit designation, is this pattern or orderedness of the sustained relationships of change. These configurations or ensembles of sustaining have been called "process-units" to emphasize their organizational nature.

This temporal process of "relational sustaining" seems to be characteristic of behaviour across many dimensions, both in individual and interactional behaviour. It appears to be a feature of the basic structural logic of behavioural organization in animals in general. Insects have not been studied from this perspective as yet. For example, the word "ask" exhibits sustaining forms across multiple levels simultaneously. These are illustrated in parts II and III of Fig. 1. Behaviour is thus also integrated hierarchically in that *while* these lower-order organizations are sustaining their relationships, there are concomitant wider sustainings across different temporal dimensions which, however, still maintain an ordered relationship with the lower dimensions. It is a hierarchic integration of the ordered forms of change of the body so that different ensembles of the body fill these forms as the emergent order requires. There are varying relationships of relationships having interlocking temporal regularities. It is as if the body were outwardly reflecting an internal system. There are relationships of speech/body change being sustained together at the minimal level and *while* these are being sustained, relationships of speech/body features are simultaneously being sustained together across still wider temporal dimensions and *while* these are being sustained yet wider forms are being sustained together. They are all there together and each is discriminated as a pattern of relationship in contrast to the rest. The lower order forms were not combined to create the higher nor were the higher there first. No one of them has a privileged position in relation to the rest. Forms of organization are discovered to interpenetrate other forms of organization as if forms of order posed no isolating boundary surfaces to other forms of order. They can often be seen to share features from a different, contrastive perspective, revealing still different patterns. Aspects of one pattern can be seen to share similar aspects within another pattern, revealing a third pattern. All of this along multiple interpenetrating dimensions comprises a description of behaviour. Figure 2 below exemplifies this hierarchic organization of behaviour.

The word "keeping" in Fig. 2 illustrates the rhythmic, hierarchic integration of the relation of the patterns of change of body motion with those of speech. There are five relatively minimal sub-forms of body motion which co-occur with relatively minimal articulatory features. Body motion forms also occur isomorphically with the syllabic aspects /kkkiiipp/ and /p'ɨ̇ɨ̇ŋŋŋ/. There is an incline left (QL) of the head accompanying /kkkiiipp/; and a downward movement of the head (D) plus rapid wrist flexion (Ff) accompanying /p'ɨ̇ɨ̇ŋŋŋ/. The word as a totality is precisely accompanied by flexion of the right wrist. That wrist had been extending but flexes exactly at the onset of "keeping" and continues flexing until the end of the word where it again extends. This organization was discovered in the behaviour and in terms of the "discrete-like" forms revealed there, not from the study of *a priori* categories. The thought intended here is that body motion and speech are a unity, expressing a hierarchic flowing unity of the organism and

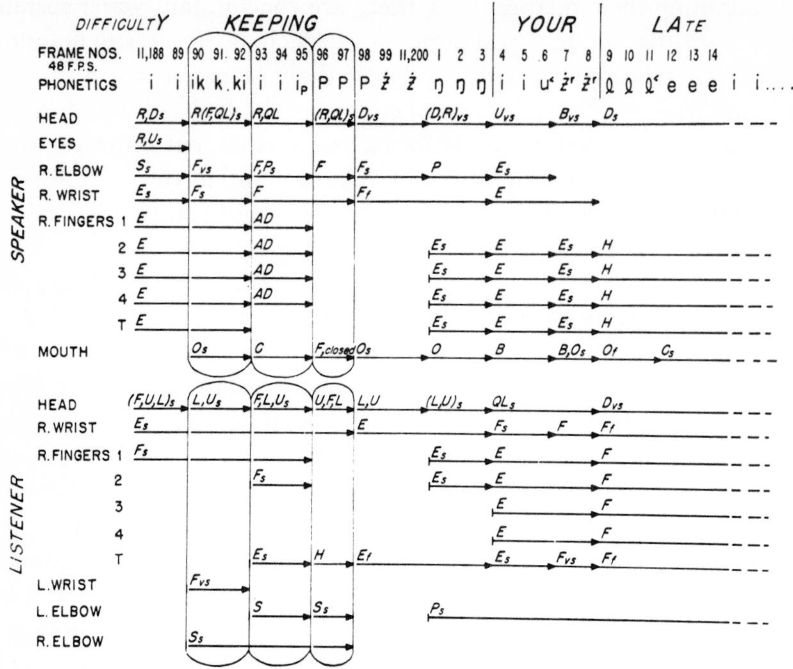

Fig. 2. The hierarchic organization of speaker behaviour.

not a hierarchic integration of two separate systems (body motion and speech) by a third, the brain. Behaviourally, speech and body motion are a unity even though they can also be studied independently. Synchronous timings across multiple levels of organization appear to be a central feature of behaviour. The rhythm hierarchy of speaker behaviour is analysable into integrated speech and body motion patterns across the following relative levels: (1) phone types, (2) syllables, (3) words, (4) a one/half-second cycle, and (5) a one-second cycle (Condon, 1970).

When one conceives of a sentence as constructed by putting phone types together to form syllables, syllables together to form words, words together to form phrases, and finally phrases to form sentences, it is difficult to find the glue which holds it all together in meaningful, syntactic unity. The view expressed here is that a spoken sentence is both discrete-like and continuous simultaneously, without contradiction. Lower dimension relationships of sustaining and change of behaviour appear to be "organized together" by wider, simultaneously occurring relationships of change, etc. This is all being done as it is occurring. All these parts being simultaneously "held together" in relation to each other is what constitutes integrated behaviour. These comments on the hierarchic organization of speaker micro-behaviour were made to illustrate continuities and levels of continuities. This may be a useful analogue in terms of which other continuities in human existence can be analysed.

Interactional Synchrony

Continued, frame-by-frame analysis of sound films of human interaction led to the surprising observation that a listener moves synchronously with a speaker (Condon, 1963, 1964; Condon and Ogston, 1966). The listener was observed to move in organizations of change (often including intensity of change as well) which were isomorphic with the articulatory patterning of the speaker's speech. The ordered way the simultaneously moving body parts of the listener change in relation to each other follows the articulatory pattern of the speaker's speech. Recent work in the study of nerve cell assemblies suggests a similar isomorphism between neurological processing and peripheral stimuli.

> "These findings (histogram tracings) indicate that the incoming information *modulates* the neuronal activity of the territory into which it arrives, in such a way that the total spatial and temporal distribution of excitation and inhibition within the territory corresponds to the characteristics of the peripheral stimulus" (Verzeano, 1970).

Interactional synchrony, however, suggests that incoming information, particularly speech, modulates the pattern of the organization of change of the total organism even as it is incoming. The listener moves in synchrony with the speaker's speech almost as well as the speaker does. Interactional synchrony is possibly a sub-class of responding. We are dealing, it seems, with the continuity of man's information-processing relation to Nature, including other human beings. There is a physical continuity in the flow of sound between interactants. The ear drum of the listener oscillates rapidly and synchronously in relation to the impinging sound waves. Assemblies of cells further reflect the structure of that peripheral stimulus. After only 50 msec the organization of change of the body motion of a listener wholistically reflects the organizations of change of the stimulus, at least with respect to speech.

Figure 3 illustrates the responsive precision which is characteristic of interactional synchrony. A black graduate student is talking with the white president of an industrial corporation. They had never met prior to the filming. They were told that the sound film (which was taken at 24 f.p.s.) was being taken to study human communication. The student

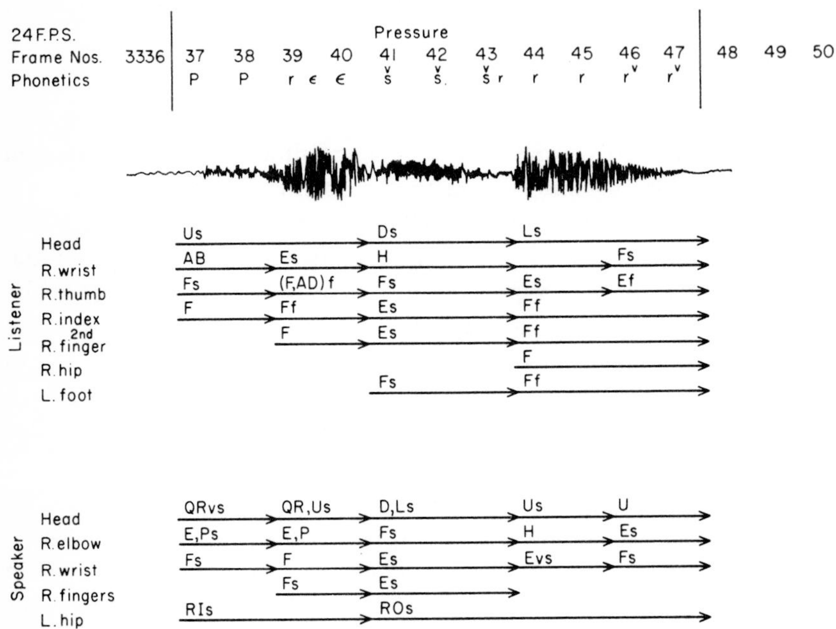

Fig. 3. Interactional Synchrony: the organization of change of the listener's behaviour is isomorphic with the structure of the speaker's speech. The oscilloscopic display of the word "pressure" is presented above the microanalysis of the listener's behaviour.

is saying, "When I.B.M. and other corporations are asking for degrees they put the *pressure* on the people on the job market for degrees." The word "pressure" /ppresssrrrr/ exhibits a contrasting sequence of voiced/unvoiced phone types. The voiced /$\wedge$/ sound terminating "the" is followed by /p/ which is unvoiced and lasts two frames (two twenty-fourths of a second). This is then followed by voiced /re/ also lasting two frames which is then followed by the unvoiced /s/ lasting three frames. Finally, the voiced /r/ occurs, lasting four frames. It takes eleven frames for the emission of the word "pressure" or just slightly under $\frac{1}{2}$ second.

For greater accuracy in segmenting speech a sound film was made of an oscilloscopic display of this speech with the sound of the speech being simultaneously re-recorded onto the sound track of the film of its own display. Speech was thus segmentable down to the level of one sixtieth of a second or better, and could be correlated with the body motion. Sound can actually be segmented to a finer degree than body motion since the sound track is relatively continuous compared to a film frame which is the lower limit at which body motion changes can be detected. (High speed films can be obtained which permit a finer analysis of body motion but beyond 94 f.p.s. it becomes quite difficult to detect changes.) Reliability studies on the degree of accuracy in determining the onset of both speech and non-speech sounds were carried out by independent judges. There was a high degree of accuracy with 98% agreement at a hundred and twentieth of a second and 100% agreement at one sixtieth of a second using 30 f.p.s. film.

The organization-of-change of the body motion of the listener can be seen to change isomorphically and in an ongoing, tracking fashion with the forms of change of the word "pressure". This seems to be a form of responding on the part of the organism well below the level postulated by the traditional stimulus-response model. Interactional synchrony is also illustrated in Fig. 2. It must be emphasized that the criteria for such synchronization depend on units of behaviour interpreted as forms of ordered patterns of change. What is being postulated is a profound continuity of perceptual processing in relation to the structure of the surround. One of the implications of interactional synchrony as a form or sub-class of "response" is that the concept of "response" may need to be conceptualized as a *process*, not as an event, although certain points along its path may stand out more than others.

The relatively immediate "response" to sound occurring in interactional synchrony appears, to reiterate, to be an *organizational* response. There can be a relatively continuous yet constantly varying stream of speech which is almost simultaneously being continuously and organizationally tracked as expressed in the varying body motion of the listener. The tracking in interactional synchrony may be an early, yet prominent system in relation to other systems of the response process.

The preceding section has illustrated continuities within the behaviour of the normal individual and the continuity of the normal individual with the surround, including other human beings. "Having" a world involves having a naturally organized surround and a responding and processing organization that is properly linked with that surround. Interactional synchrony is probably only a particular manifestation of a much wider synchronization or continuity of the organism with the surround. All of the sensory modalities may exhibit such tracking to some degree.

Dysfunctional Behaviour

The ethological study of dysfunctional child behaviour and interaction led to observations which further support the hypotheses presented in the preceding section, particularly the concept of interactional synchrony as revealing a possible early phase in the responding process. Several years of intensive sound-film analysis of autistic-like children led to the observation that these children seemed to be responding to the same sound *multiple times* (Condon, 1974). The rationale for postulating such multiple responses were *later* body motion patterns (entrainments) which were isomorphic with earlier occurring sound patterns. (These later movements looked jerky and bizarre and seemed to have no relationship to the surround.) The criterion of such later "response" was derived, again, from interactional synchrony; an organization of change of body motion that was isomorphically entraining with the organization of sound—except that in this case the sound had occurred earlier, even as long as a full second earlier. Most of these children who exhibit the delayed entrainment with sound probably do not actually hear sounds multiple times, yet some of them may. What seems to be happening is a separation or delay of the synchronized response which normally follows the impingement of sound waves upon the ear drum.

Autistic-like Children. Prominent characteristics of the kinesics of autistic-like children are sudden and rapid movements which, as mentioned, appear to bear no relation to the environment. An example may illustrate the phenomenon. An autistic-like child throws a block on a table and it bounces three times then falls to the carpet below. He sits relatively still while this happens. At a certain time period later, in the present case 16 frames ($\frac{2}{3}$ second), the child's body suddenly jerks three times at intervals which precisely reflect the intervals between the earlier actual bounce sounds. Further striking evidence is provided by having the sound on the film delayed the appropriate amount by a film laboratory. The sound on a copy of this child's film was delayed 16 frames so that the sound now occurred with the later body movements. It is quite startling to see the child move in precise synchrony with these now delayed sounds which actually occurred 16 frames earlier. Such isomorphism remains systematic and exact down to the level of one twenty-fourth of a second for most of the sounds throughout the film. When a loud sound occurs on a non-delayed film one can count out for 15 frames from the onset of the sound and predict that precisely on the 16th frame the child's body will usually jerk as if at the onset of a sound. No actual sound is occurring at this later time, yet the child's body moves as if sound were occurring. Some dysfunctional children look around as if to see where the sound is coming from and seem puzzled.

Figure 4 shows the results of a microanalysis of the response to sound of a normal 12-year-old girl compared with the response of an autistic-like 12-year-old girl. The film of the autistic-like girl was analysed for response in relation to 60 selected sounds when they actually occurred.

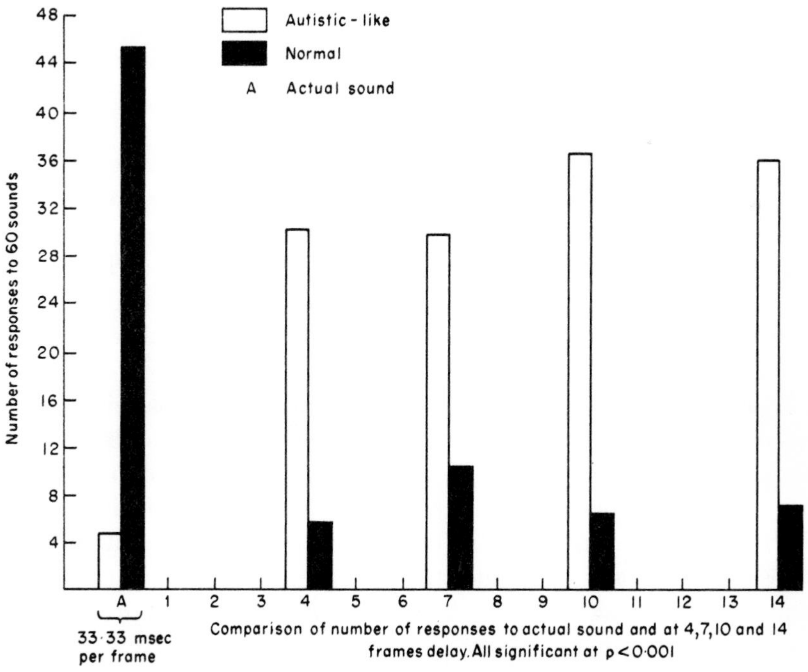

Fig. 4. Comparison of response to sounds between a 12-year-old autistic-like girl and a 12-year-old normal girl.

Response was also studied in relation to these same 60 sounds delayed. The sound was systematically delayed frame-by-frame out through 15 frames, and at each of these frames response to the same 60 sounds was again analysed. There were only five responses to the 60 sounds when they actually occurred. However, four marked delay-response times were observed, at 4, 7, 10, and 14 frames, with the last being the most synchronous. There seemed to be a reverberation or cycling of the delayed responses, each approximately 117 msec out from the last. The responses of a normal control were similarly analysed in relation to 60 selected sounds when they actually occurred and at delays of 4, 7, 10, and 14 frames respectively. Figure 4 illustrates these comparisons, all of which were significant ($p < 0{\cdot}001$). The normal girl had 46 responses, each within 50 msec, in relation to the 60 sounds when they actually occurred. This illustrates the entrainment with actual sound characteristic of normal behaviour. The figure also shows the delayed and repeating entrainment characteristic of the autistic-like children.

It must be emphasized again that the criterion of "response" used was that described in interactional synchrony: the serial entraining of the body with the transformations of the sound. In this respect the study of pathology strongly, but indirectly, supports the hypothesis of interactional synchrony. It reveals that the organism moves in organizations of change which are isomorphic with those of sound, even though at a much later time. An intensive, naturalistic study of pathology thus led to unexpected observations reflecting normal processes in distorted form. The displaced synchronization observed in pathological behaviour also provides further support for the postulate of an early stimulus tracking phase of the response process. Thirty autistic-like children have been studied thus far and all have exhibited this "multiple response to sound".

Reading-problem Children. Continued intensive microanalysis of other dysfunctions in children, particularly reading-problem children, led to the discovery that they too exhibited the multiple response to sound. At the present time approximately ten sound films of children with reading disabilities have been studied. These children all appear quite normal. They speak well and can understand complex verbal statements. They seem to be of average or above average intelligence except that they are one or two years behind in reading. It is difficult to detect anything unusual in their behaviour even when watching them closely. A frame-by-frame analysis of a sound film of their behaviour, however, reveals marked asynchronies. It was, frankly, a shock to discover that they too displayed the multiple response to sound. There is a marked difference, however, between the autistic-like and the reading-problem children. The latter exhibit much less intensity of response at the delay times than do the autistic-like children. They also have much more synchrony with the actual sound than the autistic-like children. A variety of children with other dysfunctions were also filmed and studied. All manifested the multiple response to sound. They included two hyperactive children, three retarded children, and two aphasic children.

The relevance of these further findings for the present discussion is that dysfunctional behaviour resembles normal behaviour but in the characteristic distorted form of a multiple response to sound. That the multiple response to sound occurs in a *variety* of forms of childhood dysfunctions ranging from severe to mild and differs in its degree from severe to mild provides further support for interactional synchrony as a phase in normal information processing. The existence of a spectrum of differing childhood dysfunctions all manifesting varying degrees of a similar form of dysfunction that resembles a postulated normal process but distorted lends support to the probable existence of such a normal process.

Infant Synchronization

The next question was how early in human life interactional synchronization might be detected. Sixteen normal neonates (from one- to four-days old) were sound filmed with live human voices and voices from a tape-recorder, including Chinese speech. These films were studied intensively. All of the infants were found to move synchronously with adult speech (Condon and Sander, 1974). The synchronization was sustained and precise for long intervals. In one instance it occurred across the emission of 89 consecutive words by an adult. The baby is born, it seems, with an ability to steadily track subtle auditory speech variations with almost as great an ability as that of an adult. There is, apparently, a major continuity of infant "response processing" with the surround almost as soon as it is born.

An attempt will be made to explore some of the features of this infant entraining process, although these must be considered tentative and speculative. An example may help illustrate what appears to be happening. The infant sustains a given relationship of movement (or configuration of change) isomorphically with a relatively uniform speech sound-type emitted by the adult, such as an /s/. When this changes to another sound type, for example an /o/, the infant's organization of movement also changes, sustaining a new organization until a different sound occurs, etc. Let us assume the adult had said the word "so", with a silence after the /o/. The onset of silence is also a change point. The infant seems to sustain the same body motion configuration as long as the sound seems to remain the same, changing when the sound changes. This is implicit in adult behaviour also as seen in the entrainment of the listener with the word "pressure" (Fig. 3).

When a sound film is played in reverse the terminations of sounds are then met as onsets. In the present example there would be silence, then the /o/ would be heard followed by the /s/. One can go through an entire film in this reverse fashion and characteristically see normal infants initiate movements at these "onset" (actually termination) points. This indicates that the infant had been entraining across the terminal sound and had changed configuration with the onset of the silence.

The process of analysing sound films in reverse is particularly convincing and striking with respect to the multiple response phenomenon in autistic-like children. In that situation, using the film that had the sound track deliberately delayed, the autistic-like child can be shown to move at the "onsets" (actually terminations) of these now delayed sounds. The co-occurrence of change points and sound onsets in a film with a sound track deliberately delayed 16 frames and then analysed in reverse is one more piece of evidence for the hypothesis of entrainment. It thus supports the thesis that certain dysfunctional children entrain much later with the structure of earlier sounds. It also supports the general thesis that entrainment, as such, occurs.

The infant organism when tracking with speech may be functionally reflecting these discrete-like sequencings *as* discrete-like. Discrimination is, perhaps, beginning to be achieved in a rudimentary way during this entraining stage of processing. The central hypothesis emerging is that interactional synchrony may be an indication of a primary phase of the responding process and that this phase is simultaneously the beginning of a discrimination function, laying an essential organized groundwork for later operations. This would also apply to the adult responding process as well. A different way of stating it may be that interactional synchrony is an early stage in the discrimination/cognition process. The organizational "entraining-along-with" the structure of the incoming signal is, ethologically, how the infant is behaving in relation to some of the auditory aspects of the surround. To call what he is then doing *a* response does not particularly add greater information about the nature of that process. The human neonate may, and probably does, have far greater abilities than we have imagined. The human organism as a behavioural unity entrains with the micro structure of speech within as short a time as 50 msec and a one-day-old infant is capable of this. A breakdown of this process might result in severe perceptual disabilities; this seems to be the case with autistic-like children.

Sensitivity. The preceding discussion dealt with the hypothesis of a possible primary phase (within 50 msec) in the human responding process. This was derived from the concept of interactional synchrony and from the study of dysfunctional child behaviour. A process of stimulus entrainment, which was also felt to be an incipient form of discrimination, was ascribed to this phase. Both adults and infants exhibit this process. A remarkable feature of man's responsivity to sound, especially at the micro-level, is his degree of sensitivity, particularly to human speech. One of the marked characteristics about the hypothesized later "response" of autistic-like children in relation to earlier occurring sound is the degree to which they appear to be dominated by it. They often literally jerk this way and that in precise later synchrony to even slight sound stimuli which occurred earlier. They seem oblivious to their own bizarre movements and do not appear to be able to shut them off. In essence, they do not seem to be able to "habituate" at these later times in relation to whatever in the earlier sound stimuli has dysfunctionally led to the later isomorphic body jerks. Many of these children also seem hyper-responsive to sound when it actually occurs. Thus both normal and pathological behaviours exhibit marked sensitivity to auditory stimuli. There is a sense in which the constant and precise entraining of interactional synchrony could be inferred to be a pre-habituation or relatively non-habituating process. In other words, at this early phase of the responding process there appears to be little decrement of response in relation to relatively continuous speech stimulation on the part of the whole animal. Human speech seems to be highly species-meaningful in contrast to many inanimate sounds. Adults characteristically appear to ignore most of the inanimate sounds around them when they are engaged in conversation. Preliminary work suggests that neonates entrain much more readily with adult speech than with inanimate sounds, particularly with the rhythmic aspects of speech. This is illustrated in Table 2 of Condon and Sander (1974).

There have been several attempts to define and clarify the nature of habituation and its role in information processing. Habituation was defined by Thorpe (1963) in the following way: "The relatively permanent waning of a response as a result of repeated stimulation which is not followed by any kind of reinforcement. It is specific to the stimulation and relatively enduring" (p. 61). Thompson and Spencer (1966) described nine parametric characteristics of habituation on which they felt there was general agreement. They are often cited by other investigators. Hinde (1970), in an excellent and thoughtful paper, carefully examined the propositions of Thompson and Spencer, indicating that habituation was a more complex process than they had portrayed. He says, "The question arises, however, whether the characteristics listed by Thompson and Spencer are detailed enough either to establish similarities between phenomena at different levels of analysis, or to be much guide to the nature of the mechanisms" (p. 34). More recently, an excellent two-volume work by Peeke and Herz (1973) entitled *Habituation* has appeared. Petrinovich, writing in Volume I of the above work, also emphasizes the complexity of habituation:

> "In dealing with organism–environment interactions we must accept the fact that there are a multitude of stimuli to which the organism is exposed and that each of these stimuli has a differential significance depending on such things as the state of the organism, the context within which the stimulus is embedded, and the preceding experience of the organism. In turn, the response of the organism cannot be absolutely predicted when we deal with the natural environment since it depends on a host of factors such as the behavioural supports for action available in the environment and the immediately preceding action patterns" (Petrinovich, 1973, p. 156).

Autistic-like children behave roughly like normal children in relation to sound, except that the entrainment occurs later, several times, and appears exaggerated and bizarre. They seem to be controlled by a dysfunctional sound stimulus process, whatever its cause and whether actually heard by them or not. They seem to be out-of-phase with the actual sound universe in a *hypersensitive* fashion. In a certain respect, however, the normal listener is just as "locked-in" to sound, especially human speech. Our body organization entrains with the structural variations of the speech of the person we are listening to. We may choose not to listen to that person, but if we do choose to listen it seems doubtful that we are then also able to choose not to move synchronously with the rapid and subtle variations in his speech. If one is attending to what is being said and he is also moving, the hypothesis implies that the micro-structures of his movement will inevitably entrain with the speech. The point is not that it is necessary that the body be entraining for listening to occur, but that the body does do so characteristically during listening behaviour. The organization of change of the listener's movements may be only secondarily following the structure of the speech signal. Yet it may be necessary in order for auditory discrimination to take place that the listener track the structure of the incoming signal in some organized neurological fashion. Body movement synchronization may only be a reflection of that neurological processing. The autistic-like child cannot control his delayed or reverberating entrainment and in a similar way we are not free to dispense with our own neurological-organizational tracking of incoming auditory stimuli. If such precise and alert entraining is taking place it would seem to preclude the occurrence of waning *at this level* at the same time. We can of course become bored and our attention shift but that would be at a different level.

Further Tentative Explorations. The possibility of more than a speculative connection between the dysfunctional multiple response to sound and non-habituation emerged from the study of a 12-day-old female infant who was anoxic for seven minutes at birth. There was also some damage in the right hemisphere with concomitant weakness on the left side of the body. A T.V. tape was made of this child in the at-risk nursery and a 30 f.p.s. sound film (kinescope) was subsequently made from the T.V. tape. This permitted a microanalysis of her response to sound. There was some evidence of a multiple response at 12 days but the kinescope was not of sufficient quality to confirm this. A marked multiple response to sound, with the major delay at 14 frames (fourteen thirtieths of a second) was clearly detected when the girl was filmed two months later. The initial T.V. taping at 12 days showed a very surprising inability to habituate. There may be some connection between this pathological apparent lack of habituation, the delayed response to sound, and hypersensitivity. In other words this infant seemed unable to shut off her response to tapping sounds. Tapping sounds were made on a metal table primarily for later assessment for multiple response, but it was noticed that the infant would blink systematically with each tap. If there were two taps in a row the infant would blink twice. This occurred time after time. It was almost as if there were a direct or unscreened line into the nervous system. Similar tapping sounds had been made during the filming of normal infants, and all had stopped blinking after nine or ten taps, if they even blinked at all.

Some preliminary and tentative comparisons were made which, while quite inadequate, were felt to be suggestive. These comparisons seemed to indicate the possibility of hypersensitivity in this infant which may also be a factor in the dysfunctional multiple response to sound. There is, for example, the exaggerated intensity of the delayed body motion responses to earlier sound. Many autistic-like children seem to become upset with loud sounds, putting their hands over their ears.

1. In a first exploratory study a comparison was made between the 12-day-old anoxic infant and 10 two- to four-day-old normal infants with respect to the number of eye blink responses in relation to tapping sounds. Following 188 tapping sounds the anoxic infant had 114 blinks and 74 without blinks. Following 188 tapping sounds the normal infants had 39 blinks and 149 without blinks. There was a significant difference ($p < 0{\cdot}001$).

2. A second comparison was made between the anoxic infant's blink response to taps at 12 days and her blink response to taps at two months. The number of taps from the 12-day-old data was randomly reduced to provide an equivalent population. Following 32 tapping sounds the infant at 12 days had 23 blinks and 9 without blinks. Following 32 tapping sounds at two months the infant had 2 blinks and 30 without blinks. This was a significant difference ($p < 0{\cdot}001$).

3. A third comparison was undertaken to determine whether there might be a difference between eye blink responses to onsetting speech sounds (following silence) in contrast to taps between 12 days and two months in this anoxic infant. At 12 days following 155 speech onset sounds there were 24 blinks and 131 without blinks. Following 155 speech onset sounds at two months there were 11 blinks and 144 without blinks. This was non-significant ($p > 0{\cdot}05$).

The speech onset sounds were obviously less intense than the tapping sounds and did not evoke as many blinks. This would follow from the proposition that the weaker the stimulus the more pronounced the habituation. The contrast between blink response to taps and to speech onset suggests that some "turning off" of eye blink response could take place, probably related to intensity differences. (There were also ten vowel-like sounds, each following silence, in the film of the 12-day-old infant. These were emitted by a human speaker but were louder than regular speech onsets. Of these ten vowel onset sounds, six evoked blinks.) It is also true that there was a contrast between speech and inanimate sounds as well as intensity. If the infant were hypersensitive as a result of her trauma it might account for her relative inability to shut off the blinks in relation to taps in contrast to normal infants.

In his excellent paper, J. P. Griffin reviews many studies and illustrates from his own work the thesis that lesions tend to reduce and can even eliminate habituation. The hypothesis has been put forward that this may result from a change in neurone excitability:

> "In the above investigations it was demonstrated that transection of the spinal cord 7 days after removal of the frontal cortex resulted in a spinal animal that habituated much more slowly than a spinal preparation tested under similar conditions but which had no lesions of the frontal cortex. This effect could not be demonstrated if the frontal cortex lesions were produced after transection of the cord. It has been suggested (Glaser and Griffin, 1962; Griffin and Pearson, 1967; Kugelberg, 1952, 1962) that habituation is a consequence of changes in internuncial neurone excitability. It would appear that the excitability of the internuncial neurones has been increased following lesions of the frontal areas of the cortex but not after lesions of the somato-sensory areas of the cerebral cortex, and that this hyper-excitability persisted after spinal transection" (Griffin, 1970, p. 171).

The entrainment that occurs in a delayed or reverberating fashion in the multiple response to sound appears to exhibit such hyper-excitability. The body of the autistic-like child jerks intensely at times even with slight sounds. These movements resemble unconscious startle responses. This later entrainment, including its hypersensitivity, appears to be an *organized* process. In the multiple response the body wholistically reflects the entrainment and its hyper-excitability in the same organized way that the normal listener's body reflects the ongoing structure of the speaker's speech. It is as if the early, organized, tracking phase of normal response began pathologically to repeat or reverberate, becoming hypersensitive at the same time.

4. A fourth comparison was made between the two- to four-day-old normal infants and the 12-day-old anoxic infant concerning the

rapidity with which the blink occurred following the onset of a tapping sound. Only those sound and blink onset points were selected where there was 100% agreement between independent judges. A graph of the results is presented in Fig. 5 below. There is a marked rapidity of blink response (decreased latency) to taps in this anoxic infant in contrast to the normal infants. This might be simply due to the older age of this infant but it could also be a possible added indication of hypersensitivity.

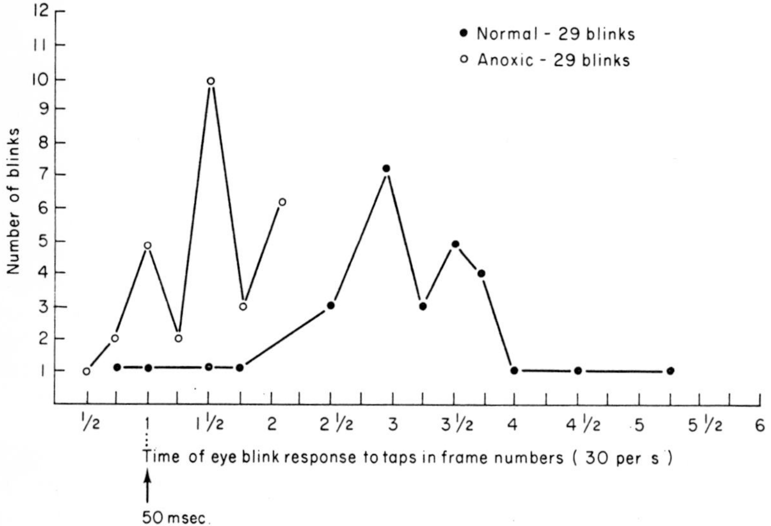

Fig. 5. Anoxic infant and normal infants compared in terms of rapidity of blinks following tapping sounds. A blink occurring one frame after a tap would indicate a latency of 50 msec.

The preceding observations on one at-risk infant are methodologically inadequate and much further work needs to be done. They were presented as tentative support and clarification of the hypothesis of an early and *organized* entraining phase in human response behaviour, particularly in infant response behaviour. The multiple response (a delayed and repeating entrainment) which appears to be a pathological distortion of a postulated similar normal entraining process was clearly observed in this two-month-old infant. A pathological occurrence of entrainment at this age lends credence to the hypothesis that it is probably also there in a normal way in normal infant behaviour at the same age.

Conclusion

An attempt has been made by the author to give some tentative theoretical formulations for the observations emerging from the microanalysis of sound films of normal and pathological human behaviour. There were two recurring and interconnected themes.

> 1. The first was the presentation of the hypothesis of a primary, organized, entraining/discriminating phase in human responding behaviour. This phase was postulated to be fully functional at birth. If this proves to be the case it will have implications for the analysis of infant abilities and development. 2. The second, a more implicit theme, concerned the presentation of an organizational perspective in inquiry as complementary to a discrete-like focus. It is not a question of either an organizational or a discrete-like perspective, but of an integrated use of both.

The infant probably does not put his world together in the way the investigator goes about dividing it in order to study the infant's reaction to it. Many things happen at once in the infant's world, yet it is complexly organized and he may be aware of ordered coherences or unities in that complexity. A gentle gaze is not the warmth of the caressing hands, the quiet voice is not touch or the smell of perfume or being held; but all of these in their coherence are the mother's presence for the child. The other sensory modalities may each track their relevant stimulus modes in a fashion similar to auditory perception and all may then be integrated together, reflecting coherent perceptual unities of the surround. An analogy with the nature of the "process units", as the logical order in seemingly diverse body part movements, may be relevant. This is the organizational emphasis that diverse features may reveal forms of order which comprise basic regularities. There may be forms of order or interactional regularities which are revealed by what at first seem to be disparate items. Eye gaze, touch, voice usage, holding, etc., including the timings of these in relation to each other and to the infant's behaviour, may form patterns in their functioning together which no one of them in isolation would reveal.

The lesson from microanalysis is that what are taken to constitute "units" and "organizations of units" is always a critical ongoing problem in inquiry.

Acknowledgements

W. S. Condon had been partially supported by the Grant Foundation and is presently supported by the Medical Foundation (through the Dr Charles H. Weed memorial award) which is The Research and Community Health Agency of United Way of Massachusetts Bay.

I am indebted to Dr Jeffrey Gould and the Neonatology staff of Boston City Hospital for part of the research described in this paper. I also wish to express my gratitude for the dedicated work of Mr Thaddeus Bartter who contributed to these studies.

References

Condon, W. S. (1963). Synchrony units and the communicational hierarchy. Paper presented at Western Psychiatric Institute, Pittsburgh, Pa. Unpublished.

Condon, W. S. (1964). Process in communication. Paper presented at Western Psychiatric Institute, Pittsburgh, Pa. Unpublished.

Condon, W. S. (1970). Method of micro-analysis of sound films of behavior. *Behav. Res. Meth. Instrn.* **2**, 51–54.

Condon, W. S. (1974). Multiple response to sound in dysfunctional children. *J. Aut. Child Schiz.* **5**, 37–56.

Condon, W. S. and Ogston, W. D. (1966). Sound film analysis of normal and pathological behavior patterns. *J. nerv. ment. Dis.* **143**, 338–346.

Condon, W. S. and Sander, L. W. (1974). Neonate movement is synchronized with adult speech: interactional participation and language acquisition. *Science* **183**, 99–101.

Griffin, J. P. (1970). Neurophysiological studies into habituation. In G. Horn and R. A. Hinde (Eds), *Short-term Change in Neural Activity and Behavior.* Cambridge University Press, London.

Hinde, R. A. (1970). Behavioral habituation. In G. Horn and R. A. Hinde (Eds), *Short-term Changes in Neural Activity and Behavior.* Cambridge University Press, London.

Husserl, E. (1913). *Ideas* (general introduction to pure phenomenology). Macmillan, New York.

Peeke, H. and Herz, M. J. (1973). *Habituation.* Academic Press, New York and London.

Petrinovich, L. (1973). A species-meaningful analysis of habituation. In H. Peeke and M. J. Herz (Eds), *Habituation*, Vol. 1. Academic Press, New York and London.

Thompson, R. F. and Spencer, W. A. (1966). Habituation. *Psychological Review* **73**, 16–43.

Thorpe, W. H. (1963). *Learning and Instincts in Animals.* Methuen, London.

Verzeano, M. (1970). Evoked responses and network dynamics. In R. E. Whalen, R. F. Thompson, M. Verzeano and N. M. Weinberger (Eds), *The Neural Control of Behavior.* Academic Press, New York and London.

Woodbridge, F. J. E. (1940). *An Essay on Nature.* Columbia University Press, New York.

8

The Infant's Stimulus World During Social Interaction:

A Study of Caregiver Behaviours with Particular Reference to Repetition and Timing

D. N. Stern, B. Beebe, J. Jaffe and S. L. Bennett

Introduction

Whatever a mother "does" with her face, voice and body provides for her infant his first and formative exposure to a human being and human communication. The flow of maternal behaviours are the very events from which the infant, through his visual, auditory and other perceptual processes, will establish a schema of the human face (Kagan, 1967); will establish schemata of human emotions as reflected in facial expressions (Spitz, 1965; Stern, 1974a); will acquire smiling and probably vocalizing as exogenous or social events (Spitz and Wolf, 1946; Rheingold *et al.*, 1959; Emde and Harmon, 1972); will begin to form bonds of attachment (Bowlby, 1969); will acquire experience with the effect of his own social behaviours (Rheingold, 1961) and experience with self-regulation of his own states of arousal and affect (Stern, 1974b). In addition, the ongoing flow of maternal behaviour gives the infant his primary experience with the "stuff" of the process of human communication through vocal and kinesic channels.

Accordingly, we must have a more detailed knowledge of the nature of the social behaviours that a mother normally performs, since these will be the actual events which organize many of the infant's crucial developmental achievements.

In this spirit, we have adopted for this chapter a descriptive approach, and examined in detail the sequential structure and temporal patterning of naturally occurring vocal and kinesic behaviours found in a few selected samples of free play. We anticipate that through such detailed analyses of the infant's actual stimulus world we can arrive at new and different perspectives on the infant's emerging constructions of his world.

This study was largely prompted by the consideration of some fairly commonplace and ubiquitous features of maternal play. One of these simple yet striking features of what a mother actually "does" during a natural play session with her infant is the repetitiveness of her behaviour. This repetitiveness is apparent both in what she says to her infant and in what she does with her face, head and body. Snow (1972), among others, has commented on the use of repetition by mothers to facilitate language acquisition and comprehension in the young child learning to speak. The phenomenon we wish to focus on, however, is somewhat different and more general, namely, that maternal behaviour manifests or utilizes repetition in all modalities: vocal; movements; facial expressions; tactile and kinesthetic stimulation. Furthermore, mothers use repetition at early points in the infant's development (it can be seen in the neonatal nursery) where considerations such as the facilitation of comprehension of a repeated element cannot be at issue. The "instructional" use of repetition may best be considered to be a special use of this more general phenomenon.

A second commonplace feature of maternal behaviours is that they give the impression of being rhythmic, whether or not there are repetitions of a given element. A description of the nature of the particular temporal patterns, which seem to be such a pervasive feature of maternal play, is also a description of the social stimulus world through which the infant must organize much of his internal experience of arousal, attention and affect. It is through the experience with these maternal behaviours that the infant gradually acquires the ability to perceive and discriminate from the ongoing communicative flow those movements and sounds that constitute the emotional and cognitive signs and symbols that allow for full membership in a human community.

This study, in providing a more detailed view of the stimulus world the infant actually inhabits during early social interaction, may further our understanding of how caregiver behaviours attract and hold infant attention under normal conditions with well babies. Such information may be crucial in designing both studies and strategies of intervention for optimizing the social interactive experiences in deviant cases.

Methodology

SUBJECTS AND DATA SELECTION

Two interactions were chosen for this pilot study. Since we were interested in potentially general features of caregiver behaviours, two different adult interactants were chosen. The dyads were: a mother with her 13-week-old daughter and an experimenter with a 14-week-old girl. These interactions were chosen from pre-recorded data. The essential feature of the recording interaction was to interfere as little as possible with the natural interactive flow. Further details of the conditions of data collection are presented elsewhere (Stern, 1974a).

Of the many interactions available those chosen satisfied the following criteria: (1) Each was considered a "good" interaction by our research team—good, meaning generally that the interaction was successful in attempting to get, or hold, the infant's attention and generate some positive affect. (2) Each interaction was considered "normal" in the statistical sense that we have seen many similar interactions. These interactions were in our experience typical rather than extraordinary. (3) The interactions consisted of at least 100 discrete caregiver behaviours. Roughly 100 sequential behaviours was the sample size. This represented interaction durations of 120 and 194 seconds. (4) We wished to have behaviours in different modalities represented. Ninety-two sequential vocalizations of the mother, and 104 sequential non-verbal behaviours (facial expressions and head movements) of the experimenter were chosen for analysis. (The analysis of sequences of tactile and kinesthetic stimuli are currently underway and will not be reported here.) Accordingly, the interactions chosen had to contain relatively uninterrupted sequences of stimulation in the chosen modality. This also necessitated that the T.V. picture or sound track be of sufficiently good quality to allow the analyses chosen. For the non-verbal (visual) interaction with the experimenter a split-screen television technique was used, which combines in one split picture the view from one camera focused on the adult and the view of a second camera focused on the infant.

DATA SCORING

The selected T.V. tapes were converted to 16 mm film for analysis. The films were seen on a projector at normal speed. Two observers watching the films each operated through a push button, the channels of an Esterline Angus event recorder (running at a speed of 12 cm/min). When the non-vocal behaviours were being scored the sound was turned off and when the vocal behaviours were scored the lamp was turned off. Before actual scoring, short sections of the film (from 3 to 10 seconds) were replayed as many as a dozen times in succession until both observers knew the section "by heart". Accordingly, when the actual scoring run was made, each unit scored was anticipated. The experimenter's own auditory and visual perceptions and short term memory were thus an important part of the scoring and coding "instrumentation". Further comment on this procedure will be made below. Operationally speaking, the units recorded were:

(1) *Vocalizations.* During a vocalization that was continuous to the E's ears, the pens of the event recorder were activated. Each continuous vocalization (which consisted of one or many words) was called a vocal phrase, the silence between phrases was called a pause. A phrase and its following pause together make up a phrase period. Appendix 1 lists all the vocal phrases and shows the duration of each phrase and pause. Interrater agreement as to the presence of a vocalization was 100% with a mean error as to the start and stop of the vocalization of less than 0·1 seconds.

(2) *Head movements and facial expressions.* Units of movement are more difficult to code because there is rarely a behavioural "silence" interspersed between an easily recognizable signal. It is here that we relied on the organized perceptual processes of the observers and their lifelong experience with human behaviour. A kinesic "phrase" was a term applied to any facial and/or head movement or constellation of movements that (1) constitutes a burst of behaviour in the sense of being

bounded by relative behavioural "rests" or appreciable decreases in activity and (2) that has the obvious intention to attract, hold or in some way alter the infant's visual attention. A kinesic phrase was considered to span in time the formation of the act and the duration of holding the fixed position (expression, etc.) once achieved. The pauses which follow the kinesic phrases were rarely without some movement, too. However, movements during pauses were perceived to be the work of "undoing" the phrase or repositioning the face or head for the next intentional act or kinesic phrase. The list of kinesic phrases, and the duration of kinesic phrases and pauses is shown in Appendix 2. Interrater agreement as to the presence of a kinesic phrase was 91% with a mean error as to the start of a kinesic phrase of less th~n 0·1 seconds and 0·2 seconds as to its stop.

The following infant behaviours were scored: infant smiling, infant vocalization, and infant gaze at mother. The association between any of these infant behaviours and the vocal or kinesic phrases could thus be determined.

Results

This section describes three structures of progressively larger size within the flow of caregiver behaviours. These are: the *phrase*; the *run*, a string of repeating phrases; and the *episode of maintained engagement*, a longer series of phrases, unusually containing several runs and bounded by shifts in maternal behaviours and often attention. These structures are illustrated in schematic fashion in Fig. 1.

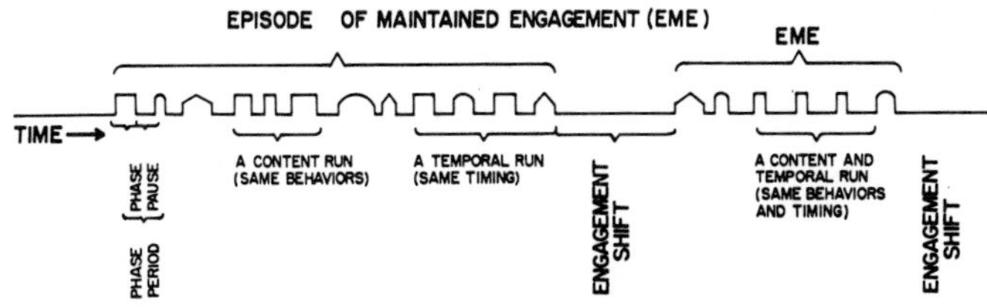

Fig. 1. A schematic representation of different structures within a sequence of caregiver behaviours. The sequence is illustrated as consisting of only three "types" of behaviour, represented here as:

⊓, ∩, ∧.

1. THE VOCAL PHRASE AND THE KINESIC PHRASE: TWO RELATED COMMUNICATIVE UNITS

There is little doubt about considering any continuous vocalization (a vocal phrase) an important communicative act and unit. Also there is general agreement about reliable methods for isolating these units of communication. The kinesic phrase and its pause are more problematical. With an adult speaker, who is also moving, it is difficult to delineate in his movements a communicative unit comparable or analagous to a vocal phrase. This is so because movement almost never stops as does sound, and because kinesic units occupy a different time frame even though they may be related through synchrony with single or multiples of vocal units. In adult communication then, we do not think of vocal and kinesic phrases as similar or equivalent communicative units. In the case of a caregiver interacting with an infant the situation is different, and the kinesic phrase and vocal phrase appear to have many more features in common as communicative units. When in the presence of an infant rather than of another adult, the caregiver produces body movements and facial expressions which unfold in more discrete and shorter bursts with more obvious "rests" in between bursts. Furthermore, these bursts of movement are generally performed with considerable exaggeration of facial display and exaggeration of body or head movement in time and space. These unusual deviations from normal adult–adult communicative and expressive behaviours have previously been labelled "infant elicited variations" (Stern, 1974b). Because of their exaggerated performance, these bursts, or kinesic phrases, are set in relief from other movements and expressions which are not intended to affect the infant socially. Accordingly, because of the more discrete on-and-off bursting pattern and the exaggerated motor performances during these bursts, the kinesic phrase as elicited by the presence of an infant is found to be a readily identifiable communicative unit between caregiver and infant.

The interesting finding is that within a caregiver's behaviour the kinesic phrase and the vocal phrase appear to be comparable communicative acts in several respects. They hold the following features in common, which can be ascertained from Appendices 1 and 2. (1) They occur roughly as frequently in the flow of caregiver behaviour, with overall rates of 43 vocal phrases per minute and 32 kinesic phrases per minute in these samples. (2) They both share the same form with respect to burst and pause, and a roughly similar distribution of time allotted to each, such that the average pause is considerably longer than the average burst. (3) The durations of the phrases and pauses are roughly similar for both kinesic and vocal acts. Kinesic phrases are 0·82 seconds long with a SD of 0·56 seconds. Kinesic pauses are 1·06 seconds long with a SD of 0·59 seconds. Vocal phrases are 0·47 seconds long with a SD of 0·32 seconds. Vocal pauses are 0·91 seconds long with a SD of 0·81 seconds. (4) The relationship of one phrase period to the next by repetition provides an additional striking similarity in structure. This is demonstrated in the following section.

These findings are not a simple "artifact" of "self synchrony" between simultaneously performed vocal and kinesic behaviours as reported by Condon and Ogston (1966). Sixty-three of the experimenter's 104 kinesic phrases had no accompanying vocalization. Similarly, many of the mother's vocal phrases, while necessarily accompanied by lip movements, contained no kinesic phrases as scored. Clearly we are dealing with two related yet different communicative acts which can be performed separately, together, or sometimes alternately. The point is that both constitute similar vehicles for packaging communication units for infants.

2. THE RUN, A SERIES OF REPEATING PHRASES

A. *Vocal Runs: Repeating What She Says*

(i) *Repetition by content (content runs)*. Appendix 1 lists all of the mother's vocal phrases, their duration and the duration of the pauses between vocalizations. Two or more phrases are considered to be part of a repeating "run" of similar content (a content run) if: (1) the word or words that make up the phrases are identical (e.g. phrases 5–8, Appendix 1), or if there is an addition or deletion of only a small part of the phrase (e.g. phrases 1 and 3), or if there is only a change in stress within the phrase (e.g. phrases 9 and 10). In the last two cases where the phrase is not quite identical it is considered part of the content run but called a variation; (2) the repeating phrase must immediately follow the original phrase with the exception that common "time marking" exclamations may intervene, such as "Hey", "Yeah", "Huh" (e.g. phrase 2).

Using these criteria, 64% of all the mother's phrases belong to content runs. Stated differently, only one-third of all her vocalizations are not repeated, or repeats. Within the 92 vocal phrases scored there are 24 content runs with an average of 2·46 phrases per run.

(ii) *Repetition by time ("temporal runs")*. If we disregard the content of the vocal phrase and measure only the duration of the utterance and the duration of the pause following it, we can establish purely temporal criteria for a repeating run, "a temporal run". (Although the rate of phrase period production is fairly regular, i.e. the duration of a phrase plus the duration of its following pause, there remains great latitude as to how much of that time is allotted to the phrase and how much to the pause. Thus the temporal pattern of phrase duration and pause duration can be similar or quite different in successive phrase periods.) Two or more phrase periods can be considered to belong to a repeating temporal run if their temporal patterning are similar enough. We established the following criteria of "similar enough" for successive phrase periods: (1) if the phrase durations were not different by more than 0·3 seconds;* (2) if the pause durations were not different by more than 0·3 seconds; (3) the repeating phrase must immediately follow the original phrase.

Using these criteria 63% of the mother's phrase periods belong to repeating temporal runs. Accordingly, by temporal criteria alone only one-third of her vocal phrases are not part of a repeating temporal sequence. Within the 92 vocal phrases scored there are 20 temporal runs with an average of 2·90 phrases per run.

(iii) *The relationship between vocal content runs and vocal temporal runs*. An examination of Appendix 1 reveals that a repeating content run need not also be a repeating temporal run and vice versa. Forty-three per cent of all phrase periods simultaneously fulfil both content and temporal criteria of a run. This concordance is not greater than that expected by chance; however, content runs and temporal runs tend to share the same boundaries.

In other words, almost one-half of what the baby hears is part of a repeating sequence in which both content and timing of the vocalizations and pauses are immediately repeated.

B. *Kinesic Runs: Repeating What She Does*

In Section A above we were considering what the mother said. This

* The choice of 0·3 seconds was influenced by known reaction time values, but is otherwise to be considered only a first approach pending further information about infant's perceptual capabilities.

involved vocal phrases and their organization into content and temporal runs. In this section we are considering the movements she makes. This involves kinesic phrases and their organization into content and temporal runs.

(i) *Repetition by content (content runs).* Appendix 2 describes all of the experimenter's movements (kinesic phrases), their duration and the duration of their following pauses. Similarity of "content" between one phrase and another appears more difficult to establish for movement than for words. However, after considerable training experience, two observers achieved a 90% agreement as to whether two kinesic phrases were identical, one a variation of the other, or each belonging to a different category. This was almost identical to the 93% agreement achieved in making the same classification of vocal phrases.

Two or more successive kinesic phrases were considered to be part of a content run if the separate facial, head and body movements that make up the phrases are identical or only slightly altered so that they are clearly related variations.

Using these criteria 70% of all the experimenter's kinesic phrases belong to content runs. Within the 104 kinesic phrases scored there are 25 content runs with an average of 2·92 phrases per run.

Thus, similar to the situation that prevails with vocal behaviours, only about one-third of the non-vocal behaviours the infant is exposed to are not repeated or repeats.

(ii) *Repetition by timing (temporal runs).* If we disregard what the experimenter did, i.e. the form of the movements she made, and measure only the duration of the movements and the duration of the following pause, we can establish purely temporal criteria for a repeating run. Using the same temporal criteria as described above for vocal phrases, 54% of all her kinesic phrase periods belong to repeating temporal runs. Within the 104 kinesic phrases scored there are 21 temporal runs with an average of 2·67 phrases per run.

(iii) *The relationship between kinesic content runs and kinesic temporal runs.* An examination of Appendix 2 reveals that a repeating content run need not be a repeating temporal run and vice versa. Forty-one per cent of all kinesic phrase periods fulfil both content and temporal criteria of a run. As with vocal phrase periods, this concordance is not greater than that expected by chance; however, here too, content runs and temporal runs tend to share the same boundaries.

In summary, almost one-half of what the baby sees (as well as hears) is part of a repeating sequence in which both the nature and timing of movements is immediately repeated.

Forty-one of the 104 kinesic phrases were accompanied by some vocalization (more often a non-word sound). The incidence of content or temporal runs was unaffected by the presence or absence of a vocalization associated with the movements.

C. *The Effect of Content Runs on Infant Smiling*

By comparing all the kinesic phrases during which the infant smiles and all the kinesic phrases which formed content runs, we determined that infant smiling was more likely to occur during the content runs. Smiling occurred during 35 of the 73 phrases that comprised content runs, and only during 7 of the 31 phrases that were not part of content runs. (Chi-square $= 4{\cdot}9$, $p < 0{\cdot}05$.) The likelihood of smiling during temporal runs was not greater, nor was the combination of simultaneous temporal and content runs more associated with smiling than content runs alone. These results, however, do not indicate whether the infant smiled more in response to content repetitions, or whether the experimenter was more likely to repeat her behaviour given the presence of an infant smile.

A comparison between the relationship of kinesic runs and infant smiling with that between vocal runs and infant smiling could not be made because of the much lower incidence of infant smiling during the selected sample of vocal phrases.

3. AN EPISODE OF MAINTAINED ENGAGEMENT

The episode of maintained engagement (EME) is the next largest structural unit. This term was chosen to imply a period of time during which both a fairly constant level of visual attention and a fairly constant rate of production of behavioural acts is sustained. It refers solely to the mother or caregiver, not the dyad nor the infant. "Engagement" was chosen as a somewhat more global term to encompass and denote the simultaneous status of maternal attention and behavioural activity. The EME is characterized by the following features, many of which are illustrated in Fig. 1 in a schematic fashion:

1. It is a definable sequence of vocal and/or kinesic phrase periods of variable length. The shortest in these samples contains six phrase

periods and the longest 34. The EME thus generally contains several or many runs.

2. The sequence of phrase periods constituting an EME has recognizable boundaries labelled "engagement shifts" in Fig. 1. Shifts can consist of: (a) an obvious change in the rate of performance of behaviours. This can occur in several ways. There can be a marked decrease in the rate, consisting of a relative behavioural "silence" (longer in duration than any of the pauses within the sequence of phrase periods that make up the EME). This relative cessation in activity gives the impression of a "time out". However, the caregiver's level or direction of visual attention toward the infant need not change during the "time out". Conversely there may be a sudden increase in the rate of performance of maternal behaviours (see 4 below). At the point that the infant looks away or toward the mother she will often change her rate without an intervening pause. (When a mother is trying to get an infant's visual attention, at the moment she does, there is no apparent consistent tendency for her to increase rather than decrease her rate of behaviour.) (b) An interruption in the ongoing level of attention towards the infant. Generally, this simply involves the caregiver looking away from the infant and refocusing her attention elsewhere. Shifts in visual attention from the infant's face to other body parts may also constitute such an interruption. In either case there need not be a change in the level of maternal behavioural activity. However, the direction or focus of her acts will be altered. (c) A change in attentional focus and behavioural activity together. A common example is when the caregiver simply sits back in her chair for a moment, quietly, often looking elsewhere, and waiting before re-engaging her attention at the previous or a different level and re-initiating a new sequence of phrases, i.e. starting the next EME. The actual duration of these engagement shifts between EMEs is shown in Fig. 2 which plots the cumulative recorded phrase periods against time.

3. The first maternal behaviours of the EME usually contain some elements of an exaggerated orienting response or greeting behaviour. The most characteristic of these behaviours is the "mock surprise face" which consists of: head up; mouth open; eyebrows raised; eyes widened. The "fish mouth face" has the same elements with the substitution of pursing the lips and opening and closing them "like a fish", instead of the open mouth of the "mock surprise face". Similarly at the onset of an EME the infant often engages in a series of orienting facial and head

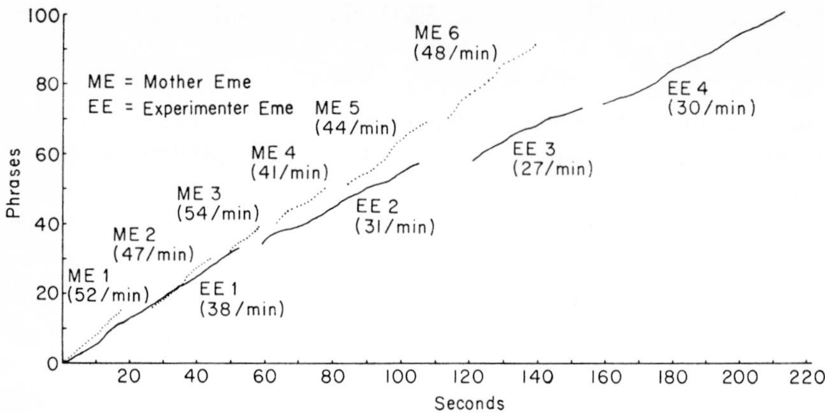

Fig. 2. Cumulative phrases (vocal for the mother and kinesic for the experimenter) plotted against cumulative time.

behaviours. Tronick *et al.* (1975) have described these infant behaviours as being specifically elicited by the expectation of a social interaction with a human adult.

4. During an episode of maintained engagement the caregiver produces phrase periods (kinesic or vocal) at a fairly regular rate. Each EME has its own tempo which is defined as phrase periods per minute. The regularity of the tempo is a function of the variability in the duration of the phrase periods. Figure 2 plots the rates and their regularity during each EME. The slope of the curve indicates the behavioural rate or tempo. The most striking feature of these curves is the regularity of tempo during each EME. In order to satisfy ourselves that EMEs did not consist of runs of rapid tempo, alternating or mixed in some fashion with runs of slower tempo, the Wald-Wolfowitz Runs test was utilized. The runs test was modified to treat all phrase periods shorter in duration than the median phrase period as one population, and all phrase periods longer than the median as the other population. No significant runs were discovered within any EME. This indicates that the mother is emitting phrase periods at a fixed tempo with only random fluctuation around that tempo. The regularity of tempo came as a surprise to us, perhaps in part because a mother can and does alter the degree of stress, or vigour, or amplitude of movements and sounds from moment to moment, thus giving the impression of constant change in the flow while not significantly altering the basic tempo.

Each caregiver can alter the tempo from one EME to the next and probably has a wide range of characteristic tempos. It is interesting to speculate whether there are characteristic ranges of tempos for individuals, or cultures, or infant ages, and what may be the developmental consequences of such differences. The important point is that, for a given dyad, once a tempo is established for a particular EME it is maintained. Accordingly, during each EME the infant is experiencing a sufficiently predictable stimulus world that he can form expectancies.

The finding of a relatively regular rate of behaving during EMEs applies to vocal as well as non-vocal behaviours, as demonstrated in Fig. 2, which plots the cumulative record of only vocal phrase periods for the mother and only kinesic phrase periods for the experimenter. Forty per cent of the experimenter's kinesic phrases were accompanied by a vocalization of some kind. The "addition" of sound to these movements did not alter the tempo. Whether speaking or just moving the caregiver provides the infant with discrete bursts of human behaviour that come at roughly regular intervals.

Discussion

Caregivers provide a highly ordered stimulus world for infants, one in which the separate stimulus events are the different human expressive and communicative acts. These acts are formed largely by different vocalizations, face presentations, expressions and gaze. The description and analyses of the temporal sequence of these behaviours has isolated three different structural units: (1) The phrase, a burst of behaviour intended to communicate at least in the sense of affecting attention. The important finding concerning this unit is the identification in caregiver behaviour of the kinesic phrase as a structurally and temporally comparable unit to the well recognized and studied vocal phrase. (2) The run, formed by repeating exactly or very closely the form and/or content of the preceding vocal or kinesic phrases. (3) The episode of maintained engagement, a larger sequence of phrase periods, usually containing several runs, during which the attentional focus on the infant is unchanged and a tempo of phrase performance is maintained.

We shall speculate on what may be some of the implications of a stimulus world that is organized in this particular fashion.

Two of the structural units, the EME and the run, may be functional units in the regulation of the interaction. During play interactions the main goal for the mother and infant is to interest and delight one another, i.e. to maintain some optimal range of attention and arousal which is affectively positive (Stern, 1974b). Such a process involves the constant mutual regulation of behaviour. On the mother's side this requires the frequent changing of modalities, of tempo, of intensity, of "strategies", so that over-shooting or under-shooting of the optimal range can be goal-corrected. The entire play session is made up of EMEs during which the caregiver has a focused engagement with the infant separated by shifts in engagement, many of which function like time-out intervals, during which there is either a relative cessation of caregiver behaviour and/or a refocusing of attention away from the infant. After the time-out interval the caregiver re-establishes a level of attention toward the infant and initiates the next EME. The EME and its time-out interval appear to function as gross re-tuning units in the regulation of the interaction. During the interval, in between EMEs, the interpersonal situation can be reassessed (almost always out of awareness), that is, the interactive trend with regard to levels and direction of attention, excitement and affect can be evaluated, and on the basis of this information new immediate goal-correcting strategies are formulated and then tried during the next EME, and so on. Each EME thus offers the opportunity of "resetting" the interaction on a different course. It is important to note that the time-out intervals between EMEs are also potentially important re-tuning or re-setting moments. Very often the caregiver uses these relative cessations in the interaction to "cool down" or resettle the interaction.

Compared to these fairly gross "tuning" units the run represents a fine tuning unit to readjust the ongoing levels of arousal and/or affect. Since the run consists of successive presentation of the same or only a slightly varied stimulus, it is ideally suited to create expectancies and then to satisfy or mildly violate them. We know that levels of attention, arousal and direction and level of affect are differentially influenced by stimulus redundancy and by the degree of stimulus-schema mismatch (Berlyne, 1960; Sokolov, 1960; Kagan and Lewis, 1965). The "run" is something like an extraordinarily richly and subtly designed series of experimental stimuli consisting of many variable elements, each of which can be slightly varied at each successive presentation so as to re-correct the ongoing interaction.

The notion that the EME and the run are functional units in the regulation of the interaction as well as structural units is readily observable and testable. The discovery that infant smiling occurred significantly more frequently during the performance of kinesic content runs by the experimenter lends support to the idea of a functional role for the run.

Caregivers provide vocal and kinesic acts in sequences which have an established, though loose, tempo. Much of human behaviour has this characteristic of unfolding at rates which fluctuate, but only within certain limits around a predictable tempo. We have the impression, though undocumented at present, that adults generally establish more regular behavioural tempos when interacting with infants as compared to other adults. In any event, an important aspect of the infant's stimulus world is the temporal patterning of that world. This applies to human behaviours as well as to all other stimulus events. It is probable that the range of rates of caregivers' behaviours and the extent of momentary fluctuations in rate are well suited to the infant's temporal perceiving and processing structures. Our knowledge of an infant's attentional and cognitive processes would predict that a generally regular temporal process with limited but almost constant variability would be better suited for attracting and holding infant attention than a precisely fixed, completely redundant process or a completely unpredictable process. We would expect that biologically important human events such as attempts to communicate and establish affectional bonds would be patterned in time so as to be well matched to the infant's innate response biases. We now accept that the genetic design of the human face is such that its visual stimulus characteristics closely match the evolved innate visual preferences of the human infant (Freedman, 1964; Haaf and Bell, 1967). We are here expanding this concept to include the temporal patterning of human social behaviours.

A further study of the temporal patterns of "effective" caregiver behaviours may provide important clues and directions of approach for the design of future experiments to explore the infant's perceptual and cognitive processes especially as they relate to time. Let us take an example. The mean duration of the mother's vocal phrases is 0·47 seconds and 0·91 seconds for her vocal pauses. The mean duration of the experimenter's kinesic pauses is 0·82 seconds and 1·06 seconds for her kinesic pauses. Similar values for adults engaged in verbal dialogue as reported by Jaffe and Feldstein (1970) are: mean phrase duration,

1·42 seconds; mean pause duration, 0·60 seconds. Comparing these adult values, from 576 thirty-minute long dialogues with our admittedly very small sample of caregiver values, it is interesting that the caregivers provide the infant with phrases that are only about one half as long as they would provide for an adult—and they separate these phrases with pauses that are almost twice as long as those given an adult. The total duration of phrase plus pause, i.e. the duration of the phrase period, is less different for adults compared to infants than is the distribution of time into phrase and pause. In other words, caregivers act as if the infant can take in smaller chunks of information and needs more time to process them before receiving the next. These comparisons may roughly reflect the developmental course of capabilities in several important psychic operations. The temporal world of human behaviours is certainly a different one for infants than for adults. A closer examination of the ontogeny of this world may prove fruitful.

The fact that vocal phrases (auditory stimuli) and kinesic phrases (visual stimuli) share similar temporal structures supports the notion that the timing of these events is an important general feature which transcends the modality of stimulation. Condon and Ogston's (1966) finding of "self synchrony" between movement and vocalization suggest that it could not be otherwise. The likelihood that caregiver stimulus events in all modalities share the same temporal pattern sheds a different light on the ready substitutability of stimulation in one modality for that in another. In this regard, the modality of stimulation may prove to be a less crucial feature of human behaviour for an infant than the temporal patterning of that stimulation. This point bears on the interpretations given to many studies that draw conclusions from data related to only one stimulus modality.

Another speculation concerning the particular organization of behaviours provided by caregivers relates to the "run", which can be created in any modality. A central feature of the run is that it consists of a stimulus presentation immediately followed by a re-presentation of the stimulus, unchanged or slightly altered. The general form can be conceptualized as statement and re-statement of a theme with or without variations. Over one half of the content runs, both vocal and kinesic, involved variations. This form of theme and variation, as created by caregivers, is ideally suited to set in motion that central tendency of the infant's mental life, namely the active process of hypothesis formation and hypothesis testing (Bruner, Chapter 11).

The activation of this mental process in the infant will enhance his acquisition of schemata of different human expressive and communicative acts. Since each act is likely to be re-presented in a varied form, the infant can accommodate more members of a single class of human events. The caregiver thus, in trying to care for and engage the infant, creates themes and variations of sound and movement which the infant's mental processes will gradually re-transpose into classes of human acts of caring and engaging.

Acknowledgements

The research has been supported by The Jane Hilder Harris Foundation and The Grant Foundation.

References

Berlyne, D. E. (1960). *Conflict, Arousal and Curiosity.* McGraw-Hill, New York.

Bowlby, J. (1969). *Attachment and Loss,* Vol. I. Basic Books, New York.

Condon, W. S. and Ogston, W. D. (1966). Sound film analysis of normal and pathological behavior patterns. *J. nerv. ment. Dis.* **143**, 338–347.

Emde, R. N. and Harmon, R. J. (1972). Endogenous and exogenous smiling systems in early infancy. *J. Am. Acad. Child Psychiat.* **II**, 177–200.

Freedman, D. (1964). Smiling in blind infants and the issue of innate vs. acquired. *J. Child Psychol. Psychiat.* **5**, 171–184.

Haaf, R. A. and Bell, R. Q. (1967). A facial dimension in visual discrimination by human infants. *Child Dev.* **38**, 893–899.

Jaffe, J. and Feldstein, S. (1970). *Rhythms of Dialogue.* Academic Press, New York and London.

Kagan, J. (1967). The growth of the face schema: Theoretical significance and methodological issues. In J. Hellmuth (Ed.), *The Exceptional Infant.* Vol. I, 335–348. Special Child Publications, Seattle.

Kagan, J. and Lewis, M. (1965). Studies on attention in the human infant. *Merrill-Palmer Q.* **II**, 95–127.

Rheingold, H. L. (1961). The effect of environmental stimulation upon social and exploratory behaviour in the human infant. In B. M. Foss (Ed.), *Determinants of Infant Behaviour* Vol. I, 143–177. Wiley, New York.

Rheingold, H. L., Gewirtz, J. L. and Ross, H. W. (1959). Social conditioning of vocalizations in the infant. *J. comp. physiol. Psychol.* **52**, 68–73.

Snow, C. (1972). Mother's speech to children learning language. *Child Dev.* **43**, 549–565.

Sokolov, E. N. (1960). *Perception and the Conditioned Reflex*. Macmillan, New York.
Spitz, R. A. (1965). *The First Year of Life*. International Universities Press, New York.
Spitz, R. and Wolf, K. (1946). The smiling response. *Genet. Psychol. Monogr.* **34**, 57–125.
Stern, D. N. (1974a). Mother and Infant at Play. In M. Lewis and L. Rosenblum (Eds), *The Origins of Behaviour*, Vol. I, 187–213. Wiley, New York.
Stern, D. N. (1974b). The goal and structure of mother-infant play. *J. Am. Acad. Child Psychiat.* **13**, 402–421.
Tronick, E., Adamson, L., Wise, S., Als, H. and Brazelton, T. B. (1975). The infant's response to entrapment between contradictory messages in face to face interaction. Presented at the Soc. Res. Child Dev. Biennial Meeting, Denver, April, 1975.

Appendix 1

A record of the content and timing of mother's vocalizations as they appeared in sequence, and the designation of her vocal phrases into two types of repeating runs.

* Italicized words are the stressed words of the phrase.
† The addition of a letter indicates that the content is considered a variation of the original phrase.

Episode No.	Phrase No.	Vocal phrase content	Phrase duration (seconds)	Pause duration (seconds)	Designated runs: Content runs	Designated runs: Temporal runs
1	1	Look at all those *colours** huh	0·7	1·1	1	
	2	*Yeah*	0·1	0·3		
	3	Look at all those *colours*	0·9	0·7	1a†	
	4	*Hey*	0·1	0·9		1
	5	*Cheryl*	0·4	1·0	2	1
	6	*Cheryl*	0·3	1·1	2	1
	7	*Cheryl*	0·3	1·1	2	1
	8	*Cheryl*	0·4	0·8	2	1
	9	Who's this	0·3	0·7	3	1
	10	Who's this	0·3	0·4	3a	1
	11	Hi *Dorothy*	0·3	0·8	4	
	12	Hi Dorothy	0·4	0·3	4a	
	13	Say *hi*	0·3	1·1	5	
	14	*Hi*	0·3	0·7	5a	2
	15	*Hey*	0·2	0·9	6	2
	16	*Hey*	0·2	—	6	2

(*cont.*)

Episode No.	Phrase No.	Vocal phrase content	Phrase duration (seconds)	Pause duration (seconds)	Designated runs Content runs	Designated runs Temporal runs
		Interruption of 8·7 sec				
2	17	*Yeah* Dorothy's looking for attention	1·0	1·0	7	3
	18	*Yeah* Dorothy's looking for attention	1·3	1·0	7a	3
	19	*Yeah*	0·3	0·5		4
	20	That's what he wants	0·5	0·8	8	4
	21	*That's* what he wants	0·6	0·6	8a	4
	22	*Yeah*	0·2	0·6		5
	23	*Huh*	0·2	0·9		5
	24	Say	0·1	0·3		
	25	Wait till I get over	0·7	0·5		6
	26	I'm going to pull *all* that hair	0·8	0·6	9	6
	27	*Yeah*	0·2	0·4		
	28	I'm going to pull *all* that hair	0·1	1·3	9	
	29	And then you're gonna *run* from me	1·0	0·5		
	30	*Yeah*	0·2	0·8		
	31	*Huh*	0·2			
		Interruption of 4·9 sec				
3	32	*Ooh*	0·2	0·6		7
	33	Look	0·2	0·6	10	7
	34	*Look*	0·2	0·6	10a	7
	35	Ooh look at all those *fingers*	1·1	0·4	11	8
	36	Look at all those *fingers*	1·3	0·6	11a	8
	37	Look up *here*	0·5	0·9	12	
	38	Look up *here*	0·6	0·4	12	
	39	*Hey*	0·2	0·5		
	40	Click, click, click, click, click, click, click	1·2	—		
		Interruption of 4·2 sec				
4	41	*Where* are you going	0·4	0·7	13	
	42	*Where* are you going	0·7	0·2	13	
	43	Huh	0·1	0·8		
	44	Where are you *going*	0·5	0·9	13a	
	45	Hey	0·2	3·0		

(*cont.*)

Episode No.	Phrase No.	Vocal phrase content	Phrase duration (seconds)	Pause duration (seconds)	Designated runs Content runs	Temporal runs
	46	Say *hi* doggie	0·7	1·2	14	
	47	Say *hi* doggie	0·7	0·5	14	9
	48	*Look* at doggie	0·5	0·7	14a	9
	49	Say *hi* to doggie	0·6	0·6	14b	9
	50	Say *hi* to doggie	0·5	1·0	14b	
	51	(Clap hands × 5)	1·2	—		
		Interruption of 5·0 sec				
	52	Get *up*	0·3	1·2	15	10
	53	Get *up*	0·3	1·2	15	10
	54	Get *up*	0·3	1·4	15	10
	55	Get *up* in that chair	0·8	1·5	15a	
	56	Get *up* in that chair	0·8	0·7	15a	
	57	*Yeah*	0·2	0·5		
	58	I thought you were *faking* it	1·2	0·6		
	59	*Yeah*	0·2	0·3		11
	60	*That's* right	0·4	0·3		11
	61	*Shake* your head yes	0·6	0·3		11
	62	*Yeah*	0·2	0·2	16	12
	63	Yeah	0·2	0·5	16a	12
	64	da (inaudible)	0·1	1·7		12
	65	*Hi*	3·0	0·8		
	66	*Hi* honey	0·7	0·7	17	
	67	*Hi* honey	0·6	1·1	17	13
	68	*Ooh*	0·5	0·9		13
	69	Ya gonna *ooh*	1·0	1·9	18	
	70	Ya gonna *smile*	0·6	—	18a	
		Interruption of 4·7 sec				
6	71	*Hi*	0·2	0·5		14
	72	*Yeah*	0·2	0·5		14
	73	*That's* it	0·3	0·4		14
	74	*Come* on	0·3	0·3	19	14
	75	*Talk* to me	0·4	0·6		14
	76	*Come* on	0·3	1·0	19	15
	77	*Come* on	0·3	0·9	19	15
	78	*Come* on	0·3	1·2	19	15
	79	*Come* on	0·3	1·3	19	15
	80	Look at those *eyebrows*	0·8	1·0	20	16
	81	Look at those eyebrows	0·7	0·8	20	16

(*cont.*)

Episode No.	Phrase No.	Vocal phrase content	Phrase duration (seconds)	Pause duration (seconds)	Disignated runs Content runs	Temporal runs
	82	Your *head*	0·4	0·2		17
	83	is going *round*	0·3	0·5	21	17
	84	and *round*	0·3	0·5	21a	17
	85	and *round*	0·2	0·3	21a	17
	86	and bobbing *up* and *down*	1·0	0·9	22	
	87	and *up* and *down*	0·9	1·8	22a	18
	88	all *all around*	1·2	1·5		18
	89	*Yeah*	0·3	0·9		19
	90	*That's* what it's doing	0·7	0·8		19
	91	*Yeah*	0·2	0·8	23	20
	92	*Yeah*	0·2	—	23	20

Appendix 2

A record of the description and timing of the experimenter's movements as they appeared in sequence, and the designation of kinesic phrases into two types of repeating runs.

* H = Head.
† F = Face.
‡ E = Expressions.
§ "Mock surprise", described in text.
¶ The addition of a letter indicates that the content is considered a variation of the original phrase.
|| "Fish mouth", described in text.

Episode No.	Phrase No.	Kinesic phrase "content" (description of movements)	Phrase duration (seconds)	Pause duration (seconds)	Designated runs Content runs	Temporal runs
1	1	H* forward, F† present left side, E‡ "mock surprise"§	2·1	0·6		
	2	H up and down	0·4	0·4	1	
	3	H up and down	0·7	2·1	1	
	4	H forward, F present left side, E smile	1·0	0·2	2	
	5	H forward, F present right side, E smile	0·8	1·7	2a¶	

(*cont.*)

Episode No.	Phrase No.	Kinesic phrase "content" (description of movements)	Phrase duration (seconds)	Pause duration (seconds)	Designated runs Content runs	Temporal runs
	6	H forward and wiggle side to side, E "kiss mouth"	1·0	0·5		
	7	H up, E kiss air	0·2	0·3	3	1
	8	H up, E kiss air	0·4	0·4	3	1
	9	H up, E kiss air	0·3	0·6	3	1
	10	H up, E kiss air	0·3	1·0	3	
	11	H forward, E "fish mouth"‖	0·8	0·9	4	2
	12	H forward and wiggle side to side, E "fish mouth"	0·8	0·8	4a	2
	13	H "fish mouth", wiggle side to side, E "fish mouth"	1·0	1·1	4a	2
	14	H up and down	0·6	1·0		
	15	H nod	0·8	1·4	5	3
	16	H nod	0·5	1·1	5	3
	17	H forward, F present left side	0·4	0·9		3
	18	H up, E "mock surprise"	0·7	1·1		3
	19	H forward and down, E purse lips and "mock surprise", finger on belly	0·3	1·0		4
	20	finger poke belly (emphasis)	0·3	0·9		4
	21	H up, E "mock surprise" and kiss air	1·5	0·8		
	22	H forward, E "mock surprise and purse mouth	0·4	1·1	6	5
	23	H tilt left, E "mock surprise" and purse mouth	0·6	1·2	6a	5
	24	H tilt right, E "mock surprise" and purse mouth	1·2	0·9	6a	
	25	H forward, E "mock surprise" and purse mouth	1·2	0·3	6b	6

(*cont.*)

Episode No.	Phrase No.	Kinesic phrase "content" (description of movements)	Phrase duration (seconds)	Pause duration (seconds)	Designated runs: Content runs	Designated runs: Temporal runs
	26	H back, F tuck chin in	0·9	0·5		6
	27	H forward	0·8	0·5	7	6
	28	H forward	0·7	0·5	7	6
	29	H forward	0·7	0·8	7	6
	30	H tilt left, F present right side	0·7	0·6		6
	31	H forward, E frown and grimace	0·9	0·8		6
	32	H forward, E kiss air	0·7	0·6	8	6
	33	H forward, and wiggle, E kiss air	0·8	1·1	8a	
	34	H forward, and wiggle, E kiss air	0·8	—	8a	
		Interruption of 6·0 sec				
2	35	H forward, F present right side	0·7	0·4	9	7
	36	H forward, F present left side	0·5	0·4	9a	7
	37	H up	0·4	0·9		
	38	H circle down, forward fast—back, up slow, E purse mouth	1·7	2·5	10	8
	39	H circle down, forward fast—back, up slow, E purse mouth	1·8	2·7	10	8
	40	H short up, E eyebrows raised, mouth?	0·2	1·2	11	
	41	H short up, E eyebrows raised, mouth?	0·3	1·8	11	
	42	H forward, F present left side	0·5	1·2		9
	43	Eyebrow flash	0·3	1·4		9
	44	H foıward, F present right side	0·3	0·6		
	45	H forward, E eyebrow flash, and mouth open	0·3	2·1		
	46	H up and back, E "mock surprise"	0·2	0·6	12	
	47	H up and back, E "mock surprise"	0·2	1·6	12	

(cont.)

Episode No.	Phrase No.	Kinesic phrase "content" (description of movements)	Phrase duration (seconds)	Pause duration (seconds)	Designated runs Content runs	Temporal runs
	48	H forward, wiggle side to side, E purse mouth	1·2	1·0	13	10
	49	H jerk forward, E purse mouth	0·9	1·0	13a	10
	50	H forward and down, E purse mouth	1·1	0·8	13b	10
	51	H forward and down, E purse mouth	1·0	1·4	13b	
	52	H forward and down, E purse mouth	1·6	2·4	13b	
	53	H forward, E "fish mouth" and frown	0·6	0·6	14	
	54	H forward, E "fish mouth" and frown	0·5	1·1	14	
	55	H forward and to side, E "fish mouth" and frown	0·6	0·7	14a	
	56	H forward and to side, E "fish mouth" and frown	0·7	1·2	14a	
	57	H up, E kiss air	0·2	2·3		
	58	E smile	1·2	—		
		Interruption of 15·0 sec				
3	59	H forward, E "fish mouth"	0·6	0·9		
	60	H up and back, E "mock surprise"	0·5	0·5		
	61	H nod	1·0	0·7	15	11
	62	H nod	0·9	0·8	15	11
	63	H nod	1·3	1·3	15	
	64	H rapid forward, E mouth open	0·4	0·8	16	12
	65	H rapid forward, E mouth open	0·4	0·8	16	12
	66	H rapid forward	0·7	1·3	16	
	67	H back to side, E mouth mouth open	0·8	1·8	17	
	68	H forward to side, E mouth open	0·6	2·9	17a	

(*cont.*)

Episode No.	Phrase No.	Kinesic phrase "content" (description of movements)	Phrase duration (seconds)	Pause duration (seconds)	Designated runs Content runs	Temporal runs
	69	H forward, E eyebrow raise and "fish mouth"	1·5	0·9	18	
	70	H forward and wiggle, E eyebrow raise and "fish mouth"	1·0	0·3	18a	
	71	H forward and wiggle, E eyebrow raise and "fish mouth"	3·5	1·2	18a	
	72	E smile	1·8	1·3		13
	73	H up, E mouth open	1·5	1·5		13
	74	E mouth open	0·5	—		
		Interruption of 5·3 seconds during which E is sitting back, waiting, and is behaviourally silent with the exception of licking lips once (behaviour No. 75 lasting 0·4 seconds).				
4	76	H far forward close to I's face, E "O" mouth	0·8	1·7	19	14
	77	H far forward close to I's face, E "O" mouth	1·0	2·0	19	14
	78	H slow forward, finger "walk" on I's belly	3·6	0·5		
	79	H back, finger "walk" on I's belly	0·2	1·1		
	80	H forward	0·6	1·6	20	15
	81	H forward and wiggle side to side	0·9	1·3	20a	15
	82	H down then up, E mouth open ("Hello")	0·4	1·0	21	16
	83	H down then up, E mouth open	0·4	0·7	21	16
	84	H down then up, E mouth open	0·5	0·7	21	16
	85	H down then up, E mouth open	0·8	0·8	21	16
	86	H down then up, E mouth open	0·9	1·3	21	17
	87	H down then up, E mouth open	1·0	1·3	21	17
	88	H down then up, E mouth open	1·2	0·8	21	

(*cont.*)

Episode No.	Phrase No.	Kinesic phrase "content" (description of movemedts)	Phrase duration (seconds)	Pause duration (seconds)	Designated runs Content runs	Temporal runs
	89	H down then up, E mouth open	0·7	2·7	21	
	90	H turn to side, short gaze aversion	0·3	0·9		
	91	E smile	0·9	1·6		
	92	Lick lips	0·4	0·3		
	93	H forward, F present left side, E "mock surprise"	0·8	1·0	22	18
	94	H forward, F present left side, E "mock surprise"	0·9	0·7	22	18
	95	H forward, F present right side, E "mock surprise"	0·9	0·7	22a	18
	96	H forward, E broad smile	1·3	1·4		
	97	H forward, E "fish mouth"	0·7	0·8	23	
	98	H forward and wiggle side to side, E "fish mouth"	1·7	1·1	23a	
	99	H forward and wiggle side to side, E "fish mouth"	1·3	1·2	23a	
	100	H up and back, E "mock surprise"	0·3	1·0	24	19
	101	H up and back, E "mock surprise"	0·4	1·3	24	19
	102	H up and back, E mouth purse	1·1	0·7	25	20
	103	H up and back, E mouth purse	1·3	0·7	25	20
	104	H turn side, gaze avert	0·7	—		

9 | Imitative Interaction

Susan J. Pawlby

Introduction

The phenomenon of imitation has been raised as a topic for discussion intermittently over a long period. Its existence and indeed its importance are rarely denied. Most studies of imitation, however, have, in our view, been limited in that their approach has been one which relies upon measuring the effectiveness of standard test situations in eliciting imitative responses from the child (Gardner and Gardner, 1970; Uzgiris, 1972; Fafouti, 1973; Maratos, 1973). We regard this approach as complementary to our own but useful only in that it tells us what a child *can* do, given special conditions, and not under what circumstances imitative acts normally occur. Our interest lies in observing interpersonal imitative activity as it occurs between a mother and her young infant. Natural and relatively spontaneous interaction episodes were thus chosen in an attempt to observe this activity.

Our study of imitative activity is set within a general approach to the systematic description of mother–infant interaction (Newson, 1974; Newson and Shotter, 1974; Newson and Pawlby, 1975; Pawlby and Jones, 1975; Newson and Newson, 1976). We have suggested that from a very early age mothers and infants can co-ordinate their activity in ways which are reciprocally adjusted, the acts of each individual being contingently geared to those of the other partner. Both partners actively and significantly influence one another, and there is a natural pattern of alternation such that the interaction can best be described as a kind of "conversation". One partner emits an act which, by virtue of being responded to by the other partner, takes on the characteristics of a "communication gesture". It is thus basic to our general approach to mother–infant interaction that we conceptualize it as an alternating sequence of communication gestures (Newson, 1974).

Imitative sequences, it is suggested, are one form of communication sequence in which one of the two partners (mother or infant) reproduces the same act as that previously emitted by the other partner, provided that the two acts can be observed as having a direct relationship with one another—i.e. that the reproduction is observed to be dependent upon the production of the initial act. An imitative sequence, thus, by definition, involves in its simplest form the production of an act by one partner and the reproduction of it by the second partner. These two acts are communication gestures and constitute a link in the alternating chain of gestures. However, as we shall hope to show, imitative sequences are not necessarily limited to a single exchange but can be made up of several such exchanges and continue until the attention of both partners is no longer on the activity in question. The focal point of the present study was thus to examine imitative sequences within this general framework of communication.

Our aim was to observe the frequency with which imitative sequences occurred within a natural interaction setting, the kinds of activities which were imitated in the sequences, the turn-taking nature of the sequences, and also the acts characteristic of communication sequences between a mother and her infant which might accompany imitative sequences, such as reciprocal attention-paying, or referential looking, or a climax of excitement exhibited when the communication sequence was in full flow.

Methodology

SUBJECTS

Eight mothers volunteered, in response to an advertisement in the local newspaper, to take part in the study with their infants. All the infants were 17 weeks old at the beginning of the study and came to the laboratory for weekly sessions until they were 43 weeks old. Five of the infants were boys, three were girls. They varied as to family position, five being first born, one second, one third and one fourth born. They were predominantly middle class with one clear exception being working class.

PROCEDURE

All the mothers were initially visited in their homes and told a little about the study. They were told that we were interested in how mothers and their infants played together and in how they communicated with one another. *However, no mention was made of our interest in imitation.* All eight volunteers were asked to bring their infants to the laboratory at weekly intervals over a period of 26 weeks. Time was spent each week in making the mothers and infants feel at ease before the observation period began. The observation session took place in a room 2·4 m × 3·6 m (8×12 feet). The room was made to look as welcoming as possible without having too many distracting features in it. On one wall was a mirror. The infant was seated in a baby chair with his back to this mirror. His mother was seated at his right hand side at a distance of about 45 cm (18 inches), facing both him and the mirror. Thus positioned the image of her face in the mirror could be seen through the camera at the same time as the infant.

The only piece of technical equipment inside the room was the camera. This was placed at the end of the room opposite mother and infant. The video-recorder and monitor were operated from outside the room. Mother and infant were left alone to play together as they wished, except that the mother was asked not to lift the infant out of the chair unless he was very fretful, in which case the recording would cease. In practice, this was never in fact necessary.

Two toys were available for the mother and infant to use in their play if they wished, though each mother was told that we were just as interested in how they played together with toys as without. All mothers spent some time in interaction with their infant without and some time with toys during each session. The actual toys used were changed every four weeks to give some variety. The choice of toys was made on the basis of the infant's age and also with the aim of providing two different types of toy, e.g. one noise producing and one aesthetically appealing.

During the time mother and infant were playing a consecutive ten-minute recording was made of their play. A digital clock showing units down to 0·1 seconds was superimposed on the video-tape recordings. Ten-minute recordings were made in this way of all eight mother–infant pairs over a period of 26 weeks. Some pairs missed occasional sessions because of illness or holidays. However, no pair was absent for more than one week consecutively and none missed more than a total of four weeks in all. A total of 191 sessions were recorded.

Written records of the infants' development were kept throughout the study which confirmed that all the infants were "normal". At the end of the study each mother was given a short interview. The main aims of this were, firstly, to ensure that none of the mothers was aware that imitation had been the focal point of interest in the study, and secondly, having revealed this to the mothers, to gain an insight into their own views on the importance of imitation in their interaction with their infants.

ANALYSIS OF VIDEO-TAPE RECORDINGS

Analysis was made at three different levels:

(i) All imitative sequences which occurred during the play sessions were determined, according to the definition of imitative sequence given in the Introduction. It should be remembered that this definition included all sequences where acts were imitated either by the infant or by the mother. The boundaries of the imitative sequence were determined, beginning from the moment when the act, which was then imitated, was initially made and extending until the last production of that act before both partners' attention turned to some other activity. For the purpose of further analysis transcription was begun two seconds before the start of the imitative sequence and was ended two seconds after it had terminated.

(ii) For each imitative sequence the stream of activity was coded in terms of 64 sub-categories both for the mother and for the infant. The 64 sub-categories, grouped under four main headings, are listed in the Appendix. For each one-second interval throughout all imitative sequences the appropriate coding for both mothers' and infants' activities was entered on a running record sheet.

(iii) In addition to the written record of coded variables a narrative account of each imitative sequence was made.

Our aim in carrying out analyses at these levels was to provide ourselves with as detailed a record as possible on paper of what actually happened during each imitative sequence as it appeared on the video-screen.

Results

OCCURRENCE OF IMITATIVE SEQUENCES

Initial analysis of the video-tape recordings rapidly confirmed that imitative sequences were by no means a rare occurrence in interaction between a mother and her infant.

During the 191 ten-minute play sessions which were recorded a total of 1651 imitative sequences were observed to occur, ranging from 0–30 sequences per session (mean 8·6). The modal number of imitative sequences fell between 5 and 8 per session. Out of a total of 191 sessions there were only 5 where no imitative sequences occurred at all.

All eight mother–infant pairs participated in imitative sequences, the total number per pair ranging from 111 to 348 (mean 206·4). Although there were individual differences in the number of imitative sequences observed between mother–infant pairs it is important to emphasize that *all* pairs in our sample often participated in imitative sequences. The mean number of sequences for each individual pair per session ranged from 4·4 to 14·5.

In determining whether or not an imitative response was made no time limit was imposed; thus imitative sequences varied in duration. The number of seconds devoted to an imitative sequence ranged from 2 seconds to 226 seconds. The mean length of an imitative sequence for each mother–infant pair ranged from 4·2 seconds to 16·4 seconds (overall mean 11·3 seconds). The mean amount of time per ten-minute session devoted to imitative sequences for each individual pair varied from 52 seconds to 154 seconds (mean 97 seconds, which implies, on average, 16% of each observation period).

KINDS OF ACTIVITIES IMITATED

A total of 49 different activities were observed to be imitated either by the mother or by the infant in the course of the study. Table I gives a list of the different acts classified into 5 groupings: the first includes acts which involved facial or head movements; the second, acts which involved manual or body movements; the third, acts involving speech sounds; the fourth, acts involving non-speech sounds; and the fifth, acts involving manipulation of objects. Groups I–IV include those acts which involve direct interaction between the mother and her infant.

Table I

Imitated activities (with the frequency with which each occurred in the course of the study)

I. ACTS INVOLVING FACE/HEAD MOVEMENTS	II. ACTS INVOLVING HAND/BODY MOVEMENTS	III. ACTS INVOLVING SPEECH SOUNDS
opens mouth wide (40)	waves (4)	vowel-like sounds (480)
smiles (20)	arm movements (8)	early consonantal sounds (65)
pokes tongue (3)	scratches (2)	late consonantal sounds (140)
purses lips (5)	covers face in peep-bo manner (2)	
frowns (2)	tickles (1)	
puts head on one side (6)	bangs (295)	
shakes head (7)	claps (22)	
nods (5)	hand game (35)	
	finger movements (7)	
	hits own hand (3)	
	moves backwards (3)	

IV. ACTS INVOLVING NON-SPEECH SOUNDS	V. ACTS INVOLVING MANIPULATION OF OBJECTS
whimpers (34)	sucks object (4)
laughs (112)	gives object (7)
blows raspberries (23)	pushes/rolls object (50)
coughs (23)	shakes object (16)
sighs (21)	presses object parts (42)
yawns (11)	bangs two objects together (15)
smacks lips (4)	takes object out of another (18)
panting sound (36)	puts object into another (6)
sneezes (4)	builds (1)
hiccoughs (4)	spins object (44)
clicking sound with tongue (3)	stops object spinning (1)
snuffling sound (2)	bounces object (4)
	puts object to mouth appropriately (3)
	turns pages of book (7)
	uncovers object to find it (1)

Group V includes acts involving indirect interaction between the mother and her infant, usually through the use of a toy.

Table I also shows the frequency, in brackets, with which each activity was observed to be imitated. The frequency varied from 1 instance to 480 instances. Relatively few activities were imitated with high frequency. The number of activities which each individual mother–infant pair was observed to imitate ranged from 21 to 33 (mean 25·9). Of the activities which occurred in more than 15 sequences 19 were imitated by 75% or more of the mother–infant pairs, thus showing that these 19 frequently imitated acts were not peculiar to just one or two pairs. Activities from each of the five groups described above were among the 19 imitated with most frequency by 75% or more of the sample.

There were, however, differences in the frequency with which each grouping of activities was imitated. Table II shows these differences. These results overall indicate the salience of speech sounds in imitative sequences, whereas the imitation of facial acts was relatively infrequent. However, there were individual differences between pairs, suggesting that for some pairs the imitation of, for example, activities involving the manipulation of toys was a more frequent phenomenon than the imitation of speech sounds. This may possibly have implications for the infants' later development.

Table II

Percentages of sequences per subject pair observed to occur in each of five groups of activities

Group of activities	Subject pair								
	P1	P2	P3	P4	P5	P6	P7	P8	Mean
I (facial)	4	2	16	3	1	16	2	6	5
II (manual)	24	32	21	53	11	7	38	21	23
III (speech)	30	35	17	17	72	30	32	52	42
IV (non-speech)	22	21	11	8	12	30	11	16	17
V (object)	20	10	35	20	5	17	17	5	13

IM/MI DISTINCTION

We have so far deliberately made no distinction as to which partner initiates the imitative sequences and which partner gives the first imitative response. However, two types of sequence can be distinguished and we shall now refer to IM sequences where the infant initiates and the mother follows and to MI sequences where the mother initiates the sequence and the infant gives the first imitative response.

Out of the total 1651 imitative sequences observed for all pairs 1308 (79%) were of the type IM and 343 (21%) were of the type MI. The number of IM sequences per pair ranged from 79 to 323 (mean 163·5) and of MI sequences from 25 to 67 (mean 42·9).

Table III shows the number of IM and MI sequences for each mother–infant pair. Using the Wilcoxon Matched-Pairs Signed-Ranks Test we find that there is a significant difference between IM and MI sequences ($\alpha = 0{\cdot}01$): IM sequences occur much more frequently than MI sequences when observed within a mother–infant interaction setting.

Table III

Total number of IM and MI sequences for each pair of subjects

Mother–infant pair	IM sequences	MI sequences
P1	152	40
P2	175	54
P3	80	31
P4	79	41
P5	323	25
P6	161	43
P7	112	67
P8	226	42

Each activity was examined to determine whether it occurred within both IM and MI sequences. Of the 49 different activities 31 (63·3%) appeared in both types of sequence, 16 (32·7%) were found only to occur in IM sequences, and 2 (4%) were only found in MI sequences. Of the 19 frequently occurring activities mentioned earlier, 17 occurred in both IM and MI sequences. The other two (whimpering and sighing) only occurred in IM sequences. One suggestion why these two activities are only found in IM sequences is that the mothers, although they themselves imitate their infants' production of these acts, do not elect to initiate and encourage their infants to imitate them because they are regarded as socially unacceptable. The other 14 activities which are found only in IM sequences occur relatively infrequently (see Table I). The 14 are pokes tongue, frowns, puts head on one side, nods, scratches, moves back, yawns, smacks lips, sneezes, hiccoughs, snuffles, sucks objects (inappropriately), builds, stops toy spinning.

The 16 IM-only activities were found to occur in a total of 107 sequences (8·2% of all IM sequences), whereas the 31 activities which were found to occur in both IM and MI sequences occurred in 1201 (91·8%) of all IM sequences. This suggests the relative infrequency with which activities which only appear in IM sequences occur. Fafouti (1973) and Maratos (1973) have both shown that an infant is capable of imitating most of these IM-only activities at the stage of development which we are studying. This adds further weight to our suggestion that the mother elects not to encourage her infant to imitate these activities and thus they are never found in mother-initiated sequences and only rarely in infant-initiated sequences.

Only two activities were found to occur in MI sequences and never in IM sequences. These were tickling and uncovering an object to find it. In both cases the activity occurred in only one sequence, giving a total of 2 instances where activities occurred solely in MI sequences. The 31 activities which were found in both IM and MI sequences were present in 341 MI sequences (99·4% of all MI sequences). The rarity of activities occurring only in MI sequences is testimony to the fact that the mother hardly ever initiates imitative sequences with activities which are not already in the infant's repertoire and which she herself does not imitate.

Most activities which appear in imitative sequences do so in both IM and MI sequences. Where activities do occur in only IM or MI sequences they do so with considerably less frequency. In other words it appears that mothers and infants tend to imitate the same activities.

DEVELOPMENTAL CHANGES

(a) *Number of imitative sequences.* In order to see whether there were any differences in the number and type of imitative sequences as the infant increased in age, the observation period was divided into three equal time periods—period I, when the infant was aged 17 to 24 weeks, period II, when the infant was aged 26 to 33 weeks, and period III, when the infant was aged 35 to 42 weeks.

Table IV shows the mean number of imitative sequences per session

Table IV

Mean number of imitative sequences per session for each subject pair at each of three time periods

Subject pair	Time period I	Time period II	Time period III
P1	5·5	13·8	6·9
P2	7·9	12·9	10·7
P3	1·9	4·7	6·9
P4	1·9	6·7	6·9
P5	12·1	15·3	17·6
P6	8·8	6·6	8·6
P7	5·2	8·7	8·6
P8	7·0	13·6	11·2
Mean	6·3	10·3	9·8

for each pair at each of the three time periods. Using the Wilcoxon Matched-Pairs Signed-Ranks Test the difference between the number of imitative sequences in the first and second time periods was significant ($\alpha < 0{\cdot}02$), but there was no significant difference between the second and third time periods.

(b) *IM and MI sequences.* Similar tests were carried out on IM and MI sequences separately (Table V). Using the Wilcoxon Matched-Pairs

Table V

Mean number of IM and MI sequences for each pair at each time period

Subject pair	IM sequences, Time period I	IM II	IM III	MI sequences, Time period I	MI II	MI III
P1	4·5	12·3	4·6	1·0	1·5	2·3
P2	6·7	9·9	7·6	1·2	3·0	3·1
P3	1·4	3·3	5·3	0·5	1·4	1·6
P4	1·0	4·7	4·5	0·9	2·0	2·4
P5	11·6	14·4	15·7	0·5	0·9	1·9
P6	7·9	4·3	6·8	0·9	2·3	1·8
P7	3·5	5·9	4·6	1·7	2·8	4·4
P8	5·9	12·0	8·9	1·1	1·6	2·3
Mean	5·3	8·4	7·3	1·0	1·9	2·5

Signed-Ranks Test no significant difference was found to occur in the frequency with which mothers imitated their infants' acts between the first and second time periods nor between the second and third time periods.

In the case of MI sequences, the Wilcoxon Test showed a significant increase between time periods one and two ($\alpha = 0{\cdot}01$) and also between time periods two and three ($\alpha = 0{\cdot}05$).

The data thus show that the mothers imitated their infants' acts with much the same frequency throughout the period of study. On the other hand the infant uses an imitative response to his mother's introduction of an act with increasing frequency as he gets older.

(c) *Number of different activities.* The number of different activities imitated during each time period varied. Figure 1 indicates that over all pairs there is an increase in the total number of different activities observed in imitative sequences between the first and second time periods, with a levelling off between the second and third time periods.

In IM sequences the number ranged between pairs from 3 to 11 in the first time period, in the second period from 9 to 16 and in the third period from 10 to 20. In MI sequences the numbers ranged from 2 to 6

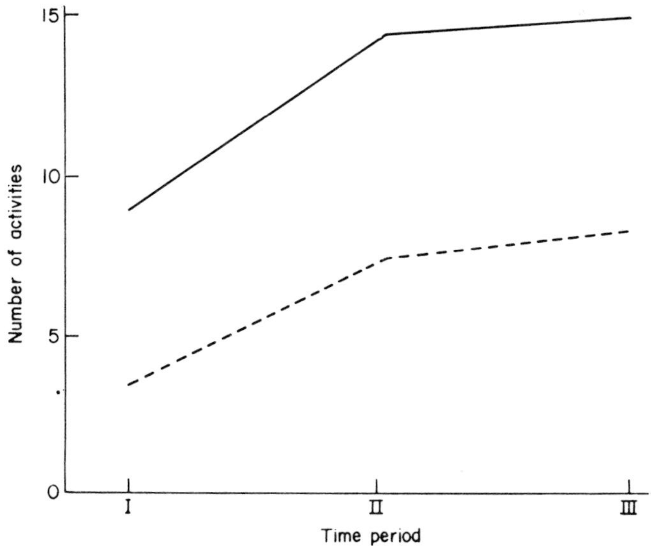

Fig. 1. Mean number of different activities imitated in IM sequences (solid line) and MI sequences (broken line) over all pairs at each of three time periods.

in the first period, 4 to 9 in the second and 5 to 13 in the third. The Wilcoxon Test was used to ascertain whether there was a significant difference in the number of different activities imitated over time. Table VI shows the number of different activities imitated by each subject pair during each of the three time periods for IM and for MI sequences. Using the Wilcoxon Test a significant difference was found between the number of different activities imitated between the first and

Table VI

The number of different activities for each subject pair which was observed to be imitated in IM sequences and in MI sequences at each of three time periods

Subject pair	IM sequences			MI sequences		
	Time period			Time period		
	I	II	III	I	II	III
P1	10	13	12	5	5	5
P2	7	14	18	5	9	13
P3	4	16	20	4	9	8
P4	5	9	12	3	4	7
P5	10	13	12	2	4	9
P6	11	11	14	2	8	7
P7	3	10	10	3	7	10
P8	9	15	13	6	6	8

second time periods in both IM ($\alpha = 0{\cdot}02$) and MI ($\alpha = 0{\cdot}05$) sequences. However, no significant difference was found in either IM or MI sequences between the second and third periods, thus confirming a levelling off in the number of different activities imitated. In all three time periods, however, the number of different activities found in IM sequences was significantly higher than the number of different activities found in MI sequences ($\alpha = 0{\cdot}05$ in the first period, 0·01 in the second and 0·02 in the third).

Analysis of each activity over the whole time period revealed that some activities which were imitated more frequently in the beginning did not appear in imitative sequences later on. Other activities were imitated with most frequency towards the middle of the study and others not until towards the end. The five groupings of activities mentioned above (Table I) were examined to see if there were any differences in the frequency with which each group was imitated over time. Table VII shows the total number of IM and of MI sequences observed for each of the five groups of activities at each of the three time periods. In both IM and MI sequences the number of imitative

Table VII

The total number of times each group of activities occurred in IM and in MI sequences at each of three time periods

Group of activities	IM sequences Time period			MI sequences Time period		
	I	II	III	I	II	III
I (facial)	32	24	15	9	5	1
II (manual)	33	137	65	17	50	43
III (speech)	175	187	226	14	19	20
IV (non-speech)	64	115	68	4	6	5
V (object)	2	24	60	8	34	77

sequences in which manual activities and non-speech sounds occurred rose to a peak in the second time period and then showed a decline. The imitation of facial activities declined over time in both IM and MI sequences, whereas that of activities involving the manipulation of toys and those involving speech sounds increased over time. The frequency of occurrence of each group of activity followed the same trend over time for both IM and MI sequences.

We suggest from these findings that, although the types of activities which are imitated change over time, imitative sequences of some kind occur during each time period, thus emphasizing the importance of imitative sequences in an interaction setting regardless of the type of activity being imitated.

TURN-TAKING NATURE OF IMITATIVE SEQUENCES

Imitative sequences by definition must involve the production of an activity by two partners. Inasmuch as the imitative act produced by one partner must be dependent upon the initial production of that act by the other partner the sequences necessarily involve turn-taking. In its simplest form an imitative sequence will consist of just two acts involving one interchange, or exchange of turns. However, our study has revealed that imitative sequences are not necessarily limited to just one interchange. Like other communication sequences (Newson, Chapter 3) they can be made up of a number of imitative acts which form links in a chain of interdependent action and reaction. In other words, an imitative act may not only be a response to the preceding gesture but it may also be a signal eliciting a further response which may in turn be imitative. Preliminary analysis of the data has shown that the number of interchanges within an imitative sequence ranged from 1 to 67. Table VIII shows the frequency with which sequences with a given number of interchanges occurred for each mother–infant pair. The proportion of sequences with only one interchange varied between pairs from 48% to 66% (mean 57%); the proportion with two interchanges ranged from 6% to 31% (mean 17%); and the proportion with three or more interchanges ranged from 19% to 36% (mean 28%). Examination of Table VIII shows remarkable consistency, in that all pairs in our sample not only imitated acts in simple interchange sequences but all used sustained interchanges.

Summary of Results

Our findings can be summarized as follows:

1. Imitative sequences occurred within almost all the observed interaction episodes between mothers and their infants and on average occupied 16% of interaction time.
2. The number of infant-initiated, mother-imitated (IM) sequences was greater than the number of mother-initiated, infant-imitated (MI) sequences. However, the number of MI sequences increased as the infant grew older whereas the number of IM sequences stayed relatively constant throughout the observation period.
3. A total of 49 different activities were found to occur in imitative sequences. The frequency with which activities occurred in imitative sequences varied but almost all activities which were found in MI sequences also occurred in IM sequences. A number of activities only occurred in IM sequences and it is suggested that these activities are deliberately not encouraged by the mother initiating them.
4. Speech sounds took place most frequently in imitative sequences throughout the whole period of study. Imitation of facial acts was

Table VIII

Frequency of imitative sequences for each subject pair according to number of interchanges

Subject pair	Number of interchanges																					
	1	2	3	4	5	6	7	8	9	10	11	12	13	14	15	16	17	18	19	20	21+	Total
P1	101	28	25	10	12	2	4	1	0	2	1	1	0	2	1	1	0	0	0	0	1	192
P2	126	34	25	16	9	4	5	0	2	0	2	0	1	1	1	2	0	0	0	0	1	229
P3	56	34	11	3	4	0	1	0	0	1	1	0	0	0	0	0	0	0	0	0	0	111
P4	69	23	15	8	0	0	1	2	0	0	1	1	0	0	0	0	0	0	0	0	0	120
P5	231	21	39	11	12	6	7	0	7	2	3	3	0	0	2	0	3	0	0	0	1	348
P6	122	32	13	12	8	4	6	3	1	1	0	1	0	0	0	0	0	1	0	0	0	204
P7	86	28	20	15	9	4	2	5	1	1	1	2	1	1	0	0	1	0	0	0	2	179
P8	147	51	25	21	10	5	1	2	1	2	1	1	0	0	0	0	0	0	1	0	0	268
Total	938	251	173	96	64	25	27	13	12	9	10	9	2	4	4	3	4	1	1	0	5	1651

infrequent but occurred most often when the infant was between 4 and 6 months. Imitation of manual movements and of non-speech sounds was most frequent when the infant was between 6 and 8 months. Imitation of activities involving the manipulation of toys increased over the study period and was most frequent when the infant was between 8 and 10 months, i.e. towards the end of the period under study.

5. Imitative sequences show some of the characteristics which have been suggested for other communication sequences. Turn-taking is one example. Imitative sequences are not necessarily limited to one single interchange. The number of interchanges varies but sustained sequences are often observed.

Discussion

Our observation of imitative sequences within an interaction setting has revealed that such sequences are not only a frequent phenomenon but have characteristics similar to other communication sequences.

In their interaction with one another a mother and infant are attempting, we suggest, to promote shared understanding of events (Newson and Pawlby, 1975). The infant cries, the mother responds by picking him up, or by feeding him, until he no longer cries. The mother imputes meaning into the infant's signal; she regards his action as if it were a meaningful request for reciprocal action on her part and this is the natural beginning of two-way communication. Similarly a mother says, "No!" as her infant puts a forbidden object to his mouth. The infant withdraws it. Communication is deemed to have taken place.

It is implicit in the writings of many developmental theorists that the sharing of meaning comes only with the onset of language, i.e. when a common verbal code is set up between an adult and a child. However, it is suggested here that a great deal of mutual understanding obviously comes about well before even the passive understanding of words. It can be seen in one of its earliest forms in the infant's ability to imitate his mother.

When a baby bangs a drum upon seeing another person bang a drum, it is a considerable strain on scientific credulity to assume that the mere sight of such an action is simply and automatically encoded into an appropriate pattern of complex and co-ordinated muscle twitches the first time it happens, and that this facility is just an inherent property of the human nervous system which will be called into play without the infant having had an enormous amount of previous communication experience. In any case, one thing that immediately falsifies such a simplistic viewpoint is that the actual pattern of muscular contraction will hardly ever be the same twice running. What the baby is imitating is not a precise movement pattern at all. It is, rather, an event sequence, the main defining criterion for which is that it has a specified end point, that is it results in a satisfying "bang". In practice the object with which the infant bangs may well not be the same object as that used by the person who is demonstrating the action of banging. It may be held by the baby in quite a different form of grip; it will probably be banged in a different place, a different number of times and with a different rhythm. Despite all these dissimilarities of action between the two persons involved we are still normally prepared to judge that the infant is, or is not, attempting to imitate the action of banging. In this particular example, therefore, to say that the baby imitates is to say much more than that he goes through a precise sequence of motor movements. What we are suggesting is that once a baby can spontaneously imitate some pattern of behaviour which is offered to him when his mother enacts it or models it for him, he must be well on the way to comprehending that action, or at least in some way be able to share its meaning with her. The ability to imitate an action is acquired gradually, but can clearly occur long before the child has any real knowledge of words.

The phenomenon of imitation in early infancy can thus be thought of in terms of establishing a non-verbal communication code between an infant and an adult, and it is perhaps only through the use of such codes that the two are able to test the extent and nature of their mutual understanding.

Our observations suggest that the ability to imitate actions does not appear suddenly in development or occur simply as a function of maturation. On the contrary, it emerges only gradually in the context of the reciprocal pattern of social interplay between mother and child as a result of the mother's intention to communicate. However, we have observed that quite complicated imitation sequences are possible well before the child can have any secure knowledge of words.

But where does imitation begin? Paradoxically our study suggests that the whole process by which the infant comes to imitate his mother in a clearly intentional way is rooted in the initial readiness of the *mother* to imitate her infant. In other words, almost from the time of birth there seems to be a marked tendency for mothers to reflect back to their infants certain gestures which occur spontaneously within the baby's natural repertoire of activities. She appears, however, to select actions which she can endow with communicative significance, especially vocalizations, and it is these acts which the infant may first perform inadvertently or unintentionally that are automatically reflected back as if the infant had deliberately initiated them for the purpose of social exchange.

Even more strikingly, in circumstances where it is predictable that an infant is likely to repeat one particular action for a second or third time—in a kind of repetitive ritual—we have observed that a mother may skilfully insert her own copy of that action between two of his repetitions and hence create a simulation of a deliberate act of imitation on the infant's part. The way in which such interventions are made suggests that they serve an important functional purpose for the mother in helping her to sustain a more meaningful dialogue with her baby. But in addition they also facilitate the development of more deliberate imitation because the mother's answering gesture provides the infant with an interest-holding event which is in fact temporarily contingent upon his own performance of a similar event.

Our study confirms that babies do pay special attention (in that they laugh and smile and appear to be pleased) when the mothers themselves imitate an action which the child has just performed. His action is thus "highlighted" or "marked out" as something special. This may be what leads to the infant's more deliberate production of the action. Since the mother has repeatedly reflected back an event which he himself has just performed and since he finds this pleasing and attractive, the same action is produced by the child on a different occasion *in order that* his mother does likewise. Learning sequences of this sort have been observed to occur in our study remarkably early on, even within the first half of the first year. This in turn suggests that the natural social situation in which a mother is spontaneously communicating with her infant and treating him as a responsive human being provides a context within which learning of this kind can be extremely rapid and effective.

However, because mothers are continually striving to improve communication between themselves and their children it would be highly misleading to conceptualize "learning to imitate" as a simple or once-for-all phenomenon. Mother and infant become progressively more skilful in their exchanges. A mother is likely to become highly sensitive to those moments when her child is about to produce some action or gesture which she has previously endowed with special social significance and reflected back to him. She thus knows how to anticipate actions which her child is about to perform, and again in endeavouring to sustain a dialogue she produces selected actions just before the child himself does, thus creating yet another form of simulated imitation. Observations of this kind naturally suggest to us that the mother's timing and placing of her reproductions is a matter of crucial importance in understanding the development of a child's ability to imitate on his own at a later stage.

Having studied many instances of imitation in the making it now seems obvious that it is only through this social interplay, which includes monitoring by the mother of the child's spontaneous activity, that the infant's ability to imitate actions becomes reliable in the sense that these actions are finally brought under his own voluntary control. Once this is achieved the mother merely has to perform an act and the infant is able to respond by imitating it. He has learned that this is a desirable response and is automatically rewarded at three different levels. Firstly, his mother goes on paying him attention, i.e. his action helps sustain the communication dialogue. This a child probably finds rewarding in itself. Secondly, he begins to understand and to make more sense of the world. New shared meanings established with the help of other human beings have their own cognitive pay-off. Enlightenment is self-rewarding. Thirdly, whenever he produces a recognizable new form of imitation his mother will normally react with excessive pride and manifest pleasure at his "cleverness" in having understood what she was trying, and previously failed, to communicate. Verbal commentary such as the following, as well as smiles and a general tone of encouragement, were frequently recorded when the infant imitated an action produced by the mother:

> "Go . . .", as mother demonstrates. "You do that!" Child imitates action. Mother continues, "ooo! There's a good boy, there's a good boy! That's quite clever."

Such a definite sense of special achievement is almost inevitably conveyed to the child—perhaps because mothers are always looking for reassurance that their children are becoming capable of genuine communication at last. In answer to the question, "Why do you want N to imitate you?" participant mothers replied along much the same lines:

> "I suppose it's the way they learn, isn't it?"
> ". . . you're trying to teach him. I suppose it's progress . . ."
> ". . . it's just sort of nice to see that she reacts, not that she's just continuing in her own little world, and she's taking notice of what our world is."

Such reactions on the part of mothers are understandable. After all, communication ability provides the only satisfactory guarantee that her baby is becoming a real human being and will not for ever remain an egocentric bundle of needs and wants.

On the whole it would seem that, although mothers are delighted when their children demonstrate the ability to imitate, they are by no means fully aware of the processes by which the ability comes about. The mother's imitation of her child's actions appears to be an automatic and largely unconscious reaction unless attention is specifically drawn to it. However, at least one mother in our sample was aware, on reflection, that she did unconsciously imitate her child and that this was important. In answer to the question, "Can you think of any example of when N imitates you?" she replied:

> "Well, it's a very complicated thing this, because I've found out that she . . . I mean sounds, for instance, let's restrict ourselves to sounds—she suddenly discovers a sound and it rather fascinates her and I reinforce it; I make the sound as well. And that tends to make her want to do it more. And then perhaps on a different occasion when she's forgotten all about it, if I make that sound she will imitate it. But the sound seems to have to come from her in the first place."

Obviously one cannot rely on an insightful comment by one single mother to confirm a theoretical view about how imitation normally originates. Our study has, however, helped to confirm that a communication context may provide a useful way of looking at the problem.

References

Fafouti, M. (1973). Unpublished M.A. Thesis, University of Nottingham.

Gardner, J. and Gardner, H. (1970). A note on selective imitation by a 6-week-old infant. *Child Dev.* **41**, 1209–1213.

Maratos, O. (1973). The origin and development of imitation in the first six months of life. Unpublished Ph.D. Thesis, University of Geneva.

Newson, J. (1974). Towards a theory of infant understanding. *Bull. Br. Psychol. Soc.* **27**, 251–257.

Newson, J. and Newson, E. (1976). On the social origins of symbolic functioning. In P. Varma and P. Williams (Eds), *Piaget, Psychology and Education.* Hodder and Stoughton, London.

Newson, J. and Pawlby, S. (1975). On imitation. Unpublished paper, University of Nottingham.

Newson, J. and Shotter, J. (1974). How babies communicate. *New Society* **29**, 345–347.

Pawlby, S. and Jones, O. (1975). Preverbal mediation of the infant's social environment. Paper presented to I.S.S.B.D. Conference at University of Surrey.

Uzigiris, I. C. (1972). Patterns of vocal and gestural imitation. In F. J. Monks, W. W. Hartup and J. de Wit (Eds), *Determinants of Behavioural Development.* Academic Press, London and New York.

Appendix

The coded variables used in analysis of the video-tape recordings

I. EYE DIRECTION

1. Mother/infants face
2. Mother/infants body
3. Mother/infants hands
4. Own body
5. Own hands
6. Room
7. Toy held by self
8. Toy held by mother/infant
9. Toy on table
10. Eyes closed
11. Other (state)

II. ARM/HAND MOVEMENTS

12. Arms stretched up
13. Arms stretched down
14. Arms stretched out
15. Arms stretched in
16. Hands apart
17. Hands together
18. Touching self
19. Touching mother/infant
20. Touching table
21. Holding object
22. Manipulating toy (state)
23. Sucking toy
24. Sucking fingers
25. Reaching
26. Waving
27. Pointing
28. Giving
29. Taking
30. Banging
31. Hitting
32. Tickling
33. Clapping
34. Other (state)

III. FACE/MOUTH MOVEMENT

35. Closed mouth
36. Open mouth
37. Smiling
38. Laughing
39. Crying
40. Frowning
41. Sneezing
42. Coughing
43. Yawning
44. Tongue poking
45. Raspberry blowing

46. Smacking lips
47. Sucking
48. Sighing
49. Singing
50. Kissing
51. Squealing
52. Vocalizing (state)
53. Verbal question
54. Verbal comment
55. Verbal invitation
56. Verbal command
57. Other (state)

IV. BODY/HEAD MOVEMENT

58. Distance short
59. Distance long
60. Nodding
61. Shaking head
62. Leaning forward
63. Leaning back
64. Other (state)

IV | Communicative Performance

10 Descriptive Analyses of Infant Communicative Behaviour

Colwyn Trevarthen

Introduction

Experiments on the abilities of infants to discriminate stimuli, to perceive objects in space, or to control reinforcement and learn have gained much ground in recent years. Now the specialists, even those who lean strongly to the empiricist philosophy, speak of the infant as highly competent—as endowed with complex functional abilities, and with outlines of much more in the way of *potentialities* for psychological action. Most of all, infant man is now seen as a sensitive and impressionable perceiver.

Many reviewers and teachers speak loudly of the advantages of rigorous experimental procedure and of the great risks of description or anecdote. But, if one reviews this recent, highly fruitful period and awakening of interest in infant psychology it may be seen that the art of the new experiments is in letting infants express themselves more naturally, and in recording their choice of reaction more directly than before. Unfortunately, when controls and recording devices are set up to obtain quantitative data on a restricted range of questions, the findings may give a distorted view of infant intelligence. Putting an accent on discrete problem-solving and task-perceiving powers of infants, both problem and task being set by the experimenter, as well as emphasis on conditioning as a mechanism for developmental change, have obscured the spontaneous, innate aspects of infant behaviour, by which the mind of an infant regulates its own growth in more complex circumstances. This was, of course, clearly stated long ago by Piaget in his criticism of the behaviourist approach to the development of intelligence (e.g. Piaget, 1950).

What is found out by experiment answers logical questions about the preferences or limits of intelligence one by one. Experimental technique is always selective. If the questions are well posed, and if the techniques for channelling the activity of the subject to answer each question are well chosen, then the findings permit sound inferences of what may happen in the infant's brain. But there is always a danger that the experimenter will not know the differences between a genuine correspondence of *his* purpose with the functions of the "subject" and a spurious or trivial coincidence between them, a coincidence which misleads about what the infant was doing when he formulated acts to the stimuli in some consistent measurable way.

For example, if differential orienting responses are obtained to two stimuli, which stimulus dimensions and what features of the temporal occurrence or change in the stimuli are important to the infant perceiver? A constellation of tests may clarify this question. Invariably, when this is done, the answers have been surprisingly complex, the infant showing himself to be making elaborate integrative reactions to events, and guiding his perceptual development by asking progressively more complex questions of the world in which he acts (Bower, 1974). Then, how do ordinary infants employ a demonstrated ability in a world where those precise stimuli may never occur like that? Is information about changes in the frequency of a response (on which inferences about learning, habituation, etc. always depend) relevant when that particular act never occurs, at least not isolated in that way? What is the importance of unnoted and unreported acts of complex regulated form which accompany the one repeating movement or reaction that has been chosen by the experimenter as the measured response?

Usually these and other questions about integration are not answered by selective experimentation. A literature composed of hundreds of studies of one question at a time produces a disintegrated impression. This is not to say that experimental technique is invalid or that it may be dispensed with to gain understanding. It does indicate, I believe, that a different kind of research, less analytical *at the start* is a necessary complement to experiment in scientific study of intelligence, especially for the early developmental stages when great impressionability of memory is controlled by innate forms of action. This alternative method attempts to capture regular patterns in spontaneous action and tailors experimental intervention to what is discovered, to determine how the activity may change to overcome an obstacle, avoid an impasse, transform a less favourable situation into one in which it is well adapted, or how behaviour may be completely reformulated to create a new kind of opportunity. The essential difference resides in an emphasis on generative or structural and functional complexity in the subject who thus becomes a free-acting agent. Even the neonate is capable of formulating and controlling psychological activity, in and of itself.

DIFFICULTIES IN THE STUDY OF GROWING PSYCHOLOGICAL STRUCTURES

Growing biological systems have one unique property which is paradoxical in comparison with non-living systems to which they are often compared for purposes of experimental analysis. They predictively generate structures as a means for transforming function. Any immature organism will show organs in a strange anticipatory state of adaptation, with intrinsic organization in excess of essential function at that time. This prefunctional determination of parts, much of which is invisible or ultra-microscopic, is essential for development—it is what drives the process along a predictable plan or course, often in opposition to circumstances.

To observe this kind of predetermination in developing psychological systems is very difficult because the prefunctional and generative components are, generally, not known. They cannot be identified as physical elements in the brain. We must see them indirectly, reflected in the dynamics of psychological action. Organization of percepts in a coherent space referred to the body and detection of stable objects in space can only be inferred from what infants do in selective response to complex changes or patterning of events in the stimulation around them. Any elementary movement of an infant is evidence of psychological control of action only if it is seen in dynamic combination with many other movements.

If the brain at birth were an unorganized collection of simple elements then a neonate would make nothing but jangled irregular reactions or clockwork repetitions of movement. This would be so even if these elements were as complex as reflex arcs built into the anatomy of the lower levels of the central nervous system and wired precisely in relation to a delicate anatomy of receptors, muscles and bones. Proof of coherence or directedness of movements over even a few seconds is proof of neural integration far above the level of a reflex. To see more of integration the infant must be left free and with appropriate conditions to develop the highest possible levels of spontaneous organization. To record and measure integration and control we have to follow patterns in the dynamics of what the infant does.

When we do the appropriate recording, regular, repeatable and effective sequences of movement come to light. By means of these actions the infant governs the essential internal conditions for its growth, and regulates the intake of information for growth from ordered structures in the world. They are also the embryonic form of acts that will be conscious and voluntary in adult life.

PURPOSIVE MOVEMENTS IN EARLY INFANCY

Human movements, even the acts of adults which have clear purpose, are much harder to perceive than is generally understood. One can see the approximate course and end effects of an act, and often make sound inferences about its purpose or goal. But until the invention of cine photography the details of movement were as far from human vision as were the planets before the invention of the telescope. Now we possess elaborate physical devices for gaining detailed information about how the body and its parts move, but we are still far from seeing the integrations of movement accurately or clearly. This may explain why most of psychology is concerned with perception, learning and motivation—notions about kinds of functions which apply to the results or conditions of movement. We do not really have a psychology of movement itself, one which explains how the astronomical number of alternative muscle contractions are ordered into effectively evolving patterns of force and displacement. We do not know how the body and its parts move co-operatively together. I believe that psychology is wrong to assume that this is a secondary problem, or a physiological one, and in the future much more attention will have to be paid to it.

The Russian physiologist Bernstein (1967) has pioneered in this nearly vacant field. He claims that great rewards come if we defy our blindness of what movement is like, to precisely measure details of action in short intervals of time. He shows that most studies are not accurate enough to bring out the underlying structure of movement. He elegantly proves that all voluntary action is built on images or templates which determine, within the brain and in advance of actual limb displacement, what the component movements will be. The familiar reflexes of the motor physiologist are special and limited elements of movement. They cannot be the units out of which voluntary acts are built. This was also Lashley's (1951) argument.

Bernstein logically concludes that the cause of the co-ordinating images of movement lies in *biodynamic structures* of the brain that grow and develop. Developmental studies which he made support this theory well. Perception of physical space for movement and of objects as goals for particular movements is, he argues, linked to these growing movement-image systems in the brain. Percepts are defined as much by structure within the determining nerve circuits of action, as by structure in the information that the sense organs pick up from the environment. If this is so, we cannot ever explain perception by studying the structure of receptor organs and the layout of stimulus events alone. Even unit reactions to stimuli will be highly unpredictable because the subject is organizing his movements from within as well as from without.

Obviously this theory is not compatible with a strict behaviouristic view of psychological development, and Bernstein, being a Russian, was obliged to explain with great tact how his ideas differed substantially from those of Pavlov. Nor is it the same as the idealized cognitive or perceptual psychology of mental functions which is much in vogue at the present time.

Application of Bernstein's techniques, in simplified form, to young infants shows that they, like adults, possess programmes of motor action, and strongly suggests that at the start of life these programmes are very little influenced by perception of the external world.

Detailed analyses of spontaneous movements to look at and to touch or grasp, described elsewhere (Trevarthen, 1974a, c; 1976), show that the brain of a newborn specifies the outline of a unified *space* for acts of separate body parts. Moreover, selective detection by the various special organs of sense, operating in different physical *modes* of afference, is co-ordinated in this space from the start. Infants look, listen, touch or taste in an outline of one field of orienting movement. Attending in one mode at a time, e.g. vision, therefore becomes a particular figure of moving, a figure differentiated out of the total pattern of action. As Gibson (1967) puts it, we see because we look—that is, because we move to favour pick-up of information by eye. How this is achieved by the developing brain is suggested by observation of the hierarchical structure of neonatal acts, and the separate development of different levels of action in the course of the first year after birth.

The movements of infants also show remarkable temporal regularities or measured cadences which prove the existence in the brain of a physical regulation of *time*. Close comparison of the output units in movement of the limbs of young infant and adult shows that both operate on the same basic elements of ballistic or pre-programmed action, and that these elements are knit together, at least in general outline, in a hierarchy that remains throughout life (Trevarthen, 1976).

These findings suggest that, of all the basic components in intelligence, those concerned directly with the generation of spontaneous movement are the most completely determined in the newborn human being. Perception must be prepared by elaborate functional input-processing systems in a newborn, and we have direct psycho-biological evidence that this is so. But perceptual access to environmental stimuli depends on how the baby moves to adjust receptors to be prepared for location and change of stimuli. We may call these patterns of action rudimentary intentions because they are directed to the obtaining of particular kinds of consequence, or particular directions of experience.

If this is accepted, then we must conclude that the material basis of intention is innate in the brain. Furthermore, the extraordinary memory functions of the growing brain, which continuously improve the adaptiveness of behaviour throughout life, depend on and grow out of the pre-wired yet changing mechanisms of intention.

INTENTIONS TO COMMUNICATE

If newborns exhibit rudimentary intentions to move in controlled manner towards objects, do they also show intentions to communicate? If so, by what features would communicatory intentions be distinguished from those directed to objects?

Human communication is not simply a matter of reaching to sign stimuli or to conditioned stimuli. It is a highly controlled and co-operative spontaneous use of a large number of muscles of expression. It transmits and responds to mental or subjective information—

information about feelings, intentions and the contents of awareness. The most significant movements of expression, such as those of the face, are uniquely adapted to affect other persons, but communication is also furthered by perception of the direction, intensity and plan of co-ordination inherent in any purposeful movement. We must therefore look, first, for special expressive movements in infants like those of adults, second, for sensitivity of infants to these movements when adults make them and, third, for awareness of the purpose of movements made by others towards objects.

One class of acts of emotional expression relates to the progress of communication itself, i.e. they signal comment on the process of personal relationship. Thus surprise, humour, disdain, disbelief, pride, annoyance, approval, sadness, anger and so forth qualify what is taking place in an actual communication. Such meta-communicative functions may also be present in infants.

Language, the most complex and most powerful form of communication, is based on speech which requires exceedingly refined co-ordination between movement of chest, throat, vocal cords, tongue and lips. It depends also on grammatical rules of relationship between acts of communication embodied in speech, now thought by many psychologists to be innate to man on the same criteria as those employed by Darwin in his study of the evolutionary origins of emotional expression and its variation in different races of man. It is necessary, therefore, to determine how speech movements develop in infants and how infants respond to or make speech in relation to the whole of the intersubjective context of communication behaviour. The question of the origin of language is changed if it be demonstrated that infants already use rules of communication with persons before they understand words or are capable of uttering them. Furthermore, there is no reason to insist that the movements of speech are absent from behaviour of infants when they are too young to use the movements with adequate control to articulate sounds of speech.

We are applying descriptive methods to detect communicative intentions in babies too young to utter words. Our method is to record favourable instances of communication as completely as possible, and then analyse them in detail. The immaturity of voice in the first months has led us to concentrate first on visible communications, many of which occur in the absence of vocalizations of any kind on the part of the infant.

The responses of infants to persons to be described below show that they may not only express communication to persons when less than two months old, but that they perceive well and quickly locate communicative acts of an attentive partner. A precocity of awareness for adult communication in infants has been evident in the results of rigidly structured experimental tests of visual or auditory discrimination. Very young subjects have consistently exhibited preferences for physical constellations of stimuli that, in the ordinary world, are unambiguous signs of persons attempting communication.

Physical aspects of persons which infants prefer even when they are experienced in isolation include rhythms of movement contingent on the infant's own acts, nearby presentation of an upright full view of a face-like shape, especially if there are dots representing eyes, raised eyebrows, etc., movement of the mouth and cheeks in the smile, pitch and articulation of the voice as in "baby talk", including certain categories of syllabic pattern in speech. To some extent these stimuli may be represented in non-living objects moved by hand or by machine or in artificial patterns of light or sound, or in drawings. It is important, however, to emphasize that the responses of young babies to real persons shows that they are better able to recognize and respond to these physical features when they are combined in dynamic patterns that can only occur in the activity of a person willing to communicate. Experimental procedures generally work against recognition of this important effect.

Exchanges between two-month-olds and their mothers tend to be precisely patterned in time. The nature of the patterning shows that it is a mutually generated effect, in which the intentions of both partners are essential, and both may adjust their acts to obtain better fit to those of the other. This aspect has also been lost in experimental studies.

It is not surprising that experimental reports rarely consider the possibility that infants may have intentions to communicate.

METHODS IN OUR RESEARCH

In the film studies of infants responding to persons a number of technical conventions have been found necessary.

To observe communication, both partners must be clearly seen. The infant is filmed directly over the mother's right shoulder, and a large vertical front-surface mirror inclined at about 60° to the camera axis allows inclusion of an almost front-face view of the infant and a $\frac{3}{4}$ front-face view of the mother in the same picture frame. The infant's eyes, the mother's eyes and the camera are set as near as possible to the same level (Fig. 1). This arrangement also allows us to screen out one or other partner during analysis and to direct attention to the behaviour of one at a time.

The infant chair we use is developed from one designed for this work at the Center for Cognitive Studies in Harvard (Fig. 1). The infant is held firmly by an elastic stomach band to a flat upholstered back which is cut away to permit full freedom of arm movement. The buttocks of the infant are perched on a small padded seat. For neonates, the chair is inclined at about 25° and the head rest has two padded side pieces to stop the infant tilting the head strongly to left or right. It is frequently difficult to get neonates (up to five weeks after birth) to remain still and relaxed in an upright position. Because the newborn *actively* curls up in a vertical chair, we conclude that firm support of the trunk and back is important, not so much because the infant is weak as to avoid attempts it makes to roll over. These movements are probably adapted to seeking warmth and safe support at a time when most of the baby's life is spent in dozing or feeding, in bed or against the mother's body. Beyond six or eight weeks the infant is usually comfortable in a seat near upright. By the age of three or four months the seat back may be set at about 5° to the vertical.

Films are taken with ample lighting, including soft spotlights to obtain a well modelled image of the face and limbs of the subject, at 24 frames/second, with a telephoto lens. Time is calibrated with an electric clock.

It is usually not difficult to obtain a friendly response from an infant of eight weeks, but underlying mood is vital to the success of the kind of communication we describe. The baby must be contented and alert. Behaviour of the adult making advances must fall within an adequate range of gentleness and responsiveness. Unresponsive behaviour of the mother leads to disruption or distortion of the infant communication as described below.

Analysis is performed with a Perceptoscope Analysing projector through which the film may be viewed frame-by-frame or at a wide variety of slow-motion rates. Observation of the structure of action is greatly facilitated by slowing to $\frac{1}{4}$ the actual rate (6 frames/second). After the general dynamics of the movement have been seen, they may

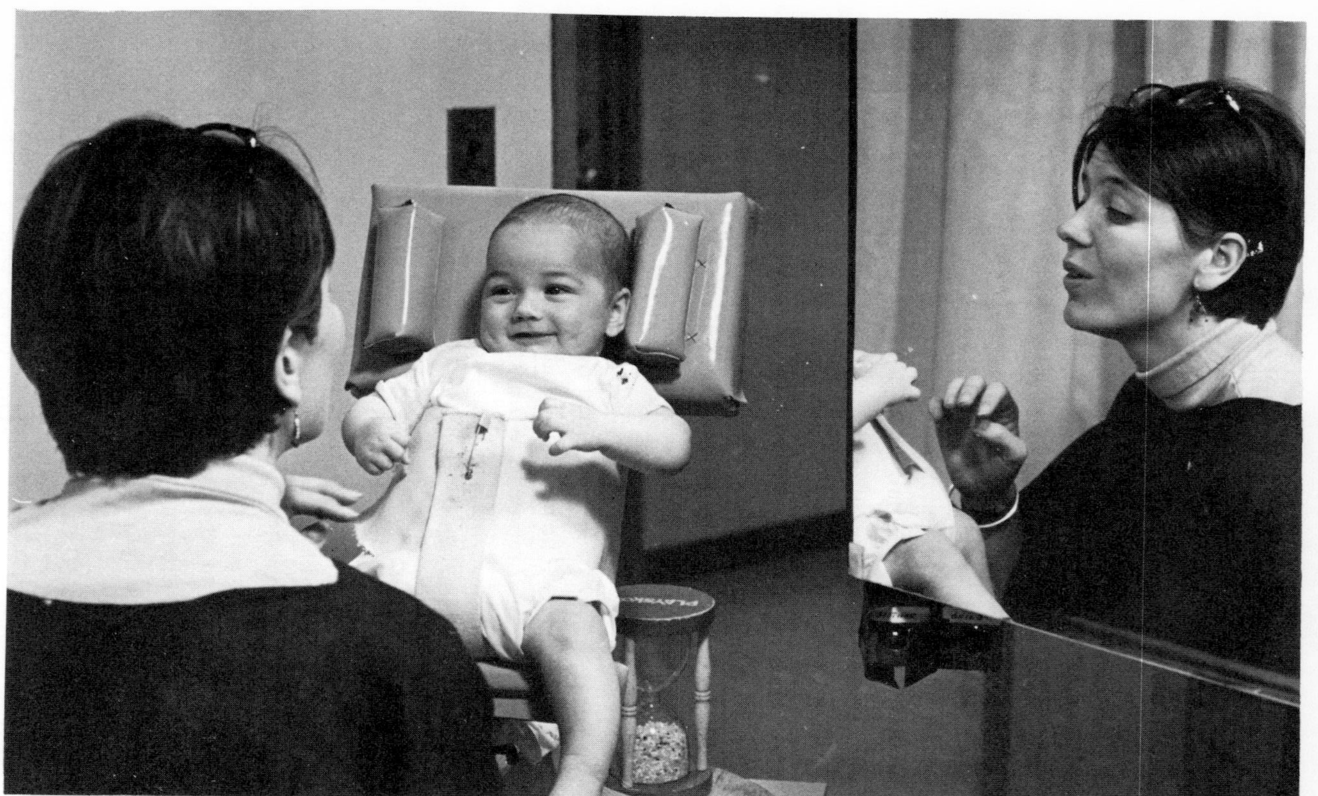

Fig. 1. Placing of mother, baby and mirror for films of communication. The specially designed chair gives the baby support without restricting limb movements. Nine-week-old boy.

be selectively analysed at slower speeds. We have built a system of front-surface mirrors and a glass-topped desk to obtain a correctly oriented picture approximately 40 cm × 60 cm, projected from below onto drawing paper. With this we may quickly trace a sequence of positions of parts of the body to get a montage drawing that shows the rate and form of movement and the combinations of movement of different parts.

Trajectories of the arms and movements of the hand are plotted by marking successive positions of the centre of the wrist and the tip of the nose. To follow details of displacement, positions of every frame are plotted, but for most purposes the pattern of movement of the hand, for example, is best shown with drawings of one frame each $\frac{1}{4}$ second. Climax positions (e.g. top of wrist trajectory, hand most extended in gesturing) or start positions (the first frame showing extension of the fingers) are taken as origin for plots of $\frac{1}{4}$ second steps. All plots or drawings of gesture or expression are made to the same time and distance scales. Accurate alignment to a fixed baseline (usually by reference to the top of the chair) is essential if movements are to be correctly represented in the plots.

The Growth of Communication

In the second and third month the reactions of infants to persons become effective in an intricate prototype of human communication. Although a few accurate and detailed descriptive studies of elements of this behaviour are available (e.g. Spitz and Wolf, 1946; Washburn, 1929; Wolff, 1963, 1969) and aspects of this major psychological development have been recorded in experimental studies aimed to test the perception or conditioning capacities of infants (e.g. Ahrens, 1954; Brackbill, 1958; Eisenberg, 1975; Gewirtz, 1965; Rheingold, 1961; Rheingold *et al.*, 1959; Watson, 1973), a coherent description of the earliest forms of human communication does not exist. It requires detailed analyses of natural exchanges, when the infant is responded to and encouraged by an unconstrained adult partner.

The situation shown in Fig. 1 for filming or video-taping mothers and their infants is, of course, somewhat artificial, with unusual conditions imposed to aid filming. But the two partners are free to express themselves to each other as they will. The communications which we obtain are rich enough in structure to establish that human infants are endowed with a specialized mechanism for human behavioural exchange and that their expressions may exercise a powerful control influence over those of an adult partner when the infant is no more than eight weeks of age.

Detailed analysis of film samples reveal a number of stereotypic acts of communication and a subtle control process linking the acts of the two human beings. We are surprised by the similarity of basic features of form and rate in acts of adult and infant. Infant and adult meet as generally similar and mutually reactive intentional agents, both accepting communication as an attractive goal in itself. This would appear to explain why co-operative exchange is mutually reinforcing between them.

The analyses do not support the contention that this similarity of action is built up from a few inbuilt reflexes by a process of imitation or learning on the part of the child as has been proposed by psychologists of behaviourist persuasion (e.g. Bijou and Baer, 1965; Gewirtz, 1961), for such a process would not result in complementary behaviour, mutually completing a transactional activity in which the infant is an active generator from the start.

In the communication behaviour of infants 6–12 weeks of age the pattern of action is normally sustained by the mother following and complementing the infant's acts at particular points. She is the mimic more often than the infant. This is not to say that the infant is not dependent on social stimulation and making precise demands on the mother's acts. Indeed, our recent work shows that disturbances of the feedback of communication from the mother, made artificially, may cause the infant to change dramatically and predictively in emotional state. The reactions of the infant to unfriendly or unresponsive behaviour of the mother prove that the normal act of communication is highly regulated, and that adaptive acts of expression, indicating emotions of distress, are available to the infant to favour re-establishment of the process if it fails to fit within a prescribed format.

PRIMARY INTERSUBJECTIVITY

My first scientific experience with the specific communication function of young infants arose from comparison of the activities of infants confronted with their mothers, who were simply asked to talk to their baby, with the activities of the same infants on occasions when a small toy was dangled in front of them. A few minutes in each condition, and two or three alternations between the conditions, were filmed once a week during the first six months of life of five infants.*

A pronounced difference in responses to objects and persons was seen when the infants were two months old. I noted a number of forms of action of body, hands and face that were associated with the infant's smile and vocalizations to the mother. Differences were also present in the manner of response of the different mothers and we gained a clear impression that each mother–infant pair was developing a different style of mutual activity. In spite of these differences a general pattern of development in social behaviour was common to all five infants. I became convinced that an exceedingly complex innate mechanism foreshadowing the co-operative intelligence of adults, and more general than the mechanism of language, was already functioning in early infancy. The responses of the infants to persons were different in kind from those to objects, and they were pre-adaptive to reception and reply by persons.

Analysis of a typical friendly diadic exchange between a two-month-old infant boy and his mother is shown in Fig. 2. It reveals a number of the special features of such exchanges. Both partners are engaging in a number of comparable forms of social expression, and they do so alternately, but with brief periods of overlap in which they move together. The infant produces two long bursts of animated behaviour and one short one which is abruptly terminated by a shift of gaze away from the mother. In between these "displays" the infant looks attentively at the face of the mother who, at these moments, is calling or speaking to the baby. At the start both smile in recognition. The mother tends to follow the infant, and she responds to excited calling out and hand waving by smiling, shaking her head or speaking with head held back. Detailed analysis of the periods when both are active reveals that the mother is studiously imitating the infant's expression with a lag of between 0·2 and 1·0 seconds. The infant is evidently calling the tune (Fig. 3).

Photographic samples show how a mother may adopt postures and

* This work was done at the Center for Cognitive Studies, Harvard, in collaboration with Dr T. Berry Brazelton and Dr Martin Richards within a project on infant development organized by Professor Jerome Bruner and supported by the N.I.M.H.

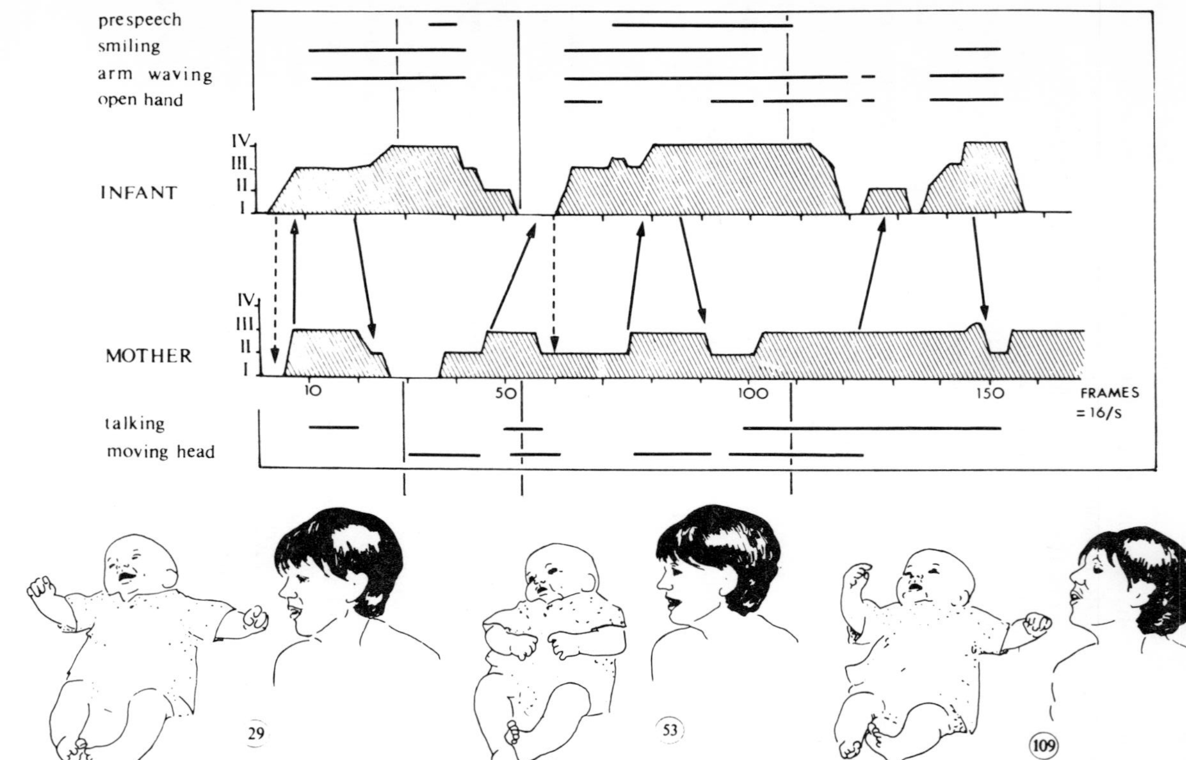

Fig. 2. Conversation-like exchange of 12-week-old boy with his mother. Periodic excitement and expression in vocalization, prespeech and gesture by infant is waited on and gently supported by the mother, who speaks most when the infant is quiet.

expressions to closely mirror what her baby does (Fig. 4). The intense mutuality or harmony of the behaviour comes initially from the infant responding to the mother's friendly behaviour in kind. Then the development is principally due to the mother accepting the expressions of the infant as models for her expression, or, rather, as indicative of an emotion which she may both share with her infant and express in like manner.

Examples of extremely close co-ordination of the infant's rudimentary vocalizations of pleasure or excitement with the baby talk of the mother are shown in Fig. 5. Apparently both partners are participating in a single rhythmical beat, as in music. Such timing of the acts of the infant to engage in the same rhythm as that of the mother's actions has been encountered in the majority of the detailed analyses we have made of fully developed communication. Thus the infant and mother generate a pattern of intention together. Condon and Sander (1974) have presented evidence that neonates synchronize climaxes of movement with speech of the mother, leaving the implication that the infant is entrained by a passive imitation to fit the mother's behaviour. We do not find synchrony as a rule, but by mutual regulation infant and mother appear to achieve a more complex co-operation which only occasionally results in synchrony of individual acts when mother and infant overlap to the same beat. Usually their acts alternate or complement one another.

We have now examined a large number of exchanges of infants at this age with their mothers in America and in Scotland. While almost all the mothers are from a middle social class they come from a variety of cultures and possess a wide range of knowledge of infants and of psychology, and a wide range of ideas about how infants become human. The general form of communication is the same.

I believe a correct description of this behaviour, to capture its full complexity, must be in terms of mutual intentionality and sharing of mental state. Either partner may initiate a "display" or "act of expression" and both act to sustain a sharing and exchange of initiatives. Both partners express complex purposive impulses in a form that is infectious for the other. It is difficult to perceive any content in the communication except the exchange itself—it is essentially phatic. The infant, at this age, does not appear capable of attending to acts of the mother that are directed towards objects. However, at certain points when engaged in elaborate expression the infant withdraws his or her

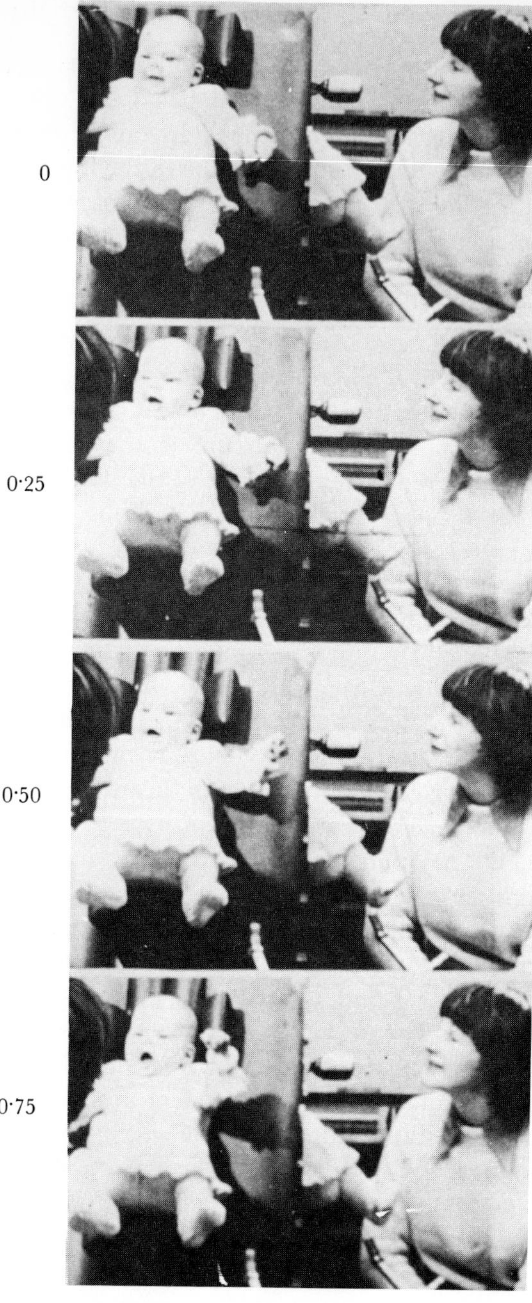
0
0·25
0·50
0·75

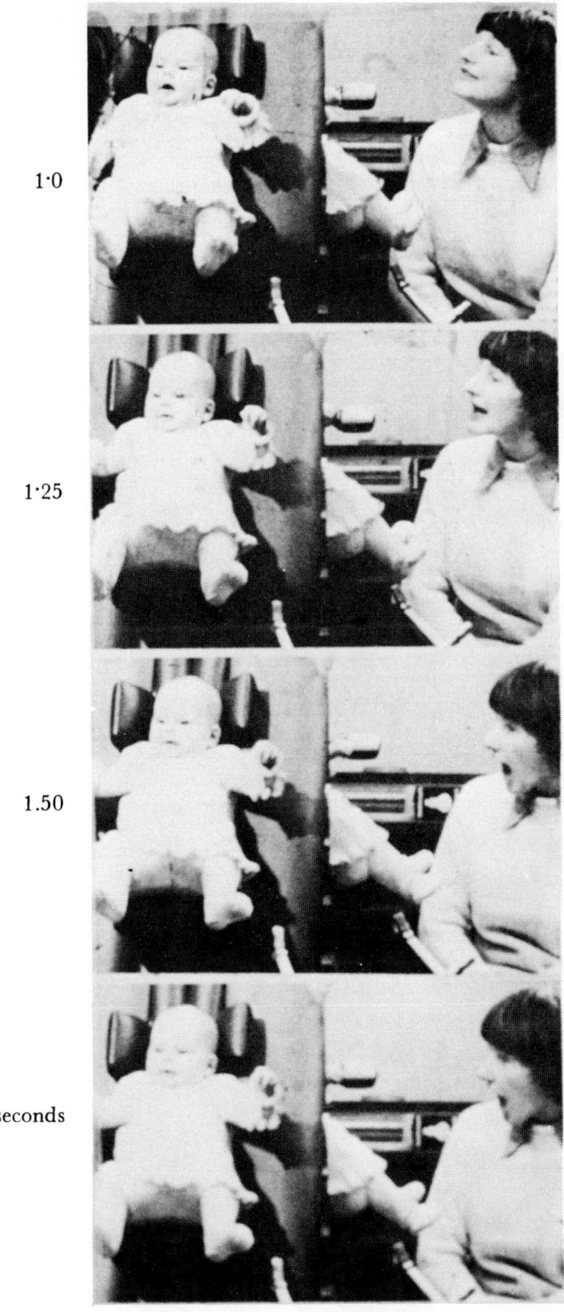

1·0

1·25

1.50

1·75 seconds

Fig. 3. Imitation of infant by mother. A typical cycle of calling out with arm-waving is followed by the mother giving an exaggerated vocalization. From a film. Baby girl of nine weeks.

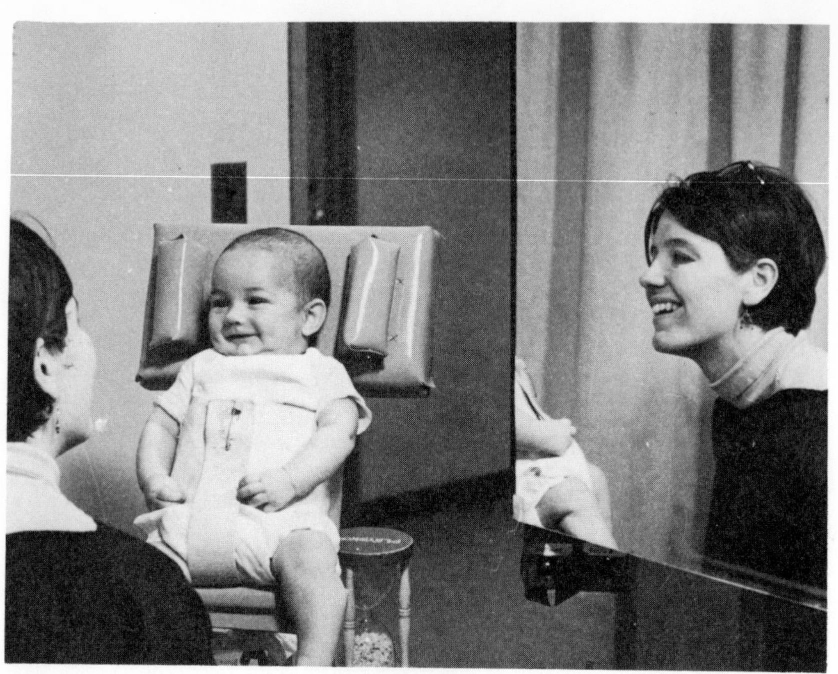

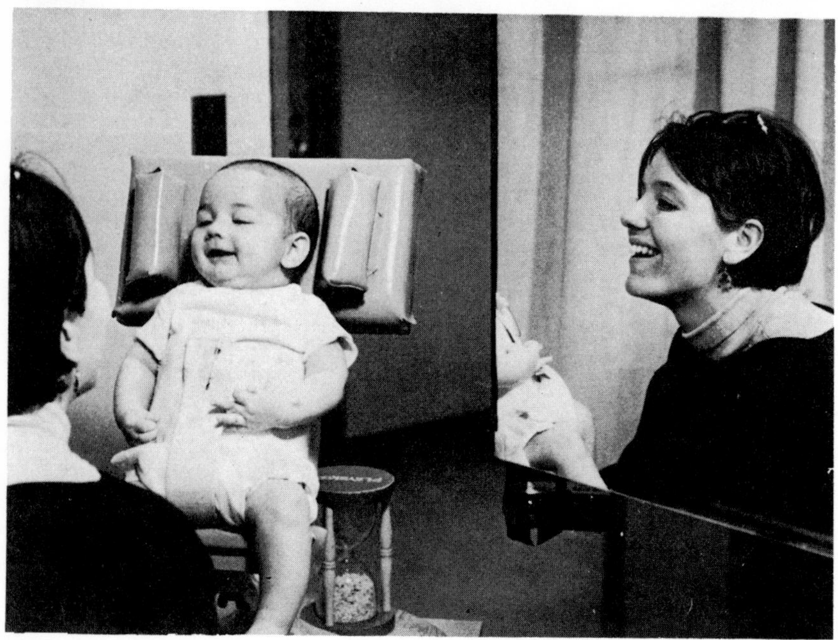

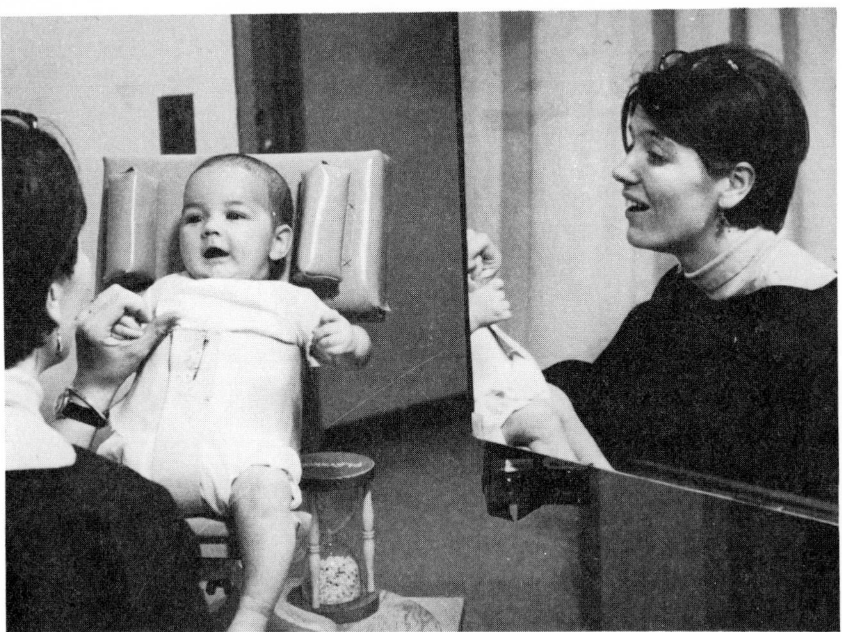

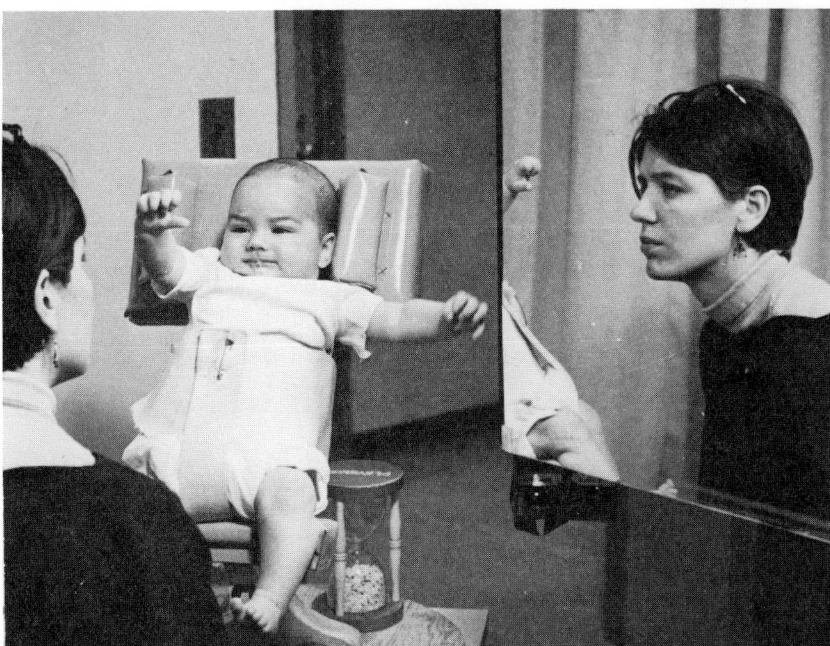

Fig. 4. Close imitation of baby by mother who is clearly dependent on the initiative of her nine-week-old boy.

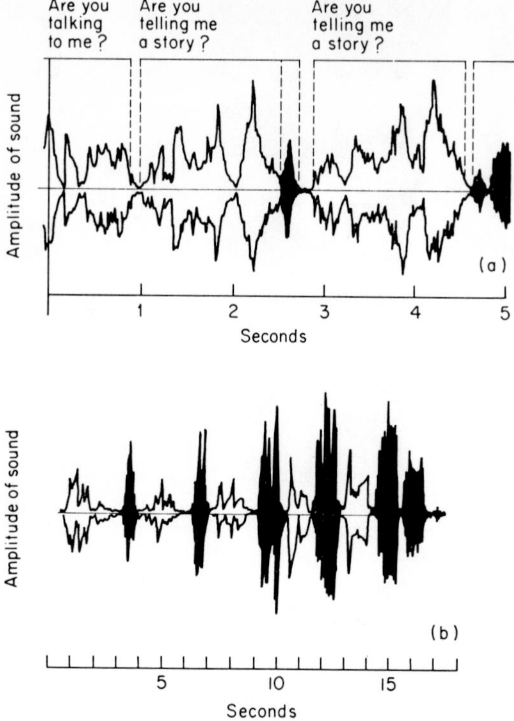

Fig. 5. Examples of behavioural co-ordination between mother and infant, recorded in sound. Traced from photographs of records transferred from tape to a storage oscillograph. Mother in white, baby in black.

(a) Nine-week-old baby boy responds with small cooing sounds to rhythmic and repeated baby-talk questions of mother.

(b) A 22-week-old joins in a game with her mother. The mother says, "You're a *cheeky* girl" repeatedly, bringing her face towards the baby each time she does so. Gradually her utterance becomes compacted and emphatic until she is saying "cheeky-girl" as one word. Her baby chuckles then giggles and, in the last three repetitions shown, laughs loudly. As in (a) the vocalizations of mother and baby are precisely alternated in time.

Mother (a) is a Scot, recorded in Edinburgh.

Mother (b) is an Australian, recorded in Melbourne.

gaze for a moment from the mother. I believe these moments of looking away, at something other than the mother, will develop, when the baby is older, into important initiatives of a different kind, to bring a topic into the communication. The evidence for this change is presented below.

The conversation-like exchanges which we are selectively recording under specially contrived conditions are, I believe, the most elaborate forms of joint action in which the infant is the leading partner. The feeding situation, where, as Richards (1974) and others have insisted, the mother must react co-operatively with the baby's behaviour, is a far less complex form of activity from a psychological point of view. A two- or three-month-old child expressing what Harriet Rheingold (1961) refers to as the "spontaneity, vivacity and delight" of communication with a person, is achieving an intricate control over the intentions and experiences of an individual of much more complex mentality. This may be achieved with nothing but auditory and visual contact between the partners. Accurate analysis of this process cannot be made in terms of a few stereotyped social reflexes which are extended by imitation and by conditioning in the presence of adults.

IMITATION

With recent verification that very young infants may imitate specific acts of adults (Uzgiris, 1974; Maratos, 1973) we might be encouraged to believe that the social acts reflect the remarkable learning activities of neonates. Our films include a few clear cases of specific imitation by infants of tongue protrusion, mouth opening, head movement and smiling. However, the details of the behaviour reveal that, far from explaining the intersubjective exchange, it is a particular by-product of a generative process which the infant could not learn (Trevarthen, 1974b, 1975).

It has often been noted that young infants tend to imitate acts that are within their own spontaneous repertoire. These are taken up by adults and then reproduced for the infant in a specific demonstrative manner. Imitation of very young (three or four weeks old) subjects may occur without clear localization of attention to the model. With babies two months old we find imitation occurs after a period of intense attention to a carefully demonstrated act by the mother who becomes a teacher in response to the infant's interest in her reproductions. When the infant is being more expressive and demonstrative, similarity between what the baby is doing and what the mother is doing is invariably due to the mother adopting the role of the mimic. In addition, as we shall see, some kinds of infant social expression are unique to them, or very rarely produced by the parent. Since models are not given, these acts must originate spontaneously.

Peter Wolff has described, with masterly clarity, the emergence of positive interpersonal communication between infants and adults in the fifth and sixth week (Wolff, 1969). Our studies of this change and the immediately subsequent highly sociable period lead us to describe the second and third months as the period of *primary intersubjectivity*, when sharing of intention with others becomes an effective psychological activity of the mind of a child.

PRESPEECH AND EARLY GESTICULATION

All normal human adults speak and at the same time they make complex changes of facial expression and they gesticulate with their hands. Charles Darwin (1872) made the first, and almost the last, thorough comparative study of human expression, and he concluded that the basis is innate and common to all races. (See Ekman, 1973 for an historical appraisal of the neglect of this field, and an account of highly significant work of the last decade.) Speech which is subtly integrated with emotional expression is cultivated into the great variety of languages, and gesticulation is accentuated in some cultures, kept subdued in others. A number of gesticulatory sign languages exist.

At points in intersubjective exchange between mother and two-month-old, when both partners are fully engaged in the process of sharing and reciprocally sustaining the communication, the infant periodically emits extremely complex expressive acts that are like acts usually thought to be learned conventional signs in human social exchange. These behaviours develop at about the same time as others that are accepted to have innate foundation.

Smiling, which has been extensively studied, and which is generally acknowledged to be a species-specific social signal acquired through evolution (as Darwin claimed), becomes clear and highly functional in the second month. It signs both pleasure in recognition or "mastery" (emphasized by Piaget, 1962) and readiness to communicate, this latter function being little understood. Smiling to voice appears at the normal time in blind babies, then diminishes through lack of visual support (Fraiberg, 1974). Eyebrow movements making quizzical, startled, angry or concentrated expressions are very clear with some infants. Sad or angry moods are also indicated by the set of the jaw and mouth, and the sound of crying has been shown to convey a number of messages concerning the needs or condition of the baby to which experienced caretakers respond in quite specific ways. Other more pleasurable vocalizations may be distinguished in the first month and they become much clearer and highly effective as definitely social acts, directed to persons and reinforced by reply vocalizations, in subsequent weeks.

Associated with smiling and pleasure vocalizations made with open mouth are more subtle figures of mouth and tongue movements which are generally performed silently. We give particular attention to these because they occur in a phase of the integrated communication act which endows them with special communicative significance (Fig. 6).

The normal pattern of response by an infant of two months to an attentive, talking mother is as follows—altering of expression and orientation to her face, focalization on her eyes, smiling, increase in body activity, vocalization, often accompanied by a shift of gaze from eyes upwards to the hair, down to the mouth or away from the mother's face to somewhere in the background. This is the sequence remarked upon by Rheingold (1961) as occurring again and again in the social responses of infants. It may be divided into a phase of orientation, a sign of recognition, then an expressive phase, and a close or termination which may take the form of a withdrawal or a return to orientation and recognition (cf. Fig. 2). When showing recognition, the infant is highly receptive to expressions or "messages" of the partner.

In the expressive phase, in which vocalizations are conspicuous, there may alternatively be elaborate grimacing with small movements of the lips, extensions of the tongue to between the lips, into the lower lip, arching of the tongue to meet the tucked in upper lip or gum, lip-pursing etc. The movements are due to rapid successions of small contractions among the complex muscles of lips and tongue. They are generally performed with the face unsmiling and the eyes may be on the eyes of the mother. Often when most "taken up" or "carried away" by the behaviour, an infant will glance upwards away from the mother's face. These movements are outside the range of face expressions described as "emotional", though they grade into emotional expressions of disgust, disdain, surprise, etc.

As a rule, the mother shows marked sensitivity to the baby's intensity and quality of effort, and frequently the mouth movements, even if they are quite silent, are interpreted by the mother, spontaneously, as attempts to talk (Sylvester-Bradley and Trevarthen, 1977). Thus she may say, "What are you trying to tell me?" or "Oh, what a lot you have to say!" Generally the mother's comments are made immediately *after* the infant has stopped moving in this way; they constitute replies. Often a succession of addresses and replies between the partners succeed

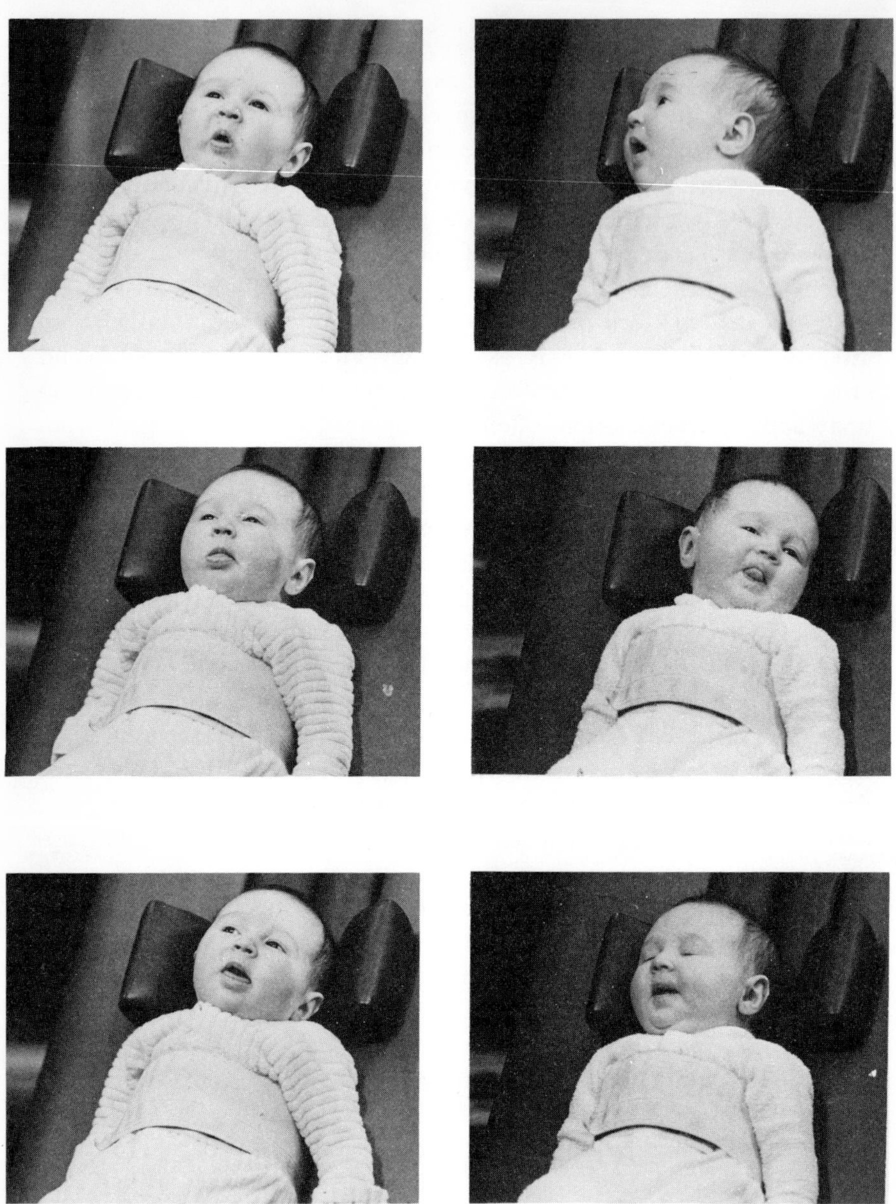

Fig. 6. Prespeech movements of lips and tongue. Seven-week-old baby girl.

one another in a temporal configuration of behaviour remarkably like that of a conversation between adults. We therefore agree with those authors who describe such behaviour as "proto-conversational" (e.g. Bateson, 1971).

Sound recordings displayed on an oscilloscope show how the baby may respond with small sounds in accurate co-ordination with repeated musical questions of the mother's baby talk (Fig. 5a). These sounds of the baby are made at the same locus in communication as are the movements of lip and tongue which we first detected by observing silent ciné films.

Since the psychological situation for the baby's expressive mouth movements is, in general, similar to that between two persons engaged in speaking together, and since the movements of lips and tongue resemble the movements adults make with the mouth while speaking, we feel justified in labelling this weakly voiced mouth activity of the infant *prespeech*. We think of it as an embryonic form of the act of speech. Preliminary observations of respiratory movements made by the two partners support the hypothesis that the prespeech movements are made in association with breathing adjustments like those which are essential to the controlled voicing of adult speech. We are beginning a study of the way in which vocalization is mastered and drawn into prespeech to create the varied articulation of speech sounds by movement of jaws, tongue, cheeks and lips. Remembering that young infants lack teeth, we conclude that the movements of prespeech anticipate many of the movements essential to the formation of forward vowels and front sto-consonants. From film, we cannot easily make inferences about sound made by the tongue moving in the back of the mouth.

Accompanying prespeech and vocalization to persons are movements of the whole body—changes in head position, trunk movements, movements of all the limbs. Most conspicuous among these are hand and arm movements which are frequently closely synchronized (to within 0·1 seconds) with utterances or grimaces. Self synchrony of acts of speech, posture and gesture is characteristic of communication behaviour (Birdwhistell, 1970). It depends on the rhythmic generators of action that regulate all voluntary co-ordination. Synchrony between communicators (Condon and Sander, 1974) requires a co-ordination of similar rhythms of action in each of them.

Vigorous calls or shouts are generally combined with longer movements including waving of the hand with palm directed forward from a position above shoulder level. Prespeech is frequently combined with more complex and individuated finger movements, including pointing with the index finger (Trevarthen, 1974a). We are now of the opinion that these acts will be found to recur in highly regulated patterns that may be identified as autonomous hand signs made spontaneously by the baby. Although different infants move their hands in different ways, most show hand-waving, index-finger pointing and fingertip-clasping movements near the face while they are animated to make expressive vocalization and prespeech. We therefore call these hand patterns *gesticulation*, and we regard them as genetically determined or innate in basis, though they are certainly open to modification by imitation. They have apparently, at this stage, no specific reference to things outside communication. Each gesture signals a particular change in the level or direction of communication itself.

Among the acts of adults that young infants have been found to imitate are mouth and tongue movements, vocalization and hand movements. All of these are acts employed in some form by infants spontaneously when they are socially excited. I believe the hand movements which infants imitate should be regarded as gesticulation for which they possess an innate co-ordinating substrate. Most of the patterns of gesticulation which we have studied with two- or three-month-olds were clearly not imitations of the adult partner, who was doing nothing resembling them. Nor could the adult easily be imagined making movements of that kind except in excited communication with other adults. Fraiberg (1974) reports "hand language" in blind babies, a language which mothers have to be taught to see and use in aiding their infants.

For a long time we did not see the gesticulations in our films and mothers appear to react to them in a quite unconscious way. However, comparison of behaviours of different infants reveal that some form of gesticulation is present in all by two months, and that stereotyped patterns such as waving and pointing occur over and over again.

Now that we know when to expect them and what to look for we detect weaker signs of gesticulation in the social responses of neonates (Fig. 7). We believe, therefore, that these expressive behaviours follow a course of development close to smiling which is at first produced only weakly as a social response. Their outline is present at birth and they apparently emerge from a latent state to active, elaborate, effective and

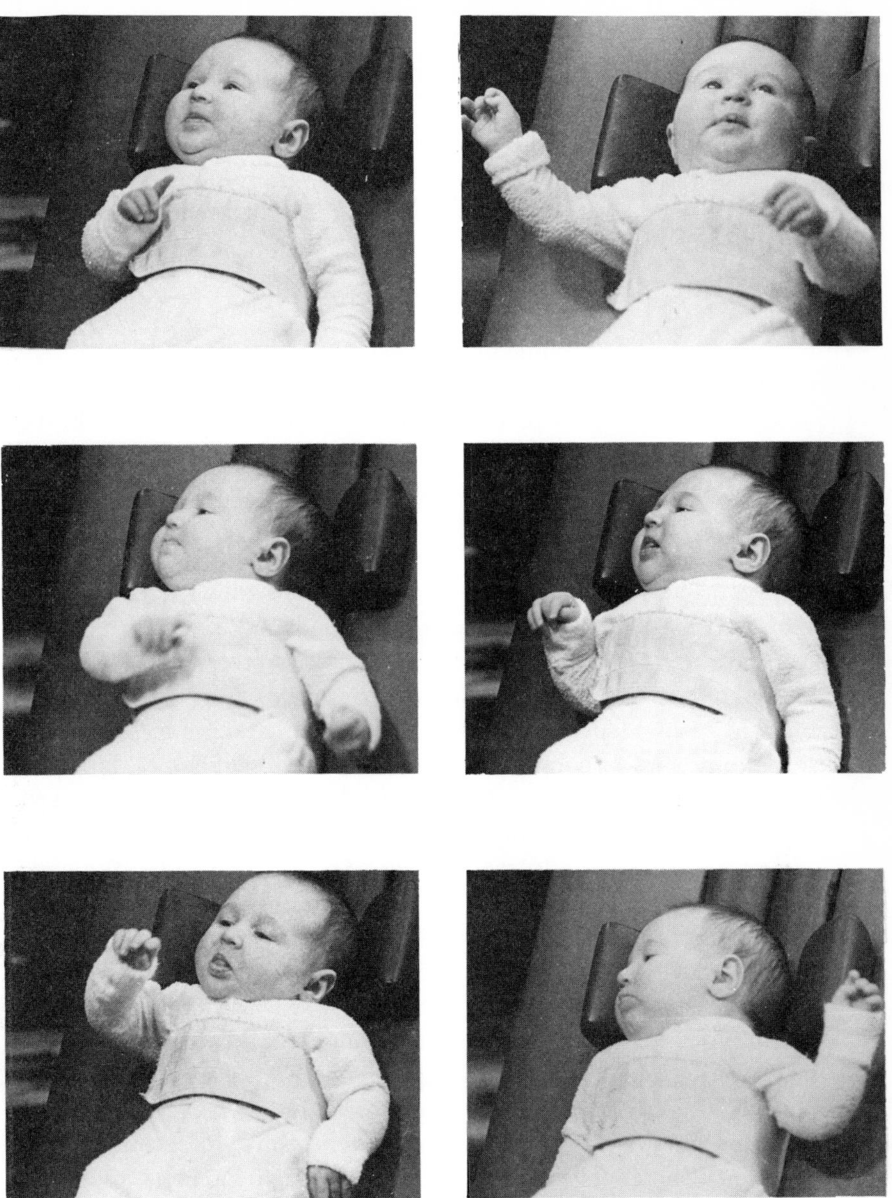

Fig. 7. Infantile gesticulation and gesture. Seven-week-old baby girl.

more specifically responsive form in the fourth and fifth week following birth. As with early smiling and vocalization, prespeech and hand gesticulations, which become well integrated in social exchange, may also occur without a stimulus as stereotyped expressions of "need to function" or as spontaneous generators of specific reafferent effects (circular reactions).

INTEGRATION OF EXPERIENCE WITH COMMUNICATION OF INTENT

However rich and satisfying in itself, communication with an infant under six months of age is essentially devoid of reference to things in the objective world. It is preoccupied with intersubjectivity itself. To become communication of or about experiences between the partners, the process must be changed to encompass an external topic, by adding a predicative function that diverts attention from time to time out of the diadic pattern. Psychologically, initiative and experience are complements, and throughout the development of knowledge, assimilation of information from the world depends upon adjustment of subjective initiatives of action to the layout of objective information. In the shared initiative of communication, experience of surroundings must be brought in by a specific act that refers to or attaches to something outside the process of communication itself.

The subjects we have studied longitudinally all show a marked change in manner of communication at the time they attain workable control of prehension, at 16 to 18 weeks (Trevarthen, 1976). We were surprised at first to discover 20-week-old infants making persistent refusals of their mothers' approaches by withdrawing gaze from them and looking pointedly elsewhere. We noted that at the same time they were still prepared to engage in friendly exchanges with much vocalization, smiling and gesticulation or reaching out in response to *other* familiar adults. This finding is in agreement with paradoxical findings concerning the development of "fear" or "strange" reactions, which occur first in marked form not to distorted human faces but to the mother when she changes her appearance. Both phenomena appear to be due to a specific development with reference to the most familiar person, to whom the infant has the clearest "attachment". All considered, "attachment" is not a good word for the psychological functions involved—"personal relationship" gives a better description of the communication process which has grown up between the infant and mother or other most attentive person.

Follow-up research has taught us to regard the coldness towards an attentive mother at five months to be a prelude to highly co-operative behaviour of a new kind which is characteristic of 9- to 12-month-olds. This development brings together the new achievements of manipulation and object perception and the highly articulate and personal communicative system that infant and mother or other principal companion have built between them.

In this work we obtain information both from the acts of the infant and from the speech of the mother who comments on the action, giving her linguistic interpretation of the purposes and acts of the baby and of her reactions (Sylvester-Bradley and Trevarthen, 1977). However, the principal new functions that lead to the formation of a new form of communication may be seen in the acts mother and infant perform together with objects. We therefore add to the filming situation some toys or other small objects on a table surface within reach of both mother and infant.

Guided by our findings with younger infants we have paid careful attention not only to the initiatives of the mother in starting, extending or redirecting play, but of the infant in accepting or refusing her offers, and in making offers or independently starting other acts with respect to the mother and her manifest interest.

Figure 8 illustrates our main conclusions with regard to this important psychological development. We know that in detail the process is much more complex than shown by this simplified example, but the essential process is one of two developmental phases in the initiatives of the infant. Adaptation of the mother to these changes ensures that communication will remain, and that it will be transferred into a prototype of an instructional exchange which is also a game.

MOODS OF PLAY AND DESPAIR

Understanding that communication between mother and infant consists in a process of shared initiatives provides models for a variety of different kinds of mutual exchange or shared state. We find that mood or affect changes of the infant may be regulated by the manner in which the mother organizes the infant's intentions in complement to her own.

Play, leading to a structured game and laughter, develops hand in hand with primary intersubjectivity. It is characterized by ritual organization of exchange through a predictable sequence to a climax.

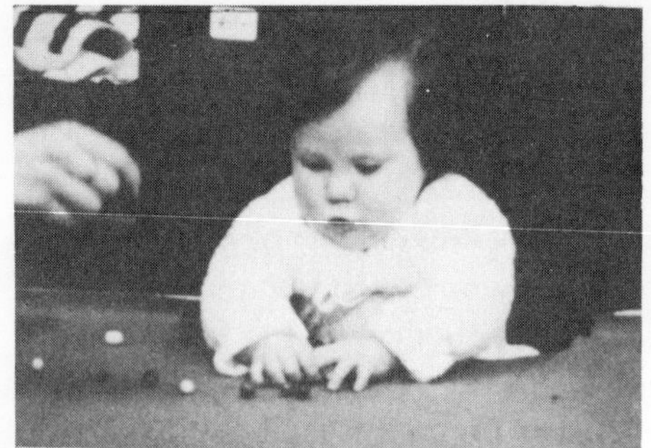

0 seconds

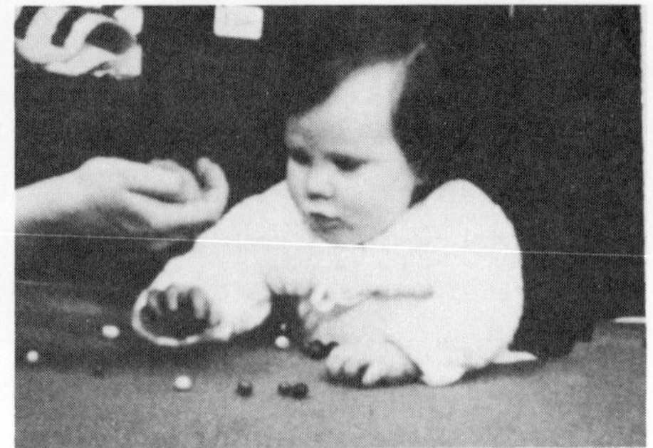

1·0

2·0

3·0

4·25

4·50

4·75

5·25 seconds

Fig. 8. Changing communication behaviour of baby girl following the development of reaching to objects. Transition from primary (diadic) to secondary intersubjectivity.

(a) Baby of 26 weeks avoids looking at mother and pushes away an object which she offers.

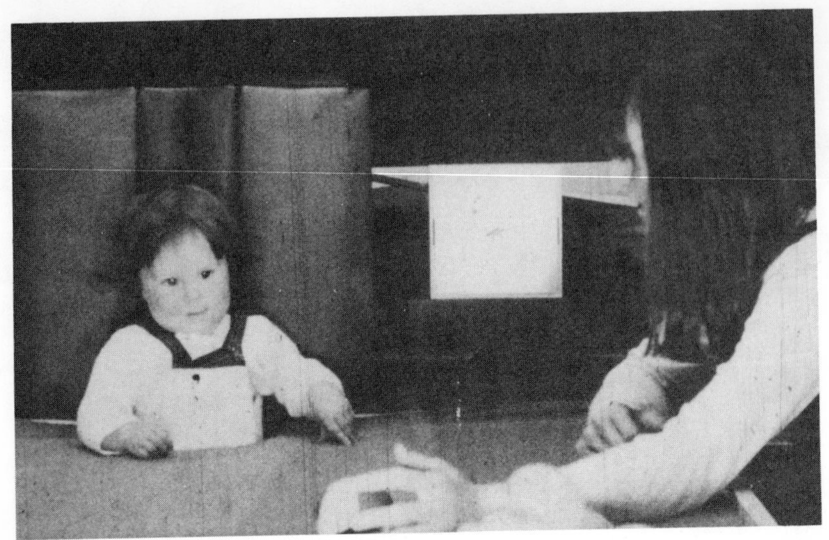

0

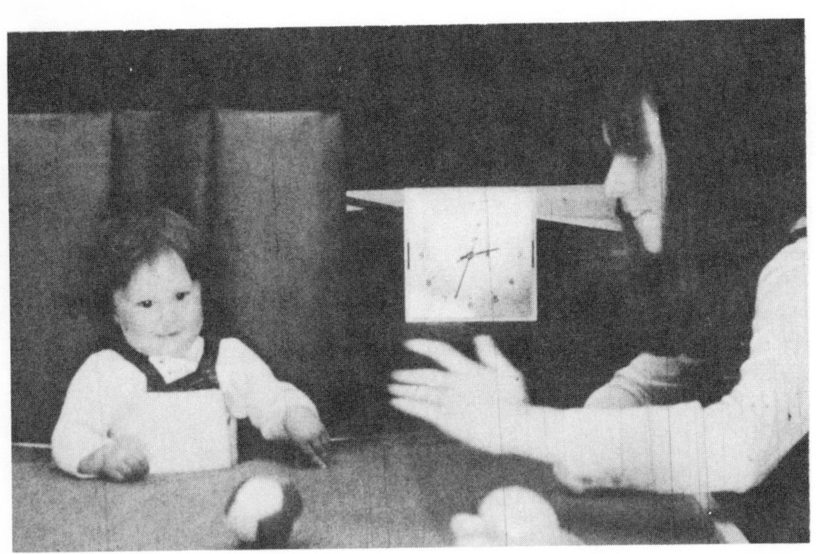

1·0

2·0

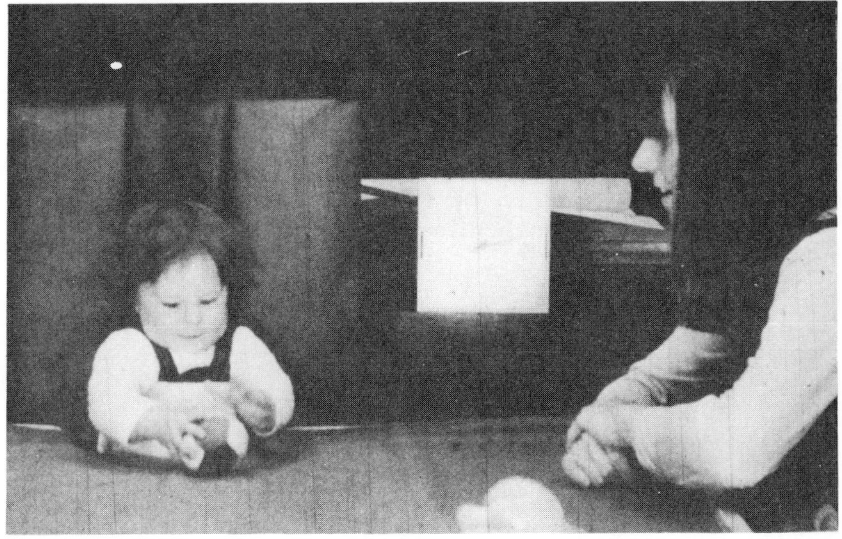

2·5 seconds

Fig. 8 (b) The same little girl of 47 weeks happily accepts an object offered by her mother.

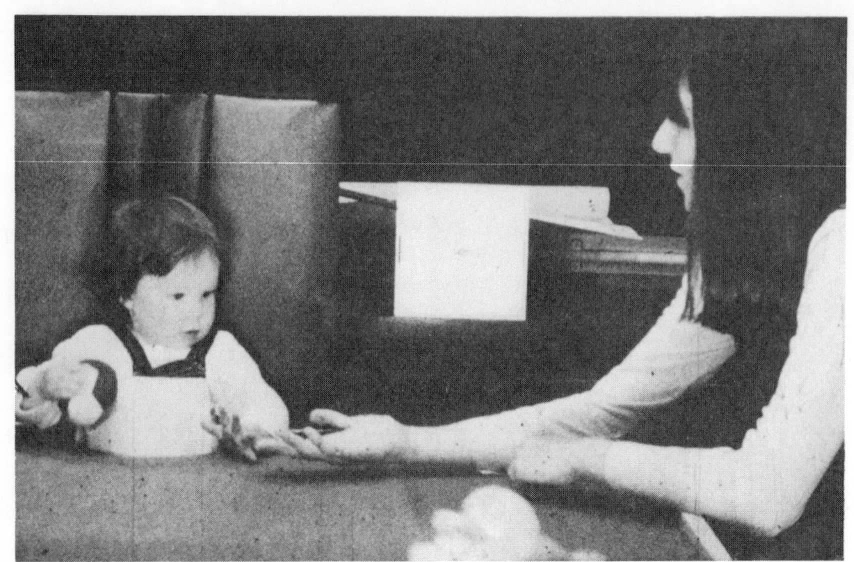

0 seconds

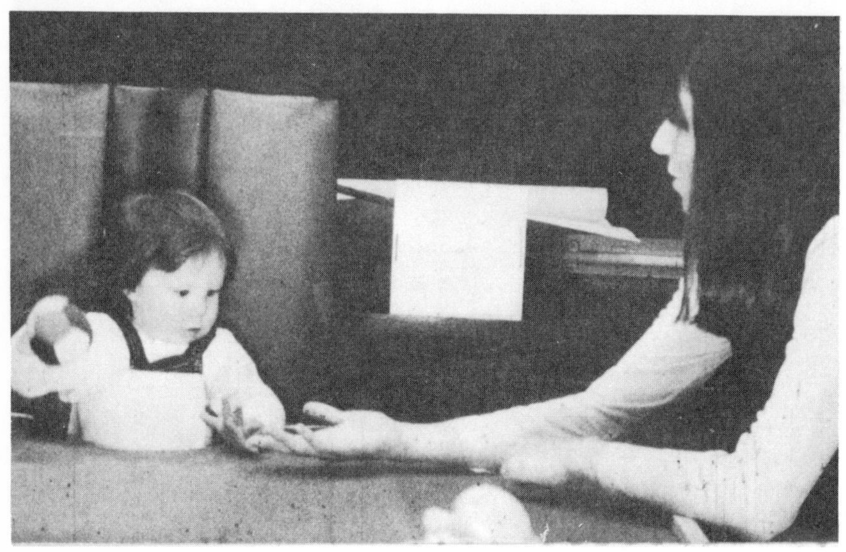

0·25

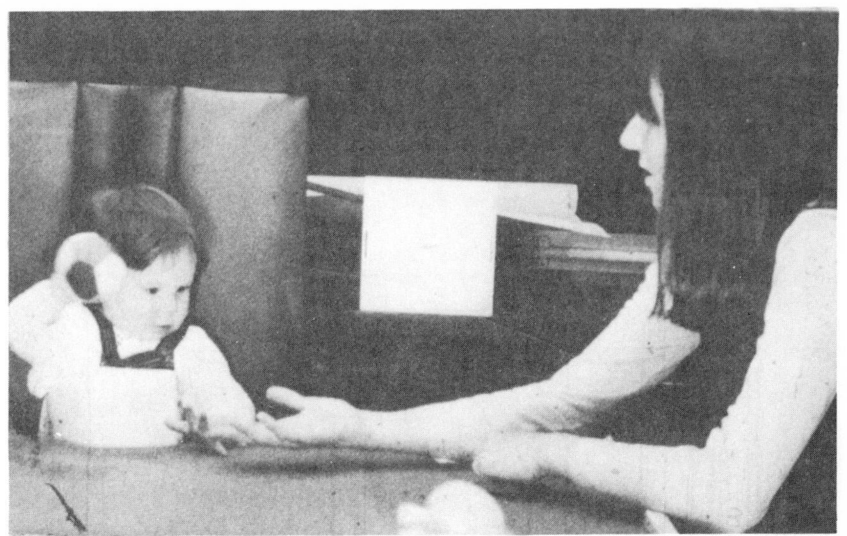

0·50

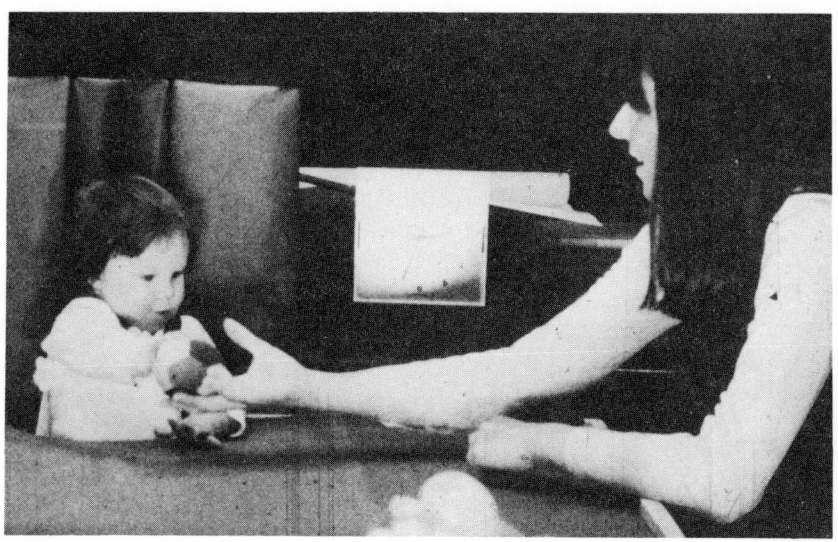

0·75

Fig. 8 (c) See legend p. 263.

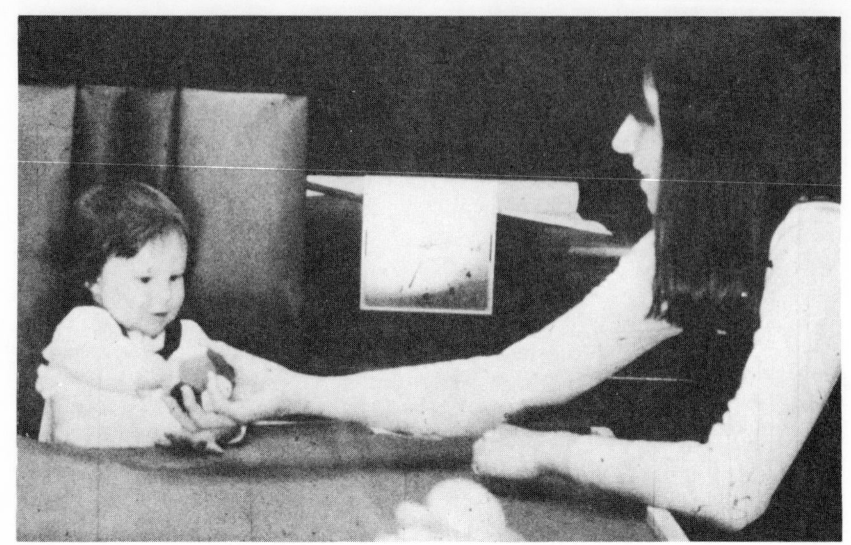

1·00

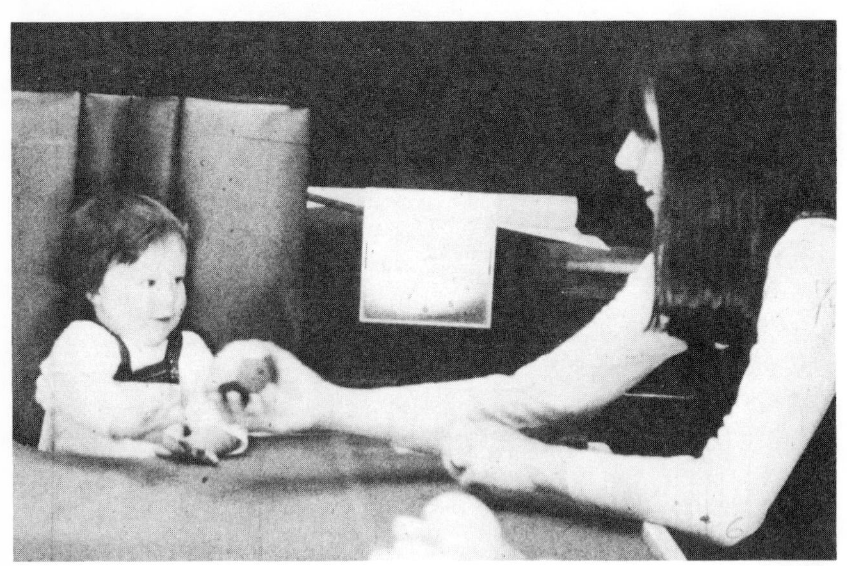

1·25

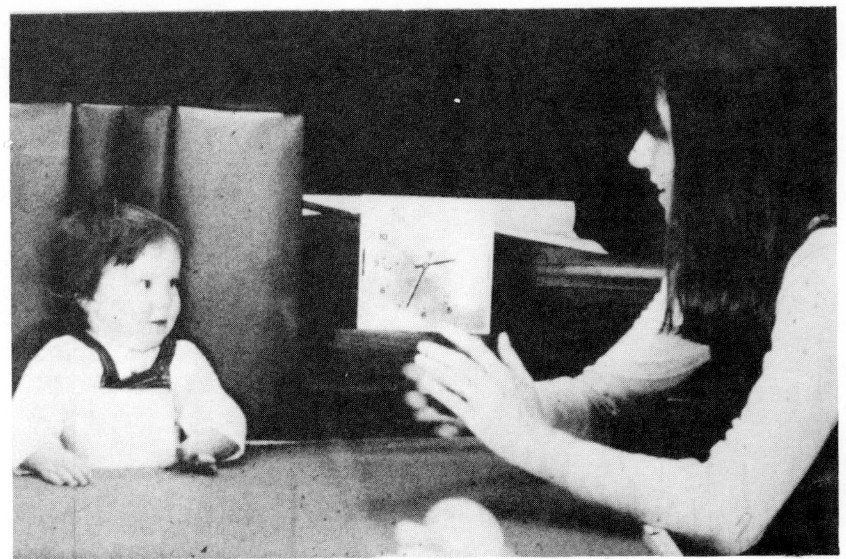

1·50 seconds

Fig. 8 (c) She will also give an object with a smile at this age (47 weeks).

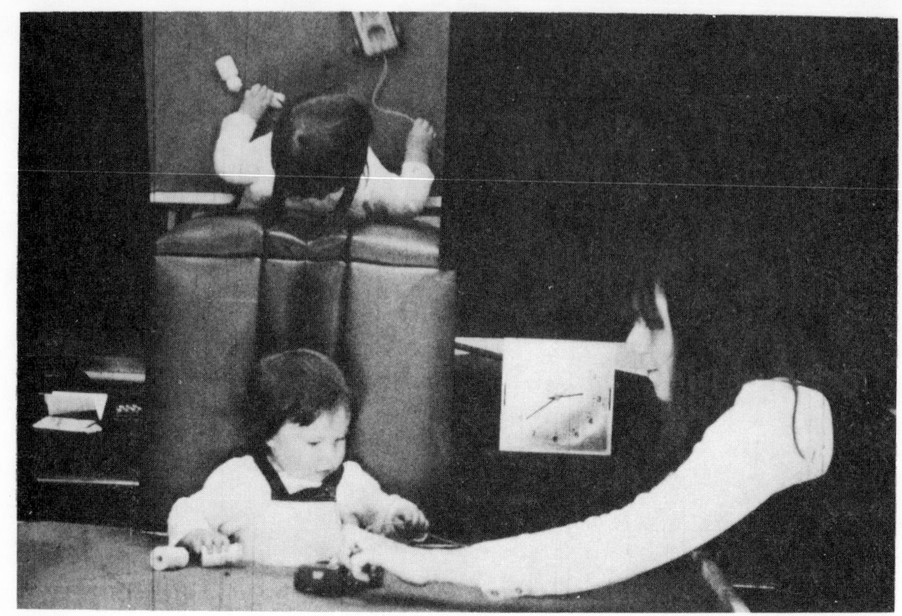

0 seconds

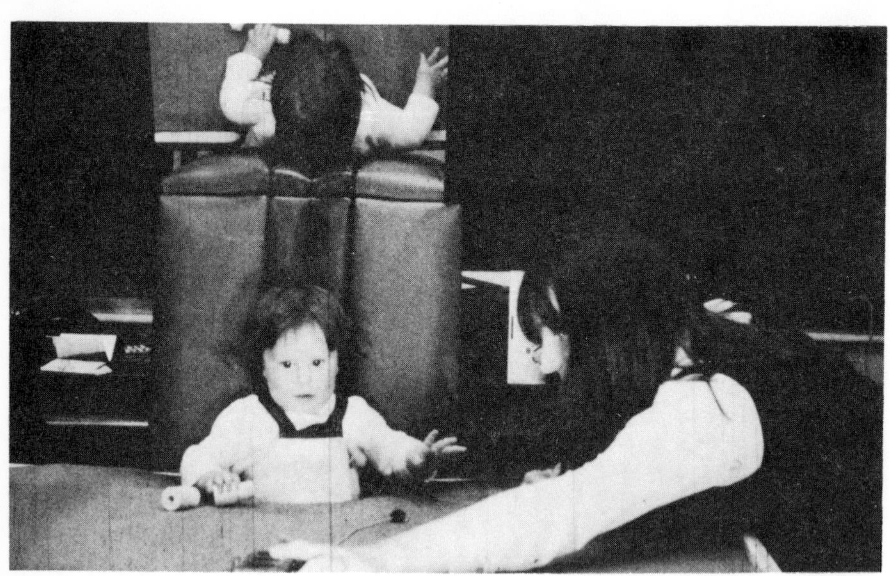

0·50

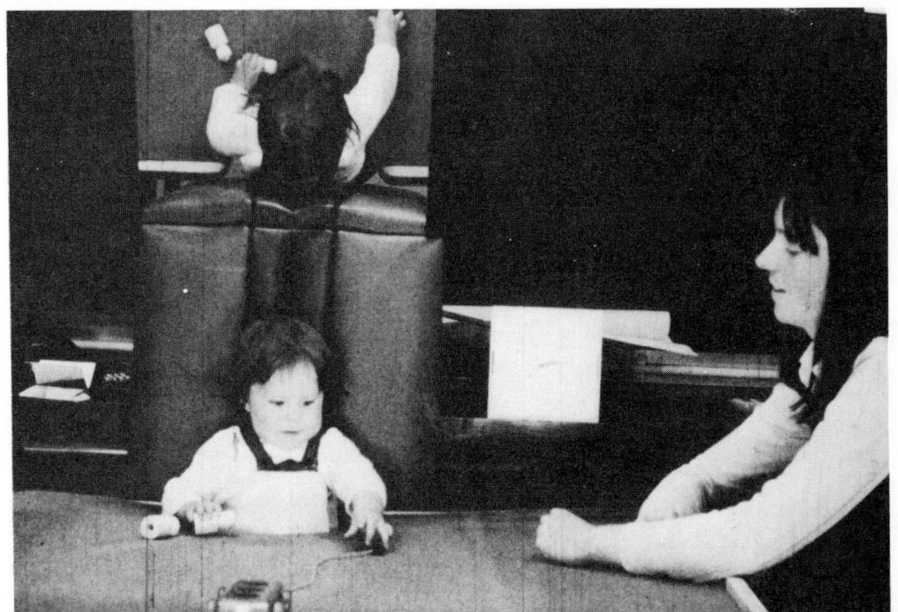

2·50

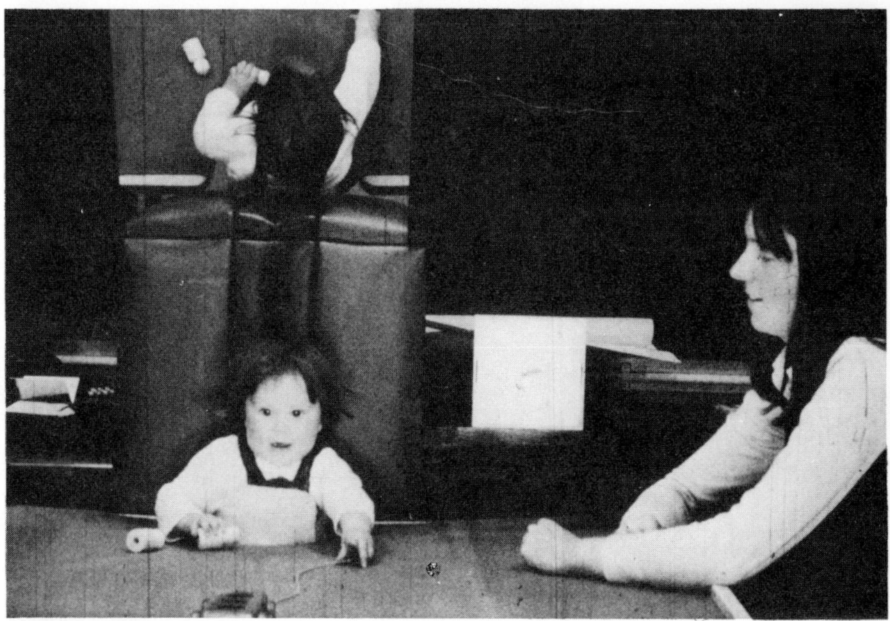

3·00

Fig. 8 (d) See legend p. 266.

5·00

6·50 seconds

Fig. 8 (d) Watching her mother show how, then using an object in play (47 weeks).

An example of this build up, and of the close temporal integration achieved between the partners, is shown in the voice record of Fig. 5b. In all techniques to elicit laughter from babies the partner must lead the positive social response of the baby to a point at which both are experiencing some twist of their relationship intensely and synchronously. In the classic game of pat-a-cake this pattern is clear. Wolff's (1969) description of the earliest stimuli to laughter indicate that they consist of a deliberate aiming of touch stimuli to particular parts of the infant's body. Marilyn Elliot (working in our laboratory) finds that natural social play of mothers with their eight-week-old babies always consists in simple stereotyped moulding of social exchange, so that attention is directed strongly to key events in the mutual contact itself. The mother makes a rhythmic, repeating build-up of social expectancy. If there is not careful integration of the play with the baby's own social signs then the game is a frustrating failure.

Thus the first games are essentially social. Games with toys arise through the development of sharing experience of objects that has been outlined above. They become a characteristic part of the social life of infants 9 or 12 months of age.

John Tatam and Lynne Murray in our laboratory have found with eight-week-olds that failure of communication due to lack of response or paradoxical response of the mother may lead to expressions of confusion, distress and crying, inert dejection, or withdrawal into self. Very slight, temporary and subtle changes in the mothers' actions, made experimentally over one minute, produce strong but entirely reversible changes in the infants' communication. Tatam switched the mother's attention from the infant to another adult by means of a change of lighting either side of a partially reflecting window. The infant, who continued to see the mother, showed strong reactions of puzzlement and unhappiness when her communication behaviour switched to adult discourse and became non-contingent with respect to the infant's actions.

Murray has employed voluntary immobilization of the mother's face to observe stereotyped expressions of unhappiness in infants of 7–12 weeks. The baby becomes unhappy, looks puzzled, stares at his fisted hand, avoids the mother's eyes but makes quick glances at them, and makes contorted grimaces. She has also studied the effect of interruptions of communication by a third person coming to speak to the mother. These are much less disturbing for the infant.

These studies, with very brief perturbations, well within the range of events that might occur easily in the home with a mother who has many things on her mind and several persons to attend to, demonstrate the sensitivity of analyses of infant emotionality based on films. The techniques of diagrammatic representation and selective sampling which we have developed to understand communication have become extended in this way to study emotional functions within the repertoire of a young human being. We feel we have obtained strong evidence that emotion or mood is very much tied in with sharing and co-operating from the early months of life.

Conclusions

It has been my main purpose in this paper to emphasize what can be learned from detailed descriptions of natural communicatory acts of infants with the aid of film or T.V. Of course, a good dose of theory is important in any observational work. There is no reason why experimental or analytical tests cannot be performed on the behaviours described. But the experiments attempted will determine what will be found, and no one is going to experiment with the complex generative structures of infants if these structures are assumed not to exist in their own right but to be passively registered from experience. This is why we feel there is a prior need for observation and description.

The descriptive studies show what a range of questions we should be asking when we resort to experiment in order to iron out ambiguities in detailed interpretation. They also provide a general map of the main developmental process which has a definite form, independent of events, because it is regulated from inside the growing brain of the child.

Acknowledgements

The research at Edinburgh on which this paper is based has been supported by the S.S.R.C. The manuscript was prepared at La Trobe University, Bundoora, Victoria, Australia and I am very happy to thank the Department of Psychology there for generous provision of facilities. I wish also to thank Dr Beryl McKenzie who made many helpful comments while writing was in progress.

References

Ahrens, R. (1954). Beitrag zur Entwicklung her Physiognomie und Mimikerkennes. *Z. Expti. Angew Psychol.* **2**, 412–454.

Ambrose, J. A. (1961). The development of the smiling response in early infancy. In B. M. Foss (Ed.), *Determinants of Infant Behaviour*. Methuen, London.

Bateson, M. C. (1971). The interpersonal context of infant vocalization. *Quarterly Progress Report, Research Lab of Electronics, M.I.T.*, No. 100, 170–176.

Bernstein, N. (1967). *The Coordination and Regulation of Movements*. Pergamon Press, Oxford.

Bijou, S. W. and Baer, D. M. (1965). *Child Development: II. Universal Stage of Infancy*. Appleton-Century-Crofts, New York.

Birdwhistell, R. L. (1970). *Kinesics and Context*. Univ. of Pennsylvania Press, Philadelphia.

Bower, T. G. R. (1974). *Development in Infancy*. Freeman and Co., San Francisco.

Brackbill, Y. (1958). Extinction of the smiling response in infants as a function of reinforcement schedule. *Child Dev.* **42**, 17–26.

Condon, W. S. and Sander, L. W. (1974). Synchrony demonstrated between movements of the neonate and adult speech. *Child Dev.* **45**, 456–462.

Darwin, C. (1872). *The Expression of the Emotions in Man and in Animals*. Appleton and Co., New York (Reprinted University of Chicago Press, Chicago, 1965).

Eisenberg, R. B. (1975). *Auditory Competence in Early Life. The Roots of Communicative Behaviour*. Univ. Park Press, Baltimore.

Ekman, P. (1973). *Darwin and Facial Expression: A Century of Research in Review*. Academic Press, New York and London.

Fraiberg, S. (1974). Blind infants and their mothers: An examination of the sign system. In M. Lewis and L. A. Rosenblum (Eds), *The Effect of the Infant on its Caregiver*. Wiley, New York.

Gewirtz, J. L. (1961). A learning analysis of the effects of normal stimulation, privation and deprivation on the acquisition of social motivation and attachment. In B. M. Foss (Ed.), *Determinants of Infant Behaviour*. Methuen, London.

Gewirtz, J. L. (1965). The course of infant smiling in four child-rearing environments in Israel. In B. M. Foss (Ed.), *Determinants of Infant Behaviour*, Vol. 3. Methuen, London.

Gibson, J. J. (1967). *The Senses Considered as Perceptual Systems*. Houghton, Mifflin and Co., Boston, Mass.

Lashley, K. S. (1951). The problem of serial order in behavior. In L. A. Jeffress, (Ed.), *Cerebral Mechanisms in Behavior*. Wiley, New York.

Maratos, O. (1973). The origin and development of imitation in the first six months of life. Ph.D. Thesis, University of Geneva.

Piaget, J. (1950). *Psychology of Intelligence*. Harcourt Brace Jovanovich, New York.

Piaget, J. (1962). *Play, Dreams and Imitation in Childhood*. Norton, New York.

Rheingold, H. L. (1961). The effect of environmental stimulation upon social and exploratory behaviour in the human infant. In B. M. Foss (Ed.), *Determinants of Infant Behaviour*, Vol. 1. Methuen, London.

Rheingold, H. L., Gewirtz, J. L. and Ross, H. W. (1959). Social conditioning of vocalizations in the infant. *J. comp. physiol. Psychol.* **52**, 68–73.

Richards, M. P. M. (1974). The development of psychological communication in the first year of life. In K. J. Connolly and J. S. Bruner (Eds), *The Growth of Competence.* Academic Press, London and New York.

Spitz, R. A. and Wolf, K. M. (1946). The smiling response; a contribution to the ontogenesis of social relationships. *Genet psychol. Monogr.* **34**, 57–125.

Sylvester-Bradley, B. and Trevarthen, C. (1977). "Baby-talk" as an adaptation to the infant's communication. In N. Waterson and K. Snow (Eds), *Development of Communication: Social and Pragmatic Factors in Language Acquisition.* Wiley, London. In press.

Trevarthen, C. (1974a). The psychobiology of speech development. In E. H. Lenneberg (Ed.), *Language and Brain: Developmental Aspects. Neurosciences Research Program Bulletin.* **12**, 570–585.

Trevarthen, C. (1974b). Intersubjectivity and imitation in infants. *Proc. B.P.S. Annual Conference,* April, 1974, Bangor, p. 33.

Trevarthen, C. (1974c). L'action dans l'espace et la perception de l'espace; mechanismes cerebraux de base. In F. Bresson *et al.* (Eds), *De l'Espace Corporel a l'Espace Ecologique.* Presses Universitaires de France, Paris.

Trevarthen, C. (1975). Basic patterns of psychogenetic change in infancy. To be published in the *Proceedings of the O.E.C.D. Conference on "Dips in Learning"*, St. Paul de Vence, March, 1975.

Trevarthen, C. (1976). Intentional movements of infants (in preparation).

Uzgiris, I. E. (1974). Patterns of vocal and gestural imitation in infants. In L. J. Stone, H. T. Smith and L. B. Murphy, *The Competent Infant.* Tavistock, London.

Washburn, R. W. (1929). A study of the smiling and laughing of infants in the first year of life. *Genet. psychol. Monogr.* **6**, 397–535.

Watson, J. S. (1973). Smiling, cooing and "the game". *Merrill-Palmer Q.* **18**, 323–339.

Wolff, P. H. (1969). The natural history of crying and other vocalizations in early infancy. In B. M. Foss (Ed.), *Determinants of Infant Behaviour,* Vol. 4. Methuen, London.

Wolff, P. H. (1963). Observations on the early development of smiling. In B. M. Foss (Ed.), *Determinants of Infant Behaviour*, Vol. 2. Methuen, London.

11 | Early Social Interaction and Language Acquisition*

Jerome S. Bruner

Introduction

In several of my articles discussing cognitive development in infants I have explored the manner in which early intellectual growth depends not only on absorbing information about the environment but also on *acting upon* that knowledge—storing a model not only of the world but of one's effect upon it brought about by active intervention in it. My emphasis was principally upon the way in which, through development of successive hypotheses about the world and how our actions affect it, the child climbs stepwise up the ladder of competence. The steps may be considered as constituent skills for coping both socially and physically. Progress or growth consists of sufficient mastery of these constituents so that, in time, they can be combined into longer, more comprehensive skill sequences directed toward longer tasks involving remoter goals with delayed rewards.

I should now like to carry the matter one step further—to go beyond the acquisition of individual skills to consider the basis in language for achieving co-operation in skilled action, which in the case of the child consists of learning first how to achieve co-operative action with his mother. I hesitate a little about reminding the reader that, quite obviously, man as a species is notable for his initial helplessness, and I

* This paper was prepared jointly with Alison Garton and Eileen Caudill who collaborated in the research discussed and in the writing of this report.

mention it only as a reminder of the amount of "motivation" there is on the side of both the mother and the infant to enter into a co-operative relationship. There are two other rather obvious preliminaries worth mentioning. The first is that much of the initial acquisition of communicative skill occurs in the context of mother and infant carrying out *tasks* jointly—one or the other trying to get help in achieving some goal, be it getting something to eat, retrieving a dropped object, or getting a "game" to be repeated. As we shall see, this links early language very closely to the requirements of joint action. And indeed it may well be the case that the very structure of human language reflects this initial requirement, as well as the broader evolutionary requirement that man communicates effectively in order to carry out his brand of social-technical existence. The second point has to do with the acculturated or conventional ways in which human tasks are accomplished. In many of them it is almost more important that we agree to do things in a certain way than that we do the particular thing, i.e. it is more important that we *agree* in Britain to drive on the left than that the choice was for the left side.

The ambience of play is of central importance in providing the context for numerous joint activities between mother and child and in providing "tension-free" opportunities for exercising one's combinatorial abilities for dealing with the social and physical environment (Bruner, 1974). Indeed, play is serious business, not only in terms of maturing the child's skills but also in permitting him to interact with other members of the species, particularly adults who serve to "model" for the child the approved forms of getting on with others. There is a curious anomaly about play. It is plainly pleasurable and provides the kind of unbounded joy that is not usually associated with the serious undertaking I am sketching here. But what is particularly interesting about play is its role in language acquisition and its provision of the opportunity for mastering rules and conventions. Peekaboo, give-and-take, joint constructing, games involving anticipation to tickling ("Round and Round the Garden") give the child not only pleasure in rules but also endow him with a subtle sense of when to use and when to protest at infractions. When the child gets to the point of playing pretend games with others, moreover, he soon learns that not only actions are rule bound but that even the products of fantasy are governed by formal requirements. Two sisters decide to *play* "Sisters", a game governed by a rule of equal shares of everything—hardly like life. Or a child can be induced into foregoing his favourite candy once it is embedded in the game of "Poison".

I mention all of this before turning to language acquisition proper in order to emphasize the aspect of conventionalization that enters into human joint activity and to remark upon the distinctive sensitivity of our species to rules and rule-boundedness. For I think these eventuate in the child learning not only about rules but, more important, learning rules about making rules.

Now let us turn to language itself.

The dominant view of the last decade has been, of course, Chomsky's, based on his so-called Language Acquisition Device. But the central feature of that device—that the child in some sense "has a knowledge" from the start of the universal rules of language and that he generates from this knowledge hypotheses about the local language encountered around him—while boldly suggestive, is plainly insufficient in the light of the past years of research. A more realistic approach to language acquisition must surely examine what the child learns that helps him pass from prespeech communication to the use of language proper, lest we leap too easily to Cartesian conclusions about innateness. For principally as a result of the studies of Brown (1973) and his students, it has become increasingly apparent that language acquisition is enormously aided by the child's pre-linguistic grasp of concepts and meanings and that many of the organizing features of syntax, semantics, pragmatics, and even phonology may have important precursors and prerequisites in the prespeech communicative acts of infants. And whilst language in its formal sense is mastered swiftly—at least its phonology and syntax—its semantic meanings and pragmatic uses for "getting things done with words" come much more slowly and only with experience. This suggests that some of initial language acquisition must be primed by an evolutionary history that makes certain structural properties "easy" but their appropriate uses difficult—a peculiar state of affairs to which we shall return later.

Yet, experience shows that little is served by trying to isolate what is learned from what is innate in language. It would be absurd to imagine that even a Chomskean innate Language Acquisition Device operates without considerable experiential input achieved during the period preceding the use of articulate, phonetic grammatical speech. Chomsky comments (1965), "The real problem is that of developing an hypothesis about initial structure that is sufficiently rich to account for acquisition of language . . ." Perhaps that structure is not so much "initial" in the innate, as in the pre-linguistic, sense. That, in any case, is what I shall try to illustrate, for I shall argue that what the child learns about communication before language helps him crack the linguistic code. For communication is converted into speech through a series of procedural advances that are achieved in highly familiar, well learned contexts that have already undergone conventionalization at the hands of the infant and his mother (or other caretaker).

Specifically, mother and child develop a variety of procedures for operating jointly and in support of each other. At first, these joint actions are very direct, specially geared to assistance and comfort. In time, the two of them develop conventions and requirements about carrying out joint tasks. The structure of those tasks, as we shall see, may shape the structures of initial grammar by the nature of the jointly held concepts it imposes. The evolution of grammar may then be only a reflection of the changing requirements of joint action between members of the evolving hominid species. It would not be surprising, then, if the ontogenetic development of joint action between mother and child contributed to the mastery of grammar, to the cracking of its code. If this is so, and I am taking it as a working hypothesis that it is, then one would have to understand the child's acquisition of the rules of joint action before one could understand the nature of grammatical acquisition—and I shall indeed be arguing that the mastery of procedures for joint action provides the precursor for the child's grasp of initial grammatical forms.

Since space is limited, I shall concentrate upon three topics that hopefully shed light on the transition from prespeech communication to early language: (1) the nature of early reference; (2) the precursors of predication; and (3) the pragmatics of language in the regulation of joint action.

Reference

Traditional philosophical discussion of reference most often begins with the example of a hypothetical infant learning that a given sound, word, or gesture "stands for" something in the extra-linguistic environment. I doubt such efforts are based on observations of the infant's real problems in mastering reference. I find myself strongly in agreement with Harrison's (1972) contention that the psychological (and even arguably the philosophical) problem of reference is not one of linking signs to objects but of developing *procedures for constructing and using a limited taxonomy* for distinguishing among limited arrays of extra-linguistic objects to which the child relates in his commerce with adult members of the linguistic community. What adults do for the child is to co-operate with him in constructing and using these taxonomic procedures for joint reference in relatively well established situations until, finally, the child can operate referentially with larger arrays of objects in novel situations. The initial procedures of reference, I believe, are generative. It is not a procedure limited to bananas or rattles or whatever, but to distinguishing among alternatives. The problem of the communicator in the mother–infant dyad is how to differentiate initially among a set of possible present objects, and how eventually to refer more precisely to any single one with minimal reliance on context. Associative theories of naming or reference presuppose that a sound or a gesture emitted in the presence of a referent leads to automatic recognition by the child that the name stands for something at the focus of the child's attention. That is plainly not so, at least not until quite late. Whatever the reference triangle is (Ogden and Richards, 1923), it is plainly not an isolated bit of mental furniture produced by the linking of a sign, a thought, and a referent. *The objective of early reference, rather, is to indicate to another by some reliable means which among an alternative set of things or state or actions is relevant to the child's and mother's shared line of endeavour.* Exactitude is initially a minor issue. "Efficacy of singling out" is the crucial objective, and the procedures employed are initially quite independent of the defining or essential properties of objects singled out. If what I have asserted here is so, we must look at the growth of procedures used by the infant and adult in indicating and differentiating the arrays of objects with which they traffic.

I shall want to deal with three aspects of early reference procedures, and for convenience I shall give them labels. The first we may call *indicating*, and it refers to gestural, postural and idiosyncratic vocal procedures for bringing a partner's attention to an object or action or state. The second is *deixis* and refers, of course, to the use of spatial, temporal, and interpersonal contextual features of situations as aids in the management of joint reference. The third involves the development of standard lexical items that "stand for" extra-linguistic events in the shared world of infant and caretaker and I shall call the process *naming*. We shall consider in detail only the first of these, touching lightly on the second and third.

Studies by Collis and Schaffer (1975), by Kaye (1976), and by Scaife and Bruner (1975) all point to a highly primitive initial form of indicating that can be observed early in the child's first year. Collis and Schaffer have shown the extent to which the mother's line of regard follows the infant's, she is constantly monitoring and following where the child looks as an important feature of inferring what is at the focus of his attention. Kaye has shown the extent to which mothers, asked to teach their child a simple task of taking an object from behind a transparent barrier, actively direct a child's attention by "marking" the target referent in various ways—e.g. touching it, shaking it, etc. Kaye's findings indicate that they know how to use effective procedures for establishing joint attention. Scaife and Bruner provide the final piece in this picture. Not only, as indicated by Collis and Schaffer, does the mother follow the child's line of regard as an indicator, but in our experiment the infant is found to be able as early as four months to follow and increasingly does follow an adult's line of regard when it is turned toward a locus removed from the child. And the child too can use devices for marking further what is at the focus of attention—by holding up an object for view, by patting or touching it, by vocalizing in a characteristic way. Thus, there is present from a surprisingly early pre-linguistic age a *mutual* system by which joint selective attention between an infant and his caretaker is assured—under the control either of the caretaker or of the child.

What has been mastered at this first stage is a *procedure* for homing in on the attentional locus of another. It is a disclosure and discovery routine and not a naming procedure. It is, as noted, highly generative within the limited world inhabited by the infant in the sense that it is not limited to specific kinds of objects. It has, moreover, equipped the child with a technique for transcending egocentrism, for insofar as he can appreciate another's line of regard and decipher their marking intentions, he has plainly achieved a basis for what Piaget has called decentration, using a co-ordinate system for the world other than the one of which he is the centre.

There is a further procedural accomplishment implied by Kaye's (1976) study of the "implicit pedagogy" of mothers, their use of "marking" in indicating not only an object or event to be attended to, but an action to be taken toward it. Without going into details, it is plain that mothers of six-month-olds succeed in getting their infants not only to attend to but also to capture the object behind the barrier. Mothers not only mark objects, as indicated, but use effective procedures for indicating the action called for: by a process of tempting as by putting the object nearer to the edge of the barrier, by modelling the behaviour themselves, by putting the child's hand closer to the object. Indicating procedures involve not only "highlighting" the target of the task but exaggerating the structure of acts to be performed in the task. In a manner we shall consider later, mothers are helping to structure tasks, helping to give them an "external status" that permits them too to become objects of joint attention and reference.

Generative procedures for indicating what is being attended to undergo three striking changes over time: *decontextualization*, *conventionalization*, and increased *economy*. Decontextualization involves the development of indicating strategies that are not so closely linked to the specific situations and action patterns in which they are embedded. Rather than marking a target by exaggerating his reach for it and by fretting, the child now uses a more peremptory reach toward the object while looking toward the mother's face. The extended hand becomes an external pointer in place of line of regard and the manoeuvre of looking *en face* at the mother serves as an indicator of intention in a shared and familiar routine. This step, of course, effects an enormous increase in economy of indicating. Conventionalization is reflected in the mother and child developing by the second half of the first year ritualized procedures, most often in play, in which agreement concerning how something is to be done becames more important than what is actually done.

The emergence of deixis and of naming can only be touched on here. Certainly, the results thus far discussed (particularly those of Collis and Schaffer, Kaye, and Scaife and Bruner) suggest that a basis for deixis is present from early in the first year. Deixis implies the capacity of a speaker to appreciate and mark appropriately for an interlocutor, the shared properties of time, space and roles—e.g. *before* what reference time, *in front of* what reference in space, *you* or *us* or *them* with respect to what systems of roles. We shall consider the last of these in connection with exchange and reciprocation in the final section. With respect to space and time, they seem, for their linguistic representation, to depend massively upon extra-linguistic conceptual development gained in interaction with the environment, as Sinclair (1969) has so carefully documented, yet once language has developed to serve as a representational system, it may permit new leaps forward in the handling of such forms of deixis. It suffices to note that it comes into evidence only when other indicating and primitive deictic procedures have been well established.

So let us now turn to predication.

Predication

In its linguistic sense, "predication involves affirming or asserting something of or about the subject of a proposition" (Wall, 1974, p. 9). It might seem then somewhat jejune to inquire about the precursors or even the prerequisites for predication in the pre-linguistic child, for surely he can in no sense be thought to be dealing in propositions. What has made the issue of pre-propositional predication a persistent and interesting one, however, was the early insistence of DeLaguna (1927) that the single words of holophrastic speech could profitably be treated as compacted sentence forms, and that single words could be conceived within that framework as comments upon extra-linguistic topics inherent in the contexts in which the child found himself. The primitive topic, then, was implicit rather than explicit. Like DeLaguna, investigators such as Bloom (1973), Greenfield and Smith (1976), etc. became interested in the manner in which the "unmentioned" topic finally found its way into explicitness to be represented by a nominal or other grammatically interpretable form that could carry language development beyond dependence on unspecified context—DeLaguna's famous claim that language development could be conceived as a process of decontextualization.

McNeill (1970a, b) carried the argument one step further. Arguing from the existence of the predicational postpositions in Japanese, *ga* and *wa*, indicating respectively extrinsic and intrinsic predicates, the latter being habitual or essential and the former temporary or transitory, he proposed that initial predication with unmentioned topic could be conceived of as the intrinsic form, while extrinsic predication was more of the *ga* type. In Japanese, the postpositions could be noted by the contrast: "The dog-wa has hair", versus "The dog-ga is on the chair". He found that for both Japanese and English speaking children, early sentences contained about twice as many intrinsic as extrinsic predications, and that subject noun phrase topics that referred to the speaker were particularly rare. This led him to conclude that "holophrasic utterances consist largely, if not exclusively, of intrinsic predicates . . . Children would add subjects to predicates . . . when the predicates become extrinsic. Such an event appears to happen first when the children are 18 to 24 months old" (McNeill, 1970b, p. 1093). To this interesting finding (or contention) should be added two others. Quite counter-intuitively, Wall (1968) found that the mean length of dialogue between children and parents was shorter than dialogues between the same children and strangers. Chafe (1970) had, meanwhile, urged that one must make the contrast between "new" information and "old" or shared information, that the two are handled grammatically in different ways. Wall (1974, pp. 232–3) makes the point, "It seemed possible that the difference in utterance length might well be explained on the basis of presence or absence of shared information between participants in the conversations. That is, it is necessary for relative strangers to state explicitly whatever it may be that they are trying to communicate verbally for efficient information transfer, whereas among friends and close associates remarks are often greatly abbreviated with little or no resulting loss of information transferred."

We may now, in the light of the foregoing, consider afresh the significance of established, mutual-action formats between mother and child. They constitute the implicit or shared topics on which comments can be made by the child without having to be mentioned. These are the implicit topics about which comments can be made. And as these formats become differentiated into reversible or complementary roles during the growth of exchange and reciprocal modes, implicit topics become that much more contextualized in the action that adult and child share. I use the three terms, division of labour, exteriority, and constraints (see discussion below) to characterize the nature of the shared action formats that develop during the onset of the reciprocal mode—terms borrowed, of course, from Durkheim's (1933) characterization of the requisite properties of social norms—to specify the manner in which formats seem to take on a shared existence binding the two partners in discourse. And it is this development that is, in my view, crucial to the course of pre-linguistic predicational activity to which we now turn—particularly to the development of intrinsic predication in McNeill's (1970b) sense.

What, we may first ask, are the forms of "comment" that can be made pre-linguistically (or pre-propositionally) on such shared topics as the joint action patterns? Before we can answer this question, we must first consider the function of predication in a communicative act. The discussion will be limited to two functions: (a) to specify something about a topic that is explicit or implicit, and (b) to do so in such a way that topic and comment can be rendered separable (e.g. *John is a boy* and *John has a hat*).

The first and perhaps simplest form of comment is, I think, giving indication that a topic is being shared in joint action, and it is principally revealed in the child's management of gaze direction. Typically in our own protocols the child, when involved in a transaction over some object or activity, looks up at some juncture and makes eye-to-eye contact with the mother, often smiling as well. The topic is the joint activity, the comment is the establishment of "intersubjective" sharing in connection with that activity, after which the activity goes on. A good example is provided in the account of glance management in an exchange game reported by Bruner (1975). The "comment" consists of noting whether both partners are "with it", engaged in the game.

This form of confirming comment is supplemented and extended at around the ninth month by the emergence of a form of vocalization we have dubbed "proclamative". It occurs at two points during joint action sequences: first, at a point where the infant is about to undertake his part of a jointly attended action, seemingly as an accompaniment to intention; second, when the act is complete. The vocalized babbling may be coincident with the child looking back at the mother or may precede it. The vocalization, in short, appears to be initiating or completive with respect to an act embedded in a jointly attended task. In this sense, it may be considered as a "candidate-comment" on an implicit topic. In time the pattern becomes further elaborated, and the child may not only vocalize in these positions and make gaze contact, but also hold up an implicated object to show the mother, as when picking up a brick and placing it on a pile.

Secondly, a word about the separability of topic and comment achieved in predication. It is by now a common observation that the child's play with objects takes one of two forms (a point also noted for chimpanzees by Köhler, 1926, and commented upon by Bruner, 1972,

1973). An *object* is successively mouthed, squeezed, banged on the table, thrown down, called for, etc. Or an *action* is fitted to as many different objects as it will accommodate: successively a cup is banged, then a spoon, then a doll, then any other loose object to hand. These play patterns, while in no sense direct precursors of propositional predicating, are nonetheless striking examples of separation and variation of comments on topics, with either the object serving as topic and actions-upon-it as comments, or the action serving as organizing topic and a variety of fitting objects as comments. Typical of the play of both higher apes and children (Loizos, 1967), this focus-variation pattern should not be overlooked as a factor that predisposes action, attention, and eventually language to the pattern that at the propositional level we call predicational.

In conclusion, I find myself in strong agreement with Lyons (1966, p. 131) when he comments:

> "By the time the child arrives at the age of eighteen months or so, he is already in possession of the ability to distinguish 'things' and 'properties' in the 'situations' in which he is learning and uses language. And this ability seems to me quite adequate as a basis for the learning of the principal deep-structure relationship between lexical items (the subject-predicate relationship), provided that the child is presented with a sufficient amount of 'primary linguistic data' in real 'situations' of language use."

Before he reaches 18 months, indeed during the second half of his first year, he is well on the way toward conceptual mastery of these concepts in the extra-linguistic sphere.

Language and Joint Action

We come finally to the last topic—language and joint action. You will already have seen how central I believe this relation to be.

From the start, the child is well equipped with communicative procedures for eliciting help from others in what we shall call the *demand mode*, many of them derived from innate patterns of expressing discomfort that activate adults. By the third or fourth month of their baby's life, most mothers claim to be able to distinguish several forms of demand calling, and though they can be distinguished phonologically, they are heavily dependent on context for interpretation. Demand cries of this kind are insistent, have a wide spectrum acoustically, and show no pauses in anticipation of response. When such expectancies are established there is the beginning of what may be called a *request mode*. The cry becomes less insistent, has a more limited time span and becomes segmented with pauses in anticipation of adult response. A variety of studies point to the importance of a consistent caretaker in the transition from the demand to the request mode (e.g. Sander *et al.*, 1970; Ainsworth, 1975).

The change to a new mode after five or six months is not so much in vocalizations but in their placement into new, joint action patterns. There first emerges an *exchange mode*. The child not only requests and receives objects, but now offers them back with the expectancy of exchange. In this period, from eight to ten months particularly, he uses his request vocalizations (much conventionalized) not only to request desired objects, but to call attention to an object he is proffering, to direct attention to his exchange intention, to confirm receipt or delivery of an object by looking at or vocalizing toward the mother, etc.

The exchange mode is gradually transformed into what may be called a *reciprocal mode*. Interactions are now organized around a *task* that possesses *exteriority*, *constraint*, and *division of labour*. The two participants enter upon a task with reciprocal, though non-identical roles. The task and its constituent acts and objects become the objects of joint attention and anticipation. Increasingly, communication by gesture and by vocalization becomes slotted into these task frames or action formats. It is in this context that the child is learning what might be properly characterized as the pre-linguistic prototype of case grammar: who is the Agent, what is the Action, the Object, the Recipient of Action and how these may be exchanged and substituted—as well as some rudiments of the case forms that will later be Possession and Location. He is learning not only how to carry out joint action, but how to represent its relevant segments and how to signal appropriately about them.

An example of this progression is contained in observations from the children in a current study at Oxford. The material is taken from observations of "Give and Take" made during the pre-linguistic period from three to 15 months and is based mainly on data from a longitudinal study of one mother–infant pair, though substantiated with data from a cross-sectional study of 20 mother–infant pairs.

Give and Take is operationally defined as exchange of an object between two people, with one person (the Agent) surrendering possession of the object and with the other person (the Recipient) gaining possession of the object. Accordingly, *agent* is the possessor of an object and, when exchange of an object occurs, loses possession of it. *Recipient* of action receives the object surrendered by the agent. Lastly, *initiator* of the exchange is the person who indicates (gesturally and/or verbally) that (a) he wishes to take over possession of the object retained by another, or (b) he wishes to give an object to the other person or (c) he displays his object to the other person.

To apply the name "Give and Take" to the exchange of objects between a mother and her three-month-old infant is somewhat of a misnomer. For early instances of Give and Take are more properly glossed as "offering and grasping" and appear notoriously one-sided: the burden of the exchange resting heavily on mother. Characteristic of this early period of exchange is mother's utilization of an array of attentional devices that make up the "offering" and "giving" phase of the Give and Take. This phase is often quite lengthy with the mother (M) manoeuvering the object in a space approximately 12 to 24 inches in front of the child (C). M's manipulation of objects is frequently accompanied by verbal highlighting, primarily in the form of interrogatives and tag questions: "Do you want this?" "You want your rattle, don't you?" Moreover, the object being offered provides an additional source of stimulation for C. With the brightly coloured, noisy rattle, for example, M has an ideal object with which to capture and sustain his attention. Frequently she is observed shaking the rattle, looming it close to C's face, gently rubbing it up and down C's stomach—such endless variety in technique has the common purpose of activating C and, perhaps more importantly, M "sees" him as taking his turn in the "game".

M's attempts at offering are usually limited to a single object for long periods of time, being concluded, more often than not, by M shoving the object into C's fist-shaped hand. In turn, this grasping period ordinarily ends with C dropping the object. Seldom does M attempt to remove the object from C's tight grip; and if M is so bold as to do so, her removal is predictably followed by a burst of tears from C. M's options regarding further play include re-offering the same object, introducing a new one, or moving on to a different game—in the latter case, often with the same object previously employed in the Give and Take.

As C approaches the age of six months, the offering phase has considerably diminished in emphasis when compared with the three-month-old. Likewise, many of the attentional devices characteristic of the early period have become abbreviated with the focus residing on the C's reach toward the proffered object. We may now refer to this joint activity by a more appropriate label: offering and taking. The offering phase thus becomes considerably more condensed—M's demonstrative "Look!" as she proffers an object is generally sufficient to capture C's attention and to activate his secondary circular reaction, for C immediately reaches out for the object. Likewise, M's face is employed less frequently in the task of maintaining C's attention. Often, M sits behind C holding the object in a range whereby he will be able to spot it. She introduces a variety of different objects with the object itself quickly capturing C's interest. Moreover, a new level of complexity enters the Give and Take as C is confronted simultaneously with two objects in a choice situation.

There are considerable differences between M's actions in the aftermath of a take by C at six months and those at three months. M no longer provides the constant vocal stimulation prevalent in the earlier period but expects C to respond accordingly. It is now his turn in the exchange, and M's function is to scaffold (see Wood *et al.*, 1976) and to aid C in his self-directed activity. For example, if C drops the object M often waits for him to pick it up. Or, if M does take the object from him, she is most likely to initiate another out-of-reach game in which C must signal (by reaching outward) that he wants the object. Indeed, M has become more demanding of C's role and, as for C, he is no longer showing total reliance on M. Noticeably, his attention is directed outward and he is freely reaching toward objects. In one respect, Give and Take remains fairly primitive for C in that he merely *takes* at this stage compared to his later *giving* of objects, yet it is well on its way of developing into a reciprocal game for M and C alike.

By about seven to eight months of age, M is still Initiator and Agent of action with C remaining Recipient. His role as Recipient is becoming more distinct as reflected in his vocalizations and gestures, both taking on more stylistic characteristics. One of our children, for example, now pounds and beats with his left hand when M delays in giving the proffered object. As for M, her attentional devices have decreased considerably (as noted above) and she now expects C to make the effort, or, as one mother put it, the "ultimate effort"! Once C has possession of the object, M begins to allow him more time for inspection and manipulation of it. In turn, C becomes quite possessive of objects, wanting them for himself although still expecting M to be the supplier of the objects he wants, and he effectively employs his differentiation of vocal calls to express his approval/disapproval of these objects.

In the 10 and 11 month periods Give and Take becomes more fully developed with C's vocalizations (in particular "da" and "gu") regularly inserted into the "game". (These vocalizations lack the specificity that later becomes so characteristic of C's marking of appropriate segments within the game.) C himself has become noticeably more sociable as expressed by his outward gazing, smiling, greetings and other vocalizations directed toward the adults present in the room. At 10 months there is an explosion of activity on C's part as he assumes a more extensive role in the Give and Take: C begins to act both as the Initiator and as Agent of the action as first exemplified in his showing and offering of objects. On M's request for an object, C turns round and hands it to her. M comments that C is giving back all the time now and the Experimenter "tests" this new development by inducing C to play a prolonged game of exchange. That C has not completely come to terms with his new role is indicated by the hesitancy in his participation and his constant checking between object and adult (as if uncertain of the next "move" within the game). Nonetheless, C has come a considerable distance in Give and Take and now it is simply a matter of time and practice before his roles and the game itself become polished and open to diversity. Some of the most interesting later developments include the simultaneous offerings by the Experimenter and C, the choice situation as proffered by the Experimenter, and the combining of objects by C. In one instance when offered a choice of objects, C first takes one of the objects (a rattle) and places it inside the other object (a nesting cup) and then takes both of them.

By 12 months the task structure of Give and Take has become quite evident and, increasingly, C dominates the game. Not only is Give and Take played for considerably longer periods, but C now assumes the initiative much more than before—both in offering and showing the objects in his possession to the adults present and in completing the give. C's earlier hesitancy and checking are superseded by routinized and confident turns. Strikingly (as we observed at 12 months, 3 days) the *task* itself, for example exchange for the sake of exchange, gains paramount importance.

C's possession time in holding objects has decreased from 27·6 seconds (9 months, 3 weeks) to 11·7 seconds (12 months, 3 days) (see Fig. 1), while the number of exchanges and proffering of objects initiated by him has increased dramatically from no first offering to approximately 50%. Give and Take has become a game involving reciprocal roles and a game with exteriority and constraint. We see this most clearly at 13 months when, in a spontaneous experiment, the child, his mother and the experimenter are involved—C, M, and E. M and E hand an

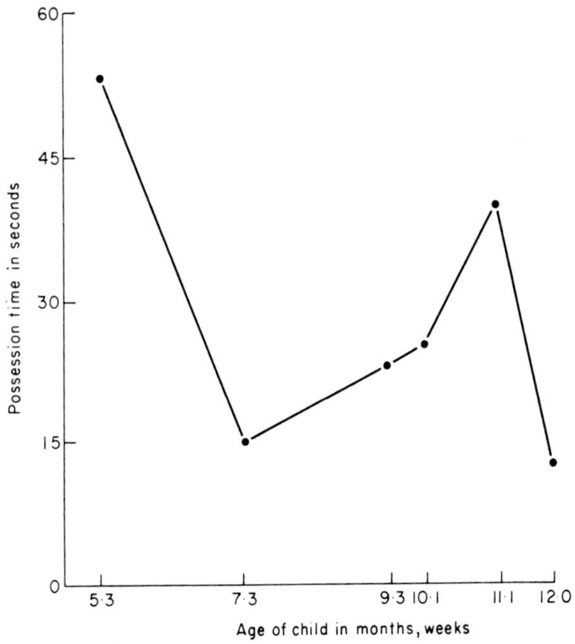

Fig. 1. Changes with age in possession time during Give and Take games.

object back and forth several times in front of C, with C intently watching. When M next hands on the object to C, he then spontaneously hands it to E and participates correctly in a circular exchange several times. Moreover, C's vocalizations increasingly mark crucial junctures in the give and take routine.

Before leaving this discussion of Give and Take two further developments in the game deserve mention. At the age of 13 months, 1 week, the finger point has been incorporated into the game with C clearly indicating the object of desire. Between 14 and 15 months there is embedding and combining of the exchange into a full hierarchical structure of games, as exemplified by reciprocal ball-rolling, the simultaneous offerings by E and C (as previously mentioned), etc.

Conclusions

We have spent a great deal of time investigating formats such as Give and Take for they provide us with a useful structure with which to approach the pre-linguistic period. The action seen in play between a mother and her child serves a pragmatic function and such rule-bound sequences as we find in Give and Take provide a solid basis for language to enter the routine and, eventually, for language to become the "carrier" of the action. The regularized pattern of a task within a format and its rules enable the mother to mark important segments or juncture points in the action, gesturally and/or vocally . . . in time, the child comes to do so. An established, familiar context is then available for the child to first use his initial babbling sounds (as part of the action pattern), later his more differentiated vocalizations, and finally his standard lexical words—all prior to the "linguistic" period. The structure of Give and Take, for example, is well worked out by mother and child in his early months. When holophrases and other lexical items appear, their order reflects the order of the action. As for the basic game of Give and Take, it becomes very regular, highly developed and sophisticated and serves as a firm foundation for other more complex and elaborate task structures.

The child is learning first how to get different things done jointly and concurrently learning to use appropriate communicative devices and conventions to signal his partner to help in the process. But if there is one point that deserves emphasis it is that language acquisition occurs in the context of an "action dialogue" in which joint undertakings are being regulated by infant and adult. The joint enterprise sets the deictic limits that govern joint reference, determines the need for a referential taxonomy, establishes the need for signalling intent, and eventually provides a context for the development of explicit predication. The evolution of language itself, notably its universal structures, probably reflects the requirements of such joint action in our species and it is probably because of that evolutionary history that its rules are mastered with such relative ease, though its theoretical explication still eludes us. But however much language-susceptibility has an innate component, its final expression is achieved by virtue of the child working his way through a series of precursors that, in effect, make possible the gradual cracking of the full language code.

Finally, to return to play, let me only note that the kinds of behaviour to which we have been referring take place principally in what can only be called a playful ambience. When things become too "serious" and intention-bound, communication regresses to the level of demand and counter-demand. The simulative, conventionalized, and rule-sensitive spirit of play seems to be a *sine qua non* for language learning.

References

Ainsworth, Mary D. Salter (1975). Social development in the first year of life: maternal influences on infant–mother attachment. Paper presented at Geoffrey Vickers Lecture, London (Unpublished).

Bloom, Lois (1973). *One Word at a Time: The Use of Single Word Utterances Before Syntax.* Mouton, The Hague.

Brown, R. (1973). *A First Language: The Early Stages.* Harvard University Press, Cambridge, Mass.

Bruner, J. S. (1972). The nature and uses of immaturity. *Am. Psychol.* **27**, 1–22.

Bruner, J. S. (1973). Organisation of early skilled action. *Child Dev.* **44**, 1–11.

Bruner, J. S. (1974). Child's play. *New Scientist* **62**, 126–128.

Bruner, J. S. (1975). The ontogenesis of speech acts. *J. Child Lang.* **2**, 1–19.

Chafe, W. L. (1970). *Meaning and the Structure of Language.* University of Chicago Press, Chicago.

Chomsky, N. (1965). *Aspects of the Theory of Syntax.* M.I.T. Press, Cambridge, Mass.

Collis, G. M. and Schaffer, H. R. (1975). Synchronization of visual attention in mother–infant pairs. *J. Child Psychol. Psychiat.* **16**, 315–320.

DeLaguna, Grace (1927). *Speech: Its Function and Development.* Yale University Press, New Haven, Connecticut.

Durkheim, E. (1933). *The Division of Labor.* The Free Press, Glencoe, Illinois.

Greenfield, Patricia M. and Smith, J. H. (1976). *The Structure of Communication in Early Language Development.* Academic Press, New York and London.

Harrison, B. (1972). *Meaning and Structure.* Harper and Row, New York and London.

Kaye, K. (1976). Infant's effects upon their mothers' teaching strategies. In J. C. Glidewell (Ed.), *The Social Context of Learning and Development.* Gardiner Press, New York.

Köhler, W. (1926). *The Mentality of Apes.* Harcourt Brace, New York.

Loizos, C. (1967). Play behaviour in higher primates: a review. In D. Morris (Ed.), *Primate Ethology*. Weidenfeld and Nicolson, London.

Lyons, J. (1966). General discussion to D. McNeill's paper, The creation of language. In J. Lyons and R. Wales (Eds), *Psycholinguistic Papers*. Edinburgh University Press, Edinburgh.

McNeill, D. (1970a). *The Acquisition of Language: The Study of Developmental Psycholinguistics*. Harper and Row, New York.

McNeill, D. (1970b). The development of language. In P. H. Mussen (Ed.), *Carmichael's Manual of Child Psychology*, 3rd edition. Vol. 1. Wiley, New York.

Ogden, J. C. and Richards, I. A. (1923). *The Meaning of Meaning*. Harcourt Brace Jovanovich Inc., New York.

Sander, L. W., Stechler, G., Julia, M. and Burns, P. (1970). Early mother–infant interaction and 24-hour patterns of activity and sleep. *J. Am. Acad. Child Psychiat.* **9**, 103–123.

Scaife, M. and Bruner, J. S. (1975). The capacity for joint visual attention in the infant. *Nature* **253**, 265–266.

Sinclair-de-Zwart, Hermina (1969). Developmental psycholinguistics. In D. Elkind and J. H. Flavell (Eds), *Studies in Cognitive Growth: Essays in Honour of Jean Piaget*. Oxford University Press, New York.

Wall, Carol (1968). Linguistic interaction of children with different alters. Unpublished paper. Davis, University of California.

Wall, Carol (1974). *Predication: A Study of its Development*. Mouton, The Hague.

Wood, D., Bruner, J. S. and Ross, Gail (1976). The role of tutoring in problem solving. *J. Child Psychol. Psychiat.* **17**, 89–100.

12 Vocal Interchange and Visual Regard in Verbal and Pre-verbal Children

H. Rudolph Schaffer, Glyn M. Collis and Gayle Parsons

Introduction

Interpersonal synchrony in the behaviour of mother and infant can be found from birth onward. Were it not so, caretaking activities vital to survival would be hazardous; some mutual pre-adaptation is required in view of the urgency of providing appropriate care to a young and helpless organism. Responses such as sucking may initially need a certain amount of "priming" (Gunther, 1961), but from the beginning their organization is such that intertwining with caretaker activities can occur (Kaye, Chapter 5).

With increasing age, however, the nature of interpersonal synchrony changes drastically, becoming increasingly diverse and progressively more complex. This applies particularly to the first two years, during which time the various perceptuo-motor and cognitive abilities that become newly available at different stages of development get implicated in the manner in which mother and infant regulate their behaviour towards one another. Thus in due course multiple channels come to function—often simultaneously—to promote the infant's communication with others, involving such means as touch and movement, visual contact and vocalizing.

The latter in particular is of interest, because verbal exchanges among older individuals is the means *par excellence* of communication. Yet vocalization in infancy has rarely been examined in an interpersonal context. Detailed attention has been given to various types of vocalization to be found at different ages (see Irwin, 1960), and more recently the receptive abilities of infants to various speech sounds have also been investigated (see Doty, 1974). The only studies to approach vocalization from a social point of view, however, are conditioning studies (e.g. Rheingold *et al.*, 1959; Weisberg, 1963), which have made the useful point that the consequences of the response affect the frequency of its occurrence but have not gone beyond this quantitative statement to throw light on the interactive process as such.

It is only recently, however, that speech itself has come to be examined in an interpersonal context instead of being regarded merely as a behaviour system exclusively the property of individuals. This applies particularly to theories about the developmental origins of language: as long as these considered speech to arise *de novo*, based on magical acquisition devices, there was little point in considering the communicative context within which it occurred, let alone that for pre-verbal vocalizations. Yet as Jaffe and Feldstein (1970) have put it so well, the dialogue and not the monologue is the basic speech unit; the monologue is merely a special instance of a dialogue with one partner absent or silent. And from the beginning infants are involved in the to-and-fro of dialogues, albeit of a non-verbal nature, providing them with the opportunity of exchanging meanings with the other person and learning about the most effective means of bringing about such exchanges.

Are these early, pre-verbal dialogues already marked by the same formal characteristics that one finds in later communicative situations based primarily on speech—characteristics that are basic to the interaction in that without them the dyadic relationship could not occur with the smoothness that is its hallmark? In this report we shall accordingly search for two of these features in the vocal interchanges of mothers and children: first, the extent to which the two partners are able to regulate their vocalizations by taking turns and thus avoiding overlapping behaviour, and secondly the manner in which the child's looking at his mother is integrated in the vocal interchange. We shall carry out this search at two age levels, namely a pre-verbal and a verbal one, and although our intention is primarily to present some descriptive data on these aspects of early dyadic behaviour it is hoped that the inclusion of the age comparison will provide the means of examining further the basic issue of communicative continuity.

Methodology

SUBJECTS

Sixteen mother–child pairs were the subjects of this study. Their names were obtained from the records of several local Child Welfare Clinics, each with a predominantly middle-class catchment area. One subject pair was replaced in the sample on the grounds that the mother spoke too little during the observation session (just seven utterances).

The children fell into two age groups: the one-year-group, with a mean age of 13·5 months (range 12 to 15 months), and the two-year-group, with a mean age of 24·5 months (range 23 to 27 months). Each group comprised three males and five females. Mothers' reports and observations of performance during the session indicated that the younger group's vocalizations were almost entirely pre-verbal, while the older children had mostly acquired a fairly extensive vocabulary which they could combine into simple utterances.

PROCEDURE

Mothers were contacted by telephone and asked to participate in a programme of research into child development. On arrival at the laboratory the mother was told that we were particularly interested in examining how children of different ages played, and that we therefore wanted her to accompany the child to a play room where he would be quite free to roam about and play. She was asked to behave as naturally as possible and talk and play with the child as she wished, the one constraint being that, as far as possible, she should remain seated on the chair provided.

The observation session took place in a room 3·5 × 2·0 m, furnished with two low tables placed together and two chairs, one for the mother and the other as an obstruction to prevent the child getting into the one corner of the room where he would be out of camera-view. A number of toys were placed on the tables, namely a set of nesting cubes, a doll, a mickey mouse, an elephant which could squeak, and a hard ball with a bell inside.

The session was video-recorded from behind a one-way window which extended virtually the length of one side of the room. Two cameras were used, obtaining a split-screen display. One camera, positioned to look virtually over the mother's shoulder, was used to track the child, while the other was focused on the mother and had a digital counter reflected into one corner of its field of view to provide a real time reference in 0·1 second time units. Added to the recording in the same way were two indicator lights which could be activated by observers at the time of the observation session whenever the child looked at the mother and the mother looked at the child.

Recording started as soon as mother and child were settled in the room and continued for ten minutes.

A transcript was subsequently prepared for each mother–child pair. This, together with the video-recording, formed the basis for all data extraction procedures.

Turn-taking

A great deal of interactive behaviour is based on the alternation of the participants' roles. In dyadic situations, particularly those involving face-to-face contact, it is frequently essential to the smooth course of the interaction that one individual at a time should play the active part while the other remains passive. Periodically the two participants exchange their roles, and it is the manner whereby this change is accomplished that constitutes the severest test of the ongoing relationship. Should both individuals claim the active role their responses will overlap, making it impossible for them to comprehend one another and producing—momentarily at least—a disruption in the ongoing flow. Action sequences must therefore not only be temporarily organized in such a way as to allow alternation but also be accompanied by rules for turn-taking that minimize the occurrence of overlapping behaviour. The participants must thus be aware of and comprehend the respective cues that signal the intention to assume or to yield the active role.

Such a pattern is most evident in speech, for when two people are engaged in a conversation it is clearly essential for them to avoid simultaneous talking. Not only is it virtually impossible to speak and listen at the same time, but in addition the dialogue provides a sequence where each person's contribution usually depends to a considerable extent on the nature of the previous utterance by the other participant. Turn-taking is thus perhaps the most obvious characteristic of a dialogue—no wonder Miller (1963) referred to it as a language universal! But just because it is so obvious little attention has been paid to it in the past, and it is only recently that the phenomenon, as found in the conversation of adult dyads, has come to be systematically investigated. Duncan (1972; Duncan and Niederehe, 1974) in particular has undertaken a detailed analysis of the communicative mechanism involved and accordingly specified the various behavioural cues that make it possible for a smooth change-over to occur without overlapping—cues such as intonation, pitch, syntax, shift of gaze and gesticulation. The communicative process within the dyad is thus dependent on the mutual understanding of the significance of these cues, which must be both used and responded to appropriately by each person.

In infancy turn-taking has also been observed in various situations: for instance during feeding where mothers tend to become active during the pauses that intervene between the infant's bursts of sucks (Kaye, Chapter 5); in play situations, where mother and infant may alternate in their readiness to send and receive cues (Brazelton *et al.*, 1974); and during skill teaching, when the infant's turning away from the task acts as a signal for the mother to participate (Kaye, 1976). To what extent vocal exchanges of mother and infant also conform to such an alternating pattern has, however, not been settled so far. It is true, on the one hand, that a number of writers (Brazelton *et al.*, 1974; Newson and Newson, 1976; Trevarthen *et al.*, 1975) have commented on the conversation-like nature of these exchanges and noted the tendency of an infant to vocalize more when his mother quietens and for the mother to reserve her utterances for intervening pauses. It is also true that data presented by Lewis and Freedle (1973) show mother and infant to spend far less time vocalizing together than either vocalizing one at a time or not at all (though the data, being based on one-zero time sampling of ten-second time slices, are not really fine enough to answer the questions posed here). On the other hand, both Stern *et al.* (1975) and Strain and Vietze (1975) have recently reported simultaneous vocalizing of three-month-old infants and their mothers to occur an unexpectedly high proportion of time; Stern *et al.* indeed suggest that such a simultaneous pattern may well represent a distinctive form of communication that differs both in structure and function from the alternating pattern.

Our primary aim, then, was to investigate further the nature of vocal turn-taking in mother–infant interaction. Without such an empirical basis it is hardly profitable to turn to such further problems as the origins of the phenomenon, the roles played by each partner, and the signals, cues and general rules on which it is based. On these questions we have only speculations to offer in the present report.

VOCALIZATION AND FLOOR-HOLDING DATA

It is helpful first to consider some basic data on each of the two partners' vocal behaviour. By vocal behaviour we mean all non-verbal and verbal utterances of mother and child: involuntary coughs, sneezes and prolonged audible breathing were excluded but no attempt was made to leave out any of the brief episodes of fussing or other distress noises or of laughter which occasionally took place.

The dialogic behaviour of each individual will be described in terms of two principle parameters, namely vocalizing times and floor-holding times. Vocalizing time refers to the cumulative duration of an individual's vocal behaviour and thus does not include either within-speaker pauses or between-speaker pauses (i.e. speaker-switch pauses). Floor-holding time (Jaffe and Feldstein, 1970), on the other hand, refers to the cumulative duration of an individual's floor-holding episodes each of which extends from the beginning of that individual's utterance until the start of the other person's following utterance. It thus includes all within-speaker pauses as well as the following speaker-switch pause.

For purposes of data analysis each of these parameters was recorded by two independent observers operating push-buttons while listening to the video-recording and simultaneously following the transcript. The push-buttons activated a device which provided a digital read-out of cumulative durations in one-twentieth second time units. For vocalizing times correlations between the two observers over all 16 mother–child pairs were 0·975 for child vocalizing and 0·979 for mother vocalizing. With regard to floor-holding times, the two categories (mother's and child's) are mutually exclusive and complementary. They could therefore be measured by a single observer in one operation. Thus an observer might monitor the child directly by operating his push-button during all child floor-holding episodes and then obtain an estimate of mother floor-holding times as the remainder of the session duration. For half the subject pairs in each age group one observer monitored the child directly and the other observer the mother; the two observers exchanged roles for the remaining subject pairs. It was readily apparent from the data that whether an individual's floor-holding time was measured directly or indirectly had negligible effect on the outcome. The overall inter-observer correlation for floor-holding times was 0·992. However, high inter-observer correlations do not of themselves guarantee reliability of measurement. As a further precaution against systematic bias from this source the observer variable was therefore built into the following initial analyses of the vocalizing and floor-holding data.

Table I presents the durations of vocalizing and floor-holding by the mothers and children of the two groups. The proportion of the session devoted to vocalizing, particularly in the one-year-group, may seem

Table I

Mean vocalizing and floor-holding times (in seconds) by mothers and children during observation session

	Vocalizing time		Floor-holding time	
	Child	Mother	Child	Mother
One-year-group	49·87	79·49	235·14	364·83
Two-year-group	79·74	118·30	242·17	357·78

limited, but one must bear in mind that the figures refer only to time actually spent uttering and thus leave out of account all pauses between utterances. A 2 (ages) $\times$ 2 (speakers) $\times$ 2 (observers) analysis of variance was carried out on the vocalizing times. Results show that the observer variable exerted no significant influence, either as a main effect or in interaction with the other variables. There was, however, a significant main effect of age ($F = 7{\cdot}04$; $df = 1{,}14$; $p < 0{\cdot}01$), indicating that more vocalizing occurred overall in the two-year-group. A significant main effect was also found for speakers ($F = 21{\cdot}06$;

df = 1,14; $p < 0{\cdot}01$), due to the greater amount of time spent vocalizing by mothers than by children. The age × speaker interaction, however, was not significant: in both age groups mothers vocalized more than their children. This applied to all individual mother–child pairs with just two exceptions, one in each age group.

It is particularly noteworthy that the smaller amount of vocalizing of the one-year-old infants in comparison with that found in the two-year-group was not compensated for by increased vocalizing on the part of the mothers. Not only the children but also the mothers vocalized less in the younger than in the older group, as though the increased fluency of the older child stimulated his mother into greater talkativeness too. A matching rather than a compensating phenomenon thus occurs. This is further illustrated by the significant correlation between child and mother vocalizing time across the 16 subject pairs (r = 0·639, $p < 0{\cdot}01$). These data suggest that mothers do not feel they have to fill in all the pauses but, more likely, are stimulated by the child to set up a pattern matching his own quantitative output. Findings that mothers provide younger children with shorter (as well as simpler) verbal utterances (Snow, 1972; Phillips, 1973) are indicative of the same kind of matching, though based on a different type of analysis that focuses on single utterances rather than on total time.

Turning to the floor-holding data, a 2 (ages) × 2 (observers) analysis of variance yielded no significant main effects or interactions. The lack of observer effects gives added confidence to the reliability of measurement and consequently all further analyses involving floor-holding and vocalizing times will be based on the means of the two observers' measurements. In the absence of any age difference in floor apportionment we can proceed to ask whether, over all the subject pairs, one or the other speaker held the floor more than his partner. It emerges that this is so, with mothers having significantly longer floor-holding times than their children (t = 2·96; df = 15; $p < 0{\cdot}005$).

Thus of the two kinds of measures used, vocalizing time differentiates the two age groups in showing that considerably less time was devoted to vocal utterances by the mothers as well as by the children of the one-year-group. In contrast, floor-holding time revealed no such age difference, though it did indicate a speaker difference in that mothers were found to hold the floor for longer periods than their children. This latter difference may well be simply due to the differential in vocalizing time, for floor-holding is, after all, a composite measure, the main utility of which is to facilitate the analysis of the data on visual behaviour that we shall present in a subsequent section.

THE OCCURRENCE OF OVERLAP EPISODES

We turn now to those points of the interaction where speaker-switches occurred, in that one partner yielded the floor to the other. In most cases speaker-switches were characterized by a pause between the offset of one individual's vocalization and the onset of the other's. These speaker-switch pauses were timed with stop-watches by two observers working from the video-recording and transcript in conjunction, and classified into one-second time bins, i.e. $\leqslant$ 1 second, $\leqslant$ 2 seconds, $\leqslant$ 3 seconds, etc. Inter-observer discrepancies were easily resolved by repeating the timing of the interval in question. In a few instances, however, the pauses were negative, that is the vocalizations of mother and child overlapped.

By an overlap episode we mean one or a series of simultaneous sets of vocalizations that are not interrupted by a speaker-switch pause. Their incidence in the two age groups is given in Table II, from which it is apparent that overlaps in fact occurred relatively rarely—even when, as in the one-year-group, one partner's vocalizations were of a pre-verbal nature. In the ten-minute interaction session a mean of only 11·37 overlap episodes occurred in the younger group and a mean of 12·00 in the older group. However, these means may be misleading as descriptive statistics unless one takes into consideration the amounts of vocalizations with which they are associated and which, it will be recalled, clearly differentiated the two age groups. Using an analysis of covariance procedure (Winer, 1962), with mother and child vocalizing times as two covariates, the means of the number of overlap episodes are adjusted to 14·13 and 9·24 for the younger and older groups respectively. But while these figures differentiate the two age groups more than the unadjusted scores, the difference still fails to reach significance ($F = 3{\cdot}2$; $df = 1{,}12$).

The relationship of number of overlap episodes to child vocalizing time and to mother vocalizing time in the two separate age groups is given in Table III. The pattern of relationships is similar for both groups: the incidence of overlaps shows a strong association with the duration of maternal vocalizing but does not show such an association to a significant degree with child vocalizing time. The matrix also

Table II

Overlap data for individual subjects in the two age groups

Subject pair		Number of overlap episodes	Person interrupting: Mother	Child	Simultaneous
One-year-group					
Ia		11	4	6	1
Ib		2	2	0	0
Ic		12	6	5	1
Id		3	2	1	0
Ie		27	15	11	1
If		14	9	5	0
Ig		11	5	6	0
Ih		11	5	5	1
	Mean:	11·38	6·00	4·88	0·50
Two-year-group					
IIa		8	5	2	1
IIb		6	1	3	2
IIc		17	7	10	0
IId		33	16	16	1
IIe		4	2	2	0
IIf		7	2	3	2
IIg		15	3	9	3
IIh		6	4	1	1
	Mean:	12·00	5·00	5·75	1·25

Table III

Correlation matrix of number of overlaps and associated variables[a]

	A.	B.	C.	D.
A. Number of overlap episodes	—	0·559	0·690[b]	0·816[c]
B. Child vocalizing time	0·283	—	0·481	0·814[c]
C. Mother vocalizing time	0·689[b]	0·563	—	0·596
D. Number of speaker-switches	0·591	0·703[b]	0·673[b]	—

[a] Top-right corner of matrix gives correlations for older group, bottom-left for younger.
[b] $p < 0{\cdot}05$.
[c] $p < 0{\cdot}01$.

contains one other variable, namely the total number of (non-overlap) speaker-switches. It can be expected that the more such speaker-switches occur the greater is the chance of overlaps being found. This is indeed so in the older group, where a highly significant relationship exists between these two variables; in the younger group the relationship, though showing the same trend, just fails to reach significance.

How were overlaps brought about? In Table II details are given as to who the interrupter was in each overlap episode. In some instances it was impossible to determine whether one individual preceded the other in vocalizing; these instances are therefore classified as "simultaneous", in that it appeared that both partners began vocalizing at the same time, neither interrupting the other. As to the rest, there is a fairly even distribution within each group: rather more instances of mother interrupting the child in the younger group and somewhat more of the child interrupting the mother in the older group. These differences are not significant, however, and in nearly every mother–child pair both partners were responsible for bringing about at least some of the overlaps.

The overlaps were generally extremely short—even when one takes the brevity of most utterances into account. Many lasted but a fraction of a second, as though the participants were readily able to recover without getting into any real dyadic tangle. Indeed the rhythm of the interaction showed little sign of having been upset by any of the overlap episodes, for a comparison of speaker-switch pauses immediately following overlap episodes showed no consistent trend for them to be longer or shorter than other speaker-switch pauses. Furthermore, overlap episodes rarely occurred in clusters: they appeared mostly in isolation and were fairly randomly distributed throughout the observation sessions. It is as though the various pairs took each occurrence of an overlap episode in their stride and rather quickly recovered the customary alternating pattern.

A closer examination of each episode, however, quickly made it apparent that not all instances of overlap could be regarded as a breakdown of the interactive exchange. A somewhat arbitrary, impressionistically based classification of overlaps yielded the following five categories:

1. *Warning calls*, namely those occasions when the child appeared to the mother to be in some sort of danger—when, for example, he reached

toward a radiator or electrical socket (both in fact perfectly safe!), or when he found a piece of carpet fluff and put it in his mouth. The mother would then utter a warning, usually accompanied by some other preventative action, irrespective of the child's vocal state at the time. In such circumstances the urgency of the situation overrode the customary turn-taking pattern.

2. *Distress occasions*, brought about when the child for one reason or another started fretting. It will be recalled that fretting noises were included in our definition of vocalizations, primarily because low-key distress sounds were often extremely difficult to distinguish from other vocalizations. Pauses between such noises tend to be fewer and briefer than those between other types of child vocalizations; consequently, on the relatively rare occasions that fretting did occur, the chances of mother overlapping with these noises while attempting to comfort or distract are clearly greater than normal. Yet it is interesting to note that even with crying it seemed that mothers were still attempting to take turns by slotting their utterances into the pauses between cries. With loud cries in particular this is perhaps very understandable, for her soothing words would simply be drowned were they to coincide with the child's cries.

3. *Laughter*, on the other hand, provides no reason for attempted turn-taking. On the contrary, laughing *together* is an acceptable form of social interaction; moreover, probably because of the low information content of this type of vocalization, simultaneous laughing is not disruptive in the same way as simultaneous speech. There were not many instances of laughing together in this sample, especially in the younger group, though occasionally a mother laughed on her own. The fact that such a noise tends to leave fewer and shorter periods of silence in which the partner can vocalize uninterrupted increases, of course, the chances of overlaps occurring.

4. *Chorusing* refers to another set of instances when mother and child joined forces and quite deliberately vocalized together. One child, for example, picked up a doll, held it against him and cuddled it, and at the same time came out with a prolonged "aaaaah". The mother immediately chimed in with "aaaaah" too. These instances were mostly seen in the older group and were generally instigated by the child, with the mother then joining him and copying the sound he was already making.

5. *Turn-taking failures* is a miscellaneous category that is defined

primarily by exclusion. It refers to all instances of overlap that could not be fitted into any of the above four categories and thus applies to those cases where a real and (presumably) unintentional interruption took place.

The last category is thus the only one which refers to a "true" clash of roles, for only here can one describe the interaction as having become dysynchronized. It is true that the majority of overlaps fell into this category; nevertheless, once we exclude the other categories it becomes apparent that the course of the interaction was even smoother than the number of overlap episodes given in Table II suggests. Much depends, of course, on what is included in one's definition of vocalizing: whether, for instance, laughter and crying should be considered together with babbling, cooing, and verbalizing. Here it was decided to keep the definition as broad as possible, and thus we have the opportunity of examining the occurrence of overlaps in relation to various types of vocalization. As a result we can conclude that not all overlap episodes constitute a break-down of the interactive exchange: on the contrary, as the examples of laughter and chorusing in particular make clear, simultaneous vocalizing may under certain circumstances be an appropriate and beneficial activity for the two partners to undertake.

Chorusing, let us note, appears to be equivalent to the simultaneous vocalizing described by Strain and Vietze (1975) and by Stern *et al.* (1975)—referred to as a "joining in" pattern by the former and a "co-action" pattern by the latter. The comparatively high incidence of such simultaneous vocalizing obtained in these two studies was not, however, found by us. This might possibly be due to methodological considerations, in that there is plenty of room for difference in such matters as the operational definition of vocalizing, in techniques of recording and in methods of measuring the amount of vocalizing. It may, however, also be due to the age difference in the subjects studied (theirs being only three months old). Given that turn-taking is very much influenced by the mother, it could be that at 12 months infants are expected to comprehend what is being said to them and that mothers will accordingly take care to avoid overlapping; at much younger ages, on the other hand, infants are not perceived in this way and mothers will therefore use vocalizing for different purposes best served by simultaneously occurring behaviour.

Whatever the facts of incidence, we see here the danger inherent in equating mother–infant synchrony, considered descriptively in terms of the temporal patterning of behaviour, with synchrony in a functional sense. The occurrence of some observable regularity is not necessarily functionally appropriate—two individuals who consistently spoke simultaneously could be said to be acting synchronously but would scarcely be able to communicate. Conversely a break-down of some form of interpersonal regularity, in this case the overlapping of two activities which normally alternate, is not necessarily inappropriate and indicative of dysfunction. Under some conditions an alternating pattern may indeed be appropriate, verbally transmitted information exchanges being the most obvious example. Thus in the two-year-group some children, on being confronted with a novel toy, would turn to the mother and ask, "What's that?" and then wait for the mother to reply. Interrupting the mother's answer is clearly not functional if it means some loss of the information given. Under other conditions, however, turn-taking may be inappropriate. Warning calls are a case in point, in that the imperative need for rapid one-way communication overrides the importance of regulating the two-way exchange. Somewhat different examples are furnished by the chorusing episodes, where simultaneous vocalization gave the intuitive impression of a drawing together of the two participants. The non-correspondence of the two aspects of the concept of synchrony shows how mistaken a strategy it would be to attempt to use some measure of behavioural synchrony, which is merely a descriptor of temporal patterning, as an index of the quality of the interaction in terms of its functional appropriateness.

SPEAKER-SWITCH PAUSES

Let us now examine those speaker-switches where overlaps did not occur and instead a momentary period of silence intervened. Two kinds of such pauses are to be distinguished, depending on the sequence of speakers on either side of the pause. We shall accordingly refer to child–mother pauses, where the child yielded the floor to the mother, and mother–child pauses, where mother spoke first and was succeeded by the child.

In Table IV data are given for individual subject pairs detailing their speaker-switch characteristics. The age difference between the mean number of speaker-switches that occurred during the ten-minute session, 101 and 143 for the younger and the older group respectively, is not

Table IV

Speaker-switches in individual subject pairs: number and duration

Subject pair	Number of speaker-switches	Percent more than one second: Child–mother pauses	Mother–child pauses
One-year-group			
Ia	53	31·03	53·85
Ib	75	34·21	75·68
Ic	132	21·54	62·69
Id	96	12·50	45·83
Ie	140	17·91	50·00
If	142	18·84	61·64
Ig	91	32·56	45·83
Ih	80	30·00	77·50
Mean:	101·13	24·82	59·13
Two-year-group			
IIa	145	18·57	54·67
IIb	73	35·14	22·22
IIc	126	25·81	53·13
IId	282	4·35	31·03
IIe	166	25·30	40·48
IIf	118	24·56	50·85
IIg	160	26·83	57·69
IIh	74	28·57	65·79
Mean:	143·00	27·21	46·98

significant, for the range within each group is considerable and the overlap of the two distributions more noteworthy than their difference. In so far as the number of speaker-switches within a given time period reflects the rate at which the two participants exchanged roles it appears that this rate did not vary substantially from one age to the other. In comparison with the older group the reduced amount of vocalizing of the younger children was accompanied by longer pauses, thus producing comparable floor-holding times and so providing an interactive rhythm similar at both ages despite the difference in the content of the interaction.

As could be expected from distributions of speaker-switch pauses in adults (Jaffe and Feldstein, 1970), the duration of pauses is on the whole extremely brief, the majority in both age groups being but a fraction of a second (see Fig. 1 for two representative cases). The duration depends, however, on the sequence of speakers, for mother–child pauses tend to be somewhat longer than child–mother pauses. This is brought out by a 2×2 analysis of variance on the percentages of pauses greater than one second, in which the age effect and speaker sequence are investigated. Neither the main effect of age nor the interaction term are significant; the speaker sequence variable, on the other hand, is found to be highly significant ($F = 67{\cdot}57$; $df = 1{,}14$; $p < 0{\cdot}001$), indicating the tendency for mothers to reply more quickly than their children.

This difference is perhaps best understood in terms of the bout structure of the vocal exchanges. The vocal interaction was not, of course, continuous throughout the session, for periods of relatively prolonged mutual silence occurred from time to time. It is noteworthy, however, that such prolonged pauses, when they involve a speaker-switch, were generally of the mother–child rather than the child–mother type of sequence. It appears, in other words, that bouts of vocal interaction were usually initiated by the child. It was he, therefore, who set the pace, whereas the mother tended merely to reply.

Our data are, of course, only descriptive and we do not know anything definite about the mechanisms that bring about the harmony apparent in the exchange of roles of the two participants. We shall return to this issue later; here let us note, however, the strong impression gained by a number of investigators (Schaffer, 1974; Trevarthen *et al.*, 1975) observing infants rather younger than those studied here that "proto-conversations" are brought about mostly by the mother letting herself be paced by the infant. The infant, in other words, periodically emits bursts of vocalizations, and it is then up to the mother to fill in the pauses. She alone would thus be responsible for regulating speaker-switches, and turn-taking would accordingly be brought about entirely by her initiative.

There are, as we shall see, indications that this may be too extreme a statement. Nevertheless, the very much shorter pauses characterizing child–mother speaker switches attests to the mother's considerable competence in taking over the floor from the child, and makes one wonder what cues she may be using to indicate that it is her turn to speak. Few of the cues found to be operative in this respect in adult conversations (Duncan, 1972) are likely to have played a part here, particularly among the one-year-group where syntax and paralinguistic features can hardly be used as indication that the child has come to an

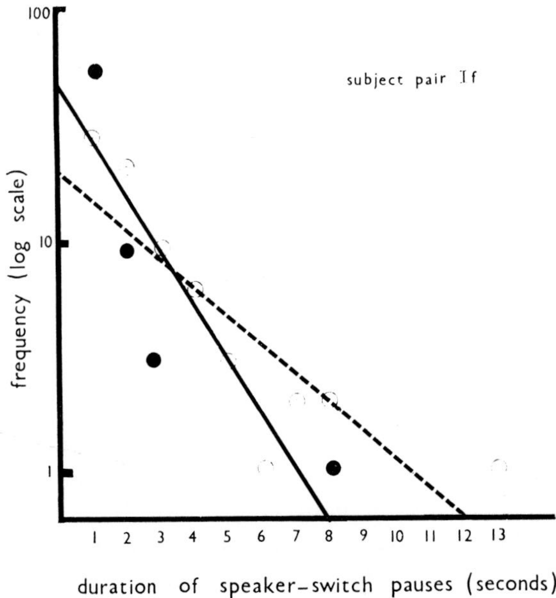

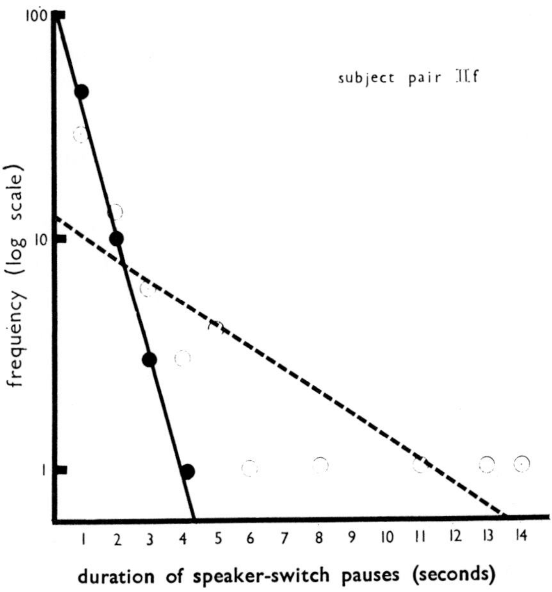

Fig. 1. Speaker-switch pause distributions for two subject-pairs. ● ———— Child–mother pauses. ◯ - - - - - - - - - - Mother–child pauses.

end of his utterance. It is true that in the two-year-group syntax and intonation may have begun to exert influence (a lot of utterances, even the one-word ones, had the rising inflection of a question and, when accompanied by pointing or holding up a toy, were clearly meant as such); nevertheless, it is interesting to note that the mothers of the one-year-old infants were no slower in answering than those in the older group.

In any case, too close a comparison with adult conversation may be misleading, as the vocal interaction we observed was far from continuous. The child's utterances tended to be discrete in nature and—particularly at the one-year level—less sequentially dependent than an adult's. Thus the mother's task in predicting whether she would be able to speak without clashing with the child is a matter of judging not so much whether the last utterance will be taken up and continued but whether the child is likely to make another, separate, utterance. What this prediction is based on remains conjectural. It seems inconceivable, however, that there are no cues in the child's behaviour during play and exploration as to the likelihood of his vocalizing. Were this to be the case the relationship between his vocalizing and other behaviour would be random—an intrinsically unlikely state of affairs. It remains for further work to clarify this relationship.

Until this has been done, it must be concluded that the most obvious cue which appeared to guide a mother's behaviour was silence: when the child stopped vocalizing she knew that she could take the floor. To do so as promptly as these mothers generally did required great sensitivity on their part; they had to be closely attuned to the child's activity to respond as quickly as they usually did. But then, as we shall mention below, these mothers were in fact extremely watchful in this situation, hardly taking their eyes off the child throughout the entire ten-minute session. Under the circumstances they were clearly well placed to ensure prompt, timely sequencing.

Vocalizing and Looking

Communication generally takes place via several channels simultaneously. For the communicative process to function properly these need to be finely integrated with one another, so that they remain in phase and no ambiguous or contradictory messages are sent. Mature interactive behaviour must therefore be characterized not only by interpersonal but also by intrapersonal synchrony.

The integration of looking with verbalizing during the conversations of adult dyads provides the clearest example of the way in which various response systems are jointly engaged in the interaction with another person (though note also the data now becoming available on the role played by body movements as part of this pattern, Birdwhistell, 1971). As the work of Exline and Winters (1965), Kendon (1967), Argyle (1972), and others has shown, looks at the other person are not randomly distributed in the course of a dialogue; they occur rather in orderly patterns and play a significant part in regulating the interactive flow. Three main functions have been suggested for dyadic looks, namely (1) expressive, in that they indicate something of the subject's attitudes and feelings, (2) monitoring, so that information may be gained as to the progress of the interaction and the way in which the partner is receiving the subject's behaviour, and (3) regulatory, whereby the behaviour of the two individuals is synchronized and the flow of the dialogue regulated. The third function is of particular interest to us, for one of the main roles that looking has been found to play is with regard to floor apportionment. Looks, that is, serve as a mutually understood cue that regulates the exchange of speaker and listener and thus helps to minimize the incidence of overlaps. One may therefore consider looking as a gesture, in that it is used both to indicate something about oneself to others and to direct the other person's behaviour.

In the study of infants' social behaviour looking at the other person has received quite a lot of attention in recent years. Mostly it has been used as an attachment index (e.g. by Coates *et al.*, 1972; Maccoby and Feldman, 1972), on the assumption that its total quantity reflects the intensity of the child's desire to be in contact with the other person. Treated in more dyadic terms, mutual gazing has come to be recognized as playing a special part in cementing the bond between mother and baby (Robson, 1967) and, moreover, has been found to show marked regularities in the interaction of even quite young infants with their mothers (Stern, 1971 and 1974). It has also been suggested that these regularities reflect a fundamental property of human interaction sequences generally and may accordingly be compared to the rhythms found in adult conversations (Jaffe *et al.*, 1973). The co-ordination of looking patterns with vocalizing, on the other hand, has so far not been studied at an early developmental level; yet, at the very least, an examination of the relationship between the two responses should tell us whether looks are randomly distributed during the vocal interchange or not. Thus the two responses, about each of which we now know quite a lot as separate systems, need to be considered in terms of their interaction in order to determine their sequential arrangement within the early dyadic situation.

BASIC LOOKING DATA

The data on each child's looks at mother were extracted from the video-recording by two observers working jointly on the basis of frame-by-frame analysis and with repeated viewing of appropriate sections. The time of initiation and termination of each look was ascertained by reference to the digital timer included in the video-record, thus yielding its duration. In addition, the ongoing vocalization state at the time of the initiation of each look was determined. Six vocalization states were distinguished: (1) mother vocalizing, (2) mother within-speaker pause, (3) mother–child speaker-switch pause, (4) child vocalizing, (5) child within-speaker pause, (6) child–mother speaker-switch pause. The first three states comprise a mother floor-holding episode, while the other three make up a child floor-holding episode. For the few cases where the moment of onset of a look was indistinguishable from the moment of change of vocalization state between pause and vocalizing, the following decision rules were adopted: when a look began at the same time as a vocalization the look was scored as starting during the vocalization; when a look began as a vocalization ended the look was scored as starting during the pause.

As can be seen from Table V, the children in the two-year-old group looked at their mothers considerably more often than the younger children (means of 54·88 and 23·75 respectively, $t = 4{\cdot}004$; $df = 14$; $p < 0{\cdot}01$). The reason for this difference must be conjectural. It is hardly likely to signify that the two-year-old children are more attached than the one-year-olds. A more likely explanation is in terms of the attention distribution that characterizes the two age levels, with the younger children showing a pattern of far greater absorption in ongoing activity relating to toys and far less ability to switch from toy to mother and back again. Impressionistically, it appeared that the older children found it much easier to play *with* the mother, that they were able to

Table V

Total number and mean length of looks at mother by individual subjects

Subject pair		Number of looks	Mean length of looks (seconds)
One-year-group			
Ia		21	1·11
Ib		27	1·29
Ic		28	1·88
Id		7	0·66
Ie		21	1·82
If		29	1·16
Ig		32	1·33
Ih		25	1·35
	Mean:	23·75	1·33
Two-year-group			
IIa		38	1·38
IIb		77	2·04
IIc		53	1·21
IId		77	0·99
IIe		43	0·82
IIf		75	1·45
IIg		55	1·62
IIh		21	1·60
	Mean:	54·88	1·39

include her in their ongoing concerns with toys and that their looking patterns thus reflected this increasing flexibility. The "obligatory" nature of attention in very young babies has been described by Stechler and Latz (1966), and for later infancy too evidence shows a growing ability to deploy attention over several features of the environment—even those not directly within the perceptual field (Millar and Schaffer, 1972 and 1973). It may well be that this development continues into the second year and underlies the difference found here.

Mean length of looks, on the other hand, did not differentiate the two ages, being 1·33 and 1·39 seconds respectively for the younger and the older group. For the majority of children the distribution of looking length was extremely skewed, with most looks being very brief and only a few sustained over several seconds. The lengths of looks initiated during the six vocalization states were compared but no pattern emerged.

The mothers, on the other hand, showed a very different pattern of looking at their children. Because the physical arrangement of the observation setting was designed primarily for accurate recording of the child's looks, those of the mother could not be so readily ascertained from the video-recordings. However, estimates were obtained from nine mothers (five from the younger and four from the older group) at the time of recording by an observer pressing a button and thus indicating the cumulative duration of these mothers' looks. These data confirmed the general impression that mothers spend a large part of the session watching their children. In all but one case the mothers looked for more than 80% of the session time, and in six cases more than 93% (giving a mean of 90% for the whole group). There was, moreover, a strong impression that looking continued as much during the mother's vocalizing as it did while she was listening to the child. This suggests a very different distribution from that observed during the conversation of adult dyads (Kendon, 1967), who look away far more during their own utterances than during those of their partner. On the other hand, such "aberrant" patterns have been described by Stern (1974), who found the gazes of mothers playing with three-month-old babies to be extraordinarily long compared to average adult gaze exchanges. This pattern means, of course, that the great majority of child looks resulted in mutual looking, and that the child was thus in a position to find out that his mother's attention was very much focused on him and more or less constantly available.

THE INTEGRATION OF LOOKING AND VOCALIZING

At what points of the vocal exchange did the children look toward the mother? This question will be considered basically in terms of a comparison between looks initiated during mother floor-holding episodes and those initiated during child floor-holding episodes. We shall ask, in other words, whether children were more likely to initiate looks in the course of their own activity or in response to the mother's, or, for that matter, whether looks were distributed randomly throughout the session.

Table VI shows the number of looks initiated by each child during the two kinds of floor-holding episodes. To evaluate these data, however, it must be recalled that mother floor-holding times generally exceeded those of the child; therefore the number of looks initiated needs to be

Table VI

The association of looking at mother with child floor-holding and mother floor-holding

Subject pair	L_{CFH}[a]	T_{CFH}[b]	L_{CFH}/T_{CFH}[e]	L_{MFH}[c]	T_{MFH}[d]	L_{MFH}/T_{MFH}[e]
One-year-group						
Ia	3	120·10	0·02	18	479·90	0·04
Ib	16	394·65	0·04	11	205·38	0·05
Ic	15	302·43	0·05	13	297·53	0·04
Id	4	269·78	0·01	3	330·15	0·01
Ie	10	192·15	0·05	11	407·70	0·03
If	4	123·08	0·03	25	476·90	0·05
Ig	18	335·58	0·05	14	264·40	0·05
Ih	5	143·33	0·03	20	456·70	0·04
Two-year-group						
IIa	19	221·13	0·09	19	378·83	0·05
IIb	28	155·08	0·18	49	444·93	0·11
IIc	26	171·05	0·15	27	428·80	0 06
IId	61	298·93	0·20	16	301·03	0·05
IIe	19	247·40	0·08	24	352·53	0·07
IIf	58	333·85	0·17	17	266·08	0·06
IIg	26	254·00	0·10	29	345·93	0·08
IIh	13	255·88	0·05	8	344·13	0·02

[a] L_{CFH}: Number of looks starting during child floor-holding time.
[b] T_{CFH}: Child floor-holding time in seconds.
[c] L_{MFH}: Number of looks starting during mother floor-holding time.
[d] T_{MFH}: Mother floor-holding time in seconds.
[e] The ratios L_{CFH}/T_{CFH} and L_{MFH}/T_{MFH} express the rate of looks per unit time of child and mother floor-holding respectively.

expressed as a rate per unit of floor-holding time. In a 2×2 analysis of variance which compared looking rates during mother's and child's floor-holding across the two age groups both main effects were significant. The age effect ($F = 19{\cdot}61$; df $= 1,14$; $p < 0{\cdot}001$) merely reflects the previously mentioned finding that, overall, the older children looked more than the younger ones. The other main effect showed that looking rates were greater during the child's than during the mother's floor-holding episodes ($F = 11{\cdot}55$; df $= 1,14$; $p < 0{\cdot}01$). However, the significant interaction of these two terms ($F = 14{\cdot}55$; df $= 1,14$; $p < 0{\cdot}01$) shows that this effect is not homogeneous across the two age groups; in fact, the simple main effect test indicates significance only for the older group ($F = 26{\cdot}02$; $df = 1{,}14$; $p < 0{\cdot}001$) but not for the younger group ($F = 0{\cdot}87$; $df = 1{,}14$). Two-year-olds, that is, are more likely to look up at the mother while they themselves are holding the floor than while the mother is doing so; one-year-olds, on the other hand, distribute initiation of looks indiscriminately over both partners' floor-holding episodes.

Similar analyses were performed on two of the constituents of floor-holding, namely vocalizing and speaker-switch pauses. As to the former (Table VII), we will again consider the rates of looking at mother per unit time. In order to interpret any age effects in these data

Table VII

The association of looking at mother with mother vocalizing and child vocalizing

Subject pair	L_{CVOC}[a]	T_{CVOC}[b]	L_{CVOC}/T_{CVOC}[e]	L_{MVOC}[c]	T_{MVOC}[d]	L_{MVOC}/T_{MVOC}[e]
One-year-group						
Ia	0	21·50	0·00	12	81·38	0·15
Ib	7	31·70	0·22	3	27·60	0·11
Ic	7	71·43	0·10	6	85·73	0·07
Id	2	78·58	0·03	2	89·28	0·02
Ie	3	73·80	0·04	5	110·10	0·05
If	1	47·83	0·02	9	105·73	0·09
Ig	8	34·18	0·23	4	72·83	0·05
Ih	2	39·93	0·05	3	63·23	0·05
Two-year-group						
IIa	9	99·55	0·09	7	143·88	0·05
IIb	6	28·53	0·21	8	72·78	0·11
IIc	10	53·60	0·19	15	156·33	0·10
IId	41	138·60	0·30	10	168·50	0·06
IIe	15	83·28	0·18	18	105·78	0·17
IIf	42	98·30	0·43	10	74·00	0·14
IIg	15	69·55	0·22	12	103·90	0·12
IIh	9	66·48	0·14	7	121·23	0·06

[a] L_{CVOC}: Number of looks starting during child vocalization.
[b] T_{CVOC}: Child vocalization in seconds.
[c] L_{MVOC}: Number of looks starting during mother vocalization.
[d] T_{MVOC}: Mother vocalization in seconds.
[e] The ratios L_{CVOC}/T_{CVOC} and L_{MVOC}/T_{MVOC} express the rate of looks per second of each vocalization type.

we need to be able to separate differences in looking rates specific to vocalizing periods from differences in the overall rates of looking irrespective of vocalizing state. Accordingly, overall rate of looks was controlled statistically by using each child's total number of looks as a covariate in a 2 × 2 analysis of covariance. As a result, no significant age effect emerges ($F = 0{\cdot}04$; df = 1,13); a difference was, however, found for the other main effect, in that more looks were initiated per unit time during child vocalizing than during mother vocalizing ($F = 6{\cdot}55$; df = 1,13; $p < 0{\cdot}05$). The interaction falls only just short of significance ($F = 4{\cdot}29$; df = 1,13), and again we find that the effect is confined to the older group ($F = 10{\cdot}72$; df = 1,13; $p < 0{\cdot}01$) and is not apparent among the one-year-olds ($F = 0{\cdot}12$; df = 1,13).

A similar analysis of covariance was performed on looks initiated during speaker-switch pauses (Table VIII). Again the main effect for age was negligible ($F = 0{\cdot}06$; df = 1,13), while the significant difference found for the other effect ($F = 13{\cdot}38$; df = 1,13; $p < 0{\cdot}01$) showed looks more often beginning during child–mother pauses than during mother–child pauses. Here too the interaction fell short of significance ($F = 3{\cdot}17$; df = 1,13), but simple main effects tests showed that the differential influence of pause types could be observed only in the two-year-group ($F = 14{\cdot}79$; df = 1,13; $p < 0{\cdot}01$) and not in the one-year-group ($F = 1{\cdot}76$; df = 1,13).

It appears therefore that, in the two-year-olds, looks are not distributed in a random fashion throughout the discourse. Instead, they showed a definite association with the *child's* vocal activity, in that they were more likely to be initiated while he was holding the floor than during the mother's floor-holding episodes. Looks at the mother, in other words, tended to begin either during or immediately following the child's utterances. In this respect there is a clear differentiation between the two age groups, for no similar pattern was found for the one-year-olds.

LOOKING AND TURN-TAKING

Given these data on the onset of looks in relation to vocalization state, what can we conclude about the function of looking at these ages? The literature on dyadic behaviour in adults suggests that looks are particularly related to turn-taking, in that they serve to indicate to the listener that the speaker has finished and is willing to yield the floor to

Table VIII

The association of looking at mother with speaker-switch pauses

Subject pair	L_{CMP}[a]	T_{CMP}[b]	L_{CMP}/T_{CMP}[e]	L_{MCP}[c]	T_{MCP}[d]	L_{MCP}/T_{MCP}[e]
One-year-group						
Ia	3	44·0	0·07	1	93·5	0·01
Ib	3	45·0	0·07	8	121·5	0·07
Ic	3	66·5	0·05	4	125·5	0·03
Id	2	52·0	0·04	1	133·0	0·01
Ie	4	65·5	0·06	4	159·5	0·03
If	3	57·5	0·05	7	147·5	0·05
Ig	7	70·5	0·10	3	90·0	0·03
Ih	2	68·0	0·03	11	248·0	0·04
Two-year-group						
IIa	7	56·0	0·13	6	151·5	0·04
IIb	15	90·5	0·17	9	71·0	0·13
IIc	15	66·0	0·23	2	157·0	0·01
IId	8	76·0	0·11	5	127·0	0·04
IIe	4	109·0	0·04	3	143·0	0·02
IIf	6	50·0	0·12	4	125·0	0·03
IIg	6	86·0	0·07	8	124·0	0·06
IIh	3	64·5	0·05	1	90·0	0·01

[a] L_{CMP}: Number of looks starting during child–mother pause.
[b] T_{CMP}: Child–mother pauses in seconds.
[c] L_{MCP}: Number of looks starting during mother–child pause.
[d] T_{MCP}: Mother–child pauses in seconds.
[e] The ratios L_{CMP}/T_{CMP} and L_{MCP}/T_{MCP} express the rate of looks per second of each pause type.

him. It is not easy, however, to find conclusive evidence in our data for such signal functions of looking, for the basic differences with the material obtained from adults are too great. For one thing, the findings on adults are explicitly based on long utterances (Kendon, 1967, used only those of five seconds or over), while child utterances in our sample are nearly all extremely brief—generally well below the five-second limit. And for another, the mother's looking pattern is, as we have seen, quite distinctive in the interaction with her child—indeed her near-continuous looking is rather like that of a permanent listener, always willing to concede to the child's right to hold the floor.

Comparisons with adult data are, in any case, probably quite misleading, for here we are dealing with a very different situation. Instead of participating in a continuous face-to-face interaction the child for his part was mainly involved in play and exploration, and, as Levine and Sutton-Smith (1973) have shown with older children, task-centred situations elicit considerably less looking than conversation-based situations.

In fact, if looking was an important regulator of vocal turn-taking one would expect less sophisticated turn-taking in the interactions of the younger group where the looking-vocalizing pattern was still undifferentiated. This, however, was not the case. Moreover, if looking functioned as a turn-taking signal we would expect child floor-holding episodes generally to be accompanied by looking. However, only a minority of such episodes (19·81% in the younger and 42·36% in the older group) contain a look. For that matter, there is no indication of the child consistently acting as a listener and watching the mother in order to obtain a cue for the start of his turn: 28·86% of mother floor-holding episodes in the younger group and 42·97% in the older group were accompanied by looks—again only a minority. In addition, when we compare those speaker-switch pauses that follow a look-accompanied child floor-holding episode with those that follow episodes not accompanied by a look, no difference in length emerges. The mother, that is, acts as promptly in the absence of the customary signal as in its presence.

It appears unlikely therefore that, in the particular situation observed, the child's looks played any important part in vocal turn-taking. This applies as much to the two-year-old as the one-year-old children, and refers to both the taking and the relinquishing of turns. In no case is there definite evidence that child looks served to regulate the exchange of speaker and listener roles and that they helped to minimize the occurrence of overlaps. This is not to deny, of course, that under different circumstances such evidence might be forthcoming: a situation without the distraction of toys and other novel features and lending itself therefore more to direct confrontation may possibly yield different looking–vocalizing relationships. It is nevertheless significant that, under the particular conditions observed here, turn-taking was brought about so smoothly without recourse to the usual looking signal.

Why then do children look at the mother? One function might be merely to check on her presence and ensure that she continues to be available. However, it should be remembered that in the small observation room used for this study the children were rarely more than a few feet away from the mother and could thus be aware of her without needing directly to fixate her. In any case, were this so looking would more likely be evenly distributed throughout the session. It is also obvious that most of the child's looks were not reactive in the sense of being a response to the mother's voice, for then they would have been initiated mainly during the mother's floor-holding episodes. Rather than looks being associated with the *reception* of vocal signals, we found them—at any rate in the older group—to be associated with their *emission*. Facial orientation toward a likely recipient will ensure that the sound is emitted in the most appropriate direction and, further, that facial signals which may augment the vocal ones are optimally apparent. Even more important, however, is that looking at the other person allows visual monitoring of his reactions: the ability to adapt communicative output according to the state of the listener is widely considered to be a major component of communicative competence, and how better to monitor the state of the listener than to watch him! It has been suggested (Carlson and Anisfeld, 1969) that speech that is clearly meant to be communicative is more likely to be accompanied by visual fixation on the other person, whereas egocentric speech lacks such focus. Mothers too probably make this interpretation. Hence looking in association with speech, as well as fulfilling a monitoring function for the child, may have signal value for the mother in emphasizing the other-directed nature of the child's vocal behaviour and consequently helping her to comprehend the meaning of his utterances.

Conclusions

Let us first resume our main findings. These are as follows:

(1) In one-year-old as much as in two-year-old children vocal exchanges with the mother are "smooth". This smoothness is indicated above all by the ability of the two partners to take vocal turns and to avoid overlapping responses. Relatively few overlap episodes occurred at both ages.

(2) An examination of the nature of overlaps shows that not all represent a break-down in the interactive synchrony of the two partners. On the contrary, simultaneous vocalizing may, under certain circumstances, help to further the interaction.
(3) Overlaps were generally of very brief duration and did not appear to throw the interactive flow out of gear. They were as likely to be brought about by the mother interrupting the child as by the child interrupting the mother.
(4) Most speaker-switch pauses were extremely brief—generally less than one second. This applies particularly to child–mother pauses, but holds also for mother–child pauses, and is evident in both age groups.
(5) Vocal exchanges generally occurred in bouts, and new bouts tended to be initiated by the child. There was some indication that it was the child who set the pace whereas the mother's function was merely to reply.
(6) The most obvious cue for turn-taking was the other person's silence. Cues said to play a part in adult conversation were not apparent here. The mothers' extreme watchfulness, as indicated by their near-continuous looking at the child throughout the session, was clearly a help in this respect.
(7) In the older group looks at the mother were not randomly distributed throughout the vocal exchange but showed a marked association with the child's floor-holding episodes, in that they tended to be initiated either during or immediately following his utterances rather than the mother's. This pattern was not yet evident in the one-year-group.

These findings are, of course, specific to the particular age range studied, namely that between one and two years. On the basis of these data it should now be possible to investigate younger infants and ascertain whether the same relationships are to be found at earlier ages. Younger infants were not included in this particular study for two reasons: first, because preliminary observations of babies within the age range of four to nine months pointed to the considerable difficulty of obtaining a sufficient number of vocalizations within a strange laboratory situation; and secondly, because the inability to locomote or even to handle toys produces a completely different situational context for the interaction with the mother that would not have justified direct comparison with older children. A rather different approach is thus required with subjects younger than those included in the present sample; their study, nevertheless, is necessary if we are to make statements about the developmental origins of the phenomena here described.

These phenomena are essentially concerned with the temporal patterning of responses in a mother–child dyadic situation. Vocal interplay has been given special attention because we wished to ascertain what indications of interpersonal synchrony are already in existence before the onset of speech. And as our findings on turn-taking indicate, one basic means whereby participants regulate their interchange marks even pre-verbal exchanges.

There are, however, two important qualifications which must be borne in mind. In the first place, whatever the frequency of turn-taking may normally be, it cannot be regarded as a *sine qua non* of all "successful" dialogues. On the contrary, the importance of some of our overlap categories such as chorusing and laughter lies not in their incidence but in the fact that they illustrate that under certain conditions (the nature and prevalence of which may well vary with age) a simultaneous rather than an alternating dyadic pattern is appropriate to the interaction. The form of such interaction, in other words, cannot be specified according to a rigid rule which insists on turn-taking; on the contrary, that the two partners can switch from one pattern to the other according to circumstances must fill one with all the more wonder at the intricacies of interactions occurring even at these early ages.

The second qualification, however, is a warning that data such as those presented here do not enable one to make any statements about *individuals* and that one cannot therefore arrive at any conclusions about the children's "ability" to take turns. Our findings about the prevalence of the turn-taking pattern refer to the dyadic situation, not to the individuals participating in it. It is, of course, significant that, even before the burgeoning of verbal development in the course of the second year, the child is already involved in interactions that share some of the formal characteristics of verbal dialogues—that in particular, at an age when the content of the child's vocalizations as yet carries no linguistic information, he is nevertheless generally found to hold the floor without interruption. But such data are only descriptive; they tell us little about the way in which turn-taking is brought about.

To answer this further question, there are at least three possibilities that need to be considered. In the first place, such a pattern may be brought about by both partners acting jointly. Each "knows" the rules and is therefore equally responsible for ensuring a smooth interaction. Such knowledge may not be conscious, of course, and the relevant behaviour may not be intentional; yet it is worth bearing in mind that mothers are frequently heard to tell children "not to interrupt while someone is talking!" Socializing pressures are thus brought to bear on children at certain ages to become aware of this general rule governing social intercourse. In the second place, one might consider that turn-taking is at first entirely due to the mother's initiative, in that she allows herself to be paced by the child and merely fills in the pauses between his bursts of vocalizations. As we have seen, there were some indications in our data that the mother does indeed have to play a very active role in this respect; on the other hand, it seems unlikely that the infant plays no part at all in the mutual regulation of the vocal interchange and that he vocalizes as though oblivious of all external considerations. The third possibility is therefore that some primitive mechanism is already present from the beginning which makes production of vocalizations and listening to other sounds inherently incompatible. Some tentative evidence to this effect can be found in studies of six- and seven-month-old infants by Webster (1969; Webster *et al.*, 1972), where it was found that auditory stimulation had a marked suppressant effect on vocalization, in that the total number of sounds produced by the subjects during periods of stimulation showed a considerable decrease when compared with base-line levels. It is true, of course, that one cannot speak and listen at the same time; Webster's findings suggest, however, that this inability may be more basic and not necessarily confined to speech: rather, one cannot vocalize and attend to external auditory input at the same time.

We are as yet in no position to decide between these various alternatives. But whatever the results of further work may indicate, it is apparent that some of the means whereby verbal interchange is made effective are already in existence well before the child actually begins to use words. The many dialogues, that is, in which he is involved even during the pre-verbal period contain features that are likely to make the transition to the new mode of communication considerably smoother. It is in this sense that there is continuity between pre-verbal and verbal stages of communicative interaction—a continuity that is inherent in the dyadic situation in which interchanges, whatever their expressive mode, take place.

The looking data, on the other hand, illustrate the need for caution in making statements about continuity of *individual* communicative skills. In our two-year-olds a definite relationship had emerged between looking and vocalizing—a relationship based on a marked tendency for looks to be initiated during the child's floor-holding episodes rather than in response to the mother's activity. In the younger group, however, such a relationship was not yet apparent: whatever precise function looks play within the vocal interchange emerges only *after* the onset of language. It seems highly likely that by the age of 12 months the child has become aware of the illocutionary force of some of his behaviour (Bates *et al.*, 1975, find evidence of such awareness as from sensori-motor stage V); it is also likely, however, that intentional signalling is not an all-or-none ability that develops at the same rate in all behaviour systems. Certainly our data indicate that the one-year-old's pre-verbal vocalizations are not necessarily accompanied by looking at the other person; at this age, it seems, he is not yet concerned to monitor the effects of his vocal activity and search for feedback. It is only in the course of the second year that visual and vocal activities become co-ordinated, assuming the kind of integration that gives speech its obviously other-directed character.

References

Argyle, M. (1972). Non-verbal communication in human social interaction. In R. A. Hinde (Ed.), *Non-Verbal Communication*. University of Cambridge Press, London.

Bates, E., Camaioni, L. and Volterra, V. (1975). The acquisition of performatives prior to speech. *Merrill-Palmer Q.* **21**, 205–226.

Birdwhistell, R. L. (1971). *Kinesics and Context, Essays on Body-Motion Communication.* Allen Lane, The Penguin Press, London.

Brazelton, T. B., Koslowski, B. and Main, M. (1974). The origins of reciprocity: the early mother-infant interaction. In M. Lewis and L. A. Rosenblum (Eds), *The Effect of the Infant on its Caregiver*. Wiley, New York.

Carlson, O. and Anisfeld, M. (1969). Some observations on the linguistic competence of a two-year-old child. *Child Dev.* **40**, 569–575.

Coates, B., Anderson, E. P. and Hartup, W. W. (1972). Interrelations in the attachment behavior of human infants. *Dev. Psychol.* **6**, 218–230.

Doty, D. (1974). Infant speech perception. *Human Devel.* **17**, 74–80.

Duncan, S. D., Jr. (1972). Some signals and rules for taking speaking turns in conversation. *J. Pers. soc. Psychol.* **23**, 283–292.

Duncan, S. D., Jr. and Niederehe, G. (1974). On signalling that it's your turn to speak. *J. exper. soc. Psychol.* **10**, 234–247.

Exline, R. B. and Winters, L. C. (1965). Affective relations and mutual gaze in dyads. In S. Tomkins and C. Izzard (Eds), *Affect, Cognition and Personality*. Springer, New York.

Gunther, M. (1961). Infant behaviour at the breast. In B. M. Foss (Ed.), *Determinants of Infant Behaviour*. Methuen, London.

Irwin, O. C. (1960). Language and communication. In P. H. Mussen (Ed.), *Handbook of Research Methods in Child Development*. Wiley, New York.

Jaffe, J. and Feldstein, S. (1970). *Rhythms of Dialogue*. Academic Press, New York and London.

Jaffe, J., Stern, D. N. and Peery, J. C. (1973). "Conversational" coupling of gaze behaviour in prelinguistic human development. *Journal of Psycho-linguistic Research* **2**, 321–330.

Kaye, K. (1976). Infants' effects upon their mothers' teaching strategies. In J. C. Glidewell (Ed.), *The Social Context of Learning and Development*. Gardner, New York.

Kendon, A. (1967). Some functions of gaze-direction in social interaction. *Acta Psychologica* **26**, 22–63.

Levine, M. H. and Sutton-Smith, B. (1973). Effects of age, sex, and task on visual behavior during dyadic interaction. *Dev. Psychol.* **9**, 400–405.

Lewis, M. and Freedle, R. (1973). Mother-infant dyad: The cradle of meaning. In P. Pliner, L. Krames, and T. Alloway (Eds), *Communication and Affect: Language and Thought*. Academic Press, New York and London.

Maccoby, E. E. and Feldman, S. S. (1972). Mother-attachment and stranger-reactions in the third year of life. *Monogr. Soc. Res. Child Dev.* **37**, 1, Serial No. 146.

Millar, W. S. and Schaffer, H. R. (1972). The influence of spatially displaced feedback in infant operant conditioning. *J. exp. Child Psychol.* **14**, 442–453.

Millar, W. S. and Schaffer, H. R. (1973). Visual-manipulative response strategies in infant operant conditioning with spatially displaced feedback. *Br. J. Psychol.* **64**, 545–552.

Miller, G. A. (1963). Review of J. H. Greenberg (Ed.), *Universals of Language*. *Contemp. Psychol.* **8**, 417–418.

Newson, J. and Newson, E. (1976). On the social origins of symbolic functioning. In P. Varma and P. Williams (Eds), *Piaget, Psychology and Education*. Hodder and Stoughton, London.

Phillips, J. R. (1973). Syntax and vocabulary of mothers' speech to young children: Age and sex comparisons. *Child Dev.* **44**, 182–185.

Rheingold, H. L., Gewirtz, J. L. and Ross, H. W. (1959). Social conditioning of vocalizations in the infant. *J. comp. physiol. Psychol.* **52**, 68–73.

Robson, K. (1967). The role of eye-to-eye contact in maternal-infant attachment. *J. Child Psychol. Psychiat.* **8**, 13–25.

Schaffer, H. R. (1974). Early social behaviour and the study of reciprocity. *Bull. Br. psychol. Soc.* **27**, 209–216.

Snow, C. E. (1972). Mothers' speech to children learning language. *Child Dev.* **43**, 549–565.

Stechler, G. and Latz, E. (1966). Some observations on attention and arousal in the human infant. *J. Am. Acad. Child Psychiat.* **5**, 517–525.

Stern, D. N. (1971). A micro-analysis of mother-infant interaction: Behavior regulating social contact between a mother and her 3½ month-old twins. *J. Am. Acad. Child Psychiat.* **10**, 501–517.

Stern, D. N. (1974). Mother and infant at play: the dyadic interaction involving facial, vocal, and gaze behaviors. In M. Lewis and L. A. Rosenblum (Eds), *The Effect of the Infant on its Caregiver*. Wiley, New York.

Stern, D. N., Jaffe, J., Beebe, B. and Bennett, S. L. (1975). Vocalising in unison and in alternation: two modes of communication within the mother-infant dyad. *Ann. N.Y. Acad. Sci.*, 1975, 263, 89–100.

Strain, B. A. and Vietze, P. M. (1975). Early dialogues: the structure of reciprocal infant-mother vocalization. Paper to Society for Research in Child Development, Denver, Colorado.

Trevarthen, C., Hubley, P. and Sheeran, L. (1975). Les activités innés du nourisson. *La Recherche* **6**, 447–458.

Webster, R. L. (1969). Selective suppression of infants' vocal responses by classes of phonemic stimulation. *Dev. Psychol.* **1**, 410–414.

Webster, R. L., Steinhardt, M. H. and Senter, M. G. (1972). Changes in infants' vocalisations as a function of differential acoustic stimulation. *Dev. Psychol.* **7**, 39–43.

Weisberg, P. (1963). Social and non-social conditioning of infant vocalisations. *Child Dev.* **34**, 377–388.

Winer, B. J. (1962). *Statistical Principles in Experimental Design*. McGraw-Hill, New York.

13 Mothers, Infants and Pointing: A Study of a Gesture

Catherine M. Murphy and David J. Messer

Introduction

Early mother–infant interaction is a largely non-linguistic communication process, but whereas a great deal of research has been carried out on the nature of verbal communication, study of the development of such forms of non-verbal communication as gestures has been much neglected.

It has been pointed out by Collis and Schaffer (1975) that mother–infant interaction frequently takes place via features of the environment, through toys, distal surroundings, etc. In order that this pattern of interaction can take place as effectively as possible, it is necessary for each partner to be able to monitor the other's interest in the environment. There are many cues available to serve this purpose, such as those described by Collis and Schaffer which give rise to visual following behaviour. In contrast, the pointing gesture is one of the most effective methods whereby an individual can register *his own interest* in a particular feature of his surroundings which enables him to take an active part in leading the interaction. The infant's comprehension of a point is the focus of the present study.

The age at which an infant understands that a point is a social signal designed to attract one's attention to a specific object is the subject of some uncertainty. Anderson (1972) reports that it is "generally believed (though no data are available) that the first year of life will pass before an infant can detach his gaze from the mother's hand, even in his own home, to look in the direction indicated". Mallitskaya (translated in Slobin, 1966), noted that "By about the age of nine months a normal child can differentiate objects and understand the gesture of pointing". Ling and Ling (1974) found that it is not until the end of the first year of life that mothers used the category demonstration—"pointing or glancing to indicate object or person"—with their infants and not until a few months later (18 months) do the infants themselves use this category to a large extent.

Previous studies have tended to examine the effect of a point on an infant in general terms, others are largely impressionistic. No account has been given of how a mother points or how this gesture is incorporated into her behavioural repertoire (where does she look? what does she say?). This study therefore set out to investigate not only the age at which a point becomes effective, but also the precise nature of the pointing phenomenon and its integration with other responses.

An observational, exploratory approach was used whereby we have attempted to look at pointing behaviour in its entirety. The mothers were, therefore, restricted as little as possible. They were asked to draw the infants' attention to the toys, with one constraint, that they should remain seated. This enabled us to determine whether, in fact, a point is the primary mode whereby a mother focuses her infant's attention on distal features of the environment. By maintaining a fairly free and flexible situation, behaviours which naturally accompany the pointing gesture, such as looking and vocalizing, could also be observed.

Method

SUBJECTS

Subjects were 24 mother–infant pairs. The infants fell into two age groups: Group A, 9-months (mean 39 weeks; range 38 to 40 weeks) and Group B, 14-months (mean 60 weeks; range 59 to 61 weeks) with an equal sex distribution. Two mothers were replaced in the sample because they pointed fewer than five times; a further two mothers were also replaced because they left their seats. The infants were selected from lists provided by local Child Welfare Clinics in predominantly middle-class catchment areas and their mothers were contacted by telephone. They were invited to participate in an infant research programme and arrangements were made to bring them to the laboratory by taxi.

PROCEDURE

On arrival the mothers were informed that we were interested in observing their infants' reactions to an unfamiliar environment. We asked them to behave as naturally as possible and endeavoured to set them at ease by talking about the long-term aims of the project before the start of the session.

The observation session took place in a room 3·5 × 2·0 m, one side of which contained a one-way window. The baby was placed in a high chair with his mother seated on a stool alongside. They faced the one-way window, suspended in front of which were three toys: a teddy bear, a rag doll and a cloth clown. The observation session lasted for five minutes and was video-recorded. Throughout the session observers stood behind each of the three toys, on the other side of the one-way window, monitoring the infants' looking behaviour. While the infant looked at a particular toy the observer pressed a button which activated a light. These lights together with a digital timer were optically superimposed on the video-recording.

In order to compensate for any differential attractiveness of the three toys their positions were systematically varied, all six permutations being used. The possibility of the mothers' position influencing the babies' looking behaviour was controlled by varying their position in relation to the baby so that half sat to the infant's left and half to his right.

VIDEO ANALYSIS

Data analysis involved frame-by-frame inspection of the video-recording, in order to time certain responses to the nearest 0·1 second. Descriptive notes were also taken. The analysis was undertaken by two observers; disagreement between them resulted in a third opinion being sought. The following responses were analysed:

A. *Mothers' Behaviour:*

1. The time of onset and duration of the mothers' points.

2. Mothers' looking behaviour at the toys and at the baby while pointing.
3. A description of the "style" of the mothers' points and of additional cues provided by the mothers while pointing, e.g. clicking her fingers.
4. The verbalizations of mothers throughout the session and particularly while pointing.

B. *Infants' Behaviour:*

1. The time of onset and duration of the babies' looks at the toys before, during, and after the mothers' points.
2. The total number of looks at each toy throughout the session.
3. The timing and "style" of the infants' pointing and reaching behaviour.

Definition of a Point: A point was considered to be the emergence of the forefinger, usually accompanied by a movement of the hand and arm, and directed at a specific object. Operationally a point began with the initial movement of the hand or arm, causing a distinct blur on the video-picture, and ended with the blur caused by retraction of the arm (or very occasionally the withdrawal of the extended index finger).
Reliability: Decisions about what time and whether the mother or infant looked in a particular direction were formulated by consulting the indicator lights on the timer (in the case of the baby), by examining the video-pictures, and finally by agreement between observers. On six occasions, (each toy position for both age groups) a test of the reliability of the indicator lights was carried out. Two observers stood behind one toy and pressed buttons as before. The reliability coefficient was calculated by dividing the number of times the lights overlapped by the number of instances of overlap and no overlap. Agreement on looking events throughout the session was 83·6%. Looks following a point were examined in more detail and a similar reliability coefficient of 81·8% was found.

The Maternal Contribution

Our observations rapidly confirmed that a point is the primary method whereby mothers attract their infants' attention to a particular object at a distance. We shall examine her part in the pointing situation before considering the effect of the gesture on the infant.

MOTHERS' POINTING

Our 24 mothers pointed a total of 428 times in all, ranging from 5 to 37 (mean 20·08) for the nine-month-olds, and from 5 to 30 (mean 15·58) for the 14-month-olds. Mean length of point per mother varied from 7·55 seconds to 56·66 seconds (mean 23·05) at nine-months and from 10·20 to 37·58 seconds (mean 20·40) for the older group.

A brief description of the style of each point was noted as the data analysis was carried out. There were, of course, individual idiosyncracies, but two major types of points emerged: the mother held her outstretched arm towards the toy or bent her arm at right angles at the elbow. These two methods were used by mothers of both age groups; 382 of the 428 points were made with the mother using the arm furthest away from the baby. This was true irrespective of which side of the baby the mother was seated. Twenty-six of the exceptions were accounted for by one mother who rested her nearest arm on the tray in front of the baby and pointed from this position.

The three toy positions produced three discrete forms of pointing. The mother pointed *across* the baby to the toy on his side, sideways *away* from the baby to the toy on her side, or *forwards* and slightly upwards to the toy in the middle of the array (see Fig. 1).

The mothers' pointing behaviour was examined to determine whether there were any age differences with regard to:

(a) The total number of points per mother.
(b) The mean duration of mothers' pointing.
(c) Any toy preferences both within and between mothers.
(d) Any positional preferences while pointing.

One might have expected that there would be a difference in the number of points between the mothers of the two age groups, with the mothers of younger babies pointing proportionally more to compensate for the relative immaturity of their offspring. Similarly one might expect them to point for a longer period of time in order to increase the likelihood of their infants attending to them.

As the task of visually following the three types of points appeared to differ in complexity, the analysis of the babies' following behaviour

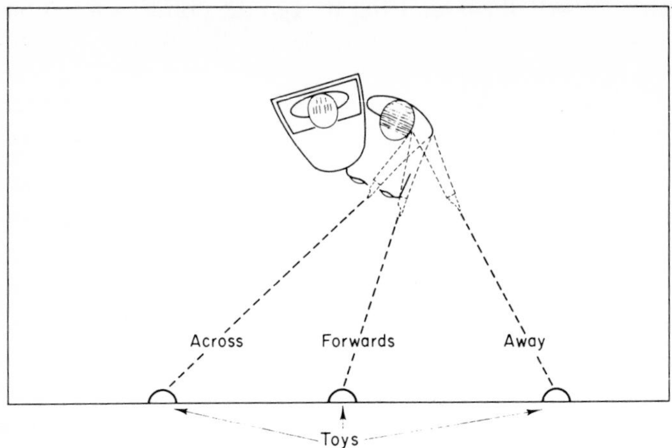

Fig. 1. The three types of points that occurred during the observational sessions.

was carried out according to the direction of each point. It was important, therefore, to consider whether the mothers showed any marked, differential pointing behaviour with regard to particular toys or the direction of the point.

Analyses of variance, two ages × three toys, showed no systematic differences on either number or mean duration of points, so it appears that neither the particular toy nor the age of the infant significantly influenced the mothers' pointing. Similar analyses, ages × directions, showed no significant effect on the number of points. The only significant effect on mean duration of point was a main effect of direction, $F\ (2{,}44) = 5{\cdot}36$, $p < 0{\cdot}01$, which inspection of the data indicated was due to points in the *away* direction being longer.

It was expected that, because their gestures are less effective, mothers of younger babies might tend to point where the baby was already looking. In order to discover whether this was, in fact, the case we employed the method of analysis that Collis and Schaffer (1975) used to test whether mothers tended to look where babies were already looking. For each mother–infant pair a contingency table was compiled in which each point was cross classified according to (a) which of the three toys the point was directed at, and (b) the direction of the babies' visual regard at the instant in time at which the point started, i.e. toy 1, toy 2, or toy 3, or none of these. The three cells on the diagonal of the resulting 3 × 4 contingency table contain the frequencies with which a mother started to point at the same toy that the baby was already looking at. The hypothesis that these frequencies exceeded those expected by chance was tested by summing the probabilities of each possible arrangement of cell frequencies (assuming fixed marginal totals) in which the sum of the three cells on the diagonal equalled or exceeded that observed.

Table I shows that some mothers did point to toys at which their

Table I

Number of instances when mothers point where the infant is looking

Mother–infant pairs 9-month group	Total number of mother's points	Number of points following infant's looks
A1	20	5[a]
A2	37	3
A3	5	2
A4	34	7
A5	10	0
A6	7	0
A7	18	4
A8	25	7
A9	16	3
A10	22	1
A11	20	4[a]
A12	25	2
14-month group		
B1	16	4
B2	19	7[a]
B3	12	5
B4	11	3[b]
B5	8	1
B6	16	2
B7	30	5
B8	14	4[a]
B9	23	7[b]
B10	6	0
B11	5	2
B12	26	14[c]

[a] $p < 0{\cdot}05$.
[b] $p < 0{\cdot}01$.
[c] $p < 0{\cdot}001$.

infants were already looking, including those mothers whose infants were able to follow a point. The fact that this occurred more frequently in mothers of the older group may reflect their knowledge of their infants' capabilities which leads them to build the interaction around the babies' interest in the toys. This pattern of pointing behaviour often occurs at split second intervals, and at normal speed of observation this often appears to be the baby closely following the mother's point; only when fine-timing analysis is carried out does it become apparent that in these cases it is the baby that is leading the mother.

MOTHERS' VISUAL BEHAVIOUR

It is obvious that the pointing gesture is not a simple process of the forefinger being extended towards an object but is rather composed of a number of behaviours, each of which contributes to the "pointing gestalt".

Mothers' points and looks were remarkably well synchronized (see Fig. 2). The onset of pointing was accompanied, to the same 0·1 second in many cases, by the beginning of a look at the toy. A glance at the object at which mothers were pointing appeared to be an integral part of pointing behaviour, for although mothers presumably quickly learned which toy was where, in 75·2% of instances they looked at the object before looking at the baby when pointing. In the remainder of cases they looked at the infant first but soon after looked at the toy. Only three of the 428 points were unaccompanied by looks at the toy whereas 45 points (for both age groups) were unaccompanied by looks at the baby. This pattern of behaviour was consistent between the two age groups.

The consistent pattern of looking at the object at the same time as pointing at it was followed by a marked tendency for the mothers' gaze to return to the infant. As seen in Fig. 3 this peaks at 1·1 seconds after the onset of pointing. As we shall show later, the babies' looks at the relevant object peak at 0·4 to 0·6 second for the older group, and at 0·8 to 1·0 second for the younger. The mothers thus look back in time to see that the infants who do follow are looking in the relevant direction. This indicates that the mother is continually monitoring her child's interest in her gesturing. Her attention is diverted for little more than a second before she returns to assess the effect of her behaviour on the infant. Mothers' pointing behaviour is thus accompanied by a consistent

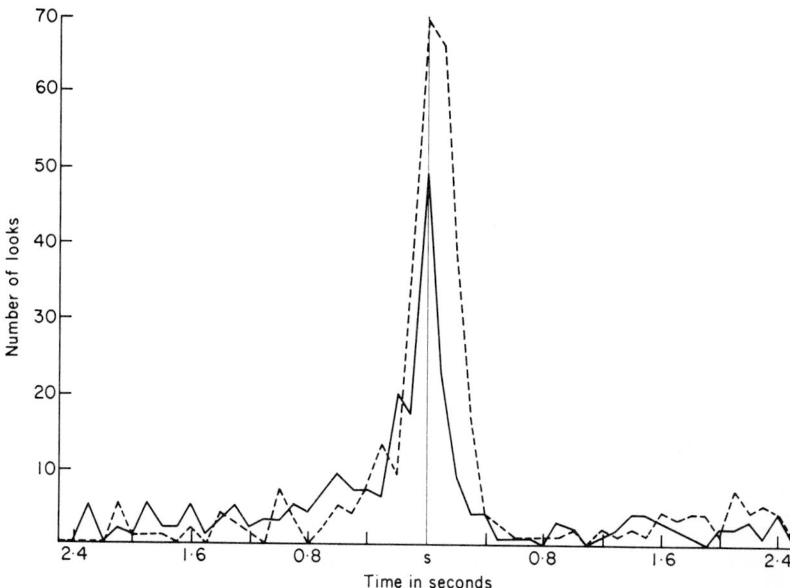

Fig. 2. Looking patterns of mothers of nine- and 14-month-old infants towards the toy at which they are pointing. The total number of looks by each group is plotted against the time at which a look *started*. S indicates the start of points; figures to the left of S indicate time before the point and those to the right of S time elapsed since the onset of pointing. ------------ Nine-month group; ———— 14-month group.

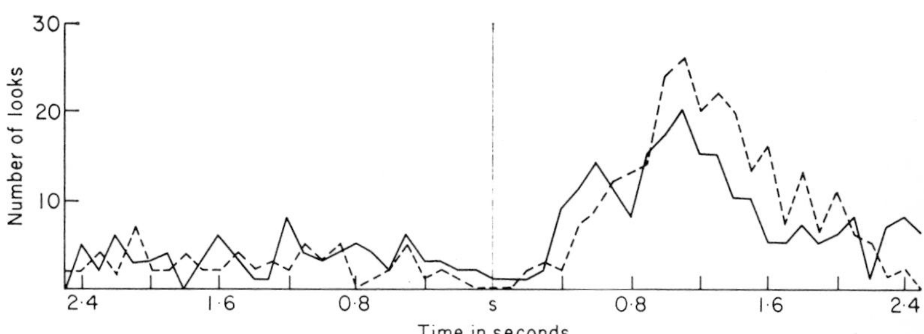

Fig. 3. Looking patterns of mothers towards their infants (nine- and 14-months) before and after pointing. The total number of looks by each group is plotted against the time at which a look *started*. S indicates the start of points; figures to the left of S indicate time before the point and those to the right of S time elapsed since the onset of pointing. ------------ Nine-month group; ———— 14-month group.

looking pattern, the main features of which occur, almost invariably, in the space of two seconds.

MOTHERS' CUEING BEHAVIOUR

Mothers appear to have a good idea of whether the pointing gesture is meaningful to their infant. Many mothers of nine-month-old babies (and also of younger ones whom we brought to the laboratory) reported that normally they simply do not attract their babies' attention to objects at a distance but rather bring them to the child. This resulted in two mothers being replaced in the sample, because throughout the session they repeatedly got up from their seats for long periods in order to attract the baby's attention to toys by playing with them and by pulling them towards him, despite instructions to remain seated.

An attempt to observe mothers of much younger babies (four–six months) was abandoned because, when obliged to attract the attention of babies of this age to distal objects, the mothers pointed in a completely different way. They spent a lot of their time placing a finger in front of the babies' eyes, clicking their fingers, and slowly drawing the hand towards the object. It was observed that, in desperation, these mothers might even physically turn the babies' head in the direction of the finger. Such behaviour we termed "cueing", i.e. providing additional cues to the point. We examined its occurrence among the mothers of the two age groups in this study (see Table II).

The mothers of 14-month-olds cued less and the cues they used tended to be of a less forceful nature. Their behaviour largely consisted of a quick tap on the hand or arm—a very effective method of indicating to a child that his mother is about to do something to which she wants him to attend. The mothers of the younger group employed this tactic to a greater extent and also the nature of their tactile contact was much more vigorous. They shook their infants' arms, grabbed their hands, etc. There was little difference between the two age groups in the number of visual cues used, primarily because the younger babies' attention must be on the pointing finger before any distal cue of this type is effective and also because the mothers of the older babies cue less anyway. Similarly the mothers of younger babies resorted to clicking their fingers in an attempt to attract their children's attention to the finger. It is as if the younger babies must first be attracted to the fingers and then to the object, whereas it is sufficient for the mothers

Table II

Type and distribution of mothers' cueing behaviour

Mother–infant pairs	Total number of cues	TACTILE CUES	VISUAL CUES	AUDITORY CUES
9-month group				
A1	3	Touches baby's arm; grabs his hand; turns his head with her hand.	—	—
A2	6	Taps baby's fingers (twice); taps cheek; taps his hand (twice); touches baby's trunk.	—	—
A3	0	—	—	—
A4	5	Shakes baby's arm; taps his nose.	Holds hand in front of infant; holds finger in front of his eyes (twice).	—
A5	4	—	Rotates finger up and down.	Clicks fingers (3 instances).
A6	3	Taps baby's arm.	Rotates finger.	Clicks fingers.
A7	0	—	—	—
A8	0	—	—	—
A9	1	Touches baby's arm.	—	—
A10	5	Touches nose; hand; arm and trunk; directs baby's arm to the toy.	—	—
A11	4	Taps baby's hand (3 instances).	Rotates finger.	—
A12	2	Touches baby's hand; taps his arm.	—	—
14-month group				
B1	2	Touches baby's arm.	—	Rattles fingers on tray of baby's high chair.
B2	1	Touches baby's hand.	—	—
B3	1	—	Moves finger up and down.	—
B4	1	Taps baby's arm.	—	—
B5	0	—	—	—
B6	0	—	—	—
B7	1	—	Moves hand up and down.	—
B8	1	—	Rotates finger.	—
B9	2	Touches infant's shoulder; touches hand.	—	—
B10	0	—	—	—
B11	0	—	—	—
B12	0	—	—	—

of 14-month-olds to "prod" their babies into attentiveness and then go on to point with very little additional cueing. The effect of age differences on the mothers' cueing behaviour is a clear indication that they perceive the pointing gesture to be appropriate to the older infants.

MOTHERS' VERBAL BEHAVIOUR

The verbal behaviour of mothers of both age groups was examined in order to investigate a fourth element of the "pointing gestalt". It is possible that, after a certain age, an infant is directed towards a particular toy not only by a point and his mother's looking behaviour, but also by her verbal exchanges with him. This is especially true of the 14-month-old age group who are fairly near the beginning of language production (a few had started) and, it is well known (e.g. Shipley *et al.*, 1969) that in most areas of language behaviour comprehension precedes production by quite a considerable margin. Mothers of the older group may not only be responding to the fact that the point is fairly meaningful to the child but also to the increasing salience of the vocal channel for communication purposes.

If the mothers of the older group perceive this greater ability on the part of their infants one would expect their speech to differ to some extent from that of the mothers of the younger group. In order to assess whether there were any such differences, utterances which overlapped with the mothers' points were transcribed (only 5 of the 428 points were unaccompanied by verbalizations). These, together with the utterances made throughout the session, were analysed according to the following criteria:

1. Incidence of Toy Naming:
   The number of times each toy was mentioned individually by some sort of name.
2. Incidence of Questions:
   The number of utterances in which the interrogative was used or in which there was a marked rise in the intonation contour.
3. Incidence of Commands:
   The number of directives used.
4. Incidence of Descriptive Comments:
   The number of descriptions of the toys which were of a fairly elaborate nature. A number of very common adjectives, namely

nice, wee, bonny, big, lovely, pretty and funny, were used by the mothers of both age groups with great frequency. As they did not clearly distinguish between the two groups they were excluded.

5. Incidence of Interactive and Relational Comments:
The mother's attempts to get the child to interact with the toys, e.g. "Wave to teddy", "Say bye-bye to teddy", or the number of times she tried to relate the toys to the infant in some way, e.g. "Is that like your dolly?", "That's the same as your teddy, isn't it?".

A single utterance was defined as a word or group of words, separated from others by a pause which usually occurred as a noticeable, natural break in conversation. One utterance could include several of the above speech categories. For example, "Wave to teddy" is a command, an interactive comment and an instance of toy naming.

The number and total duration of utterances were obtained for each mother by the use of a cumulative counter. As can be seen in Table III, no significant differences were found between age groups in the number of utterances ($U = 69{\cdot}5$) or total duration of utterances ($U = 69{\cdot}0$).

As there was little difference in the amount or duration of the mothers' speech, we proceeded to look at any differences there might be in content. It was expected that the mothers of the older group, realizing that they were more effective in drawing their infants' attention to the toys, needed to concentrate far less on this task and so would use speech categories 4 and 5 (descriptive comments and interactive/relational comments) more than the mothers of the nine-month-olds. The mothers of the older group would also expect to be able to hold their infants' attention and maintain their interest throughout the session by going on to describe the toys in more detail. On the other hand it was considered that the mothers of the younger children would spend more time getting the child to follow the point and would thus be confined rather more to naming the toys and commanding the child to attend.

A Mann-Whitney test was carried out to determine whether there was any differential use of categories in the mothers' speech according to age (see Table IV). The mothers of 14-month-olds did, in fact, engage more frequently in descriptions of the toys than those of the younger infants (14·6% vs 7·8%). The number of interactive comments also differed significantly between age groups, this category being almost non-existent in the younger age group (9% vs 1·9%). Nelson

Table III

Amount of speech by mothers during session

Mother–infant pairs	Total number of utterances	Total duration of utterances (seconds)	Mean duration of utterances (seconds)
9-month group			
A1	125	96·00	0·76
A2	65	60·70	0·93
A3	64	47·80	0·75
A4	112	131·60	1·17
A5	150	92·00	0·61
A6	134	188·50	1·40
A7	109	129·60	1·18
A8	117	134·30	1·14
A9	73	144·00	1·97
A10	187	101·20	0·54
A11	96	231·60	2·41
A12	82	109·00	1·33
14-month group			
B1	113	128·70	1·14
B2	112	163·20	1·46
B3	71	51·70	0·73
B4	110	79·10	0·72
B5	54	112·50	2·08
B6	99	134·80	1·36
B7	144	189·60	1·32
B8	100	99·20	0·99
B9	119	119·70	1·00
B10	192	170·60	0·88
B11	93	44·00	0·47
B12	130	157·90	1·21

(1973) found insufficient data for a "descriptive" category until her subjects reached two years of age, when it accounted for 7% of mothers' utterances. She does not, however, define descriptions very clearly. Contrary to expectations there is no differential toy naming between age groups (45·6%—14 months vs 41·8%—9 months). On reflection our general impression is that the difference is more likely to be qualitative than quantitative. The mothers of younger children use less elaborate language than those of older babies and thus confine their toy naming to direct utterances such as "Look at dolly" or simply "dolly". On closer examination the mothers of the older group do name the toys

Table IV

Incidence of utterance types throughout the session: an age comparison

Speech categories	9-month group Mean number of utterances	Range in the number of utterances	14-month group Mean number of utterances	Range in the number of utterances	Mann-Whitney U-value
Toy naming	45·8	18·5–84·0	50·8	10·0–152·0	67·0
Questions	38·1	16·5–51·0	44·6	26·5–95·0	64·0
Commands	18·5	1·0–42·5	14·0	4·5–27·0	54·0
Descriptions	8·6	0·0–31·5	14·2	0·0–45·0	42·0[a]
Interactive/ Relational	2·7	0·0–15·5	10·1	0·0–23·5	34·6[a]

[a] $p < 0·05$.

frequently but the naming is couched in rather more complex language and is, therefore, not so predominant.

The frequency of speech categories used by the mother while she is pointing were examined to see if there were any age differences in this respect. It was expected that mothers of younger infants would use more commands while pointing because they would be more intent than the other mothers on getting the child to follow their pointing. This expectation was confirmed by the results shown in Table V.

Table V

Incidence of utterance types that accompany a point: an age comparison

Speech categories	9-month group Mean number of utterances per point	Range in the number of utterances per point	14-month group Mean number of utterances per point	Range in the number of utterances per point	Mann-Whitney U-value
Toy naming	1·09	0·20–2·60	0·85	0·20–1·80	56·5
Questions	0·62	0·00–1·61	0·72	0·33–1·60	68·5
Commands	0·95	0·02–2·30	0·37	0·00–0·75	38·5[a]
Descriptions	0·13	0·00–0·92	0·30	0·00–1·40	54·0
Interactive/ Relational	0·02	0·00–0·27	0·06	0·00–0·37	N.S.[b]

[a] $p < 0·05$.

[b] Due to high number of 0's the Mann-Whitney Test was inappropriate therefore the Median Test (Ferguson, 1966) was used.

Nelson (1973) suggested that there is a negative relationship between the number of questions and the number of commands made by mothers of 13-month-old children. No such negative relationship was found in the data from this study. Ryan (unpublished) in a study of six-, 12- and 30-month-old infants found only one significant relationship (at six months) between questions and commands and this was positive. Nelson's study of 12- to 15-month-olds (mean 13 months) found a higher percentage of commanding (what she calls directives) in her mothers. Thirty-five per cent of their utterances were commands, whereas in this study at 14 months the percentage was 12·6 and at nine months 16·9. The percentage of questioning was quite similar—Nelson 32% (13 months), in our study 40% (14 months), 34·8% (nine months). At two years the proportion of questioning in Nelson's sample had risen to 37%.

The Infant's Contribution

DOES POINTING ELICIT VISUAL FOLLOWING?

The style, number and duration of the mothers' points is similar for nine- and 14-month-olds. Pointing, for both age groups, is accompanied by the mothers' verbalizations and by a consistent pattern of visual behaviour. Finding no major differences in pointing we examined the infants' visual response.

In order to ascertain whether infants do indeed follow a point it is necessary to compare the probability of them looking at the appropriate toy immediately after a point, with an estimate of the probability that they would have looked there anyway even if the point had not occurred. A 2·5 second period from the start of point was chosen because the peak of looking at the object being pointed at occurred in this time (see Fig. 4). Basically the procedure used involved comparing the probability of the infant starting to look in a particular direction during the 2·5 second period of time following the beginning of a point (the observed probability) with the probability of the infant starting to look in a particular direction outside these periods (the expected probability). In each case the probability of looking in a particular direction is simply the number of looks in that direction divided by the

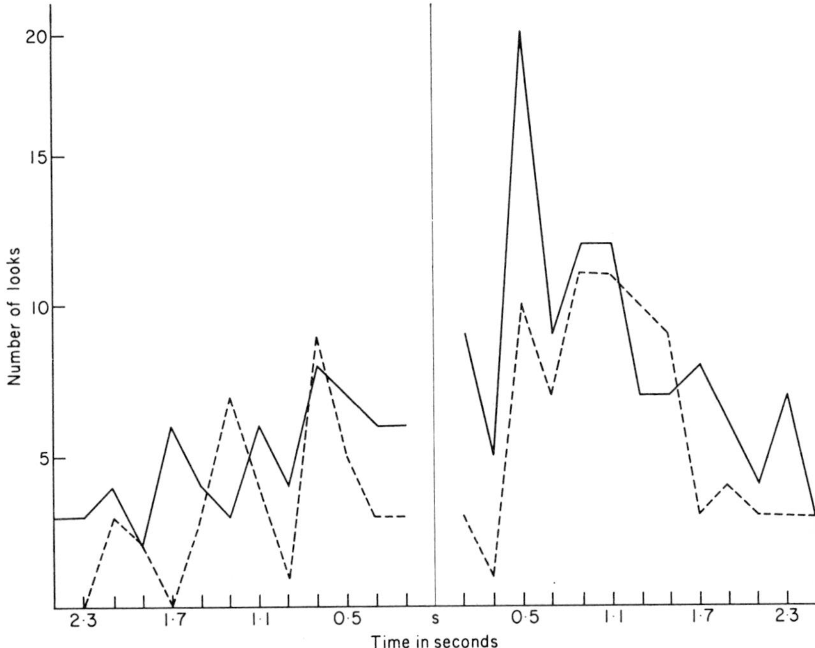

Fig. 4. The total number of infants' looks (nine- and 14-months) towards the toy at which their mothers are pointing. The total number of looks by each group is plotted against the time at which a look *started*. S indicates the start of the mothers' points; figures to the left of S indicate time before the point and those to the right of S time elapsed since the onset of pointing. Each time division includes a cumulative count of looks 0·09 seconds preceding the division until 0·1 second afterwards. ------------ Nine-month group; ———— 14-month group.

total number of looks being considered. Observed and expected probabilities for each direction of point and each age group were compared using the randomization test for matched pairs (Siegel, 1956). The observed and expected probabilities are listed for each subject in Table VI together with the results of the age group comparisons.

Table VI shows that for the nine-month-old group there was no significant difference between the observed and expected probabilities except in the *away* position. The three types of points appear to increase in difficulty for the nine-month-old infants. They significantly follow the mothers' points *away*, some follow their points *forwards*, but, except for two subjects, there is a very definite lack of ability to follow points directed *across* the babies' midline.

Table VI

A comparison of the observed and expected probabilities of the infants' looks at the three toy positions

	ACROSS		FORWARDS		AWAY	
Subjects	Expected	Actual	Expected	Actual	Expected	Actual
9-month group						
A1	0·16	0·00	0·39	0·50	0·43	0·75
A2	0·19	0·00	0·45	0·75	0·35	1·00
A3	0·33	—	0·33	0·50	0·32	0·66
A4	0·21	0·00	0·64	0·50	0·14	0·77
A5	0·09	0·00	0·44	0·00	0·46	0·66
A6	0·10	—	0·25	1·00	0·64	—
A7	0·10	0·00	0·57	0·50	0·31	0·80
A8	0·21	0·00	0·47	0·37	0·30	0·66
A9	0·16	0·00	0·20	0·37	0·63	1·00
A10	0·25	0·00	0·38	0·40	0·36	1·00
A11	0·43	1·00	0·34	0·40	0·21	0·00
A12	0·30	1·00	0·34	0·50	0·34	1·00
	$p < 0{\cdot}342$		$p < 0{\cdot}185$		$p < 0{\cdot}001$	
14-month group						
B1	0·21	0·66	0·43	0·66	0·34	0·71
B2	0·34	1·00	0·42	0·80	0·23	0·66
B3	0·18	0·40	0·50	0·60	0·32	0·75
B4	0·20	0·00	0·66	0·33	0·12	1·00
B5	0·17	0·33	0·35	0·00	0·46	0·50
B6	0·19	1·00	0·23	0·66	0·57	0·80
B7	0·31	0·33	0·27	0·66	0·40	0·55
B8	0·22	1·00	0·39	0·66	0·37	0·66
B9	0·34	0·54	0·41	0·61	0·24	1·00
B10	0·22	0·50	0·48	1·00	0·28	1·00
B11	0·20	—	0·41	0·66	0·37	1·00
B12	0·22	0·40	0·47	0·00	0·29	0·40
	$p < 0{\cdot}004$		$p < 0{\cdot}093$		$p < 0{\cdot}002$	

If the baby fixates on the mother's hand when she points the toy is in the same visual field as her hand when she points *away* from the baby, so it takes only the slightest shift of gaze for the infant to have followed this point. When the mother points *forward* the infant must shift his gaze from the hand to a greater, though still not very large, extent. In order to follow a point *across*, however, the infant must usually move his gaze through an angle of 90°. This supposition is given support by the fact that in all but two cases a point *across* eliminated all following behaviour. A point *across* often resulted in the younger children looking at the mothers' arm and then to the object beyond the arm, which was the toy in the middle position. This effect, however, failed to reach significance ($p < 0{\cdot}15$).

At nine months the infants appear to be beginning to respond to the pointing gesture, as their gaze is directed by points in the *away* position. They may be aware that the hand is a salient feature but are, as yet, unable to utilize the signal fully. This may be because the younger infant attends to the hand and arm and not to the more specific directing element of the finger, and can thus only follow points in favourable circumstances.

The 14-month-olds are successful in adapting their visual following schema to include the three types of points produced by our situation. Whereas the three types of points appear to increase in difficulty for the younger infant, the older group appear to be able to follow points *across* with more facility than points *forward*: following in this direction was significant only at $p < 0{\cdot}09$. Examination of individual infants reveals the origin of this discrepancy. One subject failed to follow his mother's directives when she pointed *forwards* and *across* but complied when she pointed *away* from him. A further two subjects in the older group failed to follow points in the *forwards* position but followed points in the *away* and *across* positions, though it should be noted that the differences between the observed and expected probabilities in these cases are marginal. These three subjects appear to have an incomplete understanding of the pointing gesture.

As the 14-month-old infants showed a better understanding of the point, we decided to examine whether their following response was quicker than the younger group. The mean latency of the first look at the pointed object was calculated for each infant within 2·5 seconds from the beginning of the point. A comparison of the mean latency of looking between the two age groups (nine months: mean 1·39 seconds; 14 months: mean 1·16 seconds) revealed a significant difference (Mann-Whitney $U = 38{\cdot}5$ $p < 0{\cdot}05$). The older infants, therefore, not only follow more points but also react more rapidly than the nine-month-olds.

Two 2×3 analyses of variance, with repeated measures across (a) toys and (b) positions were carried out to determine whether there were any differences between or within age groups in the looking behaviour of the infants toward a particular toy or toy position. There was on positional preference in looking behaviour between groups, though all subjects looked at the *across* position least (F (2·44) $= 18{\cdot}72$ $p < 0{\cdot}01$). No evidence was found of any toy preferences on the part of the infants nor any age differences in this respect.

INFANTS' GESTURING

It was interesting to note that of the 14-month group eight of these infants themselves exhibited pointing behaviour during the observational session and one of the remainder was seen to point outside the session. Of these subjects, the number of points ranged from 2 to 28 with a total of 75 points. A point was similarly defined for an infant as for the mother, but 13 of the points made by the 14-month-olds were not very well directed at an object whereas mothers' points were always clear in this respect. Some points were also vague, in as much as the infant pointed at an object, looked at that object and then looked away leaving the pointing finger still directed at the toy in which he no longer appeared to be interested. Three of the 12 infants in the nine-month-old group also pointed but with a total of only five points, two of which were not very well directed.

We also observed a substantial amount of what we have called "reaching" behaviour. This was defined as an arm extension towards a toy which gave the impression of being intentional, intentionality usually being indicated by visual fixation of the particular toy, sometimes also being accompanied by body movement towards it.

Of the nine-month-olds, the subjects who pointed also showed reaching behaviour with a total number of 12 reaches. All but two of these were well directed at an object. Nine out of 12 of the older group exhibited reaching behaviour with a total of 45 reaches, only one of which was not very well directed. Two of the subjects in the older group who did not point reached five times each. Only one subject who pointed did not also reach.

THE INFANTS' VISUAL BEHAVIOUR WHILE POINTING AND REACHING

We examined the babies' visual behaviour while pointing and reaching for the older group (there were insufficient data for the younger group).

Figures 5 and 6 show a very similar pattern of behaviour for the two gestures, although when reaching towards an object the infant is not so quick to look at the toy as when he is pointing. Figure 6 shows that the babies' looks at the toy while reaching do, however, continue for a longer period of time when the reaching has finished than in the case of pointing.

The infants' looking behaviour while pointing and reaching bear some similarities to that of the mothers while they are pointing (i.e. they both look at the toy at the start of the gesture) (see Fig. 2). The mothers, however, quickly turn to look at the baby (see Fig. 3) to assess the efficacy of their points. The infants' looks at the mother for feedback were too few to plot on the graph—a total of five looks while pointing and six while reaching. The baby does not visually monitor his mother's reactions to his directives, although she very often looks at the object

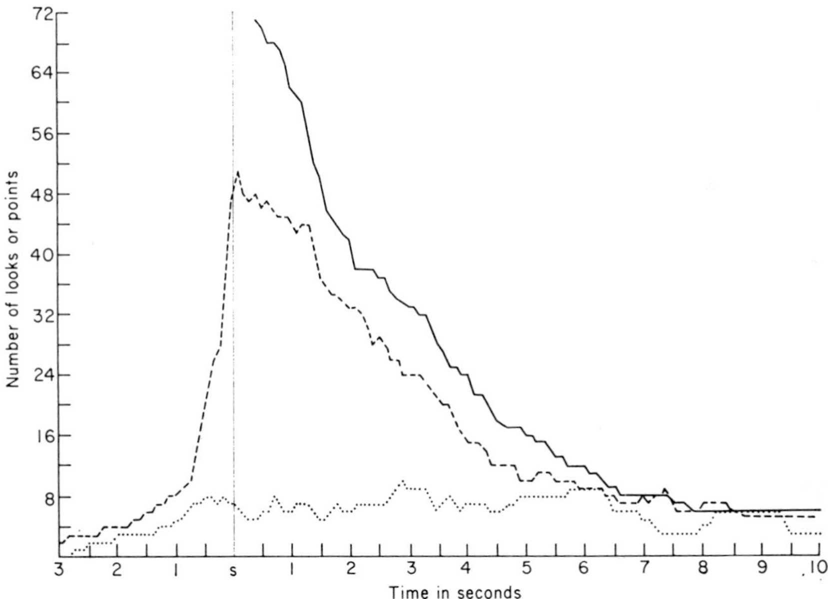

Fig. 5. Looking patterns of 14-month-old infants while they are pointing. S indicates the start of the infants' points; figures to the left of S indicate time before the point and those to the right of S time elapsed since the onset of pointing. ———— The total number of infants' points in progress since the start of all points; ------------ the total number of infants' looks at the toy to which they are pointing; .... the total number of infants' looks at toys other than the one which they are pointing at. Only those looks which overlap with pointing are included.

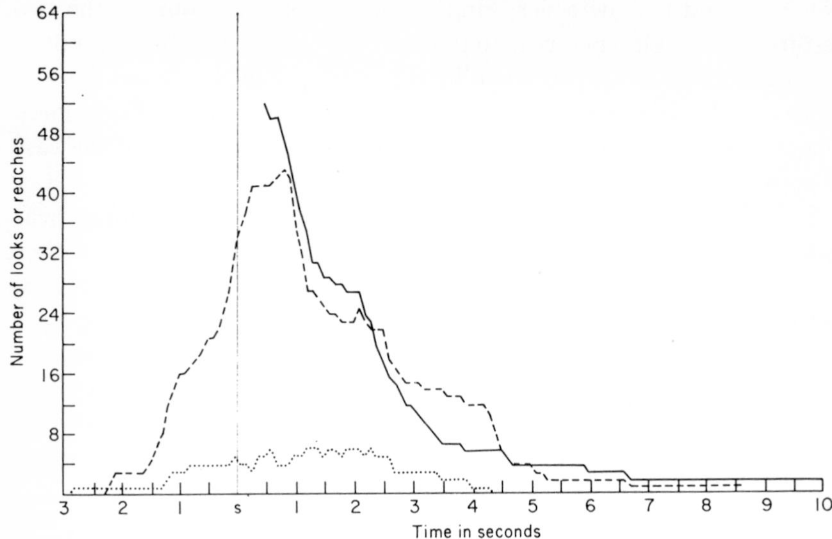

Fig. 6. Looking patterns of 14-month-old infants while they are reaching. S indicates the start of the infants' reaches; figures to the left of S indicate time before the reach and those to the right of S time elapsed since the onset of reaching. ———— The total number of infants' reaches in progress since the start of all reaches; ------------ the total number of infants' looks to the toy to which they are reaching; . . . . the total number of infants' looks to toys other than the one which they are reaching for. Only those looks which overlap with reaching are included.

unless his gesture is very ambiguous. This finding is in complete disagreement with Anderson's (1972) observations, that the pointing response always involved visual regard of the mother and that this phenomenon is one of the best indicators of who its mother is. Although Anderson was also concerned with infants who had just started to walk, these observations may be more applicable to the older infants whom he observed and to situations where there is a greater distance between mothers and infants.

DOES A POINT ORIGINATE IN REACHING?

It has been hypothesized that the baby's ability to point develops out of his capacity to reach, this ability being present in the infant within a week after birth (Trevarthen, 1974) and taking place effectively towards the end of the fourth month (Piaget, 1953). Bower (1974) points out that arm extensions which have been labelled "reaching" may not, in fact, be attempts by the infant to reach and grasp an object but "indicator gestures intended to affect the behaviour of nearby adults". He observes that "if the infants were trying to reach the distant object, the arm extension would necessarily fail. One might then expect to see some signs of disappointment or upset at the failure." He concludes that "lack of upset" and the absence of the finger adjustments made prior to grasping "would seem to indicate that the behaviour is not reaching".

Our video-recordings were not, unfortunately, able to provide us with detailed information of the finger movements of infants while they were "reaching", but at both age levels there was certainly no sign of upset when the baby was unable to attain the toy, nor any looking at the mother in a "pleading" manner. Our infants showed a slight amount of body movement forward when they reached (and also when they pointed) but not to the extent one would expect if they were seriously intending to grasp the toy. Of the older group in this study, however, seven infants both pointed and reached. If reaching is an indicator gesture rather than an attempt to get to the object, why do they not use the more sophisticated gesture? Their behaviour while using both types of gesture showed no apparent functional differences. It is also of interest to note that the three infants in the nine-month-old group who pointed were also the only subjects to exhibit reaching behaviour.

It is possible that the development of the pointing gesture takes place through the following succession of activities on the part of the infant:

1. The baby reaches towards and grasps attainable objects.
2. He then reaches towards but cannot grasp distal objects and the reach is "converted", due to lack of success, into an indicator gesture as described by Bower. An essential part of this process is the mother's interpretation of the child's gesture. By reacting appropriately, she transforms it, as Vygotsky (1966) says, into "a gesture for others".
3. The infant, meanwhile, is exposed to the conventional pointing of the mother and through the process of imitation gradually learns to indicate in a conventional manner. The infant finds this more effective in terms of the reactions of others, especially outside of the mother–infant dyad, and continues to point.

Thus, as Vygotsky says, "the pointing gesture first begins to indicate by movement that which is understood by others and only later becomes a pointing gesture for the child himself".

Conclusions

Do mothers use the pointing gesture when trying to attract the attention of their infants to distal features of the environment? This study answers the question in the affirmative, with the proviso that it depends on the age of the infant. Mothers of infants less than nine-months-old are unlikely frequently to engage in this activity as they realize that it is probably not very meaningful to younger babies. At the age of nine months a point appears to be effective in certain circumstances, but we observed mothers of infants of this age supplementing the pointing gesture with additional cues, indicating that the point was not always a sufficient directive and that the mothers realized this.

At what age are infants able to follow a point? Our answer to this question is, of necessity, conditional. It depends on the type of point and also what is meant by follow. Our observational session produced three apparently distinct types of points which seemed to present three levels of difficulty for the children. The 14-month-old age group followed two at a significantly higher than chance level and just failed to reach significance on the third. The nine-month group, however, followed significantly only those points where the relevant toy was in the same visual field as the pointing hand. When the mothers pointed across the babies' midline, all but two of the younger group failed to look in the appropriate direction.

The nine-month-old group are, therefore, able to follow a point in favourable circumstances but their "following schema" does not extend to all types of points. The majority of the 14-month-olds were able to follow all three points.

How is the pointing gesture integrated with other concurrent responses? Mothers' pointing is accompanied by a consistent pattern of visual behaviour. The onset of the mothers' points occur in remarkable synchrony with the beginning of looks at the object to which they are pointing. With similar consistency the mothers then turn to their infants to assess the effect of their gesturing. Similarly, points are almost without exception accompanied by the mothers' verbalizing. There are few age differences with respect to the quality or quantity of the mothers' utterances. The only differential level of language sophistication used by the mothers of 14-month-old infants was reflected in their greater use of descriptive language with respect to the toys and by their verbal attempts to relate the toys to their infants. The mothers of the younger group use more commands in an attempt to increase the efficacy of their directives.

The fact that mothers of nine-month-olds used more commands raises an interesting issue. One would expect them to be aware that their infants are unlikely to respond to verbal directions. Newson (1974) has suggested that mothers may attribute intentions and meaningful communication to their children's actions; an extension of this would result in the mother sometimes dealing with the infant as if he were more able to understand communications than he is, as perhaps in this case with commands. Stern (1974), however, points out that although a mother may treat her infant as being endowed with adult qualities, she does not interact with him as if he were an adult. Mothers may thus be acting towards their infants as if they were socially responsive individuals, but only slightly above the infant's present level of competence.

How does one know that it is the point and not the mothers' visual and verbal behaviour that is directing the child's attention to a specific object? As has just been shown the pointing gesture does not solely comprise of the mother extending her arm and forefinger towards the object. She also talks, looks at the object and the infant, and may use additional cues. The question is, to what extent do these other actions contribute to the effectiveness of the point?

Language could be a potential cue, especially for 14-month-old infants. If the child could match the name of a toy with his concept of that toy, this may aid his following of a point. There are several reasons, however, why such an effect is unlikely. First, the infant must match the name with the appropriate toy: this may be difficult as the clown and doll have many similar characteristics and the toys may differ from the ones that the infant has had experience with. Furthermore, if the infant were to visually search for the appropriate toy after the mother points, this would probably result in a number of looks at different toys which would reduce the difference between actual and expected probabilities (see Table VI) and thus reduce the likelihood of the infant following the point. In order for the mother's verbalizing to be effective, it would appear that the infant must remember exactly what verbal label belongs to what toy and where the toy is in the array of three before him. The possibility always remains that speech may contribute to the infant's ability to follow a point but in view of the above considerations it would seem unlikely that speech is an important element at the ages here examined.

As the mother invariably looks at the toy when she points, this may be another useful cue to the infant. Scaife and Bruner (1975) have suggested that if an experimenter first establishes eye-to-eye contact with an infant and then looks to the left or right, infants beyond a certain age are likely to look in that direction. It could be argued, therefore, that the mothers' visual attention and head-turning are further cues which the baby utilizes. Two factors may minimize this effect in the pointing situation: (1) the mothers do not generally make eye-to-eye contact with their infants before they point (see Fig. 2); (2) the evidence which Scaife and Bruner presented did not indicate that the infants looked in the precise location of the experimenter's gaze when he turned his head—an obvious requirement in this study for the infants to have followed a point. The mothers' visual behaviour showed very little difference between age groups, indicating that the mothers themselves did not perceive it to be a very effective cue.

Mothers also used other cues (clicking their fingers, tapping the child on the arm), in their attempts to help the infant to follow the points. Although these may well have helped to focus the infant's attention on his mother's hand or finger, such cues would not necessarily help the infant to look from the hand to the toy. There were more cues used by the mothers of the nine-month-olds and these infants did not show a general ability to follow points.

Although the concurrent responses of the mother while she is pointing are unlikely to be of major importance in directing the child's attention to a specific toy, they are, no doubt, additional aids, the usefulness of which is likely to increase as the child develops. The associated behaviours may help to make the point a more powerful signal.

How does an infant learn to follow a point? In learning to follow points, the infant needs to develop an awareness that the point is a directive signal and then go on to utilize the directive nature of the signal in a variety of circumstances. To perform the latter efficiently, when distances and angles between the mother, infant and object vary, is not an easy task.

The nine-month-old infants only followed points to the *away* position. It was suggested that the infant looks at the mother's hand when she points and then shifts his gaze to any prominent object which is in his visual field. The *away*, *forwards* and *across* positions result in an increasing angle between the finger and the toy and thus represent increasing levels of difficulty (see Fig. 1). It cannot be ascertained that the nine-month-old looks at the hand because he perceives it to be a signal or because it is simply an interesting event. Thus one cannot be sure that the successful following of the younger infant of points in the *away* position is the result of an "accidental" transference of gaze to the relevant toy which is in the same visual field as the hand or an ability to follow points where the angle between the hand and the toy is relatively small. Some awareness of the salience of the pointing gesture by the nine-month-olds is suggested by the fact that three of these infants could point but this could, however, also be evidence that use precedes comprehension.

As the younger infants can follow points *away* but not those to the *forwards* and *across* positions, it would seem unlikely that they have developed the ability to abstract the directive nature of a point. Millar and Schaffer (1972, 1973) suggest that nine-month-olds, while attending to one object, can learn to make a response to another object which is outside their immediate visual field. This would seem to indicate that, at nine months, an infant is capable of the association necessary to follow a point, but lacks the understanding of the directive nature of the gesture.

By 14 months the infant seems to be able to follow a greater variety of points, so it is likely that he is aware that the gesture is a directive signal and is capable of estimating the direction and angle of the object pointed at. This proficiency, however, contrasts with the fact that, while pointing, the infant very rarely looks at his mother for feedback. If he understands that a point is a communicative gesture which requires a response from one's partner, then one might expect the infant to look at his mother to monitor her attention. The infants' apparent lack of interest may be due to production preceding the full understanding of the pointing gesture or, alternatively, the child may, because of his egocentrism, assume that his mother would follow his directives.

The development of the infant's ability to follow points in a variety of circumstances probably takes place through a progression from the "easier" points when he stumbles from the hand to the relevant object, to the more "difficult" points which entail an ability to perceive that the finger is an important directive cue which is directing the infant's gaze away from the visual field of the pointing hand. It is likely that the infant's awareness of the importance of the finger as a directive signalling device develops out of his success in following points where the relevant toy is not far removed from the finger. Concurrently, the infant may start to generalize his looking response so that points where there is a larger angle between the object and the hand are now followed. This progression is facilitated by a certain amount of redundancy in the environment. There are a limited number of salient features in the surroundings to which the mother points and thus the accuracy which is required of the infant as he attempts to work out the specific direction of the point is considerably reduced.

IMPLICATIONS

This study has shown that mothers do use points to draw their infants' attention to distal objects and that by 14 months the infant is fairly proficient at following these points. Collis and Schaffer (1975) have found that during the first year of life mothers tend to monitor and follow the infants' interest in their environment so that mutual attention to a particular feature is largely a result of the mother synchronizing her looks with those of the infant. The implication of this investigation is that by the beginning of the second year of life the mother is not restricted to following her infant but can lead the interaction by directing his attention to distal objects. Instead of the mother relying mostly on her infant's interest in the distal surroundings in her interaction with him, she can now draw his attention to objects. The mother is, therefore, in a position to build on her infant's interest in an object by redirecting him to it or by directing his attention to other objects or events. Such a process may help to foster an awareness of the perspective of others; pointing also permits negotiation about topics of interaction to develop further and further.

Acknowledgements

The conduct of this research was supported by a grant from the United Kingdom Social Science Research Council to H. R. Schaffer. The authors are indebted to Professor H. R. Schaffer, and Glyn Collis for their helpful advice and criticism. Thanks also to N. Sharp for technical assistance.

References

Anderson, J. W. (1972). Attachment behaviour out of doors. In N. Blurton-Jones (Ed.), *Ethological Studies of Child Behaviour*, pp. 199–215. Cambridge University Press, Cambridge.

Bower, T. G. R. (1974). *Development in Infancy*. Freeman and Co., San Francisco.

Collis, G. M. and Schaffer, H. R. (1975). Synchronisation of visual attention in mother-infant pairs. *J. Child Psychol. Psychiat.* **16**, 315–320.

Ling, D. and Ling, A. H. (1974). Communication development in the first three years of life. *J. Speech Hearing Res.* **17**, 146–159.

Millar, W. S. and Schaffer, H. R. (1972). The influence of spatially displaced feedback on infant operant conditioning. *J. exp. Child Psychol.* **14**, 442–453.

Millar, W. S. and Schaffer, H. R. (1973). Visual-manipulative response strategies in infant operant conditioning with spatially displaced feedback. *Br. J. Psychol.* **64**, 4, 545–552.

Nelson, K. (1973). Structure and strategy in learning to talk. *Monogr. Soc. Res. Child Develop.* **38**, (1–2, serial no. 149).

Newson, J. (1974). Towards a theory of infant understanding. *Bull Br. psychol. Soc.* **27**, 251–257.

Piaget, J. (1953). *The Origin of Intelligence in the Child*. Routledge and Kegan Paul, London.

Ryan, M. L. (1976). Baby talk and intonation in adults' speech to pre-verbal infants. Unpublished Ph.D. thesis, University of Strathclyde, Glasgow.

Scaife, M. and Bruner, J. (1975). The capacity for joint visual attention in the infant. *Nature* **253**, 265–266.

Shipley, E. F., Gleitman, C. S. and Smith, L. R. (1969). A study of the acquisition of language. *Language* **45**, 332–342.

Siegel, S. (1956). *Non-Parametric Statistics*. McGraw-Hill, New York.

Slobin, D. I. (1966). Abstracts of Soviet studies of child language. In F. Smith and G. A. Miller (Eds), *The Genesis of Language*. M.I.T. Press, Cambridge, Massachusetts.

Stern, D. N. (1974). The goal and structure of mother-infant play. *J. Am. Acad. Child Psychiat.* **13**, 402–421.

Trevarthen, C. (1974). Psychobiology of speech development. In E. Lenneberg (Ed.), Language and Brain: Developmental Aspects. *Neuro Sciences Res. Prog. Bull.* **12**, 570–585.

Vygotsky, L. S. (1966). Development of the higher mental functions. In A. N. Leontier (Ed.), *Psychological Research in the U.S.S.R.* Progress Publishers, Moscow.

14 Visual Co-orientation and Maternal Speech

Glyn M. Collis

Introduction

It is now generally accepted that the very young infant is attracted to the kind of stimuli that typically emanate from other human beings and hence people tend to dominate his interest in the external world. After a few months though, the inanimate world competes more and more with people for the infant's attention and so components of the environment play an increasingly important role in the infant's interaction with people. For an adult to engage in successful social intercourse with a baby it is often necessary for an infant–environment interaction to be assimilated into the infant–adult interaction. In other words, the adult must take notice and make use of the infant's interest in the inanimate world as the focus for an interpersonal interaction.

We have previously described and quantified observations which demonstrate that mothers do, at least in some circumstances, continually monitor their babies' focus of visual attention to the environment, even when neither partner is engaged in physical contact with the object of that focus (Collis and Schaffer, 1975). In that study we observed mother–infant pairs interacting in a minimally constrained situation in which the mother had no specific task to carry out; as far as she was concerned her main role was merely to accompany the baby. The observations took place in an unfamiliar room in which, not unexpectedly, the infants spent much time visually exploring their surroundings. When we monitored the gaze of mothers and infants at four prominently placed, visually attractive toys we found that more often than not, when one individual was looking at a toy, the other was too. Examination of the sequencing of the gaze patterns showed that this was primarily the result of the mother following her baby's direction of gaze rather than *vice versa*.

Such a sharing of interest by two participants in one feature of the environment is the subject matter of the discussion to follow. What we, as observers, actually see is an orientation in common to the two subjects, hence the term *co-orientation*. With the visual sense being of prime importance in man and the orientation of the eyes being readily apparent it will not be surprising that this topic will be considered mainly in terms of *visual* orientation. Much has been written of the importance of gaze directed by one partner at his opposite number but surprisingly, until recently, very little consideration has been given to this second, arguably more important, role of gaze in social interaction.

We will consider visual co-orientation from two points of view: how co-orientation is *established* and how it is *used* in social interaction between young children and adults. With regard to the second of these points, data will be presented concerning the integration of co-orientation with maternal speech.

Establishing Co-orientation

PROVISION AND USE OF CUES

The very essence of co-orientation is that it is a dyadic state defined by the orientation of *both* partners, and it is important that it should be conceptualized as such. Nonetheless, in the mother–infant case it is understandable that there should be a particular interest in the developing capacities of the infant as a limiting factor and a source of change. There are two aspects of each partner's role to be considered, the emission of cues reflecting an interest in the environment and the responsiveness to such cues from the other individual. In the very youngest baby the main indication of localized interest is looking—cues from head and eye movements in fixation and tracking. These probably remain important sources of information throughout life but will be augmented by other cues. Firstly, swiping, reaching and grasping directed toward objects in the environment will develop. Later still comes the ability to point toward a distal object in the conventional manner and eventually the ability to label it verbally. Similarly with responsiveness to potential maternal cues: from very early on the mother can best attract the infant's attention to objects by handling them. Later, responsiveness to the direction of mother's gaze (Masangkay *et al.*, 1974; Scaife and Bruner, 1975) and the pointing gesture (Murphy and Messer, Chapter 13) will develop, and eventually the ability to comprehend the verbal representation of an object also appears (Shipley *et al.*, 1969). This is not to suggest that this progression is a simple one; the work by Murphy and Messer on the abilities of babies to "follow" pointing shows that this capacity is not unitary but is dependent upon the complexity of the task, specifically on the angular separation of the pointing limb from the target object and the presence of distracting features. There is every likelihood that an infant's abilities to follow facial and ocular orientation are similarly complex, and the same clearly holds for verbal exchanges. Neither is it suggested that the ability to follow facial and ocular orientation necessarily precedes the ability to follow a point—this is an open question, especially as the findings of Murphy and Messer would suggest that from quite early on, if a pointing hand attracted the baby's visual attention and if the target of the point was in the same visual field as the hand, then the baby's gaze would very likely transfer from the hand to the target, provided the latter was salient enough.

Whatever the details of the developmental progression, two conclusions emerge. Firstly, what we know at present of the abilities of babies to use cues in this way suggests that there are fewer constraints operating than one might expect from a consideration of Piaget and Inhelders' (1956) account of the development of understanding of the visual perspective of others. Secondly, it seems that there is a discernible trend in that, as the infant develops, object and person (mother or child) can be more distantly separated from one another yet still be brought together in interaction with the other partner. It is a familiar idea that as a baby grows older he can interact with more distal features of the environment, and so the infant–object distance in the infant–object–mother interaction can be extended. When we consider how the infant is able to cope with cues emitted by the mother about her foci of interest, it is clear that it is the mother–object distance which can be extended as the infant develops: touching and handling are only appropriate for proximal objects and looking and pointing for more distal ones, whereas language is appropriate for things which are separated from the person in time as well as space. Bullowa *et al.* (1964) remark upon this trend of an increasing separation of an object from its referent during the early stages of language acquisition: this is clearly a continuing process throughout early childhood.

These ideas concern the emergence of one of Hockett's "design features" of human communication, namely displacement—the capacity to communicate about things remote in space and time (Hockett, 1960; Hockett and Altmann, 1968). This is taken for granted as a feature of language, yet it is apparent that it begins in the social interaction of the pre-verbal child. Menzel's (1971) work on chimpanzees shows how sophisticated communication about the environment can be among non-verbal organisms.

Finally, it is as well to remind ourselves that the dyadic state of co-orientation can come about not only through one partner responding to an indication of interest by the other but also by both partners responding together to a salient event in the environment, as seen, for example, when two partners independently turn towards a third person entering the room. Such an occurrence may not be so intrinsically interesting in terms of the mechanisms by which co-orientation is brought about but it may well be important in terms of consequences, that is the use to which co-orientation is put in the dyadic exchange.

THE ROLE OF INTENTIONALITY

So far the role of intentionality in establishing co-orientation has not been mentioned. When do infants begin to "intentionally" draw their mothers' attention to an object rather than provide cues as an incidental consequence of their own interest in the world? This is a question which inevitably comes to mind when considering co-orientation from a developmental viewpoint and it raises a number of thorny issues which need to be aired. How can we distinguish intentional from non-intentional acts?

We could approach the problem by equipping a number of observers with an inventory of behavioural categories including items such as "infant intentionally draws mother's attention to X". The observers could be sent into the world of mothers and babies with instructions to record each occurrence of these categories and, with a little practice and much patience, results would probably be obtained which showed high inter-observer reliability and some understandable pattern. However, we would not be able to specify what the observers had been recording and so we could not be sure that the results could be replicated by observers from different backgrounds. This would make interpretation of the results problematic. Clearly, one would like to do better than merely obtain counts of observers' intuitions.

An alternative approach would be to adopt the control system model of intentionality as used by, for example, Bruner (1974). For Bruner, intentionality is synonymous with a system of control which utilizes negative feedback whereby the intended outcome of an act is compared with the actual outcome and the activity either adjusted accordingly or, when the goal is reached, brought to an end. Can this (very important) principle, which is discussed at length by Mackay (1972), help us with the taxonomic problem of deciding whether the result of an act was intended or not? There are a number of features which one might expect to find if such a system was operating. As the discussion on goal directedness reported by Hinde (1972, pp. 86–90) illustrates, there are considerable conceptual problems when we try to use these features as criteria for intentionality. Nonetheless, we can use the features of a feedback model to generate questions about the behaviour of our subjects which can be answered reasonably objectively. For instance, a necessary feature of the control system model is a knowledge of results, so we can look for evidence that an individual is in a position to monitor the effects of his own action on his partner. The visual sense is probably most important in this respect and fortunately the orientation of the eyes is readily apparent. Thus we can record whether pointing-like gestures are accompanied by looking toward the recipient: just such an effect is described by Murphy and Messer (Chapter 13) for mothers' pointing. We can also look for evidence that any feedback available to the senses is actually used. For example, on occasions when a mother does not follow a baby's point, does the point continue for longer, is it augmented by other referential behaviour, or are there signs of "frustration", "surprise" or "upset" (assuming these concepts could be suitably defined)? Yet another approach would be to investigate whether the nature of a child's referential behaviour varied with what we had reason to believe he knew about the competences of his opposite number, in much the same way as we ask how mothers adapt their behaviour to suit different aged infants.

What status should we give the identification of any of these features? Our understanding of the children's attention directing behaviour would be enhanced and, in so far as the data fit the model, the control system approach might provide a useful framework in which to consider the findings. However, it would be misguided to claim that such data would provide a sufficient basis for a categorical statement to the effect that the child's behaviour is controlled by a system like that postulated. In other words, although at first sight the model might appear to give a degree of precision and objectivity to the concept of intentionality, in fact it does not provide an empirical method of differentiating intentional from non-intentional behaviour. Furthermore, it hardly needs to be pointed out that behavioural phenomena which fit the control system model may well not fit the intuitive categories used by observers or, more importantly, by mothers.

In fact, it may be of more relevance to the intuitive notion of intentionality if the control systems model was applied at a higher level of analysis. Rather than viewing the execution of the attention directing action as a self-correcting system, perhaps that action should be considered as a component of a higher level system in which directing the partner's attention is but one stage in a more elaborate plan of action toward a higher level goal. For instance, we could envisage a child wanting to attract his mother's attention to an object in order that she gives it to him to play with. The task here is to specify rules for inferring the nature of the higher level goal, presumably from the context.

An alternative to concentrating on the mode of control of an activity is to rely on its content, form or topography, a commonplace basis for inference in classical ethology as well as in linguistics. I would suggest, for example, that a child who trips over an object is unlikely to be judged as having done so with the intention of drawing his mother's attention to it. Similarly, except in special circumstances, few people would judge merely looking at an object as being intended to direct the attention of others unless it is accompanied by other cues. Judgements about the economy, efficiency and appropriateness of the action to the outcome are the bases of such inferences, there being little reference to the mode of control. The implication is that we should study developmental changes in the *form* of activities of interest.

Thus the concept of intentionality has a multiplicity of connotations, and its application is far from straightforward. If we cannot do without the concept then we should be clear how we are using it. It may be, however, that once we have used the idea to generate some specific questions it may not be very useful to refer the answers back to the original concept. Indeed, of the many aspects of competence that can be seen developing in infants, there may be little utility in separating off a group of them and calling them aspects of intentionality.

The Uses of Co-orientation

We now turn from cause to consequence, from how it happens to the role that visual co-orientation plays in the interaction of babies with adults. We will primarily be concerned with consequences in terms of the immediate course of the interaction rather than with longer term developmental outcomes: we believe that observations of moment-to-moment interaction sequences have implications for our understanding of longer term processes in that they might point to imbalances and inconsistencies in our assumptions and suggest new lines of enquiry into developmental processes, but we cannot generalize directly from one time scale to the other.

As with other organisms, babies do not perform random sequences of activities; there is a degree of sequential constraint which can, in principle, be measured. It follows that another individual (e.g. mother), wishing to fit her own activities in with the baby's, would have an easier task if she carefully monitored the baby's stream of behaviour and hence had some clue about what the baby was most likely and least likely to do next. In the terminology of information statistics, her uncertainty about the baby's next action would be reduced by having monitored and knowing the baby's previous activity. Now, what babies do is not merely a function of what they did previously. It is reasonable to expect that what an infant is doing is also related to what he is presently attending to. This is where co-orientation fits in. As well as being able to use the sequential redundancy in the baby's *output*, an adult will also be able to use the redundancy inherent in the relationship between the baby's *input*—especially his visual input—and his ongoing behaviour. At some stage in development children will become able to reciprocate this process and in a similar way use these two forms of redundancy in their mothers' stream of behaviour.

Thus monitoring a baby's attention to the environment, and especially changes of interest, will enable an adult partially to anticipate changes in the baby's behaviour. There will be advance warning, as it were, which will make it possible for the adult to adapt and accommodate accordingly. There may also be a pay-off in affording anticipation of an interaction with a potentially dangerous component of the environment. A more positive aspect, however, is that the adult will be able to take notice of the focus of the baby's attention and make use of it as the focus for a social interaction. This type of social play centred around objects in the environment will provide a social context for learning not only about the environment *per se* but also about person–environment relations and especially those relations which have to do with symbolic language, a point developed by Bruner (1975) and Bullowa (1975).

When we first investigated co-orientation in mothers and babies we noted that mothers not only looked at the same toy as the baby but often went on to label it verbally and comment upon it (Collis and Schaffer, 1975). This is reminiscent of the tendency, pointed out by Brown and Bellugi (1964), to expand, elaborate or extend their children's own utterances. It would seem that mothers take note of and elaborate upon not only the speech of their children but their non-verbal behaviour as well. In the present case, they take the child's focus of attention, elaborate upon it and make it the centre of a new sequence of interaction. Bruner (1975), in particular, comments on the ubiquitous propensity for mothers to interpret the actions of children toward objects. He sees two kinds of maternal interpretation: that the child is trying to do something and that the child is trying to find out something. The second of these is most relevant here. Impressionistically, mothers seem to support the child's interest by identifying, referring to and perhaps requesting and/or providing information about the object in focus. What follows is an account of an empirical investigation into the association between visual co-orientation and maternal elaborative speech.

METHOD

Mother–infant pairs were recruited from those on a list of names obtained from a Child Welfare Clinic with a predominantly middle-class catchment area in Glasgow. The mothers were contacted by telephone and asked if they would participate in a programme of research into infant development. The initial sample comprised eight mother–infant pairs, with four male and four female babies. However, as will be explained below, the mother in subject pair E in this initial sample did not follow her infant's gaze significantly more than would be expected by chance. Consequently the sample was supplemented by a ninth pair (I) in place of pair E, so that we had eight mothers who established visual co-orientation with whom we could examine its consequences in terms of maternal speech. However, in the initial analysis which deals with the establishment of co-orientation, data from all nine pairs are reported in full. The nine babies were aged 40–46 weeks (mean = 43·3 weeks).

All the subject pairs to be reported made two visits to our laboratory, so that on the second visit they were fully at ease and familiar with the routine. On the first visit we recorded their behaviour in a situation which was an exact replication of our previous study (Collis and Schaffer, 1975). On the second visit, the results of which will be discussed here, the situation was similar except for slight changes involving the toys and their positioning.

The observation session took place in a room 3·5 × 2·0 m. A one-way window extended virtually the length of one side of the room and from behind it a video camera was focused on the subjects. An electronic video-timer provided a real time reference on the video-recording. Four visually attractive toys were positioned in dominant positions but where they would be out of reach of the subjects. The four toys were a doll's pram, a toy wheelbarrow and two dolls, similar except that one was dressed conventionally as a female doll and the other as a cowboy. The dolls were hung from the observation window so that when mother or child looked at them they were seen as looking toward the top-right or top-left corner of the video screen. Similarly, the pram and wheelbarrow were placed on two low tables below the observation window so that mother or infant, when looking at them, appeared to look toward the bottom-right or bottom-left of the screen. The two dolls were interchanged between the two positions for different subjects, as were the pram and wheelbarrow, making four combinations of toy position in all. In the sample of eight subject pairs, one male and one female infant experienced each arrangement. The ninth pair (I) experienced the same arrangement as pair E who did not establish co-orientation.

The mothers were told that we were primarily interested in the behaviour of the infants in novel environments. They were asked to behave as naturally as possible and told that they were free to talk to, play with and otherwise entertain the baby with the one constraint that, as far as possible, the baby should remain on the mother's knee. The mothers were seated on a chair placed approximately at the centre of the room and facing the observation window. The observation session began when the experimenter left the room, after settling the subjects, and continued for six minutes.

RESULTS

1. *Establishing co-orientation.* Our first task was to establish whether or not our present group of mothers did, in fact, follow the direction of their babies' gaze. Data to answer this question were extracted using stop-frame and slow-motion viewing of the video-recording. Each time the mother looked at a toy we asked the question—where was the baby looking in the same 0·1 second time-slice as the start of the mother's look? He could be looking at one of the four toys or at none of them. The data obtained were entered into a cross-classification matrix as in Table I, using a separate matrix for each subject pair. The matrix total indicates the number of looks made by a mother at the toys. The sum of the four cells on the leading diagonal indicates the number of those looks which were directed toward the same toy as the baby was already looking at. Whether this diagonal sum exceeded that expected by chance was determined using an "exact" method, treating the matrix

Table I

The association of mothers' and infants' gaze direction (data from subject pair D)

Infant looking at	Mother starts to look at: Doll	Cowboy	Pram	Barrow
Doll	(6)	2	0	0
Cowboy	1	(5)	0	0
Pram	0	0	(4)	0
Barrow	0	1	0	(2)
None	2	9	0	1

Bracketed cells indicate frequency with which mother looks where infant already looking.

as a contingency table with fixed marginal totals. Summing the probabilities of each arrangement of cell frequencies in which the diagonal sum equals that observed gives us the one-tailed significance levels that we require (see Freeman and Halton (1951) for probability formulae). Seven of the eight mothers in the original sample did indeed follow the direction of their baby's gaze significantly more often than would be expected by chance according to this model (Table II), as did the ninth mother brought in to replace the "non-follower". Thus it is

Table II

The following of infants' gaze direction by mothers

Subject pair	Infants' age (months)	Infants' sex	Mothers' looks at toys: Total number	Mothers' looks at toys: Number following infants' look
A	40	M	64	35[c]
B	40	F	13	11[c]
C	43	F	61	23[c]
D	44	M	33	17[c]
E	45	F	17	3
F	45	M	23	16[c]
G	46	M	23	10[b]
H	46	F	55	27[c]
I*	41	F	15	7[a]

[a] $p < 0{\cdot}01$.
[b] $p < 0{\cdot}001$.
[c] $p < 0{\cdot}0001$ (frequencies significantly exceed chance levels—see text).
* Subject pair I added to sample in place of subject pair E in which the mother did not establish visual co-orientation to a significant extent.

clear that, whenever a mother looked at one of the toys, her infant was more likely to be already looking at that same toy than at any other location. This is a clear replication of our earlier findings.

2. *Naming toys and looking at them.* Just as we asked whether the mothers' looks at the toys were synchronized with their infants' looks, so we can ask whether the mothers tended to verbally identify the toys when the infants were looking at them. The importance for semantic development of having verbal and visual input synchronized is self-evident.

From the video-recording, each instance of the mothers verbally labelling the toys was identified. They always referred to the doll's pram as "pram" and to the wheelbarrow as "wheelbarrow" or "barrow". However, although there were a few instances of mothers using "girl-doll", "boy-doll", "lady", "cowboy", etc., in general they did not distinguish the two dolls very much, preferring the generic "dolly". Hence, for the purpose of analysis, these various labels for the dolls were lumped into one category, together with the plurals "dollies" and (from one mother) "puppets".

Each time one of the three labelling categories (pram, barrow, dolly) occurred in the discourse, note was taken of the object of the baby's visual attention during the same 0·1 second time-slice as the naming word itself occurred—he could be looking at one of the four toys or at none of them. The object of the mother's visual attention, at the same time in the discourse, was similarly noted. The data were cross-tabulated according to which toy was named and where the infant was looking (Table III) and, in a similar way, where the mother herself was looking when she named a toy.

Table III

The association between toy naming and infant's gaze direction (data from subject pair D)

Infant looking at	Mother names: Dolls	Pram	Barrow
Doll	(4)	0	0
Cowboy	(0)	0	0
Pram	0	(4)	0
Barrow	0	0	(0)
None	2	0	0

Bracketed cells indicate frequency with which mother names a toy when infant is looking at it.

In general, the number of occurrences of naming in each subject pair was rather small. Over the group as a whole, there was a clear tendency for mothers to name toys while their infants were looking at them: 51 out of a total of 102 namings occurred when the baby was looking at the specific toy being named. This is very striking when one considers that out of 15 possible combinations of toy named and infants' gaze direction, only four correspond to naming synchronized with looking (the four bracketed cells in Table III). When the data were analysed separately for each subject pair, using the method employed above to test for co-orientation, the effect reached significance in three pairs (Table IV). Of the other subject pairs, although the number of namings was small, in all but one case 50% or more occurred while the infant was looking at the named toy. Overall, it is clear that whenever a mother named a toy, the infant was much more likely to be looking at

Table IV

Synchrony between naming and gaze direction in mothers and infants

		Infant looking at:				Mother looking at:			
Subject pair	Total namings	Named toy	Other toy	Mother	Elsewhere	Named toy	Other toy	Infant	Elsewhere
A	12	8	2	0	2	7[a]	0	4	1
B	6	3	1	0	2	0	0	6	0
C	12	9	1	0	2	5	0	6	1
D	10	8[a]	0	1	1	7[a]	0	3	0
E	5	0	1	0	4	2	0	3	0
F	16	11[a]	0	0	5	7[a]	0	9	0
G	2	1	0	0	1	2	0	0	0
H	35	9[a]	5	6	15	8[a]	1	24	2
I	4	2	0	0	2	2	0	2	0

[a] $p < 0{\cdot}05$, frequency significantly greater than that expected by chance (see text).

the toy which was being identified verbally than at any other toy. The analysis of where mothers were looking when they labelled a toy yielded a similar picture. In all, 40 namings were accompanied by the mother looking at the toy she was identifying. As can be seen from Table IV, when each mother was considered separately the effect was significant in four cases.

When we examine instances of naming while the babies were not looking at the toy named, it is apparent (Table IV) that in rather few instances was the baby looking at a different toy or at the mother; he was more likely to be looking at another, unspecified, location. In contrast, it can be seen from Table IV that mothers, when not looking at the toy they were naming, were most likely to be looking at the baby. This difference reflects the fact that for most of the session duration mothers were looking at their infants whereas the infants spent most of the time looking round their surroundings and rather rarely looked at their mothers. Moreover, it is of course understandable that mothers should look at their infants when speaking to them.

3. *Co-orientation and maternal speech.* We turn now from examining the relationship between the behavioural states of *individuals* to the relationship between a *dyadic* state (visual co-orientation) on the one hand and various behavioural states of one individual (categories of maternal speech) on the other hand. We will not include in this analysis the one mother–infant pair who did not show a significant tendency to establish co-orientation. Once again as sampling points we will use each of the mothers' looks at a toy. With the benefit of the first analysis we can now classify each of these looks as either a co-orientational (Co-) look, when the mother looks at the toy that her infant was already looking at, or as a non-co-orientational (Nco-) look. Using this dichotomy we can ask whether various maternal vocalization categories were more associated with one kind of look than the other.

Are Co-looks more likely to be associated with any kind of maternal vocalization, verbal or non-verbal, than Nco-looks? Table V gives the

Table V

Association of co-orientational looks and maternal utterances

Subject pair	Total Co-looks	Proportion with utterance	Total Nco-looks	Proportion with utterance
A	35	0·63	29	0·41
B	11	0·91	2	1·00
C	23	0·52	38	0·21
D	17	0·29	16	0·25
F	16	0·63	7	0·14
G	10	0·50	13	0·85
H	27	0·56	28	0·61
I	7	0·57	8	0·25

proportion of the total number of each kind of look in which a maternal vocalization overlaps at least some part of the duration of the look. These proportions were compared using the Mantel-Haenszel method for combining evidence from several four-fold tables (Fleiss, 1973). This procedure yields a chi-square for homogeneity which indicates whether there is significant heterogeneity among the various four-fold tables (in this case differences between the eight subjects); in none of the analyses to be reported below was this significant. Also derived is a chi-square for association which, if significant, indicates a difference between the two sets of proportions. In the present analysis this was significant ($\chi^2 = 5{\cdot}04$; df $= 1$; $p < 0{\cdot}05$). The summary odds ratio of 1·73 indicates that, overall, the odds that a Co-look would be overlapped by an utterance was 1·73 times that of an Nco-look.

Of the utterances which overlapped one or other kind of look, some included a "naming" word, as defined in the previous section. The proportions of Co-looks and Nco-looks which were overlapped by an utterance including such namings are presented in Table VI. Once again, the Mantel-Haenszel procedure shows a significant difference

Table VI

Association of co-orientational looks and toy naming

Subject pair	Total Co-looks	Proportion with naming	Total Nco-looks	Proportion with naming
A	35	0·26	29	0·07
B	11	0·09	2	0·00
C	23	0·30	38	0·08
D	17	0·24	16	0·19
F	16	0·63	7	0·14
G	10	0·10	13	0·08
H	27	0·19	28	0·29
I	7	0·29	8	0·13

between these two sets of proportions ($\chi^2 = 6{\cdot}66$; df $= 1$; $p < 0{\cdot}01$). The summary odds ratio shows that the odds that a Co-look will be overlapped by an utterance with a naming is 2·21 times that for a Nco-look. This association of naming with the dyadic state of co-orientation is consonant with the earlier result that naming tends to be synchronized with the individual gaze patterns of mother and child.

The incidence of the mothers' questions about the toys was similarly examined. The "questions" category included "Wh . . ." questions such as "What is it?" and "Where is the dolly?" plus utterances with a reversed subject-verb order such as "Is it a dolly?". However, questions in which other objects in the room were identified, for example "Is that the light?", were excluded. Decisions regarding this classification, and the "reference" category described below, were made from transcripts of the utterances without referring back to the video-recordings. The analysis showed no significant difference between the proportions of Co-looks and Nco-looks which overlapped questions. The summary odds ratio was 0·99: this is very close to unity which would indicate no difference whatsoever.

Finally, a similar analysis was carried out on utterances which included various forms of reference to the toys. This category included all the naming and questioning utterances defined above, plus utterances which referred to the infant looking or seeing things, except where an object other than one of the toys was specifically identified. The resulting odds ratio showed that the odds that a Co-look was overlapped by such a referential utterance was 1·43 times that for a Nco-look. This tendency was not, however, significant ($\chi^2 = 1{\cdot}90$; df $= 1$).

The number of words in each verbal utterance overlapping Co-looks and Nco-looks was also examined, but there was no evidence that utterance length differentiated the two kinds of look.

These results confirm that co-orientation in the dyad was indeed used as a context for vocal exchange. It would seem that, in terms of the content of the mothers' speech, co-orientation was employed mainly as a context in which to label the toys. It may be that in this situation questions about the toys, and other forms of reference, were as likely to result from the mothers' own initiatives as the infants', whereas mothers used periods of co-orientation instigated by the infants to label the toys.

Discussion

We approached the topic of visual co-orientation from two points of view: how it was established and how it was used to further the dyadic interaction. In the present study we have replicated the earlier finding (Collis and Schaffer, 1975) that, in the particular situation which we examined, visual co-orientation was brought about by the mother taking notice of the baby's focus of visual attention and looking in the same direction herself. As for the cues the mothers used, it was apparent that although they tried as much as possible to be in a position to see the child's face, this was not always possible and mothers therefore had to use cues from changes in the orientation of the head as a whole.

An examination of gaze sequences in the earlier study (Collis and

Schaffer, 1975) yielded no evidence that the infants tended to look where their mothers were already looking more often than would be expected from a chance juxtaposition of the two individuals' gaze patterns. This is not to say that the infants *could not* follow their mothers' gaze in this situation; that we do not know. The infants were, in effect, positioned between the toys and their mothers: an arrangement which is perhaps more appropriate for the mothers' following their babies' gaze than *vice versa*. Nonetheless, seating the infants on their mothers' lap is a comfortable and natural situation and has a high ecological validity.

Other authors have addressed themselves more directly to assessing the abilities of infants to follow the gaze direction of adults. Scaife and Bruner (1975) carried out an experiment in which infants were confronted with an experimenter who, having established eye-contact with the infant, looked to one side. Each infant was given one trial in which the experimenter looked to the left and one in which he looked to the right. The percentages of infants judged to have shown a positive response, i.e. looking in the same direction as the experimenter on one or both trials, were as follows: 2–4 months: 30%; 5–7 months: 38%; 8–10 months: 66·5%; 11–14 months: 100%. There was thus a clear trend for infants to be more likely to respond positively the older they were. At what stage were they responding at an above chance level? To answer this question we need an estimate of the likelihood that an infant would look in the same direction as the experimenter merely by chance. Despite the absence of information from a control condition we can obtain such an estimate provided we make a number of assumptions. Taking the authors' figure that 80% of the "negative" trials were, in fact, trials with no response at all, we have a 1:4 ratio of incorrect responses:non-responses. If the infants were equally likely to look right or left irrespective of where the experimenter was looking we have a 1:1:4 ratio of correct:incorrect:non-response, i.e. by chance 1 in 6 responses would be "positive" and 5 in 6 "negative". In two trials (assumed to be independent) the probability of both outcomes being negative (incorrect or non-responses) would be $(5/6)^2 = 0{\cdot}694$, and so the probability of at least one of two trials yielding a correct response would be $1 - 0{\cdot}694 = 0{\cdot}306$. This model would thus suggest that Scaife and Bruner's youngest group of babies performed at about chance level whereas those of eight months and older did significantly better than chance. Clearly, more information on this subject is required. The only other available source is from a task administered to rather older children by Masangkay *et al.* (1974) in which the subjects were asked to report verbally which of several toys the experimenter was looking at. The results showed that two-year-olds could readily use information from an adult's gaze direction in this way. The age at which this capacity first appears, however, must still be open to doubt.

Once a child can use information from the gaze direction of others he has the potential to benefit from the correlation between the mother's visual and vocal output, illustrated by the finding that mothers tended themselves to look at the toys that they were naming. Whichever individual witnesses the co-occurrence of looking and naming by his partner this type of redundancy could clearly be useful for resolving instances of ambiguity. Similarly, as was argued earlier, any association between either individual's gaze direction and other aspects of his ongoing and future behaviour will provide another source of redundancy. Thus our findings that mothers continually monitor the direction of their babies' gaze shows that they have available information about the infant's input as well as about his output. In principle, this could facilitate the maintenance of behavioural synchrony by permitting partial prediction of the likely future course of the infant's behaviour. Measurements of the redundancy in the input and output sequences of social interaction have mostly yet to be done, although a start has been made in the study of animal communication (e.g. Dingle, 1969). However, as well as indicating one role of co-orientation in social interaction, these considerations also underline the inadequacy of models of interaction in which each participant's interactions are considered as reactions to what the partner did previously and which, in turn, elicit a reaction from the partner in a kind of stimulus-response chain. Quite apart from the definitional contortions necessary to force the behavioural stream of a dyad into an alternating sequence in which a behavioural event by one individual is accompanied only by behavioural silence from the other member of the dyad, the fact that one participant may be able to anticipate the actions of the other before they occur potentially minimizes time-lag due to response latency and permits virtually simultaneous action by the two individuals. Expectancies by one participant about the likely future course of the other participant's behaviour cannot be assumed to be absent. Moreover, as Hinde and Herrman (Chapter 2) point out in a rather different context, it is misleading to regard the behaviour of the two individuals as independent sources of data about the dyad. One analytical model which accommodates these considerations particularly well is the conceptualization of an interaction as a sequence of *dyadic states*, a point emphasized particularly by Lewis and Lee-Painter (1974) and by Stern (1974). This approach has severe practical limitations in terms of the number of behavioural categories that can be considered before the number of possible combinations gets out of hand; nevertheless, the concept of a dyadic state is an attractive one and is illustrated by the present use of Co-looks and Nco-looks, defined by the activities of *both* partners, as a context for the mothers' speech.

Turning to more elaborate uses of visual co-orientation in furthering the interaction, we have seen that mothers use it as a context to name the object of the focus of attention that they share with their babies. The co-ordination of visual and vocal inputs in this manner clearly provides opportunities for the infant to extract from the situation information concerning the relationship between certain words and their referents. Furthermore, the looking-naming pattern is just what one would expect from Bruner's (1975) exposition of the use of joint reference in establishing the topic in a "proto-conversation". The use of co-orientation as a basis for reference in this way can be considered as but a special case of the role of behavioural context in providing or enhancing the meaning of utterances (Garnica, 1975). For context to be useful in this respect, different kinds of utterance must be related to different contexts. This is exemplified by the finding that naming was associated with co-orientation yet questions about the toys were not. In other words, co-orientation is a context which mothers selected for naming toys but which was neither selected nor avoided for questioning the children about them. This is the kind of differentiation of the content of speech according to context that is so important for verbal communication.

When we consider the implications of the content–context relationship for our conceptualization of the task faced by children who are in the process of "cracking the linguistic code", it is apparent that their task would be considerably simpler if they were to use to the full the contextual information which accompanies natural speech. Much has been written about the need to consider context when studying linguistic interaction during the period when the child is acquiring language, but it has seldom been analysed systematically enough to yield quantitative data. There is ample evidence that the structure of speech input to children is simpler than had at first been supposed and that syntax acquisition is not quite so awesome a task as it may once have seemed (Ryan, 1973). There is every reason to believe, though, that the rules and meaning of speech are not discovered solely on the basis of evidence from the auditory environment. Even in verbal communication between adults non-verbal contextual back-up makes interpretation simpler and less problematic; for young children it must be particularly important. Moreover, just as speech input to children is simpler than its adult-to-adult counterpart, so it is almost certain that the speech–context relationship is simpler too. Recently, a lot of attention has been paid to the characteristics of adults' speech to children, a line of research led by Snow (1972) and Phillips (1973). Now that there is some information available in terms of fairly global indices of the style of adult speech directed toward children of different ages, it is important to examine the moment-to-moment structure and integration of speech and context. Microanalyses of non-verbal mother–infant interaction have shown the way for this kind of investigation to proceed.

Acknowledgements

This work was supported by a (U.K.) S.S.R.C. research grant to H. R. Schaffer. I am grateful to Rudolph Schaffer for encouragement and detailed comments on the manuscript, to Gayle Parsons and Margaret Hunter for aid with data analysis and to Norie Sharp for technical assistance.

References

Brown, R. and Bellugi, U. (1964). Three processes in the child's acquisition of syntax. In E. Lennenberg (Ed.), *New Directions in the Study of Language*. M.I.T. Press, Cambridge, Mass.

Bruner, J. S. (1974). Competence in Infants. In J. S. Bruner, *Beyond the Information Given*. George Allen and Unwin, London.

Bruner, J. S. (1975). The ontogenesis of speech acts. *J. Child Lang.* **2**, 1–19.

Bullowa, M. (1975). From performative act to performative utterance. Unpublished manuscript.

Bullowa, M., Jones, L. G. and Duckert, A. R. (1964). The acquisition of a word. *Language and Speech* **7**, 107–111.

Collis, G. M. and Schaffer, H. R. (1975). Synchronization of visual attention in mother-infant pairs. *J. Child Psychol. Psychiat.* **16**, 315–320.

Dingle, H. (1969). A statistical and information analysis of aggressive communication in the mantis shrimp *Gonodactylus bredeni*. Manning. *Anim. Behav.* **17**, 561–575.

Fleiss, J. L. (1973). *Statistical Methods for Rates and Proportions*. Wiley, New York.

Freeman, G. H. and Halton, J. H. (1951). Note on an exact treatment of contingency, goodness of fit and other problems of significance. *Biometrika* **38**, 141–149.

Garnica, O. K. Nonverbal concommitants of language input to children: clues to meaning. Paper presented at the Third International Child Language Symposium, London, September, 1975.

Hinde, R. A. (1972). *Non-Verbal Communication*. University of Cambridge Press, London.

Hockett, C. F. (1960). Logical considerations in the study of animal communication. In W. E. Lanyon and W. N. Tavolga (Eds), *Animal Sounds and Communication*. Amer. Inst. Biol. Sciences, Washington D.C.

Hockett, C. F. and Altmann, S. A. (1968). A note on design features. In T. A. Sebeok (Ed.), *Animal Communication*. Indiana University Press, Bloomington, Indiana.

Lewis, M. and Lee-Painter, S. (1974). An interactional approach to the mother-infant dyad. In M. Lewis and L. A. Rosenblum (Eds), *The Effect of the Infant on its Caregiver*. Wiley, New York.

Mackay, D. M. (1972). Formal analysis of communication processes. In R. A. Hinde (Ed.), *Non-Verbal Communication*. University of Cambridge Press, London.

Masangkay, Z. S., McCluskey, K. A., McIntyre, C. W., Sims-Knight, J., Vaughn, B. E. and Flavell, J. H. (1974). The early development of inferences about the visual percepts of others. *Child Dev.* **45**, 357–366.

Menzel, E. W. (1971). Communication about the environment in a group of young chimpanzees. *Folia Primat.* **15**, 220–232.

Phillips, J. R. (1973). Syntax and vocabulary of mothers' speech to young children: age and sex comparisons. *Child Dev.* **44**, 182–185.

Piaget, J. and Inhelder, B. (1956). *The Child's Conception of Space*. Routledge and Kegan Paul, London.

Ryan, J. F. (1973). Interpretation and imitation in early language development. In R. A. Hinde and J. Stevenson-Hinde (Eds), *Constraints on Learning: Limitations and Predispositions*. Academic Press, London and New York.

Scaife, M. and Bruner, J. S. (1975). The capacity for joint visual attention in the infant. *Nature* **253**, 265–266.

Shipley, E. F., Gleitman, C. S. and Smith, L. R. (1969). A study of the acquisition of language. *Language* **45**, 332–342.

Snow, C. E. (1972). Mothers' speech to children learning language. *Child Dev.* **43**, 549–565.

Stern, D. N. (1974). Mother and infant at play: the dyadic interaction involving facial, vocal, and gaze behaviours. In M. Lewis and L. A. Rosenblum (Eds), *The Effect of the Infant on its Caregiver*. Wiley, New York.

V | Developmental Implications

15 Mother–Child Communication with Pre-linguistic Down's Syndrome and Normal Infants

Olwen H. M. Jones

Introduction

Once a communication dialogue begins to be established between an infant and some regular caretaker, it is highly likely that it will evolve through even more complex forms toward elaboration of more and more sophisticated shared understandings. Thus in the normal course of events the infant can be expected to have fairly complex communicative systems even at this pre-linguistic stage of development.

Our emphasis is on the fact that the success of the communication is dependent on the behaviour of both partners. This suggests that it need only require *one* of the partners to be insensitive to signals for the communication sequence to break down. One might expect the mother, as the more competent communicator, to have a disrupting effect on the inter-communication if she fails to respond to her child. However, this is not to say that, should the *child* have difficulty in fulfilling his role, even at this pre-linguistic stage of development, the success of the communication would not equally be disrupted. This present study was therefore set up to investigate the development of mother–child communication when the child is mentally retarded by having Down's Syndrome.

The lack of responsiveness of a mentally handicapped child might make it more difficult for a mother to keep up the kind of active informative dialogue in which most mothers engage their children. In this way the subnormal child effectively produces a less helpful and less rich environment for himself.

The relevance of pre-linguistic communication for the subsequent development of language has been emphasized by several investigators (e.g. Sugarman, 1973; Ryan, 1974; Bruner, 1975). However, despite this recognition of the salience of pre-linguistic communication skills, we still know very little about these skills in children who are known to have linguistic difficulties (see Ryan, 1975, for a review of some of the clinical studies on language retardation in Down's Syndrome). "Language remediation" is an assumed clinical necessity for nearly all Down's Syndrome children. Yet no one has so far examined the pre-linguistic communication abilities of these children in the context of mother–child communication. It may be that these mentally handicapped children communicate successfully until some specific time when "language" in all its complexities fails to develop fully. However, considering the current research emphasis on the accumulation of communication experience from birth, it would seem probable that Down's Syndrome children may show some form of communicative dysfunction long before the "first word". The major difficulties presenting themselves to investigators in this area of mental handicap research is that we have only just begun to develop techniques of analysis that allow us to observe in micro-detail the normal pattern of pre-linguistic communication in all its subtleties. We are still very much at the speculative stage concerning the relationship between pre-linguistic communication and subsequent language development, but the more we learn about the structure and development of early communication the better informed will we be to construct clinically successful theories of communication development. This particular research study therefore set out to examine the nature of interactional exchange between mothers and their normal children and to compare this to the exchanges found between mothers and their Down's Syndrome children.

Methods

SUBJECTS

Twelve children (six normal six Down's Syndrome) between the developmental ages of eight months and 19 months at the beginning of the study served as subjects. The actual chronological ages of the Down's Syndrome children ranged between 13 months and 23 months; the normal children were individually matched for developmental age (Cattell Infant Intelligence Scale), sex, family position and social class; their chronological ages ranged between eight months and 18 months.

PROCEDURE

The main source of data consisted of naturalistic observations based upon regular three-weekly video-recording sessions each lasting about 15 minutes, showing mothers talking and playing with their children in their own homes. Three toys were provided by the experimenter and the mothers were asked to find another toy from the child's own toy box that the two of them "enjoyed playing with at the moment". The mother was then instructed to play with her child as she normally would, but instead of going to their own toy box for "something else to play with" she and the child could go to the toys provided by the experimenter. When she and the child were tired of playing with each of these toys this part of the filming would cease. The mothers understood that the whole study was an investigation into ways mothers and children communicate with each other, i.e. how they talk to and play with each other. They were told that the film part was to see how the two of them would usually play together. A short informal interview on completion of the film checked how the mothers saw the play session as being "typical" of the way they play together. The film session also included a two-minute period of "play without toys" which usually took the form of general romping and ritualized lap games. Other information that was collected at the three-weekly visits included informal notes about the children's latest achievements in their general development. As well as keeping the investigator in touch with the child's rate of developmental progress, this also allowed the mother plenty of opportunity to "show-off" her child to the investigator and thus reduce this as a confounding influence in the video-tape recordings.

The films were collected for a period of 15 weeks by which time the normal children had begun developmentally to overtake the Down's Syndrome children to a significant extent.

METHOD OF ANALYSIS

The initial analysis of the video-tapes avoided the use of predetermined coding categories to prevent loss of valuable non-codable information. However, the transcription of the video-tapes was undertaken within a framework of six major areas:

(a) eye direction of mother;
(b) non-vocal activity of mother;
(c) vocal activity of mother;
(d) eye direction of child;
(e) non-vocal activity of child;
(f) vocal activity of child.

Simultaneous behaviour was recorded on the same line of the transcript, otherwise sequential behaviour was recorded on following lines. Unless events of effective communicative significance occurred within one second, in which case they were credited with separate lines, each line represented approximately one second of real time. In our view time itself is mainly relevant in as far as it leads to the identification of simultaneous and sequential events. (The time records actually kept were one-second markers on a small representative sample of the data where a digital counter marking 0·01 of a second was edited onto the tapes. Otherwise a six-second marker provided by the video-tape recorder's timeclock was included on the record sheets.)

It was considered of great importance that a record of the simultaneous behaviour of both mother and child be kept, since records which only "follow the action" as it flows between partners is an artifact of observational methods. Within the acting dyad each partner is *continuously* aware of the other's behaviour—whether it be passive or active. In a study of interaction it is therefore essential that the investigator is aware of the cues being received by both partners at any one time. Observable "listening" behaviour in the other is as important to the currently active partner as the act itself.

The next stage of the analysis was to code the behaviours into categories according to whether they were obviously invitational to the partner, effectively invitational (i.e. recognizable only by the fact that the partner responded), or effectively responsive to the other's act. Each of the initial three areas, attention, non-vocal behaviour, and vocal behaviour was coded into these categories. If none fitted they were noted simply as an "act". In this way it was possible to identify the mother's various invitational activities. Also, this made it possible to distinguish whether the mother was just responding to the infant "as if" he had invited her. This particular situation was in fact very common and, of course, salient to the child's familiarity with his communicative role. It was therefore important to note these "assumed invitations" even though this could only be done in retrospect at the point when a response was given.

DISCUSSION OF ANALYSIS TECHNIQUES

In the practical application of the analysis described above several important features of interaction became evident which forced us to be more sensitive to the subtleties of this communication process. Generally speaking, if two persons are in proximity and at least one has the intense intention to relate to the other then *continuous* interaction will occur for most of the time. It is true that much of the time may be passed in *passive* interaction, such as when a mother is watching her child's play activities, but this passivity is none the less interaction. For example, only after observing her infant's play can the mother then "mark" certain aspects of his activity by her actions and comments. Often the comment is also an invitation for the infant to share in an active interaction, e.g. a question. However, this may be so constructed that no change in behaviour is required of the child for him to complete his role. For example:

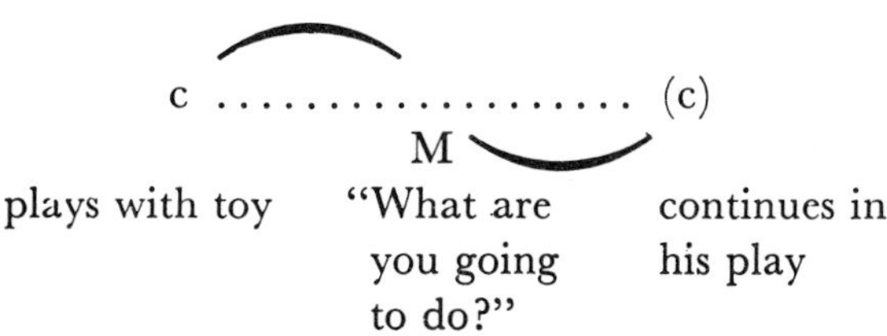

This, from the child's point of view, makes his interactive role relatively easy. Other questions from the mother may be simply dependent on the objects being played with and may specifically demand an "answer" from the child, e.g. "What is it?" These, however, seem usually to be aimed at responses that the mother knows are already in the child's repertoire. The question may be repeated if she really expects the answer, but if she is in any doubt about the child's willingness or ability to respond she may often repeat the question but make it easier to answer either by re-wording or even by suggesting the answer for him. "What is it? It's a duck, isn't it?" The last "tag" question, however, still allows the child to join in with an answer—and almost anything could be accepted as an "answer" to such a question, even a look. Thus, even when the child does not or cannot cope with the requested communicative role, his mother will utilize supportive techniques that "save his face" and maintain the communicating atmosphere.

Directly provided answers without the tag questions, such as "What colour is it? It's *blue*!", usually seem to occur in the half-way situation where the mother is not sure the child *can* answer the question, but he *might* imitate her answer. In these instances it is noticeable that the provided answer is exaggerated in its production in that it is exclaimed or elongated, thus ensuring the child's attention to this particular utterance. Selectively channelling the child's attention to his environment seems to play a major role in the mother's interactional techniques. The child's attention may be drawn to an object even when he is already attending to it, but rather than this being an unnecessary "extra" on behalf of the mother it seems to act as a warning that something important is about to happen in relation to that object.

"Difficulties" in communication are generally rare in these optimized conditions. Actual "clashes", when one partner very obviously "cannot get through" at any level, are unusual, even with the Down's Syndrome children. For the reasons we have described above, we can see that even if the child is not able or does not wish to "perform" appropriately and thus demonstrate that he understands, there are many and various ways in which this situation can be "patched up" so that some sort of communication has taken place. One of the most obvious reasons for this "break-down" is if one partner no longer attends to the other. This may be due to active attention elsewhere, or perhaps to a particularly disruptive behaviour such as autistic flapping, shouting or crying. (In this study, generally speaking, fretting occurred in children from both groups, but autistic flapping only occurred in one of the Down's Syndrome children.) Of course, there does occur the situation where the child shows no appropriate change in behaviour to a direct request from his mother, even though there is no obvious reason for him not to have heard or seen the request. In this situation we could only assume that the child does not understand, or perhaps simply does not wish to comply. These are, however, two very different levels of response. The only way to distinguish between them would be to make a subjective decision about the child's ability based on knowledge of the child and/or the mother's continuing behaviour. From the analysis point of view it was considered better simply to record this as a "missed invitation", but also to note the context of the request with respect to attentive behaviour and the mother's subsequent behaviour.

The analysis therefore needed to consider not only whether a "response was made" or "an invitation was made" or "no response to invitation" took place, but also the attentional context in which these communications occurred. One can hardly expect a response if the partner was partially or completely dissociated from the interactive situation.

In our attempt to analyse the constant ebb and flow of communication every attempt was made to preserve the totality of the interaction process and the natural continuity of its structure. However, where numbers and percentages of interactive sequences were sought it was inevitable that some sort of artificial demarcation line had to be drawn.

The diagrammatic scheme of analysis exemplified below has proved to be very useful in the identification of continuity and discontinuity in communication. The actual behaviours of the individual, however, are only taken into consideration in as far as they fall into the areas of attention, non-vocal behaviour, vocal behaviour, and whether or not the act appears to be invitational, effectively invitational, or effectively responsive.

The form of analysis used to monitor continuity of communication is based on the symbolic categories $\widehat{m\ c}$ shown above. In practice, however, it has been necessary to elaborate the system of signals in an attempt to cope, even crudely, with the complexity of communication flow. The system exemplified below (see Table I) is the one in current use. This form has been used to analyse data and some of these results will be discussed later. One of the most valuable outcomes from just attempting to monitor communication exchange in this way is that it has enabled

Table I

An example of a short section of a typical transcript record, with the symbolic system of analysis for monitoring communication flow

	TIME (seconds)	MOTHER NON-VOCAL Eye-direction	MOTHER NON-VOCAL Activity	MOTHER VOCALIZATION	CHILD NON-VOCAL Eye-direction	CHILD NON-VOCAL Activity	CHILD VOCALIZATION	DIAGRAM OF EXCHANGE	LENGTH OF EXCHANGE
Six-second time block (00–06)	00	C	Sits by C on floor		O	Sits on floor		$M - \rightarrow - c$	0
	01	T	Points to book	Oh, look!	O	Sits on floor		$M_{ao} - M_{vao}$	
	02	C	Points to book		T	Turns to book		C_{ao}	2
	03	C	Points to book	What is it?	T	Regards book		$M_{ao} - M_v$	
	04	C	Points to book		T	Regards book		( )	1
	05	C	Points to book	It's a duck isn't it?	T	Regards book		$M_{ao} - M_v$	
	06	C	Points to book		M	Look up to M	da!	$C_{am} - C_v$	
	06	C	Withdraw hand smile and nod	Yes a duck!	M	Look up to M		$M_v - M$	3
	07	T–C	Regard book and C		T	Patting book		$M - \rightarrow - c$	
	08	T–C	Regard book and C	Are you patting the duck?	T	Patting book		M_v	
	09	T–C	Regard book and C		T	Patting book		(c)	2

Key to symbols in Table I

O	Observer	
T	Toy	
M C	Mother Child	"Upper case" characters represent an invitation or a response.
m c	mother child	"Lower case" characters represent some activity; this may or may not result in being an "effective" invitation.
M - - → - C		Dotted line represents "observation", e.g. the mother quietly "observes" the child's activity.
M⁀C or M C)		A communication link in an interactional exchange is represented by ⁀ ; in the example an exchange *sequence* is occurring: the mother invites, the child responds.
M_v		Subscripts indicate "mode" of activity: attention to mother—am; attention to child—ac; attention to object—ao; vocal—v; non-vocal—no subscript. In the example the mother is making a vocal invitation (or response).
$M - M_v$		When an activity is vocally and non-vocally expressed it is linked symbolically.
M ( ))		An empty bracket indicates that a "space" has been provided for a response, but the opportunity was not used (appropriate attention, however, is assumed). This is called an "unsuccessful exchange".
M (c))		Here the opportunity for a response encloses ongoing activity—no change in the other's behaviour is required.
$m_v//c_v$		A "clash": simultaneous independent activity by both partners.
m → · ← c		Mutual attention to external object or event.
M ( )) // c		Failure to respond as above; but in this instance the other is involved in his own activity and is not paying appropriate attention.
M ( )) | M		Again the opportunity for response has not been used by the partner, but in this case the invitor then answers his own "question".
M ⋮ M		Same activity continues.

us to illuminate certain features of communication strategies that were previously masked by the sheer complexity of the whole process.

Results

The results to be presented should only be taken as illustrative at this stage. They are included primarily in order to show how our orientation can lead to quantitatively testable hypotheses. All the results to be quoted are taken from comparisons across the data available from the initial video sessions when each mother and child were playing together with the toys. (At the time of these earliest films the children were, of course, at the most closely matched developmental ages.)

INTERACTIONAL EXCHANGE

Table II shows the average rate of interactional exchanges* per minute for each mother–child pair taken from half of each individual four-minute analysis record. These figures only give us a rough guide as to the frequency of exchange sequences in this context. But we can see from the table that on average the total number of interactive exchanges (including unsuccessful invitations) is approximately 22 per minute for the Down's Syndrome Children and 17 per minute for the normal children (insignificant difference). However, if we exclude the unsuccessful invitations from the mother plus those "invitations" that did not require any change in the child's behaviour, then the overall average number of interactive exchange sequences is reduced to approximately 13 per minute for the Down's Syndrome children and 12 per minute for the normal children. Although the Down's Syndrome children therefore came up against relatively more unsuccessful sequences, overall they were involved in approximately equal numbers of interactive sequences of approximately equal length (2·2 participations long†).

These rates are possibly very specific to this age group in this context.

* An interactional exchange is an event involving both members of a dyad which invites a response or is itself a response.

† Length of exchange = the number of participations, or turns, in the exchange, e.g. $M\frown(\ ) = 1$. $M\frown C\smile M = 3$ (the number of alternations would be the number of participations −1).

Table II

Frequency of interactional exchange for each mother–child pair[a]

Child pair: matched N. and D.S.	Dev. age (months)	Toy a/b	Total No. exchanges[b]		Exchanges per min		Exchange sequences[b]		Sequences per min		Unsuccessful exchanges per min		Mean length[c] of exchange sequences	
			N.	D.S.	N.	D.S.	N.	D.S.	N.	D.S.	N.	D.S.	N.	D.S.
Pair 1	8	a	20	21	16·0	23·5	11	9	10·5	9·0	5·5	14·5	2·5	2·0
		b	12	26			10	9						
Pair 2	9	a	11	20	12·5	23·0	6	15	9·5	15·5	3·0	7·5	2·3	2·1
		b	14	26			13	16						
Pair 3	12	a	12	16	15·0	23·5	11	8	12·5	11·5	2·5	12·0	2·3	2·1
		b	23	31			14	15						
Pair 4	13	a	19	24	23·0	21·0	8	13	12·5	14·0	10·5	7·0	2·2	2·5
		b	27	18			17	15						
Pair 5	15	a	14	16	17·0	18·5	11	11	11·0	12·5	6·0	6·0	2·4	2·2
		b	20	21			11	14						
Pair 6	19	a	20	17	21·0	22·5	15	11	13·0	13·5	8·0	9·0	2·2	2·2
		b	22	26			11	16						
Mean					17·4	22·0			11·5	12·7	5·9	9·3	2·2	2·2
T (Wilcoxon)						N.S.				N.S.		N.S.		N.S.

N. = Normal children. D.S. = Down's Syndrome children.

[a] The numbers shown only represent those interactions identified in the microanalysis of two minutes of video-tape taken from the initial film session for each mother–child pair, whilst playing with the box of cotton reels (toy a) and the book (toy b).

[b] "Exchanges" include unsuccessful invitations. "Exchange Sequences" are exchanges that include a response.

[c] "Length" = The number of "participations" in an exchange sequence (e.g. m⌒c = 2, m⌒c‿m = 3).

Although the differences are small Table II indicates that the "book" toy generally seemed to encourage more interactive exchanges in general, and also slightly more successful exchange sequences, than the "box of cotton reels". But the important thing from the point of view of this study is that, given these similar developmental ages and similar contexts situations, the two groups of children show no differences, across the sampled data, in their frequency of participation in interactive exchanges in general.

However, in looking at patterns of interactional exchange some interesting differences between the groups are already evident. Some investigators (e.g. Bruner, 1975) have noted a particular division in styles of interaction that mothers tend to employ. These can best be described as whether the mother insists on directing the interactive exchanges or whether she tends to support the child's initiative. In this particular study we could divide the individual exchanges into whether the mother was directly inviting the child to do or say something (M⌒. . .) or whether she was supporting the child's initiative by, for example, just watching his play or commenting on his actions or taking up his idea and expanding it or being presented with his directive (c – ← – M, c⌒M, or C⌒. . . . .). These two styles of interaction we labelled "Mother-directed" and "Child-dependent" respectively. Obviously both categories occurred with all the mother–child pairs, but we noticed that some pairs were strikingly more at one pole than at the other.

In order to get a quick purchase on the way the mother–child pairs fitted into this division, we divided the transcript record sheet into blocks of one-tenth of a minute. This division was convenient as all the record sheets had already been marked at six-second intervals. Then, to get some idea of the relative degree to which each of these types of interaction occurred in each mother–child pair, the number of time blocks which *exclusively* contained "Child-dependent" interaction was sought. The figures in Table III can therefore be read as an approximate estimate of the proportion of time devoted to child-dependent interaction. When the data on interactional exchanges is complete a more representative analysis will measure the *proportion* of *exchanges* that are child directed (Jones, in preparation). From the table we can see that the mother–child pairs tend to divide into the more "Mother-directed" Down's Syndrome group and the more "Child-dependent" normal group, though the difference was not significant.

Table III

Percentage of six-second time blocks which contained exclusively child-dependent interaction

Child pair: matched N. and D.S.	Dev. age (months)	"Child-dependent" interaction exchange sequences			"Child-dependent" interaction observation			Total		
		N.	D.S.	Sign of difference (N.–D.S.)	N.	D.S.	Sign of difference (N.–D.S.)	N.	D.S.	Sign of difference (N.–D.S.)
Pair 1	8	29·1	2·1	+	20·8	1·4	+	49·9	3·5	+
Pair 2	9	17·8	17·2	+	3·5	9·9	—	21·3	27·1	—
Pair 3	12	9·5	5·5	+	2·7	0·6	+	12·2	6·1	+
Pair 4	13	17·8	13·0	+	23·0	9·0	+	40·8	22·0	+
Pair 5	15	18·4	19·9	—	30·5	14·4	+	48·9	34·3	+
Pair 6	19	17·7	8·5	+	7·9	4·6	+	25·6	13·1	+
Mean		18·4	11·0	+	14·7	6·7	+	25·8	9·8	+
Significance of difference between pairs (Wilcoxon)			N.S.			N.S.			N.S.	

The percentages shown in the table represent the ratio of six-second time blocks containing exclusively child-dependent interaction to the total number of six-second time blocks in the initial film session of playing with toys for each mother–child pair (average 15 minutes, therefore 150 six-second time blocks).

EYE-TO-EYE INTERACTION

Another particular pattern of interaction which we wished to study was the incidence of eye-to-eye contact in the mother–child pairs. On the transcript records we were collecting it soon became evident under the attention-direction column for the children that they rarely seemed to make eye-contact with their mothers when they were playing with toys. Considering the documented importance of eye-to-eye contact in relation to mother–child interaction (e.g. Robson, 1967; Jaffe *et al.*, 1972) we felt this phenomenon deserved special study. We were also aware from the transcript records of even less eye-contact being made by the Down's Syndrome children.

We are in agreement with Schaffer *et al.* (Chapter 12) in their findings that mothers spend much of their time looking at their children, and for this reason the onus of initiating eye-contact is mainly on the child. Thus any difference between the groups toward reduced eye-contact in the Down's Syndrome children would emphasize a lack of some skill in these children.

As a communication gesture eye-contact initiated by the child seems to have a potent effect on the interaction. The mother seems to be very sensitive to it and is usually very quick to pick it up and respond to the child. However, as we can see from Table IV, its incidence in a context of playing with toys is relatively infrequent (average 0·95/min), considering the number of exchanges that are taking place in any one minute and that it only really requires the child to glance up for this exchange to occur. But this frequency is most probably situation specific, since initial analysis of the film sessions where play occurs without toys is showing that eye-contact occurs often as much as 50% of the time during the romping and ritualized lap games that are usually observed in this part of the film sessions.

However, in our examination of the eye-to-eye contacts occurring in the film sessions with toys, we found that it was possible to identify three types of eye-contact situations. Firstly, type I occurred in essentially direct interpersonal situations. For example, the child might make eye-contact when approaching his mother for a hug, or when he wanted to be picked up, or just to stare (e.g. as he might to a newcomer). The second type (II) was more in relation to some particular game, such as peek-a-boo, or directional aiming, when throwing a ball for example.

The last type (III) is best described as a "referential" look in that

Table IV

Frequency of eye-to-eye contact for each mother–child pair[a]

Child pair: matched N. and D.S.	Dev. age (months)	Total No. eye-contacts per min		Type I "Personal" per min		Type I "Personal" % of total		Type II "Game" per min		Type II "Game" % of total		Type III "Referential" per min		Type III "Referential" % of total	
		N.	D.S.	N.	D.S.	N.	D.S.	N.	D.S.	N.	D.S.	N.	D.S.	N.	D.S.
						%	%			%	%			%	%
Pair 1	8	1·2	0·9	0·1	0·1	6	8	0	0·7	0	83	1·1	0·1	94	8
Pair 2	9	1·5	0·8	0	0·1	0	14	0·1	0·4	8	42	1·5	0·4	92	43
Pair 3	12	1·5	0·1	0·5	0·1	32	100	0·3	0	23	0	0·8	0	59	0
Pair 4	13	1·3	1·7	0·2	0·2	20	12	0·1	0·8	10	47	1·1	0·7	70	41
Pair 5	15	0·5	1·3	0·1	0·5	13	43	0	0·3	0	21	0·4	0·5	88	36
Pair 6	19	0·6	0·1	0·1	0	9	0	0·2	0·8	36	100	0·3	0	59	0
Mean		1·1	0·8	0·2	0·2	10	30	0·1	0·5	13	46	0·9	0·3	77	21
Significance of difference for pairs (Wilcoxon)		N.S.		N.S.		N.S.		N.S.		N.S.		N.S.		Sig. $\alpha = 0{\cdot}025$	

[a] These rates were taken from the transcript record of each of the initial film sessions (average length 15 minutes).

the child appeared to be making some reference to his, or her, activity by the glance up. It is typically described by a transfer of attention from the object of the activity between mother and child to the mother's face and then back to the object. Such a "look" almost invariably seems to draw a supportive comment from the mother. For example: child bangs drum, looks up pausing in activity, mother nods, smiles and says "Yes, that's right! You banged it, didn't you?" Child continues banging drum. It was almost as if the look meant "Look at me, aren't I clever?"

In Table IV we can see how often the children used these three types of eye-contact in the initial film session. We can see from this that although the rate of eye-contact is generally greater for the normal children, it is not actually significantly different between the two groups. But the rate of referential eye-contacts (type III) is on the whole considerably larger for the normal children. When we examine what percentage of the eye-contacts made by each child fall into the three groups, we can see from Table IV that type III, referential eye-contacts, prove to make up a significantly greater proportion of the eye-contacts made by the normal children.

THE COMMUNICATIVE QUALITY OF THE CHILDREN'S VOCALIZATIONS

Considering the relevance of vocalization to speech, special consideration was given to the vocalizations of the children and how these fitted into communication exchanges. All vocalizations occurring in the first two minutes' play with each of the four toys were recorded. Each vocalization was then described in relation to its approximation to:

(a) a word;
(b) a word, but unrecognizably articulated ("word" according to mother's report);
(c) intonated jargon;
(d) babble.

Each vocalization was also described by its number of syllables and whether or not it had already been heard in that play session within these eight minutes (measure of variety).

In addition the vocalizations were rated according to their communicative quality. Thus as well as a straight description of the vocalizations of the children, we were now going to take into consideration the communicative context in which the vocalization occurred. This break-down is an important one with these essentially pre-linguistic children.

The levels of communication quality used are described below in increasing order of sophistication as communication signals:

1. Vocalizations that exist only as "entertainment" for the child, in that they do not appear to be in relation to the mother's activity.
2. Vocalizations that are "picked up" by the mother, so that they are in effect enclosed in a dialogue of vocalization (c⁀M), but this is structured by the mother.
3. Vocalizations that are apparently in response to the mother's vocalization; their context is such that a vocal "dialogue" is observable, but this time instrumented, initially at least, by the child (M⁀C).
4. Vocalization by the child that seems to be a "comment" in that it is highly intonated or is accompanied by an established gesture (e.g. "Uh" plus point to desired object).
5. Vocalization by the child that is word-like, but is necessarily supported by a clear gesture ("ta" with giving gesture, "ta" with extended hand) or environmental context (e.g. "ba!" consistently means "gone" for one child when something has just disappeared according to the mother's report).
6. A word.

Each of these levels could be further sub-divided into two "context" conditions "a" and "b". These conditions are mainly relevant to levels 1–3 and they are dependent on whether the child appears to be showing some sort of consideration for his vocalizing partner (condition "a"), in that he allows a reasonable "space" for his partner to respond. This "space" was determined on the criterion of a one-second pause between utterances. If utterances followed each other within one second then the preceding vocalization was classified within the "b" condition (no space).

This one-second "opportunity-space" for the mother to respond was chosen as the criterion on the basis that this seems to be the critical unit of response time according to our studies at Nottingham. The mothers mostly responded in the subsequent second to the child's "invitation", and also seemed usually to "expect" the child to respond within this time space, in that they would leave a one-second pause, in which time, if no response was obviously forthcoming, the mothers would often go on with their suggestions for interaction. Occasionally, of course, both invitation and response would occur within one second, but this apparent rapidity of response often seems to give observers the impression that the "response" was an already forthcoming action.

Thus, if the child vocalized and then repeated his vocalization within the subsequent second (e.g. da-da-da), it gave the strong impression from the observer's point of view that the mother had not been given enough "space" to "answer". The above criteria therefore identified this situation as condition "b". Similarly, if the vocalization continued in a long stream, identifiable "pauses" were the pauses for breath (daaaaa, daaaa), and this type of vocalizing was also scored as type "b".

This division is not so relevant at the higher levels where the communication signal is more sophisticated (although one could surmise that an older child who leaves no opportunity for people to reply would be lacking some sort of communication skill). However, this particular time criterion would not be suitable with children using sophisticated strings of intonated sentence-like jargon. For this reason the particular criteria referred to above were restricted to levels 1–3 where they were most appropriate.

Table V shows the results for the children on these communication measures. The table indicates that the Down's Syndrome children showed rather more "b" type vocalizations than the normal children, especially at level 1. These children therefore tended to repeat vocalizations quickly on top of each other with little room (less than $\frac{1}{2}$ second) for dialogue, or they vocalized in long continuous strings. (Other vocal dialogue difficulties are becoming evident from further communication exchange analyses presently being carried out. The Down's Syndrome children seem to be more often involved in vocal "clashes" (C //M), that is they often vocalize *at the same time* as their mothers. This, however, does not seem to prevent the mother from "picking up" the vocalization and expanding it, but it does suggest the Down's Syndrome child is showing lapses of interactive turn-taking skills.)

Discussion

A considerable amount of data analysis is yet to be completed on our material. However, if the few trends referred to above prove to be

Table V

"Communicative quality" of the children's vocalizations

Child pair: matched N. and D.S.	Dev. age (months)	No. vocalizations		Percentage different vocalizations		1a Isolated vocalizations		1b		2a "Dialogue" due to mother's response		2b		3a Dialogue due to child		3b		4 Intonated		5 Plus gesture support		6 Word	
		N.	D.S.	N.	D.S.	N.	D.S.	N.	D.S.	N.	D.S.	N.	D.S.	N.	D.S.	N.	D.S.	N.	D.S.	N.	D.S.	N.	D.S.
				%	%	%	%	%	%	%	%	%	%	%	%	%	%	%	%	%	%	%	%
Pair 1	8	36	59	38	15	27	59	6	34	25	5	0	0	8	0	0	0	19	2	0	0	0	0
Pair 2	9	6	10	83	60	16	50	0	10	33	30	0	0	16	0	0	0	33	10	0	0	0	0
Pair 3	12	22	18	22	44	18	22	0	6	9	44	0	6	27	6	0	0	40	6	0	16	5	0
Pair 4	13	69	57	27	22	41	24	9	15	17	8	0	22	7	8	0	7	19	12	7	0	0	0
Pair 5	15	52	38	40	42	44	26	10	23	12	11	0	0	27	11	0	0	4	11	4	15	0	3
Pair 6	19	47	32	43	39	6	13	2	6	9	31	0	3	2	3	0	0	64	9	9	31	2	0
Mean		39	36	42	37	25	32	5	16	18	22	0	5	15	5	0	1	30	8	3	10	1	0·5
Wilcoxon		N.S.		N.S.		N.S.		Sig. $\alpha = 0{\cdot}05$		N.S.		N.S.		N.S.		N.S.		N.S.		N.S.		N.S.	

The figures in the table were taken from the data on the first two minutes of play with each of the four toys, in the initial film session for each mother–child pair, i.e. they are based on a total of eight minutes for each child.

consistent, there are several important conclusions that could be drawn.

Firstly, the Down's Syndrome children in this study could all participate in pre-linguistic communication with their mothers. This was true for all of them even though some were already quite severely retarded. They were all able to provide sufficient feedback for their mothers to continue to support them in interactive exchanges.

However, as we have briefly indicated, the "support" techniques available to mothers are many and various and often only require a very simple response for the dialogue to continue. It will therefore be interesting to see if the data analysis when completed indicates whether or not mothers of the Down's Syndrome children are using more of these support techniques. On the data available so far we are already showing a distinction between the two groups with respect to the amount the mothers attempt to "control" the direction of the communication, mothers of Down's Syndrome children being involved in more "Mother-directed" than "Child-dependent" interactions. The reason for this is not easily identifiable. Possibly these mothers either have more passive children or they believe their children to be passive. It does seem to be the case that Down's Syndrome children show less initiative, in that they initiate sequences less frequently than their matched normals (but then they are not given as much opportunity by their mothers). However, whoever is to blame in this "chicken and egg" situation, the *result* is that the children are not as often in situations where the mother allows them the freedom to choose the "topic" of the conversation. They also, we find, tend to come up against a greater number of unsuccessful invitations from the mother and by definition are involved in situations of dissociation or just lower level attentional responses. The normal children, on the other hand, find themselves more often in situations where they receive support and enrichment of their own activities.

The reduced use of the referential look, and even of eye-contact in general, provides another example in which Down's Syndrome children are not drawing out feedback from their mothers to the extent that normal children are. The reason for this difference is not easily explicable on developmental grounds, that is with respect to whether the Down's Syndrome children have reached that "stage" (Sugarman, 1973) when they can cope with consideration of two ideas at once, the mother *and* the toy, since the Down's Syndrome children *can* use referential looks, but generally speaking, across the whole developmental range, they use them to a significantly lesser extent than the normal children. Again, whatever the reason, the *result* is that the Down's Syndrome children are less involved in this type of supportive communication. In this particular situation, however, the onus is more definitely on the Down's Syndrome child. There are plenty of suitable opportunities available to him; he simply does not use them.

The investigation into the vocalizations of the Down's Syndrome children suggests that, although they seem to produce as many and varied vocalizations as the normal children, the context in which they employ their vocal abilities is more often relatively inconsiderate of vocal dialogue. Their vocalizations either go on relatively longer than those of their normal matched pairs or they repeat their vocalizations more often within a very short period, allowing no more than one second between breaths for the mother to respond. Despite these imposed difficulties, however, the mothers usually managed to get a response in quickly, or after the "long utterance". However, in these particular instances the mothers' comments often tended to be quick acknowledgements such as "mm", "Yes", rather than anything more elaborate. The effect of this, of course, is to reduce the richness and variety of the vocal dialogue.

This inconsideration of the mothers' communicative role on the part of the Down's Syndrome child is an example of poor use of "turn-taking" skills. Another finding that seems to be supporting this suggestion is the greater frequency of vocal clashes with the Down's Syndrome children, that is, when both mother and child vocalize at the same instance. Again, as far as we can tell with the data analysis currently available, this seems to be the child's "fault" in that it usually occurs when the mother has already started speaking. Often the mother cuts herself short to let the child "have his say". These clashes occurred across both groups—there were instances of clashes with the normal children, but fewer than those found in the Down's Syndrome children. In one mother–child pair, however, with a little Down's Syndrome girl, the mother usually completely ignored the child's vocalizations and "steam-rollered" over them with her own verbalizations (see Table IV, Pair (1): of the 59 vocalizations in eight minutes, only three were in fact responded to by the mother). But in this particular example the child's vocalizations were often socially unacceptable to the extent that they consisted mainly of deep-throated "growls" and bore little resemblance to linguistic vocalizations. In Susan Pawlby's research (Chapter 9) it was noted that mothers tended not to encourage the imitation of socially unacceptable gestures.

Conclusions

We have shown in this paper how our approach to mother–child interaction is attempting to look at communication as a feature of the interrelationship between each mother and her child. We have devised techniques of analysis that are dependent on the interactive context of the communicating pair, and by so doing we have emphasized the need to consider not just each member of the dyad separately as an independent "actor" but also the activity of one in *relation* to the other's activity. In this way the same "behaviour" may have a very different communicative meaning depending on the interactive context.

In comparing these two small groups of children we have already been able to illustrate how this sensitivity to the interactive context has illuminated differences between the groups that would otherwise have gone unnoticed. Overall frequency counts often did not show any general differences between the groups. But when the activities were considered in *relation* to the immediately preceding and subsequent inter-communicative activities, the same activity could be identified as having a different meaning and a different effect in relation to the interactive exchange enclosing it. Thus, this type of approach appears to be quantifiable and useful in its application. In this study we are now able to identify some of the very subtle, but nonetheless salient, communication skills that are available to pre-linguistic children within the supportive context of their communicating caretakers.

From the clinical point of view, any differences, however subtle, that we are able to identify between the normal children and the Down's Syndrome children will be important in helping to further our understanding of the development of sophisticated communication skills and perhaps the formulation of clinically useful communication theories.

References

Bruner, J. (1975). The ontogenesis of speech acts. *J. Child Lang.* **2**, 1–19.

Jaffe, J., Stern, D. N. and Peery, J. C. (1972). "Conversational" coupling of gaze behaviour in pre-linguistic human behaviour. *J. Psycholing. Res.* **2**, 321–329.

Jones, O. H. M. (in preparation). Mother–child communication: a comparative study of pre-linguistic Down's Syndrome and normal infants. Ph.D. Thesis, University of Nottingham.

Robson, K. S. (1967). The role of eye-to-eye contact in maternal-infant attachment. *J. Child Psychol. Psychiat.* **8**, 13–25.

Ryan, J. (1974). Early Language Development: towards a communicational analysis. In M. Richards (Ed.), *The Integration of the Child into a Social World.* Cambridge University Press, London.

Ryan, J. (1975). Mental subnormality and language development. In E. Lenneberg (Ed.), *Foundations of Language Development.* Academic Press, New York and London.

Sugarman, S. (1973). A description of communication development in the pre-language child. Study project thesis, Hampshire College, Mass.

16 Assessing the Effects of Perinatal Events on the Success of the Mother–Infant Relationship

Andrew Whiten

Introduction

Modern Western medicine, in achieving with a high degree of success the aim of reducing perinatal disease and mortality, has interfered more and more in the first social interactions of mothers and their newborn babies. Recently, sources ranging from learned journals to the popular press have given expression to the view that such interference may have psychological disadvantages which must be assessed and weighed against the medical advantages. It is possible to conceive of two principal types of disadvantage, but in the main only one of these will concern us in this paper, and that consists of *developmental* effects—those which can be traced some time after the interference.

The other type of disadvantage consists of more obviously immediate effects, with no significant developmental repercussions; as such it may be generally acknowledged as of less importance. I therefore wish to make only one comment: that it must not be completely neglected. For example, in my present study, which has been concerned with the particular intervention of separating mothers and newborns in order to provide special care for the latter, it was quite obvious from interviews that *some* separated mothers dearly wished to have more opportunity to interact with and care for their infants. Even if the distress of these mothers had no developmental consequences, it argues strongly in itself for the compassionate provision of facilities to promote contact when a mother, aware of any medical risks, desires it.

Often, however, there is a conflict between medical and potential psychological risks. A more complete understanding of the latter is therefore necessary, and this must include developmental effects. The principal concern of this paper is centred on the nature and difficulties of assessing such effects. The nature of the factors leading to differential effects is of secondary importance here, but since my study of post-natal separation will serve as concrete reference material, it must at least be described in outline.

A STUDY OF POST-NATAL SEPARATION

One of the projects which occupied me before the present one dealt with the early mother–infant relationship in gorillas. I was very struck by the contrast between the continuous contact seen here in the early months and the much lesser contact characteristic of child rearing in our culture. I therefore decided to study the latter and was soon presented with a specific topic as a result of the work of Klaus *et al.* (1972). They had studied two groups of American mothers, one of which experienced a short period of post-natal separation from the baby, as was routine in the hospital concerned. The other mothers had only slightly more contact over the first three post-natal days, yet one month later they showed a higher commitment to their infants when interviewed, and more interest in a medical examination of the infants. During a feed, they showed three times as much "en face" behaviour in which the baby was held in such a position as would facilitate eye-to-eye contact, and four times as much "fondling". It was concluded that shortly after birth there is a "maternal sensitive period" for maternal attachment to the infant.

These results were disturbing and have raised many questions, such as whether and when there is a "sensitive" period for the creation of such effects, and whether and how mother, infant, or both are directly affected. But before implementing any research on these questions, it is clearly most important to know the significance of the effects of separation in terms of their duration. The present study aimed to trace any effects up to the age of one year. Kennell *et al.* (1974) have since reported their own follow up data, and Leiderman and Seashore (1974) have studied high and low contact groups over similar periods.

The question of how long effects last was one of three principal questions which were asked because of their practical significance for paediatricians and other policy-makers. The second was related to the characteristics of Klaus' sample, which consisted mainly of young unmarried mothers of low socio-economic status. It seems likely that such mothers would have a low anticipatory commitment to their infants. Since this is not considered to be so for the majority of British mothers, it was important to see if Klaus' results would be replicated for a representative sample of them.

The separated sample included ten infants who went into the Special Care Baby Unit at the John Radcliffe Maternity Hospital, Oxford, for periods of two to 14 days. They were separated for various minor medical reasons such as prediabetic mother and hypothermia, a major criterion in their selection being that when they came out of the unit they were regarded by hospital staff as medically normal and were thenceforth not treated in any special way. Of course despite this attempt to minimize this confounding factor, no claim can be made to a study purely of the effects of separation. But this does not matter, for many people, including paediatricians, have felt that the average British mother, with a favourable home background and positive anticipatory attitude to her infant, would be able to overcome any such disadvantages as those experienced by the separated group, and would soon be interacting with her infant in a manner indistinguishable from that of mothers who had not faced these disturbances. Certainly my paediatric colleagues felt that it would be necessary to find if this were so before any properly controlled studies, with arbitrary assignation to high and low contact groups, could be warranted.

In this study a control sample of 11 subjects was matched for several characteristics likely to affect subsequent interaction (Table I), but of course the possibility remains that certain mothers and babies may be predisposed, by a common factor, both to post-natal separation and to a style of interaction different from that characteristic of the wider population. However, since this paper is in no way concerned with establishing causal relationships, we need not concern ourselves with this problem, nor with the fact that the observer knew which mothers and infants had experienced separation.

Table I

Sample characteristics

	Contact (N = 11)	Separated (N = 10)
Gestational age of baby	all 38 weeks	all 38 weeks
Mean weight of baby at birth (g)	3092	3182
(range)	(2500–3780)	(2420–3750)
Sex male/female	6/5	5/5
Bottle/breast fed	3/8	3/7
Parity of mother	all primiparous	all primiparous
Marital status	all married	all married
Length of marriage		
(years)	3·1	3·3
(range)	(1–6)	(0·8–9)
Mother's age	26	26
(range)	(20–30)	(20–33)
Length of labour		
0–6 hours	5	0
6–12 hours	3	2
12–18 hours	0	4
18–24 hours	1	1
24+ hours	2	0
(Caesarean)	0	3
Maternal age at completion of education	16	16·5
(range)	(15–18)	(15–21)
Social class of fathers (mothers' social class in brackets)		
I		1
II	3(1)	2(2)
IIIN	3(9)	1(6)
IIIM	5	5(1)
IV	(1)	1(1)
Days after birth (+ range)		
first seen	all following birth	1(½–2)
first touched	all following birth	2·1(1–5)
first fed	all on first day	2·6(1–5)
out of unit	—	5·0(2–14)
Pregnancy intended/not intended	9/2	9/1

The third question, which will occupy us for the remainder of the paper, was concerned with assessing the *nature* and *extent* of any differences in subsequent mother–infant interaction. What is required here, in order to permit comparison between experimental and control groups, is a comprehensive but sensitive description of those features of mother–infant interaction which we believe to be important in terms of their developmental significance or prominence in the everyday life of the mother and infant. Measures thus derived should be objective enough to permit quantification for comparisons, but must also be of a type about which we can make value judgements if they are to be of use in terms of informed policy-making. As such they are, of course, relevant to many types of study different to the present one, which here serves as an example only.

We shall deal as much with the problems encountered in attempting such a study as with any progress it appears to have made.

Assessment of the Success of the Mother–Infant Relationship

METHODS OF ASSESSMENT

Since in the past there had been no attempts to provide such a comprehensive account of everyday mother–infant interaction as that specified above, the principal method used was direct observation in the home. Visits lasted for most of a morning and were made at three weeks, and at 1, 2, 3, 4, 6, 7½, 9, 10½ and 12 months after the birth. During the four visits between 1 and 4 months the feed was video-taped and analysed separately. Interviews and diaries completed by the mother provided further data, but these will not be discussed here.

Direct recording was done on a sheet divided into horizontal lines, the mother's line running above the infant's. Behavioural categories were denoted by symbols which were inserted in the lines, producing a continuous analogue of the sequence of interaction being watched. An earpiece produced a tone every ten seconds to pace the recording.

Analysis of video-tapes took a similar form except that the tape was stopped at five-second intervals and categories were then entered into a grid marked in one-second intervals.

Categories of behaviour to be recorded were unfortunately, yet necessarily, finalized in little more than 150 hours of observation. An attempt was made to define categories of behaviour in the smallest meaningful, replicable and recombinable units, so as to permit flexibility in analysing the relationships between such units.

Those categories which are referred to in this paper, ranging from "smile" to "creates possibilities", are listed in the appendix.

The data thus collected relate to many aspects of the mother–infant relationship, but in this paper I shall focus on only two general areas of interaction. Both are of great interest because they are perhaps the most striking aspects of integration in the everyday interactions of mother and infant, and yet no naturalistic descriptions of them exist in the literature; indeed there are many problems in attempting adequately to assess them.

The first area is that of communication in the earliest months after the birth. The second deals with the later interactions with objects which involve both mother and infant. Here the mother may play a role in manipulating the environment from which the infant may profitably learn, providing, in Jerome Bruner's apt expression, "scaffolding" on which the infant can erect complex skills.

ASSESSMENT OF EARLY COMMUNICATION

In the initial analyses of one-month video-tapes a rather broad notion of communication was used, which involved the recording of all cases where the behaviour of one partner appeared to affect that of the other. This generally involved latencies of only a second or two. The number of behaviour categories was quite large, as is shown by Table II, which includes only maternal responses to infant behaviour. However, many of the contingencies involving specific categories were so low in frequency that it was necessary to summate some of these to permit sensible comparisons. I have classified them into four groups.

The first group consists of responses the mother made to those infant behaviours which appeared to be functional in controlling aspects of the task of feeding. At this age there were few recorded responses. During the following few months, however, the infant does come to play a significant part in controlling the structure of the feed, either directly or indirectly through communicating with the mother, and this warrants the presentation of these responses as one category.

The degree of elaboration achieved here may be illustrated by considering the behaviours recorded between the ages of one and four months which simply controlled the teat being in or out of the infant's mouth. Starting when the teat is in the mouth, the infant may directly remove it by pushing with the tongue, averting the face or pushing away with the hands. Or the mother may directly remove the teat in response to the infant grimacing, fussing, choking, or sucking too slowly or too fast. When the teat is out the mother may show the bottle to the infant, thus asking whether he wishes for more. Whether or not she does this, she may present the teat to his lips in response to his fussing, smacking his lips or sucking, making certain limb movements, or, if the bottle is visible, reaching, lunging with the head, or opening the mouth. As the teat approaches the infant's mouth he may open it, and the mother may push the teat in, or the infant may pull it in. Alternatively the infant may either keep his mouth closed, fuss, avert the head or arch away and the mother may then terminate the feed, or persevere by rubbing the teat on the infant's lips. This degree of elaboration would appear to make the feed highly significant if not unique among functional episodes (such as nappy-changing and bathing) in the opportunities it offers for early learning and integration between mother and infant in communicating about the conduct of a task of great mutual interest.

We may contrast with this type of communication that which does not appear to be functioning to regulate any immediate task. It involves such behaviours as smiling, laughing, vocalizing and touching, and is the kind of communication which we think of as being done "for its own sake"; I therefore refer to it as "purely social" behaviour. One of the groups in the analysis consists of such maternal responses to infant behaviours which I have assumed will be generally thought of as potentially purely social.

A further group, "non social", consists of maternal responses to those infant behaviours which I have assumed not to be potentially social, and which did not appear to be involved in structuring the feed, such as sneezing and defecating.

The fourth group consisted of all infant responses to maternal behaviour; these were infrequent at this age and are not shown in Table II. Of these four groups, only "purely social" showed a significant difference between the two samples at one month, the contact sample having three times as many responses as the separated sample (Table III). For certain specific types of response to "purely social" behaviours,

Table II

Maternal responses to infant behaviour during video-taped feed at age one month. Raw totals for 21 infants.

INFANT BEHAVIOURS	MATERNAL RESPONSES																
	Look	Kiss	Smile	Laugh	Talk	Reply	Imitate	Rub or pat	End rub/pat	Look out	Manipulate B's hand	Change B's position	Teat in	Offer teat	End offer	Teat out	Spoon-feed
Group 1—"Functional"																	
Fuss																	1
Fuss-face														1			1
General head															1		
General limb															1		
Suck														1			
Grunt																1	
Cough																1	
Avert				1													
Extrude				1													
Teat in				1													
Nipple out			1														
Group 2—"Non-social"																	
Cry					1				1								
Fuss				1	4			1	2		1						
Fuss-face					3												
Suck				3			3										
Burp				1													
Hiccough			1	2	2												
Frown				1													

Table II (continued)

INFANT BEHAVIOURS	MATERNAL RESPONSES Look	Kiss	Smile	Laugh	Talk	Reply	Imitate	Rub or pat	End rub/pat	Look out	Manipulate B's hand	Change B's position	Teat in	Offer teat	End offer	Teat out	Spoon-feed
Finger to mouth				1	4												
Cough					6							1					
Extrude					1												
Defecate					1												
Yawn					5												
Sneeze					1												
Choke					1				1								
State 3–4					1												
Stare										6							
Group 3—"Purely social"																	
Look		1	18		20												
Grunt	8		6	15	77		5										
Vocalize	2					15											
Smile			3		5												
Pout			2														
Open mouth			3		2												
Lip				2													
Manipulate M's hand			1														
Manipulate nipple					1												
Brow				1	1												

frequencies were high enough to permit separate comparisons, which significantly favoured the contact group (Table III).

A separate analysis of data from direct observation at the same visit revealed similar differences, contact mothers responding more by smiling and vocalizing (Table IV). Mutual looking, probably the first reciprocal communication of mother and infant and the basis on which the others seem to be established, was actually seven times greater in the contact group.

Differences in mutual looking and smiling could also be traced back to the first observation period at three weeks, which included the non-video-taped feed. At this stage a first attempt was made to determine the relative contributions of mothers and infants to these differences. Were the contact mothers more responsive than separated mothers, or did the contact babies produce more behaviour likely to elicit the responses?

This raises our first major problem, for it seems that mothers are likely to respond to such a wide variety of behaviour that it is virtually impossible to define a category of "eliciting behaviour". A mother may smile or comment on an expression which has all the appearance of being unique. As a first attempt to overcome this problem, attention was restricted to the most significantly differentiating maternal response to the commonest specific elicitor; that is, smiling in response to vocalization, which was more frequent in the contact group. It was found that the frequency of the infants' eliciting vocalizations and the proportion of these to which the mother responded by smiling were *both* higher in the contact group, though not significantly so. Thus after only three weeks it is not obvious whether the responsibility for differences lies principally with the infants or principally with the mothers. Similar analyses have yet to be done for other purely social behaviours, but we may note that in another domain of responsivity differences occur at three weeks in both mothers and infants: contact infants cried only half as much as the separated infants and contact mothers responded to a significantly higher proportion of cries.

Since the principal differences at these ages were in the constellation of purely social behaviours, analysis has first continued for these over the following months of interaction. Here we face the second major problem, for these behaviours became organized into often quite elaborate sequences which may exhibit many of the features of a conversation such as turn-taking and appropriate nuances of intonation.

Table III

Responses of mother and infant per observation hour during video-taped feed at age one month

	Contact (N = 11)			Separated (N = 10)			P(U)[a]
	Mean	Median	Range	Mean	Median	Range	
Groups of categories:							
Total maternal responses to infant "functional" behaviour	1·3	1·8	(0–3·9)	1·1	0	(0–5·5)	N.S.
Total maternal responses to infant "nonsocial" behaviour	12·1	5·8	(0–24·4)	5·0	4·6	(0–16·7)	N.S.
Total maternal responses to infant "purely social" behaviour	27·8	27·0	(5·8–66·8)	9·8	6·6	(0–36·4)	0·01
Total infant responses to mother	2·7	1·9	(0–7·5)	0·7	0	(0–13·3)	N.S.
Specific categories:							
Infant looks: mother responds by talking	3·2	3·8	(0–7·5)	0·8	0	(0–5·7)	0·025
Infant vocalizes: mother responds by talking	11·4	7·5	(1·9–38·7)	3·1	0	(0–14·5)	0·01
Infant vocalizes: mother responds by smiling or laughing	3·2	1·9	(0–10·9)	0·5	0	(0–3·6)	0·01

[a] Mann-Whitney U-test.

Table IV

Occurrences of "purely social" behaviour per hour of direct observation at age one month

	Contact (N = 11)			Separated (N = 9[b])			P(U or F[a])
	Mean	Median	Range	Mean	Median	Range	
Mutual looking (minutes)	2·9	3·4	(0–6·8)	0·4	0	(0–2·0)	0·01 (F)
"Non-elicited" maternal smiling	1·1	0·5	(0–2·9)	0·3	0	(0–3·1)	0·05 (U)
Maternal smiling in response to vocalization	0·2	0	(0–2·0)	0	0	(0)	N.S.
Maternal smiling in response to looking	0·3	0	(0–2·0)	0·2	0	(0–1·9)	N.S.
Maternal smiling in response to other behaviour	0·5	0·5	(0–1·3)	0·1	0	(0–1·0)	0·05 (U)
Total responsive smiling of mother	1·0	1·5	(0–2·2)	0·3	0	(0–1·9)	0·025 (U)
Total maternal smiling	2·1	1·5	(0–5·2)	0·6	0	(0–6·3)	0·025 (U)
Total maternal laughing	0·5	0·5	(0–5·2)	0·1	0	(0–2·0)	0·05 (U)
Maternal reply to vocalization	1·6	1·5	(0–7·8)	0	0	(0)	0·01 (F)
Reply relative to frequency of vocalization (%)	4·2	2·4	(0–13·0)	0	0	(0)	0·01 (F)
Total responses to baby's vocalization	2·1	1·5	(0–8·8)	0	0	(0)	0·01 (F)
Maximum number of turns	0·8	1	(0–2)	0	0	(0)	0·005 (F)

[a] F = Fisher Exact Test, U = Mann-Whitney U-test.

[b] Occasionally circumstances prevented observations (or video-records) being made.

They have struck me as a peak of social performance in the early months, not only in relation to other behaviour at this age but in the contrast they present to the communication I have observed between other primate mothers and infants who appear not to indulge in such conversations at all. In this connection we may note that such babbling conversations not only occur but, as far as our preliminary observations indicate, follow much the same developmental elaboration in the remote Ibo village of Owerri Ebeiri in Nigeria where this paper is being written during a pilot comparative study.

The precise developmental significance of these exchanges is unknown, but it may not be too wild a speculation that they provide opportunities for the infant to learn how to converse with another person, how not to interrupt, how to recognize the signals which indicate the other is now ready to listen, what is the correct latency for replying, what signals indicate the other is ready to speak, how to make such signals himself, what intonations and phonemes are to be used and in which accepted sequences and in relation to which expressions, gestures and other actions. If the infant does learn some of these things, he may thus be preparing for performance not only in conversational speech but, in the closer future, to play an efficient role in those turn-taking games soon to be played with the mother. These will be discussed in the next section of this paper.

How are we to assess the success of such interactions? Clearly before this can be done adequately it will be necessary to study the extent to which the above speculations are true. As a first measure of the degree of elaboration in these sequences, I have simply counted the number of responses ("number of turns") which mother and infant make alternately. This was limited to the specific categories of vocalizing, touching, smiling and laughing. Thus if an infant smiled at the mother, she then smiled at and touched him, and he then laughed and vocalized, this would constitute two "turns". A break of five seconds or more was taken to denote the start of a new sequence.

At one month of age it was rare for there to be more than one turn in a sequence (at least for these categories of behaviour). Nevertheless this measure did allow the inclusion of responses of both the mother to the infant and of the infant to the mother, and it combined different modalities, including the smiling recorded for four infants at this age. The "maximum number of turns" (in a sequence) so derived provided the most significant difference in favour of the contact group up to the age of one month (Table IV).

At two months, sequences with more than one move were more frequent, so that in addition to "maximum number of turns" the "mean number of turns" for each mother–infant pair was calculated. The differences were the most highly significant up to this age and are shown in Table V together with those for some particular types of single responses. "Number of turns" thus seems an appropriately sensitive measure for this age.

Table V

Occurrences of "purely social" behaviour per hour of direct observation at age two months

	Per hour of observation						
	Contact (N = 11)			Separated (N = 9)			P(U)
	Mean	Median	Range	Mean	Median	Range	
Baby vocalizes: mother replies	4·2	3·3	(1·0–8·6)	1·0	0	(0–4·0)	0·01
Baby smiles: mother talks, smiles or laughs	2·2	2·8	(0–6·9)	0·9	0	(0–3·8)	0·05
Mother touches or smiles: baby smiles or vocalizes	3·6	2·8	(0–11·3)	0·9	0	(0–4·3)	0·025
Maximum number of turns	2·3	2	(1–4)	0·9	1	(0–3)	0·01
Mean number of 1 or more turns	1·4	1·3	(1·0–1·8)	1·1	1·0	(1·0–1·2)	0·001

However, when the same comparisons were made at three and four months differences between the groups became insignificant (Tables VI and VII). For "purely social behaviour" then, either differences between the groups fade strikingly between two and three months post partum, or the measures used do not do justice to the significant features of the developing relationship at these later periods. Perhaps the current work of the contributors to this volume will provide the deeper understanding necessary to evaluate these alternatives.

Table VI

Occurrences of "purely social" behaviour per hour of direct observation at age three months

	Per hour of observation						
	Contact (N = 10)			Separated (N = 9)			P(U)
	Mean	Median	Range	Mean	Median	Range	
Baby vocalizes: mother replies	6·6	5·3	(0·6–20·0)	6·8	6·7	(0–14·1)	N.S.
Baby smiles: mother talks, smiles or laughs	6·1	4·8	(0–19·0)	4·5	3·8	(0–13·7)	N.S.
Mother touches or smiles: baby smiles or vocalizes	6·3	5·5	(0·5–15·5)	4·7	4·7	(0·7–10·8)	N.S.
Maximum number of turns	4·0	4	(1–7)	3·2	2	(2–8)	N.S.
Mean number of 1 or more turns	1·5	1·3	(1·0–2·3)	1·4	1·3	(1·1–1·9)	N.S.
Mean number of turns of 2 or more	—	3·0	(2·0–5·0)	—	2·0	(2·0–3·4)	N.S.
Number of sequences with 2 or more turns	5·0	2·5	(0–15·0)	3·9	4·0	(1·0–9·0)	N.S.
Total number of turns in sequences with 2 or more turns	16·7	6·0	(0–48·0)	9·9	8·0	(3·0–23·0)	N.S.

SCAFFOLDING

Perhaps one reason for the apparent ability of the separated group to "catch up" in social behaviour could have been that the contact group were experiencing a competing new interest in non social behaviour, for in the second quarter of the year there is a pronounced development of manipulative interaction with the world of objects. This may happen at the expense of purely social behaviour, but this does not mean that the mother is excluded, for mother and infant may interact through the medium of objects rather than directly with each other. In the second half-year extra behaviour categories were introduced to assess such interactions, which are significant in occupying a high proportion of the time mother and infant are together and, like those in the previous

Table VII

Occurrences of "purely social" behaviour per hour of direct observation at age four months

	Per hour of observation						
	Contact (N = 11)			Separated (N = 9)			P(U)
	Mean	Median	Range	Mean	Median	Range	
Baby vocalizes: mother replies	8·0	7·6	(0–20·6)	4·7	3·9	(1·2–10·6)	N.S.
Baby smiles: mother talks, smiles or laughs	7·1	4·4	(0–16·7)	4·7	3·9	(1·2–10·6)	N.S.
Mother touches or smiles: baby smiles or vocalizes	11·2	10·5	(0–28·2)	9·0	6·5	(0·6–22·5)	N.S.
Maximum number of turns	6·8	5	(0–11)	4·7	5	(1–10)	N.S.
Mean number of 1 or more turns	1·6	1·6	(1·0–1·9)	1·5	1·5	(1·0–2·7)	N.S.
Mean number of turns of 2 or more	3·3	3·3	(2·0–4·3)	2·9	3·0	(2·0–5·0)	N.S.
Number of sequences with 2 or more turns	8·6	10·0	(0–19·0)	5·7	6·0	(0–11·0)	N.S.
Total number of turns in sequences with 2 or more turns	31·9	30·0	(0–71·0)	18·9	20·0	(0–50·0)	N.S.

section, in immediately striking the observer as some of the most elaborate forms of mother–infant integration at these ages, despite the fact that we have no naturalistic descriptions of their development.

The categories used (see appendix) were thus necessarily experimental, although like many others in this study some were taken directly from the "ethology" of everyday classification and description of behaviour. Each category also covered a wide variety of bodily movements. This was necessary because the common features which defined each category were applied to varying, sometimes unique, environmental situations. Thus a mother might demonstrate how to stroke a kitten, yet a description of the form of this action is of little use for the majority of mothers who do not have kittens. The category of "demonstrate", however, while more difficult to define, is sufficiently widely applicable to form the basis for meaningful quantitative comparisons.

Although no analysis of the data obtained after six months of age has yet been made, some of these major categories should be mentioned before we discuss the earlier instances for which analysis is available. "Demonstrate" comprised those actions which the infant was intended to imitate. "Assist", however, consisted in helping the infant towards his own goal, as inferred by the mother. An important sub-category of assistance was "show location", originally referring to those cases where a mother drew the infant's attention to the locus for an appropriate match of two objects, but subsequently broadened to include the direction of attention to any task-relevant feature. Such categories as these appear to be significant in representing the first attempts of the mother to teach the infant, so guiding and elaborating his intellectual development, even at this tender age, in directions relevant for later success in his culture. Perhaps through such interactions the infant actually learns how to benefit from teaching. Very similar categories have been independently constructed in recent laboratory studies of the teaching strategies of mothers with small infants (e.g. Kaye, 1975; Wood *et al.*, 1975). However, these studies were concerned with a particular task set by the experimenter for the mother and the infant. What is especially notable in the free home situation is the way the mother may frequently manipulate the environment to *create* such "tasks".

"Creates possibility" is the general category which has been used to record those manipulations whereby the mother enhances the infant's scope for acting on objects. In many cases it is clear that a particular outcome is expected, and "complements" refers to the infant performing such a response. Thus the mother may "create possibilities" by building a tower and the infant may "complement" by knocking it down. Such behaviour may be repeated by both mother and infant such that turn-taking sequences are built up into games. Here we may have an important link with the topic of the previous section. Is it possible that the babbling conversations discussed there provide a framework for the regulation of turn-taking games in the second half year?

The first instances of "creates possibilities" consist simply in providing the infant with manipulable objects and initially do not involve turn-taking, although later these actions become reciprocal, leading to give and take games. Two categories were distinguished here: "give toy", in which an object was put into the infant's hand, and "present toy", in which an object was offered so that the infant had to reach and grasp it ("show toy" consisted in attracting the infant's attention to a manipulable object out of reach). Surprisingly, the separated mothers showed a significantly higher frequency of giving toy, both at the four- and six-month visits (Table VIII). This is an intriguing result, but yields no obvious interpretations. On the one hand it might mean that the separated mothers and infants were more interested in interactions via objects, thus scoring low on previous assessment of purely social behaviour. Why that would be so is by no means clear. On the other hand, we should note that at six months the contact mothers showed a higher frequency of "present toy" and a higher proportion of "present toy" in the provision of toys by giving or presenting. It could be argued that presenting rather than giving a toy creates more possibilities for the infant at an age at which he is learning so much about reaching and grasping. Thus by this interpretation there was again an inadequacy in the integration of mothers and infants of the separated group. Alternatively there may have been a difference in the infants' levels of advancement which elicited different strategies in the mothers.

Table VIII

Frequency of presenting and giving toys per hour of direct observation at four and six months of age

	Contact (N = 11)		Separation (N = 9)		
	Mean	Median	Mean	Median	P
4 months:					
Present toy	1·5	0	1·0	0·6	N.S.
Give toy	0·5	0	1·5	1·2	0·05
6 months:					
Present toy	5·2	4·0	2·9	2·0	0·06
Give toy	0·7	0	0·6	0·5	0·05

SPECIAL PROBLEMS IN ASSESSMENT

In a first attempt to assess the success of the relationship in the two main areas referred to above, many problems have been encountered and some of these have already been discussed. I shall now air some more general problems, which I shall try to formulate as specific questions.

Firstly, in the area of early communication mothers and infants may invent their own signals or variations on common signals. The meanings of conventions thus established and even their existence are not immediately obvious to the outside observer, even though he may have watched many other mothers and babies. Visits spaced at monthly intervals, even if they last a whole morning, will not be sufficient to understand and assess the success of such communication. When the aim of the study is to assess and compare mothers and infants, an important measure of responsivity is the proportion of signals responded to; this presupposes that the observer is at least as good as the mother in recognizing such signals, yet the existence of idiosyncratic conventions makes this unlikely. This difficulty is further confounded, in that it seems a reasonable hypothesis that the better integrated the communication between the mother and infant the more subtle and cursory will the necessary signalling become; a truly sensitive interaction may thus be seen as displaying less evidence of communication than a poorly functioning one. Granted that the successful establishment of communicative conventions could be a sensitive measure of the extent of mother–infant integration, how might it be possible to assess it in a study such as this, where perhaps a minimum of 20 infants must be observed?

In noting the difficulties of assessing such subtle communication, special mention should be made of tactile interactions, for there are surely many instances of successful tactile communication which are difficult, if not impossible to recognize simply because they are minimally or totally invisible. Even if such omissions are unavoidable in a comparative study like the present one, it would be healthy if we were more knowledgeable about them. What is their extent and can they be assessed in a study such as this?

Two solutions to the general problem of idiosyncratic conventions may be considered, but both have further drawbacks. The first, as a method of understanding the communication system of mother and infant, is to ask the mother about it: what does she think behaviour X meant? What enabled her to predict he would soon do Z? This can indeed be a quick way of at least generating useful hypotheses to be tested by observation, but the major drawback is that it necessarily draws the mother's attention to those aspects of behaviour which are being recorded and so may lead to her concentrating on displaying them.

The second solution is simply to make more extended and closely spaced observations. This may enable the observer to trace the development of conventions, and in general better to understand communication and scaffolding whose meaning is defined according to context or current infant competence. Yet if it is the case that in most instances the mothers' and infants' understanding of each other depends on the experience gained of each other day and night for the past weeks or months, for the observer's understanding of their communication to even approach the mothers' would require very prolonged observation indeed. In a comparative study there is competition for observation time between three demands: a sufficient number of infants to permit comparison (ideally to permit a study of the interaction of a number of causal factors, rather than the oversimplified two-way comparison used as an example here), a sufficient number of visits to permit longitudinal study of developmental effects, and a sufficient observation time at each visit to obtain meaningful measures. Since the first two could not be reasonably reduced further in this study, the only way to extend the third in a similar study would be by a heavy investment in personnel. For such a study to take adequate cognizance of the individuality of each mother and infant, it might become necessary to have nearly as many observers as babies!

Is there an alternative, in that such "pure" studies as those reported in this volume, which do not suffer from all the constraints outlined above, may through intensive observations on just a few babies provide an understanding which will reduce the necessity for similarly extensive work on the many babies essential to an "applied" study? Or does the unique nature of each mother and baby mean that there can be no such short cuts?

Creativity presents a second major problem. In studies such as those of the effects of separation on the mother–infant relationship, attention has usually been focused on simple measures of affection and attachment, such as cuddling and fondling. These are areas where separation has been shown to have effects in other species.

The two main areas of interaction discussed in this paper are perhaps no less indicative of affection, or at least of commitment and involvement. Yet it seems likely that they both, and especially scaffolding, require a certain degree of intelligence and creativity if they are to become elaborate. Are we then basing such assessments on values relevant only to the highly intelligent or creative? Or are such aspects of human mother–infant interaction appropriate and fundamental to assessment of their integration?

Acknowledgements

I am grateful to Professor J. Bruner and Dr A. MacFarlane for their encouragement and advice in the course of this study. I wish to thank Professor L. Weiskrantz and J. Bruner for provision of facilities in the Department of Experimental Psychology at Oxford University, and Professor P. Tizard, Dr D. Baum, Dr C. Robertson, Miss P. Townshend and their staff for their co-operation at the John Radcliffe Maternity Hospital. I am grateful to the S.S.R.C. for the Conversion Fellowship which made this study possible.

References

Kaye, K. (1976). Infants' effects upon their mothers' teaching strategies. In J. C. Glidewell (Ed.), *The Social Context of Learning and Development*. Gardner, New York.

Kennell, J. H., Jerauld, R., Wolfe, H., Chesler, D., Kreger, N. C., McAlpine, W., Steffa, M. and Klaus, M. H. (1974). Maternal behaviour one year after early and extended post-partum contact. *Dev. Med. Child Neurol.* **16**, 172–179.

Klaus, M. H., Jerauld, R., Kreger, N. C., McAlpine, W., Steffa, M. and Kennell, J. H. (1972). Maternal attachment: importance of the first post-partum days. *New Engl. J. Med.* **286**, 460–463.

Leiderman, P. H. and Seashore, M. J. (1974). Mother-infant neonatal separation: some delayed consequences. *CIBA Foundation Conference on Parent-Infant Relationships*, London, England.

Wood, D., Bruner, J. S. and Ross, G. (1975). The role of tutoring in problem solving. *J. Child Psychol. Psychiat.* **17**, 89–101.

Appendix

CATEGORIES OF BEHAVIOUR REFERRED TO IN THIS PAPER

Direct Observation

Some behaviours are recorded in duration; a symbol is used to record their start, and another to mark the end. They are indicated below thus: *.

A few categories are never recorded more than once in each ten-second block, and are indicated below thus: †.

Other behaviours are recorded as point events only, each time they occur.

Mother categories (M = mother; B = baby)

†look: M looks at B's face

kiss: M kisses B's skin or hair

talk to:	vocalization to the infant lasting one expiration
reply:	reply to B's vocalization, recognized on the basis of latency (about one second) and content, which is reply-like (e.g. "mm" or "yeh")
smile:	a range from narrow smile to grin: respiratory pattern does not change
laugh:	this is differentiated by the characteristic panting respiration
show toy:	a graspable object is held in front of B so he can see it but cannot reach it
present toy:	as show toy but within B's arm length
give toy:	an object is put into B's hand
spoonfeed:	a spoon of food is put into B's mouth ("during spoonfeeding" is the period between first and last spoonfuls of a session)
nipple:	M puts nipple into B's mouth
teat:	M puts teat into B's mouth
nipple out:	M pulls nipple out of B's mouth
teat out:	M pulls teat out of B's mouth
*pat:	M pats or rubs B's back to "wind" him

Baby categories

†look:	B looks at M's face
smile:	includes all expressions which could be considered as smiles or laughs

Video-tape categories

Some categories used in video-tape analysis are also used in direct observation, and so will not be repeated in the following list. This is a partial list and includes only those categories in Table III.

Mother categories

imitate:	M imitates B's expression or vocalization
look out:	M looks at what B appears to be staring at
offer teat:	teat is offered by holding it in front of B's lips
end offer:	offer is ended by removing teat from this position

Baby categories

grunt:	less speech-like than "vocalization"
pout:	B pouts lips
open mouth:	B opens mouth wide
lip:	B curls lip
brow:	B raises brow
*cry:	
*fuss:	crying and fussing do intergrade but fussing is applied to non-rhythmic whimpering and whining; crying is louder and more rhythmic

fuss-face: the contorted face characteristic of fussing, but without noise
suck: sucking or smacking of lips while there is nothing in the mouth
frown: the brow is furrowed
finger to mouth: B puts his fingers in his mouth
extrude: food is extruded from the mouth
defecate: recognized by facial expression
stare: B apparently stares at something in his surroundings, other than mother's face
state 3–4 in Table III refers to a change from state 3 (drowsy) to state 4 (alert)
general head: gross movements of head
general limb: gross movements of limbs
avert: B averts his head from an offered teat or nipple

17 Observations on the Developing Relationship between Mother and Baby in the Neonatal Period

Judith Bernal Dunn and M. P. M. Richards

Introduction

During the past six years we have been engaged in a follow-up study of 77 mother–child pairs from birth to five years, in Cambridge, England. The study was planned to assess individual differences in babies during the neonatal period, to describe early interactions between mothers and babies, and to look for continuities in both individual differences in the children and in interaction patterns from birth to five years. In this present paper we describe our observations of interaction in the first ten days of life, the period during which the initial adaptation of mother and child takes place.

Though there has been an increasing interest in observational studies of mothers and babies in recent years, relatively little work has been done in the neonatal period since the pioneering studies of Levy (1958). With the notable exception of the research by Sander and his group (e.g. Sander *et al.*, 1970), the few studies carried out in this early period look at interaction at a single point in time. Given that the mutual adaptation of mother and child takes place very rapidly, as we shall show below, such studies may give a rather misleading picture.

However, despite the relative lack of studies of this stage in the life cycle there is wide, theoretical acknowledgement of its importance; indeed some have gone as far as claiming that it represents a sensitive period during which a special relationship is formed between mother and baby (Kennell *et al.*, 1974). Though evidence for this extreme position is unconvincing (Dunn, 1975), any view that places emphasis on the interaction of mother (or any adult) and child must examine the early stages of the relationship.

There are practical reasons too for emphasis on the early phases of the relationship. For some medical and social purposes it may be useful to be able to predict the future course of a particular relationship. As there is almost always close medical supervision during the neonatal period, it would be valuable if predictive measures could be evolved for application at this time. The first step in the construction of such measures is the description of behaviour during the neonatal period. We need to know something of the extent of individual variation, factors that correlate with variation, and the degree to which an individual pair's behaviour is consistent from day to day and across different situations.

Existing data come predominantly from the study of American middle-class mothers in hospitals. We are attempting to extend the basic data by describing what happens in another country for a group of wide social background, and who unlike those in other studies were delivered at home by midwives. At the time when our data were collected about half the babies in Cambridge were delivered at home.

More specifically this paper is concerned with seven main points.

(1) *A general description of the patterning of mother and baby behaviour during feeds*. We do not place particular theoretical importance on feeding but all early interactions are organized around this activity and a mother's relative failure or success in feeding may colour much of her early behaviour with a baby. Our observations begin when a baby was picked up for a feed, and continue until the baby was back in the cot. Therefore activities such as burping and changing as well as such playful contact that may have occurred are included. However, we have concentrated on the analysis of the feeds themselves so that we have data that are comparable with previous work (e.g. Levy, 1958; Thoman *et al.*, 1972; Sander *et al.*, 1970).

(2) *Changes over the first ten days in maternal behaviour.* The first ten days represent the initial period of adaptation of mother and child and the period during which the mother (in Britain) is supervised by a midwife. We felt that it was important to describe changes over this period because without this knowledge it would be impossible to gauge the relevance of observations made at a single time or to choose a satisfactory time to use any potential assessment measure.

(3) *Co-ordination and smoothness of the feed interaction.* By attending to these aspects of the feeding situation we hope to be able to provide some objective measures of the success or failure of feeding, paralleling the analysis of Burns *et al.* (1972) and Levy (1958). Given that mutual co-ordination is much discussed as a desirable characteristic of later mother–child relationships (e.g. Ainsworth and Bell, 1961), it is important to have such measures from the earliest interactions for predictive purposes. Though mutual co-ordination may not be consistent across all caretaking and play situations we cannot test this until measures and indices are available from the relevant social contexts.

(4) *The influence of pregnancy and delivery factors on early interaction patterns.* It has long been known that some pregnancy and delivery factors correlate with the state of the baby in the newborn period (Sameroff and Chandler, 1975). As an interaction is the product of what the participants bring to the common situation, the course of the mother–child relationship will be influenced by the state of both mother and child (Bell, 1968). Indeed it has now been directly shown that the rating on the Brazelton Neonatal Scale (Brazelton, 1974) correlates with mother–child behaviour in a feeding situation (Osofsky and Danzger, 1974).

Among the many perinatal factors that have begun to be studied in recent years are obstetric anaesthetic and analgesic drugs (reviews by Bowes *et al.*, 1970; Aleksandrowicz, 1974). Some years ago Brazelton (1961) on the basis of mothers' reports showed that some drugs were related to difficulties in feeding, and more recently laboratory measures of nutritive sucking and feed intake have been found to be affected (Kron *et al.*, 1966; Dubignon *et al.*, 1969). The whole topic is very complex because drug effects are likely to interact with other aspects of the maternal and infant physiological and behaviour status and so may have widely different effects in varying situations. Also there has been a tendency among developmental psychologists to treat "maternal medication" as if it were a single unitary variable rather than a very heterogenous collection of compounds that are known to have differing effects on the foetus and infant (Anon, 1974).

In view of the potential importance of this topic and the paucity of well controlled studies it seems essential that the data from all studies of early mother–child interaction should be analysed in terms of the drugs that mothers received at delivery and other relevant perinatal factors.

(5) *Maternal affection.* In much general writing about mother–child relationships descriptive labels such as "good" or "sensitive" are often employed for mothers. Such evaluations are justified in one of two ways: it is assumed either that mothers with the desirable characteristics tend to have children with the same approved attributes or that the mothers show behaviour patterns that generally receive positive evaluation (e.g. kissing or talking to babies). Clearly there is no general agreement about what are the most desirable traits for an adult to possess and we are still very far from being able to specify which aspects of maternal behaviour are likely to foster particular traits. So beyond being fairly confident in asserting that a few aspects of parental behaviour are damaging for children (e.g. violence and other forms of abuse) we have no grounds for evaluating maternal behaviour in terms of its outcome in child characteristics. The other approach to evaluation rests on the face validity of various behaviour patterns as being indices of affection, or on measures of mutual adaptiveness (which is presumed to be good). Given the widespread use of evaluative terms for maternal behaviour, we felt it was important to see if a number of categories of behaviour that have been used as indices of affection did indeed intercorrelate.

(6) *Feeding methods.* Despite a longstanding interest in the consequences of different methods of infant feeding (e.g. Caldwell, 1964) almost no data are available on the extent to which interaction patterns might vary with breast or bottle-feeding. Given that our sample divided fairly evenly between the two methods, we are able to make this comparison.

(7) *Birth order effects.* These effects are well known in almost every aspect of adult behaviour (e.g. Zajonc and Markus, 1975) and there has been speculation about the genesis of such effects in mother–child interaction patterns. However, again, this tends to be a variable that is "controlled for" rather than investigated in studies of early interaction, though there are exceptions (Thoman *et al.*, 1971). Given that few women in our culture have much experience of handling young children before they have their own, it would hardly be surprising if there were marked

changes in behaviour as experience is gained. However, until such changes are described we are not able to begin to assess theories that link parity effects in children with differing maternal behaviour.

Methods

THE SAMPLE

Our sample was recruited with the help of District Midwives from the total population of those booked to deliver at home. Booking for home delivery takes place after a mother has been screened medically, and ideally all cases where there is thought to be any risk of complications are booked for hospital delivery. About half the total population were delivered at home at the time of this study (1967–1970). We exercised rather stricter selection criteria than those used for home booking. Ours were based on about 35 maternal, foetal or delivery factors which have been shown to be related to perinatal morbidity or mortality (Butler and Bonham, 1963; Prechtl, 1968). The parity status, method of feeding and social class distribution (based on husband's occupation, Registrar General 1970) are shown in Table I for the mother–baby pairs that make up the sample.

Mothers were approached late in pregnancy after being selected on the basis of their medical records. Less than 5% refused to take part in the study. All deliveries were spontaneous, with vertex presentation of a full term (± one week) infant.

In the results reported in this paper there are minor variations in the sample size. This is because information for the whole sample is not available for all measures and also because all cases cannot be categorized into the groups used in the analysis (e.g. in the analysis of breast-fed/bottle-fed differences we omit those babies who were only partially breast-fed or whose mothers changed to bottle-feeding during the first ten days).

PROCEDURES

An outline of the relevant parts of the study is given in Table II.

Prenatal visit. At the initial visit the project was described to the mother and an interview covering sociological questions, such as the

Table I

Composition of the sample (N = 77)

Social class	Boys				Girls			
	1st born		2nd born		1st born		2nd born	
	Breast-fed	Bottle-fed	Breast-fed	Bottle-fed	Breast-fed	Bottle-fed	Breast-fed	Bottle-fed
I and II	3(1)	1	9(1)	5	4	4	7	1
III (white collar)	1(1)		3	2	1	1	3	1
III (manual)	4		4(2)	5	2(1)	2	5(2)	8
IV	1			1	1		2	1
	9	1	16	13	8	2	17	11

Figures in brackets, in the breast-feeding columns, show the number of mothers who changed from breast-feeding to bottle-feeding during the first ten days.

Table II

Outline of procedures used in the first eight weeks

2–6 weeks before delivery	Interview of mother.
Delivery	Precoded medical information collected by midwife. Observation of first mother–infant interaction (when observer present).
Days 2, 3, 8, 9, 10	Observation of a feeding session. Collection of attitude and interview information.
Days 0–10	Continuous diary kept by mother of baby's time spent in cot, feeding, crying, bathing, out of cot.
Day 8 or 9	Neurological examination, sucking test (Waldrop and Bell, 1966).
8 weeks. 2 visits	Observation of a feeding session and two non-feeding baby awake periods. 48-hour diary kept by mother.

education and occupation of mother, father and grandparents, on the contact between various members of the family, and medical data on this and previous pregnancies was held. Attitudes and intentions about feeding and scheduling were explored.

Delivery. In a few cases one of the two observers was present at delivery. When an observer was not present, the midwife recorded some basic medical data on a precoded form. This covered the duration of the various stages of labour, drugs given to the mother, and the state of the infant at birth. The start of labour was defined by the method used by the midwives, that is the beginning of regular contractions.

Feeding observations. A full description and explanation of the observational categories is given in Richards and Bernal (1972). During a pilot phase 60 mother–infant pairs were observed for a total of about 200 hours. Based on this work, a 30-second time-grid for the observations was developed in which the occurrence or absence of each behavioural category within each 30-second period was recorded. Our categories are of three types, descriptive (e.g. mother talks to infant, infant sneezes), locational (e.g. position of infant relative to mother), and by outcome (mother stimulates infant to suck), or more accurately, by inferred intended outcome. Table III gives a list of the categories.

Reliability checks showed that agreement between the two observers (the authors) was better than 75% for each of the categories. Recording was done on duplicated sheets: symbols for each category are written in columns which are divided by cross lines corresponding to each

Table III

Some behavioural categories used in observing mother–infant interaction

MOTHER	INFANT
Rubs or pats infant.	Nipple in mouth.
Kisses infant.	Arms free (not swaddled, can touch own face).
Rocks infant.	Cries.
Changes nappies.	Fusses.
Stimulates infant to suck (e.g. by rubbing cheek or feet).	Burps.
Touches infant on bare skin.	Chokes.
Walks, carrying infant.	Sneezes.
Talks to infant.	Vomits.
Talks to another person.	Hiccups.
Looks at anything other than infant.	
Leaves room.	
Smiles at infant (and within three feet of infant's face).	

N.B.: a subdivision of "talking to infant" was "affectionate talking": talking that occurred in intervals when mother not stimulating the baby to suck, or rubbing to "burp" him, not concerned with the course of the feed.

INFANT POSITION	INFANT STATE
Cradled	1. Eyes closed, regular respiration, no movement.
shoulder	2. Eyes closed, irregular respiration, no gross movements.
sitting	3. Eyes open, no gross movements.
lying	4. Eyes open, gross movements, no crying.
	5. Eyes open, gross movements, crying.
	6. Not observable.
	7. Sucking.

30-second interval. During recording an electronic interval timer was used which gives a sound pulse in the observer's ear every 30 seconds. Anything the mother said to the baby was recorded on the margin of the observation sheet.

An observation began with the first attempt to get the baby to start sucking and ended when he was replaced in the cot; it included nappy changing and playful interaction but not bathing. The length of the observations varied. The mean length for days 2 and 3 was 20 minutes (S.D. 16 min) and for days 8 to 10 was 24 minutes (S.D. 15 min).

ASSESSMENT OF THE INFANT

Two techniques were used to assess the infant's behaviour when it was not interacting with the mother: a neurological examination (Prechtl and Beintema, 1964) and an assessment of sucking behaviour (Waldrop and Bell, 1966). We wished to assess individual characteristics that were likely to influence the style of interaction with the mother and the course of development of the infant, but until there has been much more analysis of mother–infant interaction it is impossible to specify these characteristics. As feeding is such a central issue in the post partum period for the mother, the sucking behaviour of her infant is likely to affect their interaction. The pattern of sucking behaviour is known to have wide individual variation but to show relative consistency for one infant (Halverson, 1938; Balint, 1948; Kron *et al.*, 1967; Wolff, 1968). It was assessed by the method of Waldrop and Bell (1966) during the neurological examination. A sterile teat was placed in the infant's mouth for four minutes and the number of sucks per group was recorded for each minute. After removal, the latency to the first flexion of the knee and to the first cry and the amount of crying in the following 90 seconds were noted.

DIARY

In order to study the interaction between mother and baby on a broader time scale into which the detailed observations could be set, mothers were asked to keep a continuous diary record during the first ten days. They were given paper with time periods marked out with five-minute time intervals and instructions on how to fill in categories of time spent in cot, time feeding, time bathed or changed, time crying in or out of cot, and time held or carried.

EIGHT-WEEK VISIT

This paper is concerned with the first ten-day period post partum, and analysis of the observations made later during the first year are published elsewhere (e.g. Dunn, 1975). However, results from the visit made at eight weeks are mentioned here in the context of the differences found between breast-feeding and bottle-feeding mother–infant pairs, since continuity in the early differences is of obvious interest. At the eight-week visits a feed was observed during which the methods of observations were identical to those of the first ten days.

Results

1. GENERAL DESCRIPTION OF THE PATTERNING OF INTERACTION DURING FEEDING PERIODS

Among the feeds we observed there was a great range and variation in smoothness of co-ordination and in style of caretaking. There were also some interesting changes in the patterning of the feeds over the first ten days. In the following sections we will discuss some aspects of patterning of mother and baby behaviour that emerged from the sample as a whole, and then examine some of the factors contributing to the range and variation we found. All significance values reported are two-tailed.

(a) *Analysis of interaction during feeding periods in the first ten days*. Looking first at the results for the summed information from the five feeding periods observed (days 2, 3, 8, 9, 10), Fig. 1 gives some measures of maternal behaviour. Many of the maternal behaviours happened relatively rarely, and the standard deviations were large. Table IV shows how the patterning of these was related to the baby's activity. A Wilcoxon T test was used to compare the probability of each mother activity occurring in conjunction with the different baby activities. Mothers were least likely to talk to the baby when he was sucking. Talking, then, was mostly concerned with urging the baby on when the feed was not going well. This was confirmed by an examination of what the mothers said: the most frequently used phrase was "Come on!". However, there were marked differences among mothers in the amount of "affectionate" talking, unrelated to the course of the feed, that occurred. This was defined to include any talking that occurred in an interval when the mother was not stimulating the baby to suck, or rubbing to "wind" him. This talking was often a comment on the baby's face, grimaces, sounds, etc. In Section (e) below the relationship between this measure of "affectionate" talking and other aspects of the mothers' behaviour is discussed.

Touching and looking at the baby were also patterned with his

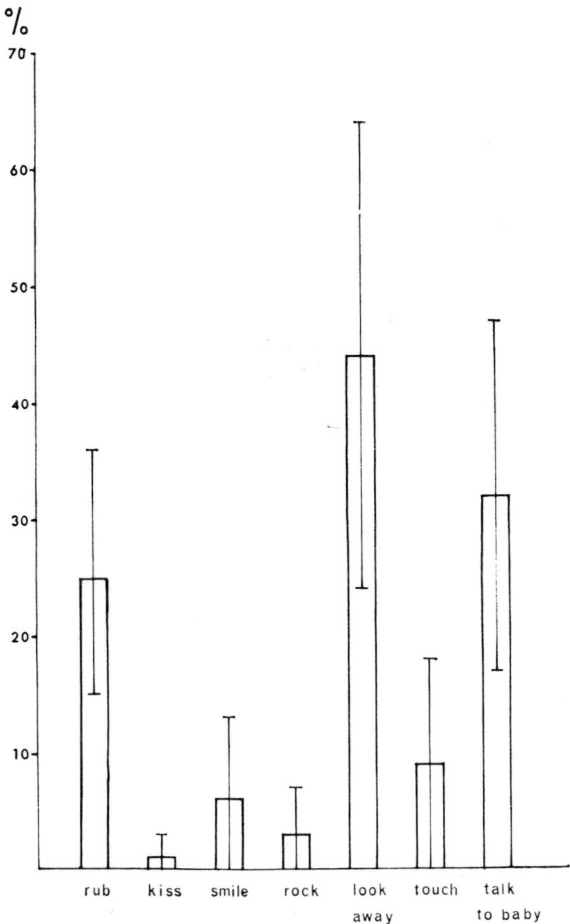

Fig. 1. Measures of maternal behaviour during feeds: mean values and standard deviation for the % of observation intervals in which the behaviours occurred. (All feeds summed.)

activity (Table IV). A mother was most likely to look at the baby if he was on the nipple but not sucking, and most likely to look away during the intervals between sucking bouts. Touching on the other hand was equally likely during sucking or intervals between the sucking bouts, but very unlikely when the baby was on the nipple but not sucking.

(b) *Changes over the first ten days in mothers' behaviour.* The patterns of maternal behaviour showed some changes from days 2 and 3 to the later days. Table V shows the analysis by Wilcoxon T test of the changes in individual mothers' behaviour from days 2 and 3 to days 8 to 10.

Table IV

Pattern of maternal activity during feeds related to infant activity
(Data summed from all feeds observed in first ten days)

(a) PROBABILITY OF MOTHER TALKING		
If baby sucking vs. if baby on nipple not sucking	0·20 vs. 0·55	$p < 0{\cdot}01$
If baby sucking vs. interval between bouts of sucking	0·20 vs. 0·43	$p < 0{\cdot}01$
If baby on nipple not sucking vs. interval between bouts of sucking	0·55 vs. 0·42	$p < 0{\cdot}01$
(b) PROBABILITY OF MOTHER LOOKING AWAY		
If baby sucking vs. if baby on nipple not sucking	0·33 vs. 0·11	$p < 0{\cdot}01$
If baby sucking vs. interval between bouts of sucking	0·33 vs. 0·44	$p < 0{\cdot}05$
If baby on nipple not sucking vs. interval between bouts of sucking	0·11 vs. 0·44	$p < 0{\cdot}01$
(c) PROBABILITY OF MOTHER TOUCHING		
If baby sucking vs. if baby on nipple not sucking	0·08 vs. 0·01	$p < 0{\cdot}01$
If baby sucking vs. interval between bouts of sucking	0·08 vs. 0·07	N.S.
If baby on nipple not sucking vs. interval between bouts of sucking	0·01 vs. 0·07	$p < 0{\cdot}01$

Wilcoxon T test, N = 68.

Table V

Changes in maternal behaviour from days 2 and 3 to days 8 to 10

	Number of 30-sec observation intervals (mean)			% of observation intervals (mean)		
	Days 2+3	Days 8 to 10	p	Days 2+3	Days 8 to 10	p
Length of observation (= whole of feed period)	40	48	< 0·01	—	—	
Mother rub baby to "wind" him	10	13	< 0·01	24	25	N.S.
Mother stimulate baby to suck	5	4	N.S.	11	8	< 0·01
Mother touch baby	3	4	N.S.	8	9	N.S.
Mother look away from baby	22	27	< 0·01	56	57	N.S.
Mother smile at baby	3	2	N.S.	6	5	< 0·05
Baby on nipple	20	27	< 0·01	52	59	N.S.
Mother alone	18	29	< 0·01	39	60	< 0·01

Wilcoxon T test, N = 49.

Scores are expressed both as absolute numbers of observation intervals and as percentage of observation period; (since the latter is based on the feed period it is variable in length, and is determined by the mother and/or the baby rather than the observer). We have presented the results in this way because both the absolute and the relative frequency of measures may be relevant: from the baby's point of view the absolute frequency of maternal activities could be very important, while changes in the percentage occurrences may reflect interesting differences between mothers. While there was no significant change in the number of observation periods during which a mother smiled at her baby during a feed, there was a relative decrease in smiles per observation period. Mothers looked away from their babies more during the later feeds, though not for a significantly greater proportion of the observation period. They rubbed their babies more during the longer observation periods on the later days, though again not for a significantly greater proportion of the time. Although mothers were more often alone with the baby at the later feeds there was no significant change in the absolute nor in the proportion of intervals during which they talked to their babies. There were, however, some changes in the patterning of the talking: on days 8 to 10, mothers were much less likely to talk to their baby during intervals when the baby was sucking (probability of mother talking when baby sucking on days 2 and 3 $= 0{\cdot}25$, on days 8 to 10 $= 0{\cdot}10$, $p < 0{\cdot}01$ Wilcoxon T test). They were more likely to look away from the baby during sucking intervals than in the early feeds (probability of mother looking away when baby sucking on days 2 and 3 $= 0{\cdot}27$, on days 8 to 10 $= 0{\cdot}40$, $p < 0{\cdot}02$ Wilcoxon T test).

(c) *Changes in the co-ordination of the feed.* There were quite marked changes in the smoothness and "success" of feeds over the first ten days.

In Fig. 2 some of these changes can be seen (analysed by the Mann-Whitney U-test). There is an increase in the time for which the baby was sucking, and a decrease in measures reflecting difficulty such as the number of intervals when the nipple left the baby's mouth, or those when the nipple was in but the baby not sucking. Another measure used to assess the relative smoothness of the feed was the ratio of the number of times the nipple left the baby's mouth to the number of intervals when the nipple was in the baby's mouth. This ratio showed a significant decrease over the first ten days. Attempts to stimulate the baby to suck, or changes in his position while the nipple was in his mouth also decrease.

Table VI

The relationship between measures reflecting difficulty during feeds, labour length, and latency to cry in sucking test

	M. stim.	M. change pos. B.	Ratio nip. out/in	Total sucking	B. on nip. not sucking	Latency to cry
Mother stimulates baby to suck						
Mother changes position of baby in intervals when baby on nipple	0·15					
Ratio of times nipple comes out of baby's mouth to intervals when nipple in	0·16	0·44[b]				
Total sucking during feeds	0·10	−0·40[b]	−0·38[b]			
Baby on nipple, not sucking	0·42[b]	0·36[b]	0·34[b]	−0·20[a]		
Latency to cry on removal of teat (sucking test)	0·02	0·10	0·01	−0·22[a]	0·09	
Labour length	0·26[b]	0·19[a]	0·06	0·11	0·20[a]	0·07

Kendall rho, N varies between 60 and 70. [a] $p < 0{\cdot}05$. [b] $p < 0{\cdot}01$.

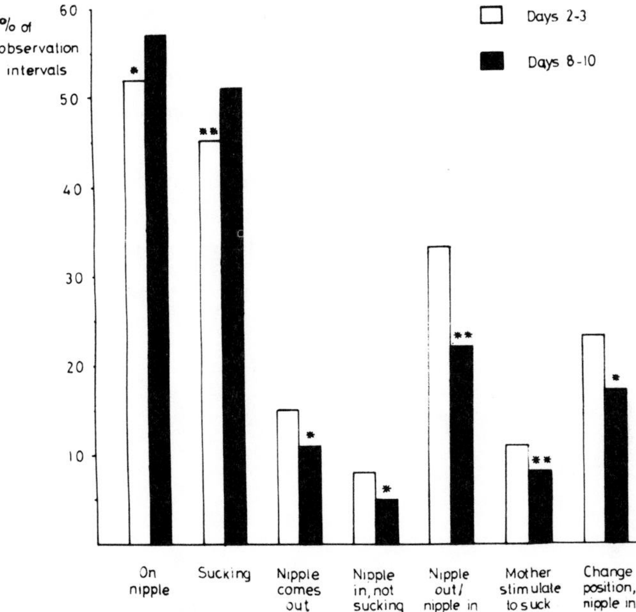

Fig. 2. Changes in the course of feeds over the first ten days. (Mann-Whitney U-test) * $p < 0{\cdot}05$, ** $p < 0{\cdot}01$.

(d) *Influence of labour and delivery factors.* Table VI shows the correlations between various measures of difficulty during the feeds. In the lower half of the table the relationship between these measures of difficulty and labour length is shown and, in Table VII, the relationship with drugs administered in labour. For the drug analysis we divided the

Table VII

Effects of medication (Pethilorfan): Measures from feeds on days 8–10 (% of observation intervals)

	No Pethilorfan N = 21	Pethilorfan N = 43	
Mother stimulates baby to suck	3·0	4·3	$p < 0{\cdot}05$
Mother changes baby's position	10·7	13·2	$p < 0{\cdot}05$
Mother talks to baby	12·8	15·2	$p < 0{\cdot}05$
Nipple comes out of baby's mouth	4·3	5·5	$p < 0{\cdot}10$

Mann-Whitney U-test, N = 64.

sample into those mothers who received Pethilorfan (meperidine (Demerol) + Levallorphan, doses range from 50–220 mgm) and those who received inhalent anaesthetic alone. In addition to these compounds a few mothers in both groups received a trichloroethanol sedative.

With a longer labour there is a heightened chance of feeds not going well. The measure of time to first cry also shows an association with difficulty in the feeds. Some of these findings are illustrated in Fig 3. They are as strong on days 8 to 10 as in the observations on days 2 and 3.

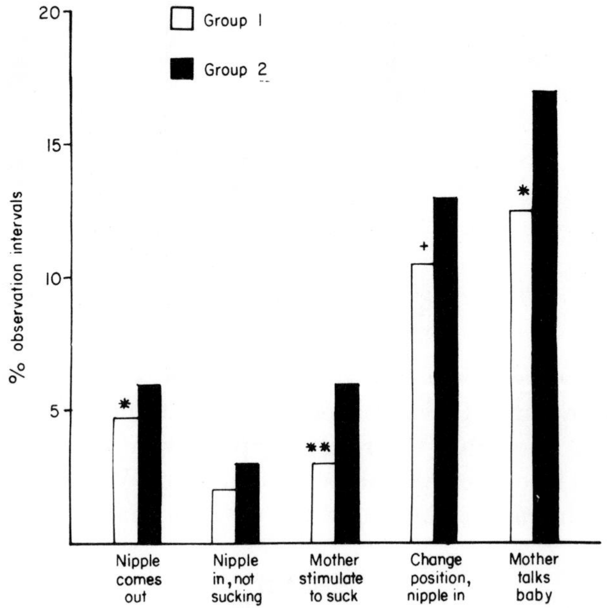

Fig. 3. Relationship between the course of feeds and the time the baby took to its first cry at birth. Group 1: Time to first cry under one minute. Group 2: Time to first cry one minute and above. Mann-Whitney U-test. * $p < 0{\cdot}05$, ** $p < 0{\cdot}01$.

When the relationship between length of labour and maternal medication was examined it was found that there was no significant difference in the length of labour of those who received Pethilorfan and those who received inhalent analgesia alone. However, when the "drug" group was divided into:

(a) those who received more than 100 mgm Pethilorfan (Group A, N = 15);

(b) those who received 100 mgm or less (Group B, $N = 28$);
(c) those who received only inhalent anaesthesia (Group C, $N = 21$); it was found that Group A tended to have longer labours than Groups B or C. The statistic used for this analysis was Gamma (Goodman and Kruskal, 1963) and the interaction was significant at $p < 0{\cdot}05$ level.

Table VI also shows that there was a negative correlation between total sucking time and a measure of baby behaviour from the sucking test (Waldrop and Bell, 1966), the latency to cry on removal of the teat after four minutes sucking. This measure shows considerable individual stability from day to day during the newborn period, but it cannot be assumed that these differences between babies are independent of post-natal experience: measures on this test are, for instance, significantly different for bottle-fed and breast-fed babies. Breast-fed babies have a shorter latency to cry on removal of the teat (Kendall's rho $= 0{\cdot}26$, $N = 63$, $p < 0{\cdot}01$); they also have a higher rate of sucking (Kendall's rho $= 0{\cdot}28$, $N = 63$, $p < 0{\cdot}01$) (see Discussion below).

(e) *Relationships between maternal measures.* We look next at the relationships between different aspects of maternal behaviour. Table VIII shows that the correlations between affectionate talking to the baby, looking at the baby, and smiling at the baby are positive, but not high. It is interesting that the measures of affectionate talk, look, and smile, are positively correlated with a measure of baby behaviour from the sucking test (see above), suck rate. When a multiple regression analysis was done for each observation variable with the "background" variables (parity, sex, feed type (breast or bottle), labour and delivery factors, neurological and sucking test measures), it was found for the affectionate talk variable that the suck rate measure was of prime importance and accounted for 18% of the variance. This suggests that differences between babies in sucking behaviour are related to the affectionate behaviour shown by the mother during a feed. Analysis of breast- and bottle-feeding pairs separately showed that the relationship was significant for both feed types, though more strongly for the breast-fed (bottle-fed $r_s = 0{\cdot}60$, $N = 19$, $p < 0{\cdot}01$; breast-fed $r_s = 0{\cdot}61$, $N = 27$, $p < 0{\cdot}001$). Table VIII also shows that the group of "affectionate" variables described above are not correlated with "touch". This was defined to include any touching of the baby not directly concerned with the course of the feed: that is, stimulating to

Table VIII

Relationship between interaction variables

	Mother touch B.	Mother smile B.	M. looks away	M. talks affect.	Time[a] spent in cot	Mean[a] length cry bout	Prob. cry[a] followed by feed
Mother touches baby							
Mother smiles at baby	0·09						
Mother looks away when alone	—0·12	—0·09					
Mother talks affectionately	0·03	0·18[b]	—0·20[b]				
Time spent in cot[a]	—0·14	—0·03	—0·01	—0·20[c]			
Mean length of cry bout[a]	—0·10	—0·04	—0·01	—0·18[b]	0·12		
Probability crying followed by feed[a]	0·02	—0·02	—0·06	—0·10	0·19[b]	0·37[c]	
Rate of sucking in sucking test	0·19[b]	0·35[c]	—0·03	0·34[c]	—0·20[b]	—0·06	—0·09

[a] The measures marked thus come from the diaries kept by the mothers, not from direct observation (see Bernal, 1972).
Kendall rho, N varies between 60 and 70. [b] $p < 0{\cdot}05$. [c] $p < 0{\cdot}01$.

suck or rubbing or patting to "burp" the baby. There is also not a close relationship with the measure, derived from the diaries, of the mothers' response to crying (probability fed if crying, and mean length of cry bout), apart from a negative correlation between mean length of cry bout with affectionate talking. This may in part reflect the possible unreliability of the crying data for this period. On the other hand neither a rating from the prenatal interview of the mother's attitude to scheduling (Bernal, 1972) nor an assessment of the actual scheduling of feeds observed showed a relationship to the affectionate measure.

2. DIFFERENCES IN INTERACTION BETWEEN BREAST-FEEDING AND BOTTLE-FEEDING SITUATIONS

The analysis of feed-type differences in interaction was done on second babies only, as there were very few first babies who were bottle-fed during the first ten days.

When the observations of feeds from five days were summed, a number of differences in interaction between breast-feeding and bottle-feeding pairs were found; it is most illuminating, however, to look separately at the observations from days 2 and 3 and those from the end of the first ten days. As breast-fed babies will be getting very little milk in the early days it is possible that the summed ten-day differences are the result of large differences on days 2 and 3 which have disappeared by the end of the week when both groups are getting comparable amounts of milk.

From Table IX it can be seen that on days 2 and 3 there are no significant differences in the number of intervals on the nipple, or sucking. But by days 8 to 10 the breast-fed babies are on the nipple longer and are sucking for longer. There are differences on days 2 and 3 in bout length of sucking, with breast-fed babies sucking for fewer longer bouts, and these differences are as strong on the later days. By days 8 to 10 there are interesting differences in responsibility for ending the bouts of sucking: in the bottle-feeding situation the mother is, in the great majority of instances, responsible for ending the sucking bout by removing the bottle teat, while in the breast-feeding situation it is equally likely to be the baby or the mother. There is a tendency for the breast-feeding mothers to kiss, rock and touch their babies more.

The differences between the two groups in touching is particularly great on the later days, during sucking and "on the nipple" intervals,

Table IX

Breast/bottle-fed differences: changes over first ten days (% of observation intervals)

	Days 2+3 (N = 35)			Days 8 to 10 (N = 35)		
	Bottle-fed	Breast-fed		Bottle-fed	Breast-fed	
Baby on nipple	48·0	53·9	N.S.	48·9	61·6	$p < 0{\cdot}05$
Baby sucking	39·0	49·2	N.S.	43·7	56·8	$p < 0{\cdot}05$
Mean length bout sucking	5·1	8·1	$p < 0{\cdot}02$	6·2	10·1	$p < 0{\cdot}05$
Mother touch	3·9	5·6	N.S.	4·4	10·3	$p < 0{\cdot}05$
Sib. present	30·1	18·3	N.S.	48·9	36·7	N.S.
Mother alone	34·3	48·4	N.S.	45·5	56·8	N.S.
Nipple leaves baby's mouth:						
% occasions mother responsible	78	55	$p < 0{\cdot}1$	82	48	$p < 0{\cdot}01$
% occasions baby responsible	7	35	$p < 0{\cdot}05$	5	41	$p < 0{\cdot}01$
Prob. M. touch if baby sucking	0·02	0·09	$p < 0{\cdot}1$	0·02	0·12	$p < 0{\cdot}01$
Prob. M. talk if gap	0·30	0·47	$p < 0{\cdot}05$	0·36	0·49	$p < 0{\cdot}05$

Mann-Whitney U-test.

and this reflects a great increase in the amount of touching by breast-feeding mothers during the babies' sucking. There are differences, in the two groups, in the patterning of mothers talking, as well as in touching the baby. Breast-feeding mothers are more likely to talk during the gaps between sucking bouts. Breast-feeding mothers are more likely to talk "affectionately" to their babies (Kendall's rho $= 0{\cdot}24$, $N = 68$, $p < 0{\cdot}01$).

Table X gives the differences between the two groups in interaction during a feed when the babies were eight weeks old. The differences in responsibility for ending bouts of sucking are still large, though the differences in lengths of sucking bouts are now not significant. Breast-feeding mothers still kiss, touch and smile at their babies significantly more, and the pattern of touching while the baby sucks remains.

Table X

Feed observation at eight weeks: Breast/bottle-fed differences in % of observation intervals

	Bottle-fed	Breast-fed	
Mother kiss	1	4	$p < 0{\cdot}05$
Mother stimulate	6	1	$p < 0{\cdot}1$
Mother touch	4	11	$p < 0{\cdot}01$
Mother smile	5	9	$p < 0{\cdot}05$
Mother responsible nipple out	87	23	$p < 0{\cdot}01$
Baby responsible nipple out	7	66	$p < 0{\cdot}01$
Mother touch if baby sucking	3	14	$p < 0{\cdot}01$

Mann-Whitney U-test, N = 45.

3. BIRTH ORDER EFFECTS

For the analysis of birth-order effects breast-fed babies only were taken, as there were very few bottle-fed first babies. When the results from the five observed feeds were summed, a number of parity differences were apparent (analysis by Mann-Whitney U-test). However, when the analysis was done separately for the days 2 and 3, and for the days 8 to 10, the parity differences with two exceptions disappeared by the end of the first week (Table XI).

On days 2 and 3, first mothers stimulated their babies to suck more, they looked away from their babies less and spent less time rubbing

Table XI

Parity differences in changes over days: % of observation intervals

	Days 2+3			Days 8–10		
	1st born	2nd born		1st born	2nd born	
Mother rubbing	12	28	$p < 0{\cdot}01$	21	24	$p < 0{\cdot}01$
Mother stimulate	22	7	$p < 0{\cdot}01$	9	9	N.S.
Mother look away	37	57	$p < 0{\cdot}05$	44	63	$p < 0{\cdot}01$
Midwife stimulate	6	0	$p < 0{\cdot}01$	0	0	N.S.
Mother alone, look away	31	46	N.S.	40	52	$p < 0{\cdot}1$

their babies to "burp" them. Their babies were less likely to be asleep when replaced in the cot at the end of the feed. The difference in number of intervals looking at the baby is in part accounted for by the presence of the elder sibling in many of the feeds for the second mother. However, when the proportion of time alone spent looking away from the baby was compared for the two groups, the difference was in the same direction.

Discussion

(a) INFLUENCE OF LABOUR AND DELIVERY FACTORS

Labour and delivery factors could be related to later differences in interaction in at least four ways. A difficult labour could lead to altered post-natal behaviour in the baby, or in the mother, or in both; it could also reflect some characteristic of the mother which independently influences her interaction with the baby later. Correlations with interaction measures from the first week such as those reported here cannot be interpreted as reflecting the effects of a difficult delivery on either the mother or the baby alone. However, the results of studies on drugs effects on babies (Aleksandrowicz, 1974; Bowes *et al.*, 1970) make it very unlikely that the correlations with medication are solely due to the effects on the mother.

The correlation between labour length and the higher dosage level of drugs could arise in a number of different ways. The drugs themselves might have an effect on labour length, either by changing the mother's psychological state, or by altering the processes controlling uterine contractions, or the correlation could arise simply because with a longer labour the mother is exposed to the possibility of being given drugs for a longer time. Caution should be exercised in generalizing from or comparing our results on medication with other studies for two reasons. Firstly, the conditions under which the drugs are administered will be very different in other studies, and secondly the compounds administered vary very much from study to study. In Kraemer *et al.*'s (1972) sample, for instance, only 7% of the subjects received Demerol (Pethidine) alone. It is important not to use "maternal medication" as a single variable comparable from study to study.

It is to be noted that the labour and delivery findings on the course of the feed fit with the studies of Dubignon *et al.* (1969), showing that nutritive sucking is affected by perinatal factors but that non-nutritive sucking rates are not. Labour and delivery factors were not correlated with differences in non-nutritive sucking rates as measured in the sucking test.

(b) RELATIONSHIP BETWEEN MATERNAL MEASURES

The analysis of these early feeding interactions for the sample as a whole raises two important points.

First, measures of maternal affectionate behaviour during this period do not covary in any simple way. There is no unitary measure reflecting "warm" mothering. The different aspects of maternal style are associated with different infant and delivery factors: success and co-ordination of the feed, for example, are affected by labour and delivery factors; total sucking, for instance, is correlated with baby differences in reactivity (latency to cry on removal of teat) and not with the measure of affectionate style and contact found here. "Touching" the baby, a variable that Levy (1958) considers to reflect maternal feeling in an important way, was not correlated with the other "affectionate" measures.

The second point raised by these findings is the importance of the baby as contributor to the early differences in mother–child interaction. It can be argued that the baby's responses in the sucking test on the eighth day are not independent of maternal treatment from birth, and that those babies who in the test react quickly to removal of the teat, or who have a lively rate of sucking, may well have been importantly influenced by their mother's style of response since birth. Whatever the origins of the baby differences, the possibility that these differences may contribute to further differences in later interaction is real. In this context correlations between the feed-type differences and the sucking test measures should be commented on. It might be thought that the associations between the sucking test measures and interaction measures were secondary to the feed-type differences in interaction. However, the multiple regression analysis showed that it was suck rate, not feed-type, that was of prime importance in accounting for the variance in affectionate talking and in total sucking.

There are a number of different possible explanations for the feed-type differences in the sucking test measures. The breast-fed babies may have sucked differently and reacted more quickly to removal of the teat because they were hungrier than the bottle-fed babies (analysis of crying behaviour and inter-feed intervals suggested that this may well have been the case (Bernal, 1972; Bell *et al.*, 1971 offered this explanation for their similar findings). Breast- and bottle-fed babies may have developed different sucking patterns as a result of the different sucking experience they have had since birth. Certainly the experience of sucking a rubber teat in the test was a novel one for many of the breast-fed babies.

Finally, the interpretation that the correlation between the sucking test measure of latency to cry and total sucking during the feeds is evidence for the importance of differences between babies' influence of the course of the feed would fit with Levy's (1958) findings. He showed that the state of arousal of the baby was of great importance in determining the course of interaction in the early feeds. The study by Osofsky and Danzger (1974) also found that neonatal characteristics were importantly related to differences in early interaction. But in their studies, as in our own, the interpretation of the direction of these effects is problematic.

(c) DIFFERENCES IN INTERACTION BETWEEN THE BREAST-FEEDING AND BOTTLE-FEEDING SITUATIONS

Far from disappearing over the first week, as lactation is established, the differences in interaction between mother and baby in the breast-feeding and bottle-feeding groups generally increase, and many are apparent at eight weeks.

The fact that breast-feeding mothers are more often alone with the baby might be important in contributing to the increased amount of touching but could not explain the patterning effects, such as the great increase in touching during sucking in the breast-feeding group. It is possible that bottle-feeding mothers touch their babies less simply because they do not have a hand free to do so. This is unlikely to be the whole story, as in many cases the breast-feeding mothers stroke and caress the baby with the hand that is holding the baby, and often use their "free" hand to prevent the breast from occluding the baby's nostrils. We have no consistent record of which hand is "touching" the baby and which is holding the baby, so cannot resolve this with our data, but it is interesting that in Levy's description of feeds (Levy, 1958), in 25 out of 37 breast-feeds the "free" hand is on the breast and is used to jiggle the breast to stimulate the baby to suck.

We have seen that in the breast-feeding situation the baby takes a great part in determining the end of sucking bouts, and that the incidence of mothers talking to the baby and touching are more patterned by the baby's activity. In discussions of early communication it is sometimes suggested that interaction where the baby is allowed an important part in patterning the interaction, and where the mother times her response to fit with the baby's behaviour, provides the best base for the development of synchrony and reciprocal exchange.

We found no later differences in interaction patterns between breast-fed and bottle-fed babies. However, it may well be that a finer level of analysis than that used in the present study is needed to examine later interaction, and the method should be sensitive to the details of reciprocal exchange such as that of Stern (1974). Other follow-up studies comparing bottle-fed and breast-fed babies have used very crude measures of infant behaviour, or suffer from methodological deficiencies (Caldwell, 1964; Richards, 1973).

(d) BIRTH-ORDER EFFECTS

In a study of a feed on the second day after birth Thoman and colleagues (1972) found marked parity differences in both breast- and bottle-feeding situations. The results of the present study illustrate how quickly mother and baby adjust to each other in the early days, and suggest it would be a mistake to relate parity differences found in very early interaction in the feeding situation too directly to later parity differences in interaction. The differences in the results from the two studies may well reflect the different effects of hospital and home environments on the first mothers. The mothers in our study delivered their babies at home, they had been constantly with their babies from birth, they were in familiar surroundings with husband and family and were supported during the early feeds by skilful midwives who had cared for them throughout pregnancy and knew them well. These circumstances may well have minimized the parity differences and helped the rapid increase in smoothness of co-ordination between mother and baby.

There were nevertheless marked parity differences in other aspects of behaviour and interaction such as crying, and the mother's response to it (Bernal, 1972).

Conclusion

We would like to emphasize three main points of interest arising from this study.

(1) There are clear associations between individual differences in babies and differences in interaction over the first ten days. It would be conceptually mistaken to describe these baby differences as congenital differences in babies independent of maternal handling. Some of the possible post-natal origins of these differences have been discussed. It is also possible that these differences develop as a result of maternal effects operating during pregnancy. For example Ottinger and Simmons (1964) have shown that mothers scoring high on anxiety ratings during pregnancy have babies who cry more in the neonatal period. There is the possibility too that differences between foetuses give rise to some differences in the course of pregnancy. Any, or all, of these processes might explain the differences found in this study, and our evidence does not allow us to distinguish between them. In most studies of mother–child interaction measures of labour and delivery and of the state of the baby at birth are not taken, and so the literature contains a systematic bias in favour of maternal effects on the infant. It is to be hoped that our study at least demonstrates the importance of collecting such information in any investigations of mother–child interaction.

Whatever their origins, these differences between babies demonstrated on the eighth day may very well contribute to later differences in interaction.

(2) The rapid increase in co-ordination and adaptation shown in the interaction measures over the first ten days suggests it would be mistaken to make wide generalizations about the relationship between mother and baby on the basis of information gathered on a single day early in the post-natal period.

At present there is much interest in deriving measures of maternal behaviour from the neonatal period that would predict later clinical

problems, for example non-accidental injury. In view of our data, and for more general theoretical reasons, we are sceptical that such attempts are likely to be successful. However, we should note that this study is concerned with a "normal" group of mothers and babies, and it is possible that useful predictions might be made if one was dealing with a sample which included mothers, or babies, who showed very pathological styles of interaction, or situations where the usual pattern of contact between mother and baby was disrupted by external factors.
(3) A number of measures were used in this study which had face validity as reflecting maternal responsiveness or affection. Our analysis does not indicate that correlations between these measures are high, and argues against the idea of a unitary attribute of maternal responsiveness at this stage.

It should be noted that our study, like all other studies, relates to a specific social and cultural context. Very little is known about differences between populations in the sort of measures we have been discussing, and great caution should be used in generalizing these results.

Acknowledgements

This project was supported by a grant from the Nuffield Foundation. We would like to thank the Midwives of the City of Cambridge and the families in the sample.

References

Ainsworth, M. D. S. and Bell, S. M. (1961). Mother-infant interaction in the feeding situation. In A. Ambrose (Ed.), *Stimulation in Early Infancy*. Academic Press, London and New York.

Aleksandrowicz, M. K. (1974). The effect of pain-relieving drugs administered during labor and delivery on the behavior of the newborn. *Merrill-Palmer Q.* **20**, 121–141.

Anon. (1974). Obstetric analgesia and the newborn baby. *Lancet* **I**, 1090.

Balint, M. (1948). Individual differences of behaviour in early infancy and an objective method for recording them. *J. genet. Psychol.* **73**, 57–117.

Bell, R. Q. (1968). A re-interpretation of the direction of effects in studies of socialisation. *Psychol. Rev.* **75**, 81–95.

Bell, R. Q., Weller, G. M. and Waldrop, M. F. (1971). Newborn and preschooler:

Organisation of behavior and relations between periods. *Monogr. Soc. Res. Child Devel.* **36**, (1–2, Serial No. 142).

Bernal, J. (1972). Crying during the 1st 10 days of life and maternal responses. *Dev. Med. Child. Neurol.* **14**, 362–372.

Bowes, W. A., Brackbill, Y., Conway, E. and Steinschneider, A. (1970). The effects of obstetrical medication on fetus and infant. *Monogr. Soc. Res. Child Devel.* **35**, (Serial No. 137).

Brazelton, T. B. (1961). Effect of maternal medication on the neonate and his behavior. *J. Ped.* **58**, 513–518.

Brazelton, T. B. (1974). *Neonatal Behavioural Assessment Scale.* S.I.M.P./Heinemann Medical Books, London.

Butler, N. R. and Bonham, D. G. (1963). *Perinatal Mortality.* Livingstone, Edinburgh.

Burns, P., Sander, L. W., Stechler, G. and Julia, H. (1972). Distress in feeding. *J. Am. Acad. Child Psychiat.* **11**, 427–439.

Caldwell, S. M. (1964). The effects of infant care. In M. L. Hoffman and L. W. Hoffman (Eds), *Review of Child Development Research.* Russell Sage Foundation, New York.

Dubignon, J., Campbell, D., Curtis, M. and Partington, M. W. (1969). The relation between laboratory measures of sucking, food intake, and perinatal factors during the newborn period. *Child Dev.* **40**, 1107–1120.

Dunn, J. F. (1975). Consistency and change in styles of mothering. In M. O'Connor (Ed.), *Parent-Infant Interaction.* Elsevier, Amsterdam.

Goodman, L. A. and Kruskal, W. H. (1963). Measures of association for cross classifications. Part 3. *J. Am. Stat. Ass.* **58**, 310–364.

Halverson, H. M. (1938). Infant sucking and tensional behavior. *J. genet. Psychol.* **53**, 365–430.

Kennell, J. F., Jerauld, R., Wolfe, H., Chester, D., Kreger, N., McAlpine, W., Steffa, M. and Klaus, M. H. (1974). Maternal behaviour one year after early and extended post-partum contact. *Dev. Med. Child Neurol.* **16**, 172–179.

Kraemer, H. C., Korner, A. F. and Thoman, E. B. (1972). Methodological considerations in evaluating the influence of drugs used during labor and delivery on the behavior of the newborn. *Dev. Psychol.* **6**, 128–134.

Kron, R. E., Stein, M. and Goddard, K. E. (1966). Newborn sucking behavior affected by obstetric sedation. *Pediatrics* **37**, 1012–1016.

Kron, R. E., Stein, M., Goddard, K. E. and Phoenix, M. D. (1967). Effect of nutrient upon the sucking behavior of newborn infants. *Psychosom. Med.* **29**, 24–32.

Levy, D. (1958). *Behavioral Analysis.* Thomas, Springfield.

Osofsky, J. D. and Danzger, B. (1974). Relationships between neonatal characteristics and mother-infant interaction. *Dev. Psychol.* **10**, 124–130.

Ottinger, D. R. and Simmons, J. E. (1964). Behaviour of human neonates and prenatal maternal anxiety. *Psychol. Rep.* **14**, 391–394.

Prechtl, H. F. R. (1968). Neurological findings in newborn infants after pre- and paranatal complications. In J. H. P. Jonxis, H. K. A. Visser and J. A. Troekshra (Eds), *Aspects of Praematurity and Dysmaturity.* Stenfert Kroese N.V., Leiden.

Prechtl, H. F. R. and Beintema, D. (1964). *The Neurological Examination of the Full-term Newborn Infant.* S.I.M.P./Heinemann Medical Books, London.

Richards, M. P. M. (1973). Feeding and the early growth of the mother-child relationship. In N. Kretchmer, E. Rossi and F. Seveni (Eds), *Modern Problems in Pediatrics, No. 15. Milk and Lactation.* Karger, Basel.

Richards, M. P. M. and Bernal, J. F. (1972). An observational study of mother-infant interaction. In N. Blurton Jones (Ed.), *Ethological Studies of Child Behaviour.* Cambridge University Press, Cambridge.

Sameroff, A. J. and Chandler, M. J. (1975). Reproductive risk and the continuum of caretaking casualty. In F. D. Horowitz, M. Hetherington, S. Scarr-Salapatek and G. Siegel (Eds), *Review of Child Development Research, Vol. 4.* University of Chicago Press, Chicago.

Sander, L. W., Stechler, G., Burns, P. and Julia, H. (1970). Early mother-infant interaction and 24-hour patterns of activity and sleep. *J. Am. Acad. Child Psychiat.* **9**, 103–123.

Stern, D. N. (1974). Mother and infant at play: the dyadic interaction involving facial, vocal and gaze behaviors. In M. Lewis and L. A. Rosenblum (Eds), *The Effect of the Infant on its Caregiver.* Wiley, New York.

Thoman, E. B., Barnett, C. and Leiderman, P. (1971). Feeding behaviors of newborn infants as a function of parity of the mother. *Child Dev.* **42**, 1471–1483.

Thoman, E. B., Leiderman, H. P. and Olson, J. P. (1972). Neonate-mother interaction during breast-feeding. *Dev. Psychol.* **6**, 110–118.

Waldrop, M. F. and Bell, R. Q. (1966). Effects of family size and density on newborn characteristics. *Am. J. Orthopsychiat.* **36**, 544–550.

Wolff, P. H. (1968). The serial organisation of sucking in the young infant. *Pediatrics* **42**, 943–956.

Zajonc, R. B. and Markus, G. B. (1975). Birth order and intellectual development. *Psychol. Rev.* **82**, 74–88.

18 Patterns of Early Interaction: Continuities and Consequences

Judith Bernal Dunn

Introduction

It is a commonplace that looking for continuities in individual differences either in intellectual abilities or in personality of children over the first two years presents huge problems. It is less often stressed that there are difficulties involved in looking for continuities in the behaviour of mothers with children, or in patterns of interaction between mother and child from the early days. And yet these difficulties pose crucial problems, problems which must be faced before we can extrapolate from observations of interaction made early in the first year. There is a growing concern among clinicians now to find indices from the earliest interaction between mother and child (Brazelton *et al.*, 1974) which could predict those relationships which are most susceptible to later disturbances. But although Stern's (1971) work has shown that mutually unsatisfying early interaction between a mother and her three-month-old may be part of a continuing pattern of difficulty, difficulties of adjustment between mother and baby at one period cannot be assumed to reflect an underlying insensitivity on the mother's part from which continuing difficulties can be predicted. In our own study we found that over the first ten days difficulties of adjustment between mother and baby during feeds rapidly disappeared, and were more closely related to labour and delivery factors than to measures of maternal interest in the baby (Dunn and Richards, Chapter 17).

One of the obvious problems in looking for continuities in interaction style is that the significance of the details of the interaction clearly changes as the child develops. One way of coping with the changing significance of the fine-grain details of interaction over time might be to look for continuities in global categories such as "sensitivity" or "responsiveness". This use of global categories raises at least as many problems as it solves. The subjective element in categorizing mothers in these terms without careful analysis at the interaction level is obvious. Behavioural scientists have expended much energy in attempting to avoid such subjectivity by specifying behavioural items for description which are intended to be "objective", observer independent, and uninfluenced by the particular context in which they occur. The attractions of this are obvious, as are its overwhelming difficulties. It is hard in principle to employ such "non-contextual" measures of interaction to specify our notions of "sensitivity" and "responsiveness", even at *one* point in development, let alone *across* points in time where a child is changing dramatically. It might be plausible, for example, to describe as sensitive a mother who goes quickly to a crying baby after it has just woken from sleep and is hungry, but who leaves him to cry when he is overtired if she has learnt that he manages the transition to sleep more quickly after a few minutes of crying alone. But a firmly behavioural measure of latency to respond to crying would not on its own provide a useful index of this. Being sensitive to a particular child's needs and wishes means in common parlance behaving in an individually differentiated way to the child's particular behaviour in a particular context.

The opposite viewpoint to the "non-contextual" approach is one where the observer records not just the behavioural items but gives the fullest possible account of the context in which the item occurs; this approach leads to an individual description of what is happening between individuals and is inevitably difficult to code in a way that makes it directly comparable to descriptions of interactions between other individuals in other contexts.

One recent line of work on mother–infant interaction in the early months which manages to retain many of the advantages of both these strongly contrasted approaches is the analysis of synchrony based on film and video-tape. It is conceivable that other sensitive but rigorous observational indices of interactive success may be attainable for interaction between mothers and slightly older children; but *a priori* considerations suggest that they could be sustained for interchange between human beings who are both competent in language only by stipulative circularity. What are to be our criteria for interactive success when the children can talk?

These problems in looking for continuities in interaction patterns from the early weeks are emphasized here not because we can go on to say we have solved them; far from it. Rather, the problems are emphasized because they do present a major difficulty that has to be faced before we can judge how far what we describe when we observe mother–child interaction in the early weeks *matters*. How persistent will the individual differences in interaction patterns be beyond the early weeks? What developmental significance can be attributed to the differences in interactional style described? As one step in considering these questions I want to discuss some data from a longitudinal study of mother–child pairs (Richards and Bernal, 1972). In the study a group of 77 mothers and babies were visited at home during the children's first five years. Details of the study, the sample and the observational methods are given in Dunn and Richards (Chapter 17).

Interaction in the First Ten Days

We have described elsewhere how our observations in the first ten days did not provide evidence for a simple unitary measure of maternal affectionate interest or warmth (Dunn and Richards, Chapter 17; Dunn, 1975); measures of maternal looking and smiling at the baby were related to the amount of "affectionate talking" to the baby, but this group of measures was not related to the amount of touching or caressing shown, nor to measures of responsiveness to crying. However, the first three of these measures were related to a measure of infant behaviour made outside the interaction situation: a test of sucking behaviour developed by Waldrop and Bell (1966) to assess individual characteristics of the newborn. The baby's rate of sucking on this test was positively correlated with the group of "affectionate" measures, a point we will discuss below. Measures of smoothness and co-ordination in these early feeds, which it has been suggested reflect underlying sensitivity on mother's part, were not related to the maternal measures described but were related to difficulties in the course of labour and delivery.

The question raised by these findings then is one of specifying which of the aspects of individual differences in interaction show continuity to later weeks, and which reflect special features of these very early feeding interactions.

Observations between Eight Weeks and Thirty Weeks

The families were next visited at eight, 14, 20 and 30 weeks, with two observations at each age. The observations were timed to fit in with the mother's convenience. We sampled at least two hours of the usual home routine when the baby was awake, but did not include feeds except at eight weeks. For some babies then our observations included long periods alone, awake in pram or cot, for others most awake-time was spent in an infant-seat in the kitchen with company. In this sense the context varied from pair to pair; we were not trying to standardize the context but to sample what was characteristic for that particular mother–baby pair.

During this period we found that mothers who were active in touching their babies were also active in talking to them and were the most responsive to their babies' vocalizations, and that these individual differences were consistent across the weeks. Spearman rank correlations between measures of maternal touch at eight, 14, 20 and 30 weeks were all positive; they ranged from 0·48 to 0·58 ($N = 55$–61) and were all significant at $p < 0{\cdot}01$ level. Similarly the rank orders of mothers on measures of maternal vocalization were consistent across these weeks (Spearman rank correlations ranged from 0·50 to 0·60, all significant at $p < 0{\cdot}01$). And correlations between measures of maternal touch and maternal vocalization at each age were positive (Spearman rank correlations ranged from 0·53 to 0·63, all were significant at $p < 0{\cdot}01$ level). The possibility is raised that individual differences in baby characteristics, as measured on the sucking test, might be contributing to the consistency in these maternal measures, in that a measure from the sucking test on Day 8 (latency to cry on removal of teat) correlated with the maternal measures in the later observations (Table I). Measures of maternal responsiveness to crying, assessed as latency to

Table I

Spearman rank correlations of latency to cry measure (sucking test, day 8) with later maternal measures (N = 60)

	Mother vocalize if present	Mother touch if present	Mother touch if vocalize
14 weeks	$-0{\cdot}30^a$	$-0{\cdot}37^b$	$-0{\cdot}36^b$
20 weeks	$-0{\cdot}16$	$-0{\cdot}22$	$-0{\cdot}29^a$

$^a p < 0{\cdot}05$ $^b p < 0{\cdot}01$

respond to crying, however, were unstable across the weeks. It was found to be important to take account of the level of irritability of the baby when comparing this latency measure of responsiveness to crying with other maternal measures; for instance, with the more irritable babies a mother who was unresponsive to crying was not necessarily unresponsive to vocalizations. For the least irritable babies a low level of responsiveness to crying on the mother's part *was* correlated with low scores on other measures of maternal responsiveness. (These results are reported in detail elsewhere, Dunn, 1975.)

How were these consistent individual differences in maternal style related to the patterns of the first ten days? The measure of touching during the early feeds was, for breast-feeding pairs, correlated with the measures of touching, vocalizing and responsiveness to baby vocalization over the 8–20 week period. However, the individual measures of affectionate talking, looking and smiling did not correlate significantly with the maternal measures from the observations at 14, 20 and 30 weeks. A factor analysis of 31 measures from the first ten-day observations had been performed (statistical package SPSSH—version 5·01; varimax rotated factor matrix). This analysis had produced a factor (referred to as Factor 2 in this paper) on which the chief loading variables were maternal affectionate talking and the suck rate measure from the sucking test on day 8. This Factor did not correlate significantly with the maternal measures at 14, 20 and 30 weeks (Table II).

These results suggest that individual differences in the ways mothers relate to their babies along dimensions of talking to the baby, touching the baby and responding to his vocalizations remain consistent as the babies grow up over the first seven months, and that these differences between mothers are already indicated, for breast-feeding mothers, in the individual differences in the mothers' touching behaviour in the

Table II

Continuities from the first ten days: Spearman rank correlations between two variables from the first ten days and maternal variables from observations at eight weeks and 30 weeks (N = 50–65)

	First-10-day: Factor 2	First-10-day: Mother touch
8 weeks:		
Mother touch	0·22	0·46[b]
Mother vocalize to baby	0·26[a]	0·23
Mother responsive to baby vocalize	0·30[a]	0·30[a]
Mother unresponsive to baby cry	—0·36[b]	0·27
30 weeks:		
Mother touch		0·37[b]
Mother vocalize		0·23

[a] $p < 0{\cdot}05$ [b] $p < 0{\cdot}01$

feeds during the first ten days. It is interesting that for bottle-feeding mothers the relationship between touching in the early feeds and the later consistent differences was not significant. We should not conclude that bottle-feeding mothers are less physically interested in their babies in the early days; rather we would stress the important differences in the context of the early feeds for bottle-feeding and breast-feeding mothers. During bottle feeds there were very often other people present, and the feeds became social occasions very different from the more private breast-feeds when the mother was almost always alone with the baby. It could well be that the physical caressing of the baby shown by bottle-feeding mothers *outside* the feeding situation would have shown similar continuity with the 8–30 weeks observations to that demonstrated for breast-feeding mothers.

We look next at the individual differences in interaction found seven months later, when the children are 14 months old.

Observations at Fourteen Months

At 14 months two observations, of at least one hour each, were made in the home, and the observations were tape-recorded. We watched the children playing in their usual routine, without structuring the situation. This usually included time when the mother was occupied with household work, and also time when she was more relaxed.

We will be discussing two sorts of data then: measures derived from the observations, based on the occurrence or non-occurrence of previously categorized behaviours within 20-second time intervals, and measures of verbal interaction from the tape-recordings. (Unfortunately the tape-recordings of many mother–child pairs could not be used as there was too much interference from the noises of the home environment—washing machine, radio, T.V. and neighbours. For this reason the N for the measures from the tape-recordings is only 36.)

OBSERVATIONAL MEASURES AT FOURTEEN MONTHS

The analysis of the observational material at 14 months showed that there were high correlations between the measures of a baby looking at, vocalizing to, and giving, showing or pointing out objects to his mother, and the measures of mother vocalizing to the baby (Table III).

Two other measures correlated with these measures:

(a) the percentage of the intervals when the baby vocalized where a mother vocalization occurred in the same or the following interval;

Table III

Spearman rank correlations between observational measures at 14 months (N = 61)

	(2)	(3)	(4)	(5)	(6)
(1) Baby look at mother	0·86[b]	0·59[b]	0·63[b]	0·49[b]	0·40[b]
(2) Baby vocalize to mother		0·60[b]	0·43[b]	0·45[b]	0·40[b]
(3) Baby show, point or offer object to mother			0·44[b]	0·45[b]	0·40[b]
(4) Mother vocalize to baby				0·83[b]	0·63[b]
(5) % baby vocalize followed by mother vocalize					0·38[b]
(6) % baby fuss followed by mother vocalize					

[b] $p < 0{\cdot}01$

(b) the percentage of the intervals when the baby fussed, where a mother vocalization occurred in the same or following interval. If mother and infant vocalization occurred together within a 20-second period we had no record of which vocalization occurred first. This means that some of the intervals included in measure (a), for example, will be intervals where the baby vocalization followed the mother vocalization. As an assessment of the likelihood a mother will "reply" to a baby vocalization this measure is clearly very inaccurate. A better measure from the analysis of the tape-recordings is reported below: the percentage of baby utterances that are given a response.

The infant measures which reflected the baby's "conversational" exchange of looks, vocalization and objects (baby look at mother; baby vocalize to mother; baby give, show, point out object to mother) were, however, *not* related to measures of the mothers touching, handling or carrying. We found in fact that two rather different patterns of maternal response were reflected in these correlations. In one pattern the response to a baby fussing, vocalizing or looking at the mother was maternal *vocalization*, and these mothers ranked high on total vocalizing and giving objects to their 14-month-olds. In the other pattern the response to a baby fussing, vocalizing or looking at the mother was maternal *touching*. There were no significant correlations between the two response patterns.

It would be tempting to stress the difference between these two patterns of maternal behaviour, particularly since, as we will see, the individual differences in the pattern of vocalizing, giving objects, and responding to vocalizing were consistent from 30 weeks to 14 months. But this separation of maternal "styles" should not be pushed too far; although maternal touching behaviour was not correlated with the measures of infant looking, showing objects and vocalizing etc., it did show a low positive correlation with maternal vocalization ($rs = 0{\cdot}45$, $N = 61$, $p < 0{\cdot}01$). That is, some mothers ranked high on both measures.

MEASURES FROM THE VERBAL TRANSCRIPTS

The verbal transcripts of the observations available for 35 of the mother–child pairs make possible another measure of the mother's response to the baby's vocalization: the percentage of the baby's utterances that are responded to. This measure is found to correlate with the measure of the amount of mother vocalizing obtained from the observations ($rs = 0{\cdot}61$, $N = 35$, $p < 0{\cdot}01$). However, it would be mistaken to regard this simply as a measure of mothers' responsiveness without regard to the characteristics of the child, since we find that the percentage of baby utterances that are responded to depends on the number of those utterances that are (or are assumed to be) demands for objects or for help. The percentage of baby utterances that are responded to is positively correlated to the proportion of utterances that are demands ($rs = 0{\cdot}48$, $N = 35$, $p < 0{\cdot}01$). The problem that measures of maternal responsiveness are confounded with individual differences in infant behaviour is one which we discuss below.

We can also use the verbal transcripts to look at the exchange between mother and child in rather different terms from the responsiveness measures used so far. Studies of the verbal development of children during the second year have examined the relation between several different indices of the mother's language and the later development of the child's language. Katherine Nelson (1973) has stressed that,

> "a non-directive parental strategy that was accepting of the child's behaviour—both verbal and non-verbal—facilitated the child's progress in language acquisition."

In order to be able to compare the "feedback" measures in mother's replies that Nelson found important in promoting language growth with other measures of responsiveness, we categorized the mother's replies to the child's vocalizations by the same classification of direction, acceptance, or rejection that Nelson used. Acceptance, the category we will be discussing here, refers to all verbal indications by the mother that she accepts or approves some behaviour—verbal or non-verbal—by the child, e.g. "Good"; "That's the way"; "Yes, it's a doggie" (Nelson, 1973, p. 68). We also examined the proportion of utterances containing object words.

The analysis showed that *how* a mother replies to her 14-month-old's vocalizations is not related to *whether* she replies. There were no significant correlations between the measures of responsiveness to baby's vocalization (from the observation or the transcripts), responsiveness to fussing, or amount of touching, and the verbal feedback measures of direction, acceptance or rejection, although the measure of acceptance showed a low positive correlation with measures of mother showing, pointing to, or offering objects ($rs = 0{\cdot}40$, $N = 28$, $p < 0{\cdot}05$). (One measure from the verbal transcripts that did relate to the observational measures was the number of mother utterances containing object words: this measure correlated with the number of intervals in which the baby showed, offered, or pointed out an object to the mother. Further analysis will indicate how far these utterances with object words were in *response* to the baby's actions.)

In looking at these differences in mothers' replies we are thus recognizing a different quality of a mother's responsiveness to her baby's words and wishes from that highlighted by the observational measures. Can we find measures in the earlier observations that relate to this aspect of mothering? Or does it reflect differences between mothers that only become apparent when the child is beginning to use language? What are the antecedents of the individual differences in the amount of "conversational" exchange of looks, vocalizations and objects reflected in the measures from the observations? We look first at the observations made at 30 weeks.

Relationship to Thirty-week Observations

Table IV shows that for the observational measures there are correlations between, on the one hand, measures of maternal vocalization response to baby vocalization and giving or showing objects at 30 weeks and, on the other hand, some measures of the interchange between child and mother at 14 months, although these correlations are low and account for little of the variance. No correlations were found between measures of the amount of baby vocalizing, manipulating objects or smiling at 30 weeks and later measures. The "feedback" differences in quality of mother's reply to baby vocalization, i.e. in the direction, acceptance and rejection categories, showed no relationship with the consistent individual differences in maternal measures from the 8–30 week period. It seems that the qualities of mothering a two- to seven-month-old baby that our observational measures highlighted, while certainly related to the amount of interchange of looks, vocalization and objects between mother and baby at 14 months, are rather different from those reflected in the way mothers reply to their 14-month-olds.

Table IV

Spearman rank correlations between maternal behaviour at 30 weeks and measures from 14 months (N = 55–61 except column C)

	14-month measures					
	A	B	C	D	E	F
30-week measures	Mother vocalize	% baby vocalize followed by mother vocalize	% baby utterance responded to (N = 35)	Baby vocalize to mother	Baby shows, points or offers object to mother	Mother shows, points or offers object to baby
Mother vocalize	0·33[b]	0·32[a]	—	0·24	—	0·31[a]
% baby vocalize followed by mother vocalize	—	0·35[b]	—	0·27[a]	0·21	0·25[a]
Mother gives, shows or points out objects	0·30[a]	—	0·42[b]	0·21	0·40[b]	0·49[b]

[a] $p < 0{\cdot}05$. [b] $p < 0{\cdot}01$.

Relationship to the Early Post Partum Period

When we turn to the measures from the first ten days we find that there are some significant relationships with the measures from 14 months. Table V shows that the factor from the first ten days on which the measures of maternal looking, smiling and affectionate talking and the baby suck rate measure were loaded (Factor 2), is positively correlated

Table V

Spearman rank correlations between first-10-day measures and measures from 14 months (N = 30)

	14-months measures			
First-10-days	Mother vocalize	% baby utterances responded to	% baby utterances as demands	Acceptance
Factor 2	0·31[a]	0·55[b]	0·39[a]	0·30
Suck rate	—	0·46[b]	0·45[b]	—

[a] $p < 0{\cdot}05$ [b] $p < 0{\cdot}01$

with the observational measure of the amount of mother vocalizing and with the percentage of baby utterances that were responded to. The baby suck rate measure is related to the maternal measure and to the percentage of demands in the child utterances. These patterns of correlations raise two points of general developmental interest: first the issue of continuity, and second the issue of the contribution of individual differences between babies to the maternal and interactional measures.

CONTINUITIES

The correlations in Table V and Table VI suggest that the individual differences in the style of interaction that the first-10-day measures were picking up *are* related to differences apparent in the interaction at 14 months, although the early differences were *not* related to individual differences in the measures of mothers' behaviour towards the two- to

Table VI

Correlations between three age periods (two selected variables at each age)

First-10-days:	(1)	(2)	(3)	(4)	(5)	(6)
(1) Mother touch						
(2) Factor 2	—					
30 weeks:						
(3) Mother touch	0·37[b]	—				
(4) Mother vocalize	0·23	—	0·63[b]			
14 months:						
(5) Mother vocalize	—	0·31[a]	—	0·33[b]		
(6) % baby utterances responded to	—	0·55[a]	—	—	0·61[a]	

[a] $p < 0{\cdot}05$ [b] $p < 0{\cdot}01$ —indicates correlation below 0·20.

seven-month-olds. The confusion in these patterns of correlations presents us with two possible interpretations. The most likely is that, although our measures of maternal behaviour across the two- to seven-month period did focus on consistent individual differences, they were insensitive to the aspects of maternal affection or responsiveness that the earlier measures were highlighting.

We originally used the measure of "affectionate talking" to focus on rather striking differences in mothers' behaviour towards their babies in the first feeds: while many mothers talked to their babies almost exclusively about the course of the feed—urging them to wake up, to suck harder, to "bring the wind up"—other mothers commented on their babies' faces, their expressions, and talked to them, as it were, conversationally rather than in order to get the feed completed successfully. These differences were consistent from feed to feed in the first ten days and were not affected by the experience of a difficult delivery. It seems plausible that the mother who "converses" in this personal way with a two-day-old will, when the child is a sophisticated communicator of around a year, be encouraging and "accepting" and responsive to his conversational initiations.

It also remains a possibility (albeit an unlikely one) that the "gap" in the continuity of individual differences is not entirely an artefact produced by the different measures used: that the initial interest in conversing with the new baby, picked up in the "affectionate talk" measure, is one that is, after the early days, much less apparent during the first seven months but flowers later in the first year when the baby is a fluent conversationalist. Given the elegant demonstrations by analysis of video-tape of the subtlety of conversational interaction between mothers and three, four and five-month-olds this seems particularly unlikely. If we had used fine-grained analysis of this sort over the 8–30 week period we might have found continuities in individual differences linking the earliest observation with the 14-month data.

MOTHER, BABY OR INTERACTION MEASURES?

The second point that must be made about these early measures concerns the contribution of the suck rate measure to the Factor 2 and to the correlations found with the 14-months measures. We have discussed elsewhere the problem of using measures as exclusively reflecting "maternal" or "infant" behaviour (Dunn, 1975). Since the "affectionate talk" measure is correlated with the sucking behaviour of the baby, and since the Factor 2 correlates with the later measures, it might be more meaningful to describe the connection across time as being between individual differences in mother–child pairs, rather than between measures of mother's or infant's behaviour.

Support for the idea that the continuity over time is better described as one of interaction styles rather than of exclusively maternal behaviour is found in the relationship between the suck rate measures on the eighth day after birth and the measures of verbal demands at 14 months. We cannot assume that this correlation reflects a continuity over 14 months in *baby* behaviour, independent of the interaction between mother and baby, any more than we can assume that a correlation between measures of maternal responsiveness over this period is independent of infant characteristics. Although the sucking test was done as early as day 8, and although it measures characteristics of individual babies that are stable from day to day over the newborn period, it cannot be taken as a measure of baby behaviour that is independent of the previous course of interaction between mother and child. (We found, for example, that breast-fed and bottle-fed babies showed consistent differences in sucking behaviour on the test, Dunn, 1975.) This means that correlations between such "baby" measures and later "maternal" measures may be due to continuity in some aspect of the mother's behaviour, the baby's behaviour, or the patterns of interaction between them.

To summarize this rather complex story:

(1) Measures of some aspects of maternal affectionate behaviour in the first ten days correlated with measures of baby behaviour at this period.
(2) These measures of maternal affectionate behaviour did not show continuity with the consistent individual differences in maternal behaviour found between eight weeks and 30 weeks.
(3) At 14 months observational measures of the mother's vocalization, her response to the child's vocalization and some characteristics of the interchange between child and mother were weakly related to the 30-week measures and more strongly to the first-10-day measures. Mothers who were active in responding to babies' utterances at 14 months had babies who made many vocal requests for objects and help, and it was this *interactive style* that was related to the early measures of mother and baby behaviour.

Consequences

The final issue I would like to raise concerns the developmental consequences for the child of the individual differences in maternal behaviour or interaction patterns we have described. We have seen that there are continuities in measures of maternal behaviour over the first 14 months, and that these continuities are related to how the 14-month-old child behaves with his mother. It would of course be very surprising if there were *no* connections demonstrated between the behaviour of the child and of his mother. What we do not know is whether or how these differences in interaction matter in terms of the child's later development.

There has been much interest lately in the importance of the attachment relationship between mother and child for the development of communication and language. Several studies have attempted to relate individual differences in intellectual competence and language development in the first two years with differences in qualities of the relationship with the mother. Ainsworth, for instance, has suggested that a relationship with a responsive and sensitive mother fosters communication skills during the first year (Ainsworth *et ai.*, 1974). Yarrow and colleagues (1972) examined the relationship between scores on the Bayley test at five months and various aspects of maternal behaviour, and found that the mother's contingent response to distress was significantly related to the Bayley Developmental Index and to measures of goal-directed behaviour.

In discussing these findings it has been suggested that the experience of a caregiver whose responses are promptly contingent upon the child's initiations and requests gives a child a sense of competence and effectance, which contributes to a developing mastery of the object world. Lewis and Goldberg (1969) formulated a "generalized expectancy model" to emphasize the role of contingent mother–infant interaction in the development of a child's belief that he can affect and control his environment.

It is, however, notoriously difficult to relate measures of competence or developmental quotients obtained in the first 18 months of a child's life to later measures of intelligence. Lewis and McGurk (1972), for instance, reiterate Bayley's views that

> "at each stage of infant development intelligence comprises a set of relatively discrete abilities. During the early period these clusters of abilities, according to Bayley, are relatively age specific, therefore there is no necessary continuity between intelligence as defined at one stage of development and as defined at another."

The discontinuity, and the stepwise property of the pattern of intellectual growth in infancy and early childhood, is now much discussed. Is there then any *a priori* reason to assume that the qualities of mothering that foster the abilities of a child during his first year would necessarily be the qualities that provide the most encouraging and formative support for intellectual development in the second or third years?

The findings of the present study are of direct interest here, since a number of measures of responsiveness are available and since the children in the sample have been followed to five years of age. At four and a half years they were tested with the Stanford Binet Intelligence test and a variety of tests of role-taking skills (Light, 1974).

None of the measures of maternal responsiveness obtained during the first year was related to the I.Q. at four and a half years. However, the measure of maternal "acceptance" in response to the child vocalizations, from the verbal transcripts, *did* correlate significantly with I.Q.

(rs $= 0{\cdot}52$, N $= 28$, $p < 0{\cdot}01$). This measure, as we have seen, was not related to the observational measures of response to baby vocalization, nor to the percentage of baby utterances responded to. In the present sample the "acceptance" measure was not related to social class as measured by husband's occupation, nor to the educational level of the mother. In the Nelson study the measure of acceptance in mother's replies at 13 months correlated with the child's use of object words and object naming at 24 months. (In her sample also the measure of acceptance was not related to the educational level of the mother or father.)

These findings suggest that for understanding the origins of individual differences in those aspects of a child's intellectual development that are assessed in intelligence tests, simple measures of maternal responsiveness during the first year are not of key importance. How much weight should we give to the association between the maternal "acceptance" measure, and the child's I.Q. at four and a half years? Of course we would not suggest any direct *causal* connection here. However, the association does indicate that the family environments that are likely to favour the child's intellectual development by four years are characterized, when the child is 14 months, by a particular style of verbal acceptance of the child's behaviour, while a generalized responsiveness plays no such role. The pattern of association *is* congruent with the ideas on discontinuity in development emphasized, for instance, by Lewis and McGurk (1972). In itself, however, the association between verbal acceptance and later I.Q. offers merely a clue as to what aspects of mother–child interaction between 14 months and four years are likely to be worth examining closely in the quest for a systematic causal analysis.

Acknowledgements

This project was supported by a grant from the Nuffield Foundation. The study was initiated by Martin Richards and all observations were carried out by the author and Martin Richards. We would like to thank the Midwives of the City of Cambridge and the families in the sample for their generous help.

References

Ainsworth, M. D. S., Bell, S. M. and Stayton, D. J. (1974). Infant-mother attachment and social development. In M. P. M. Richards (Ed.), *The Integration of a Child into a Social World.* Cambridge University Press, Cambridge.

Brazelton, T. B., Koslowski, B. and Main, M. (1974). The origins of reciprocity. In M. Lewis and L. H. Rosenblum (Eds), *The Effects of the Infant on its Caregiver.* Wiley, New York.

Dunn, J. F. (1975). Consistency and change in styles of mothering. In M. O'Connor (Ed.), *Parent-Infant Interaction.* Elsevier, Amsterdam.

Lewis, M. and Goldberg, S. (1969). Perceptual-cognitive development in infancy: a generalised expectancy model as a function of the mother-infant interaction. *Merrill-Palmer Q.* **15**, 81–100.

Lewis, M. and McGurk, H. (1972). Evaluation of infant intelligence. *Science* **178**, 1174–1177.

Light, P. H. (1974). Role-taking in four-year-olds. Unpublished Ph.D. thesis, University of Cambridge.

Nelson, Katherine (1973). Structure and strategy in learning to talk. *Monogr. Soc. Res. Child Devel.* **149.**

Richards, M. P. M. and Bernal, J. F. (1972). An observational study of mother-infant interaction. In N. Blurton-Jones (Ed.), *Ethological Studies of Child Behaviour.* Cambridge University Press, Cambridge.

Stern, D. N. (1971). A micro-analysis of mother-infant interactions: behaviour regulating social contact between a mother and her 3½ month old twins. *J. Amer. Acad. Child Psychiat.* **10**, 501–517.

Waldrop, M. F. and Bell, R. Q. (1966). Effects of family size and density on newborn characteristics. *Am. J. Orthopsychiat.* **36**, 544–550.

Yarrow, L. J., Rubenstein, J. L., Pedersen, F. A. and Jankowski, J. J. (1972). Dimensions of early stimulation and their differential effects on Infant Development. *Merrill-Palmer Q.* **18**, 205–218.

Subject Index